THE MEDIAEVAL ACADEMY OF AMERICA

PUBLICATION No. 46

THE RUSSIAN ATTACK
ON CONSTANTINOPLE IN 860

THE RUSSIAN ATTACK
ON CONSTANTINOPLE
IN 860

BY

ALEXANDER A. VASILIEV

THE MEDIAEVAL ACADEMY OF AMERICA
CAMBRIDGE, MASSACHUSETTS
1946

*The publication of this book was made possible in part by
a grant from the Reisinger Fund for Slavic
Studies in Harvard University*

GEORGE BANTA PUBLISHING COMPANY, MENASHA, WISCONSIN

FOREWORD

ONE may ask why, dealing with a single episode, the first Russian attack on Constantinople, I have not confined myself to a mere article but have instead written a book. The question is natural, and I feel that to justify writing a book on such a subject I should allege my reasons. They are as follows: First, my aim is to study this event not as a separate and isolated fact but in connection with the Viking incursions in Western Europe, in order to show that the Russian attack was one of the constituent and essential parts of general European history of the ninth century; for this purpose, I have outlined the Viking invasions in Western Europe, and particularly stressed their operations in the Mediterranean, to which I have tried to give a new interpretation. Second, I have thought it appropriate to study in detail the original sources, Greek, Latin, Arabic, and Russian, both for the West European Viking expeditions and for the Russian attack. Third, with the secondary works I have not limited myself to mere statements of titles or to a few words of summary, but I have often reproduced exact quotations, having in view that these works are not always at the disposal of the reader, and that many of them are written in Russian, a language which, unfortunately, for the time being, is not generally known. These excerpts from the secondary works have no doubt enlarged the size of my study; but the advantages for the reader which I have just mentioned will I believe justify me. Fourth, I have had to discuss several questions which are connected with the central subject of the book only indirectly, but which contribute a great deal to our better understanding of the facts of the Russian attack; for example, I have re-examined the question whether, before the year 860, the Russians had raided Byzantine territory; and I have used new material for an adequate estimate of the importance of the reign of the Emperor Michael III, under whom the Russian attack took place, and whose personality has heretofore appeared in history in a very distorted and intentionally degraded form. These reasons may, I believe, justify me in writing a book on the Russian attack on Constantinople in 860-861.

Since in my study I deal in detail with the primary sources on the Russian campaign of 860 and with secondary works on the same subject as well, and since ultimately I give my own presentation of the same event, some unavoidable repetitions are to be found in this book; and I am the first fully to recognize this particular defect of my work among many others.

First of all, I wish to express my deep gratitude to the New York Public Library and in particular to its Slavonic Room, without the use of which I could never have written this book. My grateful acknowledgments are also due the Mediaeval Academy of America, which accepted this book as an item in its Monograph Series, and to the Reisinger Fund for Slavic Studies in Harvard University which contributed substantially to its publication cost. I tender my warmest thanks to Mrs Ednah Shepard Thomas who, with remarkable conscientiousness, has revised my manuscript and corrected the inadequacies of my English.

TABLE OF CONTENTS

INTRODUCTION

IF we consider the fact of the Russian attack on Constantinople in 860 as an isolated phenomenon detached from contemporary events in other parts of Europe, it seems at first sight a very simple, even insignificant, story: the Russians attacked Constantinople and its environs, pillaged and devastated the latter, were routed, and returned home. But such an approach would be absolutely unhistorical. The attack of 860 is indissolubly connected with the general course of European events in the ninth century, and cannot be detached from the main European movement of that period. At this time Western Europe was being invaded by Scandinavian Vikings; Danes and, to some extent, Norwegians were devastating not only the sea coast but the interior of Europe. They penetrated far up the Elbe, Rhine, Seine, Loire, and Garonne Rivers, pillaged the interior of Germany and France, landed in Britain and, rounding the Iberic Peninsula, through the Straits of Gibraltar entered the Mediterranean, invaded Spain and Italy, and in their steady drive east reached the eastern confines of the Mediterranean Sea. Terrified and exhausted Europe was driven to despair, and almost hopelessly uttered a new prayer: 'Ab ira Normannorum libera nos, Domine!' The Russian attack of 860, carried out by the same Scandinavian Vikings, mostly by Swedes, was the left flank of that enormous destructive avalanche from the north which swept over Europe. After the period of barbarian migrations, mostly Germanic, in the fourth, fifth, and sixth centuries, the Slavonic penetration in the Balkans in the fifth, sixth, and seventh centuries, and the stupendous victorious expansion of the Arabs in the seventh and eighth centuries, Scandinavian aggression in the ninth century may be regarded as the last manifestation of conquest.

In 860 Russia first became involved in world politics. Of course, from the European point of view, the connection at first sight was very slight. But in the history of the Black Sea regions and the Byzantine Empire a distinctly new page was turned in this year. In addition to the Slavs in the Balkans and those permanent foes, the Arabs, who threatened the Empire both from the east and from Sicily and South Italy in the west, Byzantium faced a new foe in the north. The potential strength of this new enemy could not have been clearly apparent at the first aggression; but the Empire, anticipating the future, had to reconsider and rearrange its political relations with all its neighbours, especially with the Khazars in the north, who were at the same time the nearest neighbours of the young principality of Kiev. The Arabs, enemies of the Empire for the past two centuries, now became still more dangerous, because the Byzantine government and diplomacy had the new and strenuous task of protecting the Empire not only from the east and west, but also from the north.

At present the study of early Russian history is passing once more through a crucial period. A wave of hypercriticism has swept over the minds of several eminent West-European scholars. They classify Oleg as a legendary figure, waging a 'legendary' campaign against Constantinople. Authentic Russian history is supposed to have started only in the year 941, when the expedition of the Russian Prince Igor against Constantinople took place; everything before this date is legend, and tradition tinged with fable. I frankly confess that these statements concern me deeply, for I firmly believe in the historicity of Rurik, Askold and Dir, and Oleg. I rejoice that at least the existence of Igor and Olga, the last Russian rulers to bear Scandinavian names, has not been questioned. It is now well-established, I believe, that the Russian principality of Kiev was founded about 840; therefore we may consider 860 as an early date in Russian history, but an authentic one.

THE RUSSIAN ATTACK
ON CONSTANTINOPLE IN 860

DESIGNATIONS OF SCANDINAVIAN VIKINGS

THE Scandinavian Vikings, who in the ninth century were so bitterly dreaded in western and eastern Europe, are known in various sources by different names: Normans, Magi, Pagans, and Russians (*Ros* or *Rus*). Western Latin sources call them Normans (*Normani, Normanni, Nordmanni, Nortmanni, Lordomani, Lormanes, Leodemani,* etc.).[1] Most of them were Danes. In some Western Latin sources the Normans are called merely Pagans (pagani).[2] North African Arab historians, i.e., those of the region called al-Maghrib, and historians of Mohammedan Spain, use the name *Madjus,* 'pagans, fireworshippers,' in English *Magi,* to designate the Scandinavian pirates and invaders of the ninth century who were known in Europe as Normans, and they apply the same name in later times to the French Normans in the Middle Ages who often tried to land on the coasts of the Muslim West and make expeditions along its frontiers.[3] Only later in Arabian sources do we find the name *al-Ordomaniyun,* i.e., *Nordmanni.* This occurs first in the History of Ibn-Idhari (Ibn-Adhari), who wrote at the end of the thirteenth century, in his description of the Danish invasion in 971.[4] In Byzantine and Russian sources we find the name *Ros* ('Ρῶς, 'Ρώς) in Greek sources and *Rus'* in Russian applied to the Normans, mostly Swedes, who invaded the Byzantine Empire and especially its capital Constantinople; in other words, *Ros* and *Rus'* were the same Normans who raided East Europe. The name *Ros* or *Rus'* was unknown to the Arabs of Spain. But there are two Arab historians and geographers, al-Ya'qubi and al-Mas'udi, who identified the *Madjus* with the *Ros.* In other words, they managed to discover that both western Danish and Norwegian Vikings and eastern Swedish invaders belonged to the same racial group. In his geographical work *Book of Regions* (*Kitāb-al-Boldān*) Ya'qubi writes: 'Into this city (Ishbiliya = Seville) in 229 (= 843–844), broke in the Madjus who are called Rus.'[5] This rather unexpected statement in Ya'qubi's geographi-

[1] See R. Dozy, *Recherches sur l'histoire et la littérature en Espagne pendant le moyen âge,* third ed (Paris-Leyden, 1881), p. 300, n. 2; 302, 338. From Dozy, J. Marquart, *Osteuropäische und ostasiatische Streifzüge* (Leipzig, 1903), p. 349.

[2] See, for instance, a letter of Pope Nicholas I (Sept. 28, 865) to the Byzantine Emperor Michael III. *Monumenta Germ. Hist., Epistolae,* VI, 479–480: Migne, *Patr. Lat.,* CXIX, 954. A letter of Lothair II, of Lorraine, to Pope Nicholas I (867), Baronii *Annales Ecclesiastici,* XV (Bar le Duc, 1868), 123, no. 123 (under the year 867). On these sources see below.

[3] See article *al-Madjus* by E. Levi-Provençal, *Encyclopédie de l'Islam,* III (1936), 105.

[4] See Dozy, *Recherches . . .,* third ed. (Paris-Leyde, 1881), 298. Marquart, *op. cit.,* pp. 348–349. In French Dozy writes 'les Madjous-Normands.' Cf. A. Seippel, *Rerum normannicarum fontes arabici* (Oslo, 1896), praefatio, p. 7, note.

[5] Al-Ya'qubi, *Kitāb-al-Boldān, Bibliotheca geographorum arabicorum,* VII (Leyden, 1892), 354,

cal work may be satisfactorily explained by his biography. Living in the ninth century (he died at the end of this century) and, as a result, a contemporary of the events which particularly interest us, he prospered in Armenia and Khurasan, made a voyage to India, and then established himself in Egypt; finally he came to al-Maghrib, i.e., Western Africa. He was therefore well acquainted with both eastern and western affairs, and he has preserved in his work the tradition, prevalent at his time, that the attacks on western and eastern Europe from the north were not unconnected invasions, but were carried out by one group of Scandinavian invaders, who in the west were called by Arab historians *Madjus* and in the east by Byzantine and Russian writers *Ros* or *Rus'*.[6] Another Arab geographer and historian, al-Mas'udi, who died in 956–957, like al-Ya'qubi was very well acquainted with the Near East; he traversed the regions of the Caspian Sea and lived many years in Egypt and Syria. In his work *Meadows of Gold* (*Murūj al-Dhahab*) he identifies the Madjus who invaded Andalus (Spain) with the Rus.[7] Referring to this passage of Mas'udi, Marquart remarked: 'Mas'udi identified the *Ros* with the Danish Normans, who raided Spain and in 859 or 860 even Italy, and who were called by the Spanish Arabs *Madjus*. He indeed advances the identification of the *Madjus* with the *Ros*, of course, only as his own conjecture.'[8] I believe it was more than conjecture. Mas'udi's statement was based on his thorough knowledge of the Near East in the tenth century, when the racial connection of the Russians with the Normans in general was already well known.[9]

It would not be irrelevant to refer here to the statement of Liudprand, bishop of Cremona, who in the tenth century was twice sent to Constantinople (in 949 and 960), as ambassador to the Byzantine court, and whose

---

ll. 12–15. A. Harkavi, *Accounts of the Mohammedan writers on the Slavs and Russians* (St Petersburg, 1870), p. 63 (in Russian). A. Kunik, *Accounts of al-Bekri and other authors on Russia and the Slavs,* II (St Petersburg, 1903), 153 (in Russian). Marquart, *op. cit.,* pp. 386–387. F. Westberg, 'Beiträge zur Klärung orientalischer Quellen über Osteuropa,' *Bulletin* (*Izvestiya*) *de l'Académie des Sciences de St Pétersbourg,* XI (1899), no. 4, pp. 232–238. *Idem,* 'On the Analysis of Oriental Sources on Eastern Europe, *Journal of the Ministry of Public Instruction,*' 1908 (February), 382 (in Russian).

[6] See Marquart, *op. cit.,* p. 387. He gives a slightly different explanation, but one which does not contradict our own.

[7] Maçoudi, *Les Prairies d'or,* ed. Barbier de Meynard, I (Paris, 1861), 364–365. Harkavi, *op. cit.,* p. 129 (in Russian). Marquart, *op. cit.,* 348, 387. Westberg, 'Beiträge . . . ,' pp. 232–238. *Idem,* 'On the Analysis . . . ,' pp. 380–382 (in Russian).

[8] Marquart, *op. cit.,* p. 348.

[9] See the statement of Liudprand, given in the following note. On the basis of Marquart's passage just mentioned, a Russian scholar, A. Pogodin, makes the following sweeping statement 'It was not Italians or Spaniards who called these Germanic northern sea conquerors *Rus,* but Masudi introduced into his historical work the information that these same *Rus* had raided Italy and Spain,' A. Pogodin, 'Question of the Origin of the Name Rus,' *Memorial Volume in Honor of V. N. Zlatarski* (Sofia, 1925), p. 274 (in Russian).

stepfather had been an eyewitness of the unsuccessful attack on Constantinople by the Russian Prince Igor. Liudprand writes: 'There is a certain northern people whom the Greeks call Rusii, "rufous,"[10] from the color of their skin, while we from the position of their country call them Nordmanni. In the Teuton language "nord" means "north" and "man" means "human being," so that Nordmanni is equivalent to "men of the north".'[11] In another passage in the same work we read that from the north Constantinople is menaced by Hungarians, Patzinaks (Pechenegs), Khazars, and Rusii, 'whom we call Nordmanni.'[12] These two texts are interesting as showing that in the tenth century the identification of the *Rus* with the Normans was already widely known in Western Europe.

[10] In Greek the adjective Ῥούσιος—*rusios*, means *rufous, red, reddish.*

[11] 'Gens quaedam est sub aquilonis parte constituta, quam a qualitate corporis Greci vocant Ῥούσιος Rusios, nos vero a positione loci nominamus Nordmannos. Lingue quippe Teutonum nôrd aquilo, man autem dicitur homo; unde et Nordmannos aquilonares homines dicere possumus,' Liudprandi episcopi Cremonensis *Opera omnia. Antapodosis,* v, 15; Scriptores rerum germanicarum in usum scholarum, ed. altera by E. Dümmler (Hanover, 1877), p. 107. An English translation by F. A. Wright, *The Works of Liudprand of Cremona* (London, 1930), p. 185.

[12] 'Constantinopolitana urbs . . . habet quippe ab aquilone Hungarios, Pizenacos, Chazaros, Rusios, quos alio nos nomine Nordmannos appellamus,' *Antapodosis,* i, 11; F. A. Wright, *op. cit.,* p. 38.

THE FIRST APPEARANCE OF RUSSIANS (ROS)
IN CONSTANTINOPLE AND INGELHEIM
IN 838–839

WESTERN EUROPE made its initial acquaintance with the Russians in 839 under very interesting circumstances. In this year the Russians made their first appearance in the West under their own name; in 839 the 'Rus for the first time introduced themselves to the West.'[1] In this year the Byzantine Emperor Theophilus (829–842) dispatched an embassy to the court of the Western Emperor, Lewis the Pious (814–840). The cause of the embassy must be explained by the political situation of the Byzantine Empire, which at that time was crucial. A year before, in 838, the Caliph Mutasim had put himself at the head of a large army, penetrated deep into Asia Minor, captured Ancyra, and then, after a long siege, taken the important fortified city of Amorion (Amorium) in Phrygia, the birthplace of the ruling dynasty, 'the eye and foundation of Christianity, which, in the eyes of Christians, was nobler than Constantinople,' in the exaggerated wording of an Arabian chronicler.[2] After the capture of Amorium, Mutasim expected to march upon Constantinople itself. The disaster of Amorium, along with the steady advance of the African Moslems in Sicily and the raids of the piratical Arabs of Crete, broke Theophilus' spirit and convinced him that the Empire was unable to cope alone with the power of Islam. He turned to the Western states for help. His ambassadors appeared in Venice, in Ingelheim at the court of the Western Emperor, Lewis the Pious, and even in the far West, in Spain, at the court of the Umayyad ruler, Abd-al-Rahman II (822–852). For our topic the embassy to Ingelheim is most important.

Our best source for this embassy is the so-called *Annales Bertiniani* or the *Annals of St Bertin*, which extend from 830 to 882. They consist of three parts written by three different authors. The first, an anonymous author, describes the years 830–835; the second, Prudentius, bishop of Troyes (*Trecensis episcopus*), covers the period from the end of 835 to 861, and the third author, Hincmar, archbishop of Reims, the years from 861 to 882. Thus the story of the embassy of 839 is told by the second author, Prudentius, bishop of Troyes,[3] who occupied the see from 846 to 861.

---

[1] F. Braun, 'Varangians in Russia,' in the magazine *Beseda*, no. 6–7 (Berlin, 1925), p. 318 (in Russian).

[2] Tabari, *Annales*, ed. de Goeje, III, 1236. In French, A. Vasiliev, *Byzance et les Arabes*, I (Brussels, 1935), 294–295; in Russian, the same book (St Petersburg, 1900), appendix, p. 30.

[3] Troyes is the chief city of the department of the Aube, in France, on the Seine, 167 kilometers southeast of Paris. At the end of the ninth century the Normans captured Troyes.

That is, he was a contemporary and very reliable source.   His real name was Galindo, but his work is generally known as that of Prudentius; he was a Spaniard by origin.[4]   Prudentius' report has been many times discussed and interpreted in various and contradictory ways; and the literature on it is so immense that it sometimes obscures and complicates the story.   Let us forget for a moment what has been written on the embassy and try to explain the text itself.

Prudentius' story may be divided into two sections: the first deals with the embassy itself, the second with the Russian envoys to Constantinople. The Emperor Theophilus sent to the Western Emperor, Lewis the Pious, two ambassadors, Theodosius, the metropolitan bishop of Chalcedon (*Calcedonensis metropolitanus episcopus*),[5] and Theophanes, a spatharius. They brought magnificent presents and a personal letter from the emperor.   The embassy was authorized to confirm the pact of eternal peace and amity between the two Emperors and the subjects of the two Empires.   In his letter Theophilus announced his gratitude and joy to the Lord on account of the victories which he, with His help, had won over foreign nations,[6] and urged Lewis and his subjects, as a sign of amity (*amicabiliter*) also to express their gratitude to the giver of all victories. The Byzantine embassy was solemnly received by Lewis at Ingelheim (*Ingulenheim*) on May 18, 839.[7]   Of this reception Professor F. Braun writes: 'The palace was at Ingelheim, now Nieder-Ingelheim, a little place on the sunny slope of the left bank of the Rhine, about nine miles west of Mainz, on the way to Bingen.   The vast excavations which have been

---

[4] See the opening lines of Hincmar's portion 'Galindo, cognomento Prudentius, Tricassinae civitatis episcopus natione Hispanus,' *Annales Bertiniani, Mon. Germ. Hist., Scriptores,* I, 455; *Les Annales de Saint-Bertin et de Saint-Vaast,* publiées par l'Abbé G. Dehaisnes (Paris, 1871), p. 105.

[5] Theodosius, according to some writers, was not the bishop of Chalcedon but the patrician Theodosius Babutzikos, mentioned in Byzantine sources, who had been sent at an earlier date to Venice. See J. B. Bury, *A History of the Eastern Roman Empire* (London, 1912), p. 273, n. 1.   Cf. A. Vasiliev, *Byzance et les Arabes,* I (Brussels, 1935), 178, n. 2.   I see no reason to differ from Prudentius, since Theodosius is a very common Byzantine name.

[6] Theophilus probably referred to the Arab setbacks in Sicily in the years 836, 837, and 838, and especially the capture by his troops of Zapetra, Malatya, and Arsamosata in Asia Minor and Mesopotamia in 837, which resulted in his triumphal entry into Constantinople and various celebrations in the Capital.   It is strange that he fails to mention the loss of Ancyra and especially the fall of Amorium, which occurred August 12, 838.   On this date see A. Vasiliev, *Byzance et les Arabes,* I, 170, n. 3.   In my Russian edition of his book (St Petersburg, 1900, p. 136 and appendix, p. 157) I suggested as the *probable* date of the fall of Amorium September 24, 838.   It is almost inconceivable that Lewis, in May 839, when he received Theophilus' embassy at Ingelheim, did not know of the defeat at Amorium, which had occurred in August, 838.   Prudentius, a contemporary, would not have made the mistake of placing Theophilus' embassy in the wrong year, 839 for 838.   We can rely on his date.

[7] 'Quinto decimo kalendas junii.'   By oversight Bury gives June 17, 839 (*A History of the Eastern Roman Empire,* p. 273).

carried out here have revealed the whole plan of the palatial building. A portion of the walls of the throne room where this famous scene took place still now overhangs the modest houses of the German community of our day.'[8]

The second section of Prudentius' report, which is particularly important for us, relates that along with his envoys the Emperor sent also some men who called themselves and their own people *Rhos*; they asserted that their king, Chacanus by name, had sent them to Theophilus to establish amity (*amicitiae causa*). In his letter to Lewis, Theophilus begged him to be kind enough to help them to return to their own home through his Empire, because the way by which they had come to Constantinople was now occupied by barbarian and most ferocious peoples, and Theophilus did not wish them to incur danger on their way home. After a thorough investigation of their mission Lewis learned that they were from the nation of Sueones (Sueonum); suspecting that they might be spies of 'that and our empire'[9] rather than envoys of peace, he decided to detain them till he could be certain whether they had revealed their true purpose. Through the Byzantine envoys Lewis notified Theophilus of his decision; he wrote that in consideration of his affection for Theophilus he had well received his envoys; and if they proved trustworthy and if an occasion presented itself to send them back to their country without peril, that should be done; but, if the event proved otherwise, Lewis' envoys would return them to Theophilus in order that he might decide himself what to do with them.[10] Prudentius' Latin text is so clear that the Latin translation made at Lewis' court of the original Greek text of Theophilus' letter to Lewis must have been very well done. I can see no such difficulties as to its interpretation as Th. Uspenski writes of in one of his studies.[11]

The most significant statement for us in Prudentius' *Annals* is that upon investigation the Ros (Rhos) called themselves *Sueones*, i.e., Swedes. Here is striking confirmation of the fact that the people of Rhos in the first pages of Russian history were Scandinavians by origin. For a very long time an almost insurmountable difficulty in the interpretation of Prudentius' text was the stubborn and unyielding adherence of most

---

[8] F. Braun, 'Varangians in Russia,' *Beseda*, no. 6–7 (Berlin, 1925), 317–318 (in Russian).

[9] I.e., the Byzantine and Western Empires.

[10] *Monumenta hist. Germaniae*, I, 434; ed. G. Dehaisnes, pp. 34–35; ed. G. Waitz (1883), p. 19. I see no reason to suppose, as Vernadsky does, that the order of the Frankish emperor to arrest the Russian envoys was the result of secret advice from Constantinople (Vernadski, *Ancient Russia* [New Haven, 1943], p. 307). Theophilus' attitude towards the envoys was sincere and friendly; he really wished to help them to return safely to their own country.

[11] See Th. Uspenski, 'The First Pages of the Russian Annals and Byzantine Popular Tales,' *Zapiski of the Odessa Society of History and Antiquities*, XXXII (1914), 9 (pagination of separate reprint); cf. also p. 4 (in Russian).

scholars to the statement given by the Russian annals that the Russian state on the Dnieper was founded about 862. If this were true, who were the Russians who appeared at the court of Lewis the Pious in 839 and who pretended to be Swedes, that is, of Scandinavian origin? There would be no point in listing here various opinions on this subject, because at the present day they have no essential historical importance. We know now that Russian history did not begin with the formation of the Russo-Varangian state at Kiev, which was but a stage in a protracted historical process.[12] We know also from Shakhmatov's works that the Russian state of Kiev was founded about 840,[13] certainly many years before the traditional year 862. The question from where the Swedish *Rhos* could have come in 839 to Constantinople and to Ingelheim exists no longer; they not only *could* have come from Kiev but they actually did. They were the first representatives of the young Russo-Varangian-Swedish state in the middle part of the Dnieper which was founded there about 840, with its chief center at Kiev.[14]

Another very great difficulty in interpreting this text has for many years presented itself in Prudentius' words that the king of the *Rhos* who came in 839 to Ingelheim was called Khagan (*rex illorum Chacanus vocabulo*). It is very well known that Khagan was the title of the ruler of the Khazars, who, in the eighth and in the first half of the ninth century, played an extremely important part in the history of Eastern Europe and for a time controlled the middle course of the Dnieper, — in other words the territory which was to be the future Russian state with its capital at Kiev. According to one writer, the Russia of the State of Kiev was even to some extent a modification and development of the Khazar State.[15]

[12] G. Vernadsky, 'Lebedia, Studies on the Magyar Background of Kievan Russia,' *Byzantion*, XIV (1939), 179.

[13] A. Shakhmatov, *The Earliest Fortunes of the Russian Nation* (Petrograd, 1919), pp. 58, 60 (in Russian). A. Vasiliev, *La Russie primitive et Byzance. Premier recueil dedié à la mémoire de Théodore Uspenskij* (Paris, 1930), p. 12. Cf. G. Vernadsky, *Essay of a History of Eurasia* (Berlin, 1934), p. 54: 'In the 'fifties of the ninth century a group of Varangians took the state power at Kiev' (in Russian). Many years ago, V. Klyuchevski wrote: 'I do not think that the arrival of Rurik in Novgorod can properly be regarded as the beginning of the Russian Empire' (*A History of Russia*, transl. by C. Hogarth, I, 73).

[14] About the *Rhos* of 839 A. Kunik speculated thus almost a hundred years ago: 'The men who in 838 were sent as *amicitiae petitores* to Byzantium (perhaps by Rurik's father) are therefore to be regarded as the forerunners of Askold (*ca* 862) and of Oleg's guests in 882.' Kunik, 'Kritische Bemerkungen zu den Rafn'scher Antiquités Russes und zu dem Kruseschen Chronicon Nordmannorum,' Erster Beitrag, *Bulletin de la classe des sciences historiques, philologiques et politiques de l'Académie des Sciences de Saint Pétersbourg*, VII (1850), 214, note 43. This study is often referred to as *Remarques critiques*. By 'Oleg's guests' Kunik meant Oleg and his troops, who captured Kiev in 882 and according to legendary tradition presented themselves as traders going to Constantinople, i.e., guests, as traders are often called in old Russian texts.

[15] V. Parkhomenko, 'Kievan Rus and Khazaria,' *Slavia*, VI (1927–1928), 383–384 (in Russian).

Most recently Brutzkus wrote that even the raid on Byzantium in 860 had been made by the Khazars with the aid of Swedish warriors.[16]   Some writers have been inclined to believe that the Rhos at Constantinople and Ingelheim were the envoys of the ruler (Khagan) of Khazaria, that Russians of Scandinavian origin at that time were subjects of the Khazars.[17] But now, according to recent investigations, we learn that about the middle of the ninth century Scandinavian Varangians drove the Khazar governor out of Kiev and took possession of the city.[18]   But the Khazar influence survived in Russian terminology after the liberation of Kiev from the Khazar domination, so that in later times the title of Khagan was occasionally applied to the Russian princes even by Russian writers themselves.   In the eleventh century the Metropolitan of Kiev, Hilarion, in his eulogy of the Russian Prince Vladimir, calls him 'the Great Khagan of our country, Vladimir,' and again, 'this glorious one born from glorious ones, noble from noble ones, our Khagan Vladimir.'[19]   The same title applied to Vladimir is mentioned also in an inscription which was discovered in 1928 in the cathedral of Saint Sophia of Kiev.[20]   In his recent book on Russian culture Professor G. Vernadsky refers to the Russian principality of Kiev itself as 'the Russian Khaganate' and 'the Khaganate of Kiev.'[21]   It is not irrelevant to remember that the Arab geographer of

[16] Y. Brutzkus, 'The Khazars and Kievan Russia,' in a Russian magazine published in New York City, *Novoselye*, no. 6 (1943), p. 79.

[17] See Vasilievski, *Works*, III (St Petersburg, 1915), p. CVII (in Russian).   G. Laehr, *Die Anfänge des russischen Reiches* (Berlin, 1930), p. 16 and 122, n. 18.

[18] See Vernadsky, *Essay of a History of Eurasia* (Berlin, 1934), p. 54 (in Russian).   Cf. the preface to the recent book by M. Artamonov, *Studies in the Ancient History of the Khazars* (Leningrad, 1936), p. VI (in Russian).   Artamonov's book covers the period to the end of the sixth century, and his chronological index ends with the year 738.   As far as I know, the continuation of this study has not yet come out.   We have now a very useful bibliography, though of course not an absolutely complete one, on the question of *the Khazars* compiled by the Slavonic Division of the New York Public Library (New York, 1939).

[19] See for instance Vasilievski, *On the History of the Years 976–986, Works*, II (1), p. 97 (in Russian). A. Ponomarev, *Pamjatniki drevne-russkoi cerkovno-učitelnoi literatury*, I (St Petersburg, 1894), 70. P. Smirnov, *The Route of the Volga in Ancient Russia* (Kiev, 1928), pp. 136–137 (in Ukrainian). The eulogy was delivered by Hilarion before Saint Vladimir's tomb in the presence of the Great Prince Yaroslav.   V. Sokolov, 'On the Sermon on the Law and Divine Grace of Hilarion,' *Izvestija Otdelenija Russkago Jazyka i Slovesnosti*, XXII, 2 (1917–1918), 319 (in Russian).

[20] See G. Laehr, *op. cit.*, p. 122, no. 18.   V. Parkhomenko, 'Contributions to the question of the Norman Conquest and the Origin of Russia,' in the Russian magazine *Istorik Marxist*, IV (Leningrad, 1938), 109 (in Russian).   As far as I know this interesting inscription has not yet been published. In connection with this question cf. the statement by C. A. Macartney, *The Magyars in the Ninth Century* (Cambridge, 1930), p. 67: 'The Russian Chronicle nowhere gives us any foundation to suppose that the Russian rulers ever in reality took the title of Khagan.   If, indeed, they adopted it in the first flush of Oriental adventure, it soon fell into desuetude.'

[21] G. Vernadsky, *Links (Zvenya) of Russian Culture. Ancient Russia*, I (1938), 137, 172, 174 (in Russian).   Also in his recent book *Ancient Russia* (New Haven, 1943), *passim*.   Vernadsky prefers the spelling 'kagan,' 'kaganate' since it corresponds to that of the official title of the Russian rulers

the tenth century Ibn Rostah (Ibn Dastah) and the Persian geographer of the eleventh century, Gardisi, who repeated Ibn Rostah's information, write that the Russians had a king who was called Khagan-Rus.[22] Therefore, if Prudentius' Annals state that the King of the *Rhos* in 839 bore the title of Khagan, this does not signify that at that time the *Rhos* were subjects of the Khazars. On the contrary, the Russian envoys of 839 represented the independent Russian state with its capital at Kiev, and the Khazar title of its ruler is to be explained as a survival of the former domination of the Khazars over that region in the eighth and earlier ninth century.

Let us turn to another point. Prudentius' text reports that the *Rhos*, who had come to Constantinople from the north, could not return to their country by the same way, because it was occupied by barbarian and most ferocious peoples (*inter barbaras et nimiae feritatis gentes immanissimas habuerant*). Shakhmatov is inclined to believe that these were the Khazars, who, if they were informed of the negotiations directed against them in Constantinople, might have given orders for the seizure of the Russian envoys on their way home.[23] I cannot share Shakhmatov's conjecture, because relations between the Byzantine Empire and the Khazar Khaganate were friendly and even strengthened by marriages between members of the Imperial family and Khazar princesses. The Byzantines would never have called the Khazars 'a barbarian and most ferocious people.' These were doubtless the Magyar hordes which at that time occupied the territory of the steppes of present-day Russia and in their steady advance westwards crossed the Dnieper.[24] A Hungarian historian writes: 'In the middle of the ninth century, the Onogur-Magyars separated from the bonds of the Khazar state and, moving westward at the end of the century conquered the country they occupy today.'[25]

---

of Tmutorokan and Kiev. See his *Ancient Russia*, p. 179, n. 5. The spelling 'khagan' is a tentative transliteration of the original Turkish title.

[22] Ibn Rostah, ed. de Goeje, *Bibliotheca geographorum arabicorum*, VII (Leyden, 1892), 132. D. Khvolson, *Accounts of Ibn Dastah on Khazars, Slavs, and Russians* (St Petersburg, 1869), p. 35 (in Russian). Gardisi gives the same story as Ibn Rostah. V. Barthold, 'Report of an Expedition to Central Asia, 1893–1894,' *Mémoires de l'Académie des Sciences de Saint-Pétersbourg*, VIII e série, I (1897), no. 4, p. 100 (Persian text) and 123–124 (Russian translation). Hudud al-Alam, *The Regions of the World. A Persian Geography 982 A.D.* Translated and explained by V. Minorski (Oxford, 1937), p. 159, 432–438.

[23] Shakhmatov, *The Earliest Fortunes of the Russian Nation* (Petrograd, 1919), p. 58.

[24] See K. Grot, *Moravia and the Magyars from the middle of the ninth to the beginning of the tenth century* (St Petersburg, 1881), pp. 204, 232–233 (in Russian). G. Laehr, *op. cit.*, pp. 16–17. A. Vasiliev, *The Goths in the Crimea* (Cambridge, Massachusetts, 1936), pp. 112–113. J. Bury, *A History of the Eastern Roman Empire* (London, 1912), pp. 423–425. Vasilievski, *Works*, III, p. CXVIII (in Russian). C. Macartney, *The Magyars in the Ninth Century* (Cambridge, 1930), p. 67.

[25] J. Moravcsik, 'Zur Geschichte der Onoguren,' *Ungarische Jahrbücher*, X, 1–2 (1930), 89.

Lewis' suspicion that the Russian envoys might have been spies is very understandable, if we take into consideration the general political situation of his Empire.   It had already suffered greatly from Norman raids; since 834 the Normans, i.e., Danes and Norwegians, had been devastating, year after year, the shores of Friesland; in 838 it was decided to build a fleet and organize a coast guard against these pirates.   It is not surprising that the mysterious Russian newcomers who revealed their Swedish origin, might have been suspected of espionage, and that Lewis very carefully investigated their motives.[26]   Unfortunately we do not know his final decision and whether the envoys were allowed to proceed through his Empire in order to reach their northern destination or were returned to Constantinople.[27]   Since Prudentius never mentions that the *Rhos* envoys were sent back to Constantinople, we may surmise that they were finally acquitted of espionage and were allowed to leave Ingelheim and proceed to their own country.

Nor do we know whether they had succeeded, in the previous year, 838, in making a friendly agreement with the Byzantine government. Shakhmatov says that the embassy of 838 had two ends in view: to establish amity with Byzantium and to establish the way into Sweden through Western Europe.[28]   Ravndal remarks that 'conceivably a treaty of amity and commerce had been concluded in 838.'[29]   But there is no positive evidence for this.   From Prudentius' text, however, we may conclude that Theophilus' attitude towards the Russian envoys was benevolent, for he committed the Russians to the care of his ambassadors, and requested Lewis to facilitate their return to their own country through his own Empire.

However this was, we must recognize that the visit of the *Rhos* to Constantinople in 838–839 left no trace whatever in Byzantine sources, and when, twenty-two years later, in 861, the Patriarch Photius preached his second sermon of thanksgiving for the departure of the Russian invaders from under the walls of the capital, he called them, among many other epithets, an ἔθνος ἄγνωστον, i.e., an unknown people.   He may have been

[26] Vasilievski, *Works*, III, p. cxv (in Russian).   W. Vogel, *Die Normannen und das Fränkische Reich bis zur Gründung der Normandie* (Heidelberg, 1906), pp. 76–77 (*Heidelberger Abhandlungen zur mittleren und neueren Geschichte*, no. 14).   N. Beliaev, 'Rorik of Jutland and Rurik of the original (Russian) Annals,' *Seminarium Kondakovianum*, III (Prague, 1929), 229–230 (in Russian).   In the two last works sources and literature are indicated.

[27] In his recent work, Vernadsky writes of the embassy of 838: 'We may imagine, being eventually released by Emperor Louis, they went to Sweden and then possibly to Staraya Rusa,' *Ancient Russia*, p. 334.   Cf. also p. 343: 'We do not know whether they finally succeeded in getting back to Tmutorokan by the roundabout way — from Ingelheim to Novgorod and so on.'

[28] A. Shakhmatov, *Survey of the oldest period of the History of the Russian Language.   Encyclopedia of Slavonic Philology*, II, 1 (Petrograd, 1915), xxviii.

[29] G. Bie Ravndal, *Stories of the Vikings* (Minneapolis, Minnesota, 1938), p. 187.

using the adjective ἄγνωστος not in its original sense 'unknown, unheard of,' but as 'little known, insignificant.' His reference is: 'the people little known, who have received this name since their campaign against us.'[30]

At first sight, the period between the arrival of the Russian envoys in Constantinople in 838 and the first Russian attack on it in 860 is entirely devoid of any information on Russian-Byzantine relations. For some time it was believed that the *Lives* of St George of Amastris and of St Stephen of Surozh gave us information about Russian attacks on Byzantine territory before 860; but we know now that these deal with later times. But it is clear that, between 838 and 860, some relations must have existed between the Scandinavian Russians and Constantinople, probably commercial ones; otherwise the extensive Russian knowledge of the internal situation in the Empire displayed in the campaign of 860 would be inexplicable. It is not to be forgotten that the Arab sources supply us with very important evidence of trade relations between *Rus* and the Greeks in the ninth and tenth centuries.

A very vague memory of the relations between the Russians and Byzantium before 860 may appear in Russian annals in connection with the legendary history of the founding of Kiev by three brothers, Kii, Shchek, and Khoriv; the legend relates that Kii, 'being the chief of his kin,' went to Tsargrad to visit the Emperor, and was received by him with great honor.[31] This legend may reflect a real peaceful visit to the capital of the Byzantine Empire before 860.[32]

---

[30] ἔθνος . . . ἄγνωστον μέν, ἀλλ' ἀπὸ τῆς καθ'ἡμῶν στρατείας ὄνομα λαβόν, *Fragmenta historicum graecorum*, ed. Carolus Müller, v, pars prior (Paris, 1870), 168, no. 10. Σ. Ἀριστάρχης, Τοῦ ἐν ἁγίοις πατρὸς ἡμῶν Φωτίου πατριάρχου Κωνσταντίνου πόλεως Λόγοι καὶ Ὁμιλίαι ὀγδοήκοντα τρεῖς, II (Constantinople, 1900), 35. In *Lexicon Vindobonense* recensuit et adnotatione critica instruxit Augustus Nauck (St Petersburg, 1867), Photius' second sermon is published in the Appendix: *Photii in Rossorum incursinem Homilia II*, pp. 216–232.

[31] *The Russian Primary Chronicle*, transl. by S. H. Cross (Cambridge, 1930), p. 140.

[32] According to this legend, on his homeward journey, Kii arrived at the Danube. 'The place pleased him, and he built a small town, wishing to dwell there with his kinsfolk. But those who lived near by would not grant him this privilege.' After that he returned to Kiev (p. 140). This passage, it seems to me, shows some similarity with the story of the Russian envoys of 838–839, who were prevented from returning home by their former route.

WESTERN EUROPE AND THE NORMANS IN THE NINTH CENTURY

IN the ninth century the Normans, both Danes and (to a less extent) Norwegians, became a real scourge of Western Europe. The treaty of Verdun in 843 laid the basis for the formation of the modern nations, so that after that date in the West we can use the modern names of Germany, France, and Italy. Germany, France, and England alike were exposed to the devastating expeditions of the Normans, who did not confine themselves to the coast, but sailed up the rivers discharging into the German Sea and Atlantic Ocean, and penetrated far into the interior of the countries. They sailed far up the Elbe, the Rhine, the Seine, the Loire, the Garonne, and others, as I have said before, and burned such great cities as Cologne, Treves, Bordeaux, and Paris. Keary writes that 'the mid years of this disastrous century, 850 and 851, were years of peculiar misery for Northern Europe.'[1] A French historian, Ferdinand Lot, begins one of his studies with the following statement: 'With the summer of the year 856 opened the most disastrous period which the inhabitants of the basin of the Seine had ever suffered. During six long years, they were to endure Scandinavian occupation, and the Sovereign, paralyzed by the revolt of his subjects, was unable to relieve them, in spite of obstinate efforts.'[2] Other recent French historians entitle a chapter 'The Norman Terror' or call the Norman raids in Western France a 'campaign of terror.'[3] In his letter to the bishop of Argentoratum (Strassburg) Pope Nicholas I (858–867) defines the penances to be imposed upon a matricide; among other restrictions he was not to take up arms against anyone but the pagans. 'Pagans' must have meant the Normans, for the other pagans, the Hungarians — Magyars, were not a serious danger to Western Europe until later, at the end of the ninth and especially in the tenth century.[4] The helpless population of Western Europe, as I have noted above, added a fresh petition to their litany: 'ab ira Normannorum libera nos, Domine.' In a prayer book used near

---

[1] C. F. Keary, *The Vikings in Western Christendom* (London, 1891), p. 271.

[2] F. Lot, 'La grande invasion normande de 856–862,' *Bibliothèque de l'Ecole des chartes*, LXIX (1908), 5. See *idem*, 'La Loire, l'Aquitaine et la Seine de 862 à 866. Robert le Fort,' *ibid.*, LXXVI (1915), 473. F. Lot, Chr. Pfister, Fr. Ganshof, *Les destinées de l'Empire en Occident de 395 à 888* (Paris, 1928), p. 522: in 856 they burned Paris, in 858 Bayeux and Chartres, in 856 Orleans, in 857 Tours and Blois, in 859 Noyon and Amiens.

[3] J. Calmette, *Le Monde féodal* (Paris, s.d.), p. 27. L. Halphen, *Les barbares. Des grandes invasions aux conquêtes turques du XIe siècle* (Paris, 1926), p. 295.

[4] 'Nicolai I Papae epistolae et decreta,' *Monum. Germ. Hist., Epistolae*, VI (Berlin, 1925), 659, no. 139: 'arma non sumat nisi contra paganos.'

Tours in France there were in the tenth century three Masses *pro paganis*, the first of them explicitly referring to *Nortmannica calamitas*. In the same century also there was a special Mass, *Missa ad comprimendas gentium feritates*. A Benediction pronounced on a pagan war in England in the tenth century makes the addition: 'sive contra Danos.'[5]

In their steady advance southward the Normans raided both Christian and Mohammedan Spain. For our purpose an extremely important date was 844, when they rounded the Iberian peninsula and through the straits of Gibraltar entered the Mediterranean.

The history of Mohammedan Spain and its struggle with the Normans is closely connected with the name of a Dutch orientalist and historian, Reinhart Dozy (1820–1883), who devoted his whole life to the study of Mediaeval Spain. Mastering the Arab language, he published many new Arab texts referring to Mohammedan Spain, supplied many of them with a French translation, gave us extremely important studies in the history and literature of Mediaeval Spain, and finally crowned his career by publishing in 1861 his noted and brilliant four volume *History of the Muslims of Spain*, in which his talent as a first-class stylist sometimes overshadowed a scholar's scepticism. Many pages of this fascinating *History* are as interesting as an historical novel.[6] Most of his works Dozy published in French.[7] It is not given to many men, as one of his biographers points out, to complete so fully within their lifetimes the span of their work. At his death there was not one document in his portfolio which he had not used, or a single unfinished study. All that this extraordinary man had planned he carried out. He never did anything which did not contribute to his main object. This is the secret of the great number and perfection of his works, which even today fill us with admiration. After the completion of his *Supplément aux dictionnaires arabes*, Dozy wondered himself what more he could do. 'I have completed my program, and I have nothing important left to undertake.'[8] The charm of Dozy's talent was so strong that for nearly half a century after his death no one ventured to enter his field. To write about the Arabs in Spain after Dozy

---

[5] C. Erdmann, 'Der Heidenkrieg in der Liturgie und die Kaiserkrönung Ottos I,' *Mitteilungen des österreichischen Instituts für Geschichtsforschung*, XLVI (1932), 133, 134; cf. also his *Die Entstehung des Kreuzzugsgedankens* (Stuttgart, 1935), p. 86 and n. 3. In the tenth century *pagani* meant Normans in the west and Magyars in the east.

[6] See I. Kratchkovsky, *Arab Culture in Spain* (Moscow-Leningrad, 1937), p. 5 (in Russian).

[7] Dozy's *History* has been translated into German, English, and twice into Spanish. Now we have a revised and augmented edition of this work by E. Lévi-Provençal (nouvelle édition revue et mise à jour, I–III, Leyden, 1932).

[8] De Goeje, *Biographie de Reinhart Dozy*, traduite du hollandais par Victor Chauvin (Leide, 1883), pp. 40, 43. A. Vasiliev, *Byzantium and the Arabs. Political relations of Byzantium and the Arabs during the Macedonian dynasty* (St Petersburg, 1902), appendix, p. 46 (in Russian).

was, as one scholar said, 'to write the Iliad after Homer.' Only at the beginning of the twentieth century have scholars begun to deal with his topics.[9] I have perhaps devoted too much time to describing Dozy's work. But his studies, especially those dealing with Norman activities in the Mediterranean, are of extreme value for our own study, and as a by-product Dozy contributed to our better understanding of the general significance of the Russian attack on Constantinople in 860.

[9] Kratchkovsky, *Arab culture in Spain* (Moscow-Leningrad, 1937), p. 6 (in Russian).

SOURCES ON THE NORMAN RAIDS IN THE MEDITERRANEAN IN THE NINTH CENTURY

LET us now pass to the principal sources which deal with the Norman raids in the Mediterranean towards the middle of the ninth century. We shall begin with Arabian sources. There are three Arabian historians who are interesting for our study: Ibn-al-Kutiya, al-Bekri (Bakri), and Ibn-Idhari. The most important source is Ibn-al-Kutiya.

Abu-Bakr-Mohammed ibn Omar ibn Abd al-Aziz ibn Ibrahim ibn Isa ibn Muzahim, usually known as Ibn-al-Kutiya (Qutiyah), was born and flourished in Spain in the tenth century A.D. He lived in Cordoba (Cordova), the most civilized city in Europe at that time. His surname al-Kutiya is explained by the fact that he was of Gothic origin by a Gothic mother of royal descent.[1] His very important historical work, which has been preserved in only one manuscript in the *Bibliothèque Nationale* of Paris, is entitled *History of the Conquest of Andalusia* (*Tarikh Iftitah*[2] *al-Andalus*) and extends from the Moslem conquest of Spain to the early part of the reign of the Caliph Abd-al-Rahman III (912–961).[3] Ibn-al-Kutiya may not have compiled his historical work himself, but he delivered lectures covering the material, and then it was written down, perhaps from his dictation, by one of his students.[4] Ibn-al-Kutiya was also a grammarian, and his treatise on the conjugation of verbs was the

---

[1] P. Hitti, *History of the Arabs* (London, 1937), p. 565. In the French edition of the Encyclopedia of Islam we read: 'fils de la Gothe' (p. 424).

[2] Variant *Fath*.

[3] Abd-al-Rahman III was the first of the Umayyads of Cordoba who assumed the title of the caliph-defender of the religion of God.'

[4] The first edition of the complete text of the *History* of Ibn-al-Kutiyah was published by the Academy of Madrid in 1868. This text was reprinted with some corrections and supplied with a Spanish translation in 1926 by Don Julian Ribera, *Historia de la conquista de España por Abenalcotia el Cordobés. Colección de obras arábigas de historia y geografía que publica la Real Academia de la Historia*. Tomo segundo (Madrid, 1926). I am using this edition. The portions of this work referring to the Norman raids were also published by R. Dozy, *Recherches sur l'histoire et la littérature de l'Espagne*, 3d ed., II (Paris-Leyden, 1881), Appendice, pp. LXXVIII–LXXXI; and by A. Seippel, *Rerum Normannicarum Fontes Arabici* (Oslo, 1896), pp. 3–5. Seippel fails to mention the above-mentioned Spanish edition of 1868. The portions of the work of Ibn-al-Kutiya referring to the eighth century have been published and translated into French by M. Cherbonneau, 'Extrait du livre d'Ibn-el-Kouthya, intitulé Fotouh elandalos lilmoslimin,' *Journal Asiatique*, V-e série, I (Paris, 1853), 458–474; idem, 'Histoire de la conquête de l'Espagne par les musulmans traduite de la chronique d'Ibn-el-Kouthya,' *ibidem*, V-e série, VIII (1856), 428–482. The portions referring to the eighth century were also published by M. O. Houdas, 'Histoire de la conquête de l'Andalousie par Ibn-el-Qouthiya,' *Recueil de textes et de traductions publié par les professeurs de l'Ecole des langues orientales vivantes*, I (Paris, 1887), 217–259 (French translation), 260–280 (Arab text).

first ever composed on the subject.   He died at Cordoba in 977 A.D.[5] At
the time of Dozy, al-Kutiya's name was barely known.[6]

For our study the information given by Ibn-al-Kutiya is extremely
important and indeed unexpected.   He is the only Arab historian who,
dealing with the Norman raids in the Mediterranean writes that the pagans (*Madjus*), i.e., Normans, in their steady advance eastward reached
the country of *Rum*, i.e., Greece or the Byzantine Empire, and Alexandria.
We must not forget that Ibn-al-Kutiya lived in the tenth century; that is,
he was very close to the events which he described.   This striking evidence will be discussed later.

The second Arab writer who interests us is Abu Ubaid Abdullah Ibn
Abdul-aziz al-Bekri (Bakri), usually known simply as al-Bekri or al-Bakri,
a Hispano-Arab who lived in the eleventh century.   He was the best
known geographer in that century, and it is curious to remember that
during his long life he never left the Iberian peninsula.   But he had at his
disposal the best geographical materials referring both to his own epoch
and to the past.   Among other works, he compiled in 1067–1068 his
Book of the Roads and Kingdoms (*Kitabu'l-masalik wa'l-mamalik*), which
was divided into two parts: one dealt with Spain and Africa, the other
with other countries.   The part concerning Spain has not survived; but
that concerning Africa has been preserved in the Bibliothèque Nationale
of Paris (*Anc. f. ar. 580*) and in the British Museum (*Add. 9577*), and was
published and translated into French by Mac Guckin de Slane.[7]   The
second part of al-Bekri's historical work, which deals with other countries,
has survived in a *Codex Constantinopolitanus*, of which a copy was owned
by the famous French orientalist Charles Schefer, and in another manuscript which was discovered by a German orientalist, Landberg.   This
part has become known from the penetrating study of A. Kunik and

---

[5] On Ibn-al-Kutiya's biography see R. Dozy, *Histoire de l'Afrique et de l'Espagne intitulée al-
Bayano'l-Mogrib par Ibn-Adhari (de Maroc) et fragments de la chronique d'Arib (de Cordoue)*, I (Ley-
den, 1848–1857), introduction, pp. 28–31.   M. Cherbonneau, *op. cit.*, *Journal Asiatique*, V-e série,
I (1853), 458–460 (by misprint he gives the year of Ibn-al-Kutiya's death as 877 A.D. for 977).   A.
Seippel, *op. cit.*, pp. 20–21.   F. Pons Boignes, *Ensayo bio-bibliográfico sobre los historiadores y geó-
grafos arábigo-españoles* (Madrid, 1898), p. 83.   J. Ribera, *op. cit.* (Madrid, 1926), prólogo, pp. IX–
XXXI.   *Encyclopédie de l'Islam*, II (1927), 424; in the English edition of this *Encyclopedia* the year of
Ibn-al-Kutiya's death is incorrect: 927 for 977.   C. Brockelmann, *Geschichte der arabischen Litteratur. Erster Supplementband* (Leiden, 1937), pp. 232–233.   P. Hitti, *History of the Arabs* (London,
1937), p. 565.   A new edition of Hitti's book has been published.

[6] Dozy, *Recherches* . . . 3d ed., II, 259: 'al-Coutia, qui est encore entièrement inconnu.'

[7] *Description de l'Afrique septentrionale par Abou Obaid al-Bekri*, texte arabe par le baron de Slane
(Alger, 1857).   French translation: *Description de l'Afrique septentrionale par el-Bekri*, traduite par
Mac Guckin de Slane (Paris, 1859), an offprint from the *Journal Asiatique*, Série V, vol. 12–14
(1858–1859).   We have now a revised and corrected edition of this translation under the same title
(Alger, 1913).   The Arab text of the passages referring to the Normans in the Mediterranean is also
printed in A. Seippel, *Rerum Normannicarum Fontes Arabici* (Oslo, 1896), pp. 7–8.

Baron V. Rosen, *Accounts of al-Bekri and other authors on the Russians (Rus) and Slavs* (two parts, St Petersburg, 1878–1903). Written in Russian (the Arab original text has also been published), this study has not become very familiar to West European scholars. Besides the work just mentioned, al-Bekri was the author of a *Geographic Dictionary of Pre-islamic Arabia*, published in 1876–1877 by Wüstenfeld. Al-Bekri died in 1094 as a very old man.[8]

For our study al-Bekri is less important than Ibn-al-Kutiya, since he does not mention the Norman raids in the central or Eastern Mediterranean, on Italy, Greece, or Alexandria; but he helps us to fix the chronology of their raids in the Western Mediterranean which are connected with Norman activities in its Eastern waters just before 860.

The third Arab historian who interests us is Abu'l-Abbas Ibn'ul-Idari (Adari), a Moroccan by origin. He compiled a very important history of Western Africa and Spain. The author of the book fails to reveal his name, but says that he wrote at the end of the thirteenth century A.D. On the basis of the Biographical Dictionary of Ibn-al-Khatib, Dozy has proved that the name of the author was Ibn-Adari (Idari). We know nothing as to his life,[9] but he evidently was a very well informed concerning the works of previous writers from whom he made abundant excerpts; he particularly depended on the Arab historian of the tenth century, Arib of Cordoba, continuator of the famous annals of Tabari.[10]

The Arab text of Ibn-al-Idari was published by Dozy and translated into French by E. Fagnan.[11]

---

[8] The best information on al-Bekri is still to be found in the first edition of Dozy's book *Recherches sur l'histoire politique et littéraire de l'Espagne* (Leyden, 1849). I, 282–307. It is a great pity that in the second and third edition of this book Dozy omitted the chapter on al-Bekri. La baron de Slane, *Description de l'Afrique septentrionale par Abou Obaid al-Bekri, texte arabe* (Alger, 1857), preface. A. Kunik and Baron V. Rosen, *Accounts of al-Bekri and other authors on Russia and Slavs*, I (St Petersburg, 1878), 1 etc. (in Russian). A. Seippel, *op. cit.*, pp. 27–28. *Encyclopedie de l'Islam, al-Bakri. The Legacy of Islam*, ed. by Sir Thomas Arnold and A. Guillaume (Oxford, 1931), p. 88. The author of the chapter *Geography and commerce* in this book, J. H. Kramers, is inexact in his statement that 'of al-Bakri's voluminous work only the part concerning Africa had been edited.' He forgot the studies of Kunik-Rosen, Seippel, F. Westberg. M. Amari, *Storia dei musulmani di Sicilia*, sec. edition by C. A. Nallino, I (Catania, 1933), 48–49. Nallino does not mention Rosen-Kunik's study.

[9] See R. Dozy, *Histoire de l'Afrique et de l'Espagne intitulée al-Bayano'l-Mogrib par Ibn-Adhari (de Maroc), et Fragments de la Chronique d'Arib (de Cordoue).* Le tout publie pour la première fois précédé d'une introduction et accompagné de notes et d'un glossaire par R. P. A. Dozy, I (Leyden, 1848), introduction, 77–79. A. Vasiliev, *Byzance et les Arabes*, I (Brussels, 1935), 373; Russian edition (St Petersburg, 1900), supplement, p. 110. *Encyclopédie de l'Islam*, III, 105 (at the end of the article al-Madjus). A. Seippel, *Rerum Normannicarum Fontes Arabici*, p. 37, no. xxxix.

[10] Full information on Arib in A. Vasiliev, *Byzantium and the Arabs*, II (St Petersburg, 1902), supplement, pp. 43–58 (in Russian). Cf. the article 'Arib' in the *Encyclopedia of Islam*.

[11] *Histoire de l'Afrique et de l'Espagne intitulée al-Bayano'l Mogrib par Ibn-Adhari (de Maroc)* ... par R. Dozy, I–II (Leyde, 1848–1851). E. Fagnan, *Histoire de l'Afrique et de l'Espagne intitulée*

Like al-Bekri, Ibn-Idari describes Norman raids in the Western Mediterranean only; but, as I have already noted in the section on al-Bekri, the Norman raids on the Western Mediterranean, especially in the years 859–860, are undoubtedly connected with those in the Eastern, which are asserted in other sources. Dozy probably is too severe towards Ibn-Idari when he writes; 'But it is not to be forgotten that this writer is a mere compiler who abridges more ancient chronicles, or who copies them verbatim.'[12] In my opinion much information given by Ibn Idari is reliable and interesting, as (for instance) the conquest of Sicily by the Arabs.[13]

Passing now to the Latin sources pertaining to our study, I comment briefly on what I propose to call our major sources. The minor Latin sources will be quoted and discussed later.

The first contemporary Latin source is Prudentius' *Annals* or *Annales Bertiniani*, which I have already described. Prudentius gives a very important date by saying that 'Danish pirates' wintered at the mouth of the Rhone in 859; then, under the year 860, he mentions their attack on Pisa and other Italian cities. Accordingly this contemporary source extends as far east as Italy the raids of the Normans in 860, who were (as we know) mostly represented by the Danes.[14]

A second very important Latin source is the brief Spanish chronicle attributed sometimes to the King of Leon, Alfonso III the Great (866–910 or 912) and sometimes to the bishop of Salamanca, Sebastian, who lived at the end of the ninth century and at the beginning of the tenth. At the end of the seventeenth century Nicolas Antonio (Latin form *Antonius Nicolaus*), a Spanish scholar, wrote several pages on this question, and on the basis of the material which was at his disposal at that time, tried to prove that the author of the Chronicle was Alfonso III; among other proofs he stated that in that century there could have been no Sebastian, bishop of Salamanca, because the city itself at that time had been entirely desolated and was not restored by Alfonso III until the year 900.[15] But

---

al-Bayano'l Mogrib traduite et annotée, I–II (Alger, 1901–1904). Ibn-Idari's passages on the Normans are published in A. Seippel, *op. cit.*, pp. 25–31. In 1930 E. Lévi-Provençal published the Arabic text; *Ibn Idari al-Marrakuši, Al-Bayan al-Muĝrib*. Tome troisième. *Histoire de l'Espagne Musulmane au XIème siècle*. I. *Texte et indices* (Paris, 1930), pp. 368 (*Textes arabes relatifs à l'histoire de l'Occident Musulman*, vol. II). This text dealing with the eleventh century does not concern us.

[12] Dozy, *Recherches* . . . 3d ed., II, 283. Cf. Seippel, *op. cit.*, p. 37: 'Ibn'ul-Idari Maroccensis opus gravissimum de historia Africae occidentalis et Hispaniae composuit.'

[13] See Vasiliev, *Byzance et les Arabes*, I, 373; Russian edition, supplement, p. 110.

[14] *Annales Bertiniani*, Pertz, *Mon. Germ. Hist., Scriptores*, I (Hannover, 1826), 453, 454; ed. C. Dehaisnes (Paris, 1871), pp. 98, 102–103. The identical text we read also in *Chronicon de gestis Normannorum in Francia*, Pertz, *op. cit.*, I, 633, no. 22–23.

[15] Nicolas Antonio, *Bibliotheca Hispana Vetus* (Madrid, 1788), I, Liber VI, caput X, pp. 493–498. I am using this edition. An earlier edition also exists published at Rome in 1696.

in the eighteenth century, the famous editor of the *España Sagrada*, Enrique (Henrique) Florez (1702–1773) was inclined to attribute the *Chronicle* to Sebastian of Salamanca.[16]   Antonio's opinion proved very convincing to A. Potthast, who in 1896 declared that Alfonso was without doubt the author of the Chronicle.[17]   But some discrepancies on this question have continued to exist in the twentieth century, and in 1926, in a very well-documented article on Salamanca in the *Spanish Encyclopedia*, the anonymous compiler said that a Spanish writer and bishop of Salamanca, Sebastian, was charged by Alfonso with writing a chronicle, and composed the chronicle which bears his name (*Chronicon de Sebastian de Salamanca*).[18]   This *Chronicle* was published by E. Flores, in his *España Sagrada*, vol. XIII, under the title 'Chronicon del obispo de Salamanca Sebastian publicado modernamente en nombre del Rey Alfonso III.'[19]   It covers the period from 672 to 866 A.D. or, according to the Spanish era which the author used, from 710 to 904,[20] i.e., down to the death of the King of Asturias, Ordoño I (850–866), whose successor was Alfonso III. The Chronicle can be divided into two sections, which differ greatly as to reliability and exactness; the first part deals with the end of the seventh and with the eighth century, and the second with the ninth.   In his introduction, Sebastian complains of the carelessness and laziness of his compatriots who, he says, have written nothing on the history of Spain since the time of Isidore of Seville, a compiler of the seventh century. Sebastian admits that his story will be based on oral tradition only.   Accordingly his information on the conquest of Spain by the Arabs, for instance, can not be trustworthy.[21]   But his work on the ninth century, that is on contemporary events, is quite different.   In this section his information, although exceedingly brief, is of extreme importance for our study.   He says that, about the year 860, the Normans in their advance

[16] See *España Sagrada*, XIII (Madrid, 1756), appendice VII, pp. 464–474 (introduction to the text of the *Chronicle*).

[17] A. Potthast, *Bibliotheca historica medii aevi*, 2d ed. (Berlin, 1896), I, 37.

[18] *Enciclopedia Universal ilustrada Europeo-Americana*, LIII (Bilbao, 1926), 136 (in the article Salamanca, pp. 104–137).

[19] *España Sagrada*, XIII (Madrid, 1756), 475–489, or ed. Madrid, 1782, pp. 477–492.   The text of this *Chronicon* was also reprinted in Migne, *Patrologia Latina*, CXXIX, col. 1111–1124 (*Chronicon Sebastiani Salmaticensis episcopi sub nomine Alphonsi tercii vulgatum*). In 1871, Ramón Cobo y Sampedro published a Spanish translation of the *Chronicle*, in the *Revista de Filosofía, Literatura y Ciencias de Sevilla* (1871).   The *Chronicle* is not mentioned in M. Manitius, *Geschichte der lateinischen Literatur des Mittelalters*.

[20] The Spanish era begins with the first of January, 38 B.C.   The origin of this era has not yet been satisfactorily explained.   It can be traced from the second half of the fifth century.   In the Christian states of the Iberic peninsula the Spanish era was not repealed until the fourteenth century; it survived longest in Portugal, where it was abolished at the beginning of the fifteenth century. See F. Rühl, *Chronologie des Mittelalters und der Neuzeit* (Berlin, 1897), pp. 205–208.

[21] See R. Dozy, *Recherches* . . . 3d ed., I, pp. 14–15, 20.

eastwards in the Mediterranean reached Greece.[22] He thus positively confirms the statement of Ibn-al-Kutiya given above that the Normans raided as far east as *Rum*, i.e., Greece or the Byzantine Empire. We have no reason whatever to doubt the trustworthiness of the words of these two writers, Christian and Moslem. I will examine their statements thoroughly later.

An extremely important Latin source for our study is the so-called *Chronicon Venetum*, which was compiled by Johannes Diaconus, chaplain of the Venetian doge Pietro Orseolo II (991–1008). The manuscript of this chronicle gives neither the name of the author nor the title of the work. It presents the history of Venice from its beginning down to the year 1008.[23] The chronicle has been called by editors and scholars *Chronicon Venetum* or *La cronaca Veneziana*, because it deals with the history of Venice. The name of the author has been revealed not from the text itself, but from other documents which mention the name of Johannes Diaconus. He was chaplain of the Doge and was charged with several important diplomatic missions, notably to the court of the Emperor Otto III, who knew him very well. Johannes attended the mysterious meeting between Otto III and Pietro Orseolo at Venice, and was the one and only person who was informed of the real cause and object of Otto's arrival at Venice. He gives a detailed description of the wedding of Orseolo's eldest son Giovanni, in 1004 or 1005, to Maria, a daughter of Romanus Argyrus, a Byzantine noble, and niece of Basil and Constantine, joint Emperors in Constantinople, where the nuptials were solemnized with great pomp; afterwards, on the return of the newly wedded couple to Venice, festivities were continued. The events relating to the marriage are described by the author so vividly and with so many details that some historians think that Johannes not only was an eyewitness of the festival at Venice but also had been commissioned by the Doge to accompany his son on his wedding trip to Constantinople.[24] The detailed

---

[22] Dozy (*Recherches*, 3d ed., II, 279) quotes this statement without any criticism or interpretation· Florez writes that, living at Salamanca in the ninth century, Sebastian was able to get his information from good sources ('muy de cerca, y beber en la fuente'). *España Sagrada*, XIII (Madrid, 1756), 471. In 1851, Fr. C. H. Kruse dated this passage of Sebastian in the year 859. *Chronicon Nortmannorum* (Hamburg and Gotha, 1851), pp. 255–256.

[23] On Johannes Diaconus' biography see G. Monticolo, *Intorno gli studi fatti sulla Cronaca del Diacono Giovanni*, *Archivio Veneto*, VIII (1878), 1–45, cf. also Monticolo's 'I manoscritti e le fonti della cronaca del diacono Giovanni,' *Bullettino dell' Istituto Storico Italiano*, IX (Rome, 1890), 37–328. In a concise form *idem* in his edition of the *Cronaca* (Rome, 1890), pp. XXIX–XXXV. M. Manitius, *Geschichte der lateinischen Literatur des Mittelalters*, II (Munich, 1923), pp. 246–249.

[24] Kunik's notes in B. Dorn, *Caspia*, *Mémoires de l'Académie Impériale des Sciences de St Pétersbourg*, VIIe série, XXIII (1877), 230 (German edition); p. 373 of the Russian edition. Supplement to vol. XXVI of the *Mémoires* of the same Academy (St Petersburg, 1875). Kunik, after saying that, according to Le Bret, Johannes accompanied the Doge's son to Constantinople, remarks that

and vivid description of the wedding might at first glimpse suggest that Johannes Diaconus really was sent by the Doge to Constantinople and saw what he describes.   But, as we shall see a little later, this hypothesis must be rejected.   Perhaps he did not finish the chronicle he started. According to Manitius, 'from a rather insignificant compilation his work gradually rises to an interesting historical and political presentation.'[25] We do not know the exact date of his death, but he probably died at the beginning of the eleventh century.[26]   As we have noted above, Johannes Diaconus' *Chronicle* is now known under the title *Chronicon Venetum* or *La Cronaca Veneziana*.[27]

The most important passage in Johannes Diaconus' *Chronicle* has been discussed many times in the past hundred years.   As scholars generally agree, it deals with an attack on Constantinople by the Normans (*Normanorum gentes*) about the year 860.   Johannes says the Normans dared to approach (*adire*) Constantinople with 360 ships; but, being unable to damage (*ledere*) the impregnable city, they thoroughly devastated its suburbs, killed a very great number of people, and then returned home in

---

Johannes at any rate was present at the arrival of the Byzantine princess at Venice, and all his story of this wedding trip positively testifies that the author was an eye-witness of what he describes. Quoting Le Bret only by name without giving the title or page, Kunik evidently had in view the old book by J. F. Le Bret, *Staatsgeschichte der Republik Venedig von ihrem Ursprunge bis auf unsere Zeiten.* 3 Theile (Leipzig and Riga, 1769–1777).   Monticolo, on the contrary, says that in the *Chronicle* there is no indication whatever that Johannes took part in the negotiations between Venice and Byzantium (Preface to Monticolo's edition of the *Chronicle*, p. xxxv).   In 1938 G. Bie Ravndal plainly stated that Johannes Diaconus had accompanied the Doge's son on the latter's wedding trip to Byzantium; *Stories of the East-Vikings* (Minneapolis, Minnesota, 1938), p. 188.   On the wedding of Giovanni and Maria see J. Armingaud, *Venise et le Bas-Empire. Histoire des relations de Venise avec l'Empire d'Orient, Missions scientifiques,* IV (1864), 350–351, H. Kretschmayr, *Geschichte von Venedig,* I (Gotha, 1905), 142–143 (in 1004).   G. Schlumberger, *L'épopée byzantine,* II (Paris, 1900), 323–325.   W. C. Hazlitt, *The Venetian Republic,* I (London, 1915), 117.   A mere mention in Ch. Diehl, *Une république patricienne. Venise* (Paris, 1923), p. 27.   None of these writers raise the question whether Johannes Diaconus took actual part in the celebrations.   Among Byzantine sources on this wedding see Cedrenus, II, 452.   [25] Manitius, *op. cit.,* II, 248.

[26] See some confusion as to the dating of Johannes Diaconus' *Chronicle* in V. Mošin, 'The Normans in Eastern Europe,' *Byzantinoslavica,* III (1931), p. 36 and n. 12 (in Russian); see his own correction, *ibidem,* p. 306.   But the words (p. 36, n. 12) *Blondi Historiarum . . . decades,* p. 177 still remain unexplained.

[27] The *Chronicle* was published in Pertz, *Mon. Germ. Hist., Scriptores,* VII (1846), 4–38; reprinted in Migne, *Patrologia Latina,* CXXXIX, coll. 875–940.   The best edition by Giovanni Monticolo, *Cronache Veneziane antichissime,* I (Rome, 1890), 59–171.   *Fonti per la storia d'Italia pubblicate dall'Istituto Storico Italiano.   Scrittori, Secoli* X–XI.   Sometimes this chronicle was called *Chronicon Sagornini: a nonnullis Johanni Sagurnino, fabro ferrario, tribuitur*; Pertz in A. Potthast, *Bibliotheca historica medii aevi,* 2d ed. (Berlin, 1896), I, 666.   See, for instance, J. Armingaud, *Venise et le Bas-Empire. Histoire des relations de Venise avec l'Empire d'Orient, Missions Scientifiques,* IV (1864), 300.   W. C. Hazlitt, *The Venetian Republic,* I (London, 1915), 117: *Sagorninus Chron.,* 113, or *Sagorninus, lib.* XIII, 552.   Manitius fails to mention the title Sagorninus.   Cf. Aug. Prost, *Les chroniques vénitiennes, Revue des questions historiques,* XXXI (1882), 522.   In 1882 he wrote that the attribution of this chronicle to Johannes Sagorninus is not accepted by anyone.

triumph ('cum triumpho').[28]   This illuminating record has always been
discussed and interpreted as a companion piece to the Greek and Russian
sources on the Russian attack on Constantinople previously dated in 865,
but now generally acknowledged to be of 860.   Exact chronological dates
very seldom occur in Johannes Diaconus' *Chronicle*.   But the raid he
describes must have taken place before the year 863; from other sources
we date the events immediately following the Norman raid in his *Chronicle* in 863, and the events immediately preceding it in 856, 858, and 860.[29]
Since Prudentius dates the story of the Norman raid on Italy as 860 and
Ibn-Kutiya says that the Normans about the same time reached Greece
and Alexandria,[30] we may conclude that the raid described by Johannes
Diaconus took place most probably in 861.[31]

In interpreting this passage, I should like to lay stress upon the verb
adire.   I translate this verb in its original sense *to approach, to draw near,
to approach for the purpose of examining, to approach in a hostile manner*,
but not *to attack*.   This time the Normans failed to attack Constantinople, because they realized that the city was too strong to be taken.
Therefore they confined themselves to the devastation of its suburbs and
the slaughter of their inhabitants; after this they returned home in triumph.

Scholars have been interested in the question of the source of Johannes
Diaconus' record.   About seventy years ago, A. Kunik who, as we
know, was absolutely certain of the fact that the first Russian attack on
Constantinople took place in 865, devoted much attention to this question.   He believed — and in this respect he was perfectly right — that
Johannes Diaconus' report is an independent Italian record.   'As to
whether the chaplain of the doge Orseolo II reproduced the original record

---

[28] Pertz, *Ser.*, vii, 18.   Migne, *P. Lat.*, cxxxix, col. 905.   Monticolo, pp. 116–117: 'eo tempore
Normanorum gentes cum trecentis sexaginta navibus Constantinopolitanam urbem adire ausi sunt;
verum quia nulla racione inexpugnabilem ledere valebant urbem, suburbanum fortiter patrantes
bellum quamplurimos ibi occidere non pepercerunt, et sic predicta gens cum triumpho ad propriam
regressa est.'   [29] See Monticolo, pp. 116–117.

[30] On the subject of the Norman invasions in 858–861 see Dozy, *Recherches*, 3d ed., ii, 279–286
and 262.

[31] Fr. C. H. Kruse attributes Johannes Diaconus' story to the year 860 precisely.   *Chronicon
Nortmannorum . . .* (Hamburg and Gotha, 1851), p. 261.   Recently G. Bie Ravndal dates this raid
as *about* 860; *Stories of the East-Vikings* (Minneapolis, Minnesota, 1938), p. 188.   Like most of the
scholars who have dealt with Johannes Diaconus' passage, N. T. Beliaev in 1929 identified his story
with the expedition of Askold and Dir on Constantinople, as given in the Russian Annals, 'Rorik
of Jutland and Rurik of original (Russian) annals,' *Seminarium Kondakovianum*, iii (Prague, 1929),
241, n. 122 (in Russian).   See also G. Ostrogorsky, 'L'Expédition du Prince Oleg,' *Annales de l'Institut Kondakov (Seminarium Kondakovianum)*, xi (1940), 52, n. 16: 'The Russian attack of 860 ended,
according to the Byzantine chronography, in a complete failure of the invaders, whereas, according
to the independent and impartial testimony of an occidental author, the Russians returned *cum
triumpho*' (Joh. Diacon.).

in undeteriorated form, this is a different question. . . .   The undoubted result of my investigation,' Kunik proceeds, 'has been that Johannes used a written source for the year 865. . . .   But the whole method of presentation in the above mentioned passage is his own.   Had he given in this case his original source in a literal excerpt or translation, his record would have appeared to us in an absolutely different shape.   Then in addition we must note that his own presentation of the event of the year 865 in its sobriety of approach and its reliability is superior to the presentations of Byzantine patriotic historians.'[32]   In my opinion, Johannes Diaconus used a written Venetian source which might have been contemporary with the Norman attack.   It follows, I think, that his passage on this Norman raid plainly shows that Johannes himself did not attend the nuptials of the Doge's son and the Byzantine princess in Constantinople.   Had he been in the capital of the Byzantine Empire in 1004 or 1005, he might have learned more about Russian attacks in general; the Empire probably remembered not only the year 860 but also the Russian princes Oleg, Igor, Svyatoslav, and Vladimir, and the Russian princess Olga, who had come to Constantinople in person.   We have already noted that Johannes calls the invaders, not Russians, but Normans; in other words, he reproduced the western tradition on the Norman raids in the middle and eastern Mediterranean.   He apparently never heard of the Russian danger to Constantinople from the north.   De Boor wrote that the information given by the *Venetian Chronicle* of Johannes, whose origin cannot be verified, stands in irreconcilable contradiction with other sources, Greek and Russian.[33]   Recently another German historian, G. Laehr, has stated that the *Chronicon Venetum* of Johannes Diaconus is in complete accordance with good Greek sources.[34]   The latter statement is rather surprising; there is a striking divergence between these two sources of information.   Johannes Diaconus calls the invaders Normans, not Russians, speaks of 360 vessels, not 200, and finally uses the phrase 'Norman triumph' instead of 'Russian defeat.'   The cause of this divergence becomes entirely clear if we decide that the Greek and Russian sources, on one side, and Johannes Diaconus on the other, speak of two different events: the first deal with the Russian attack on Constantinople from the north in the year 860; the latter deals with a Norman raid in the year 861 from the south, from the Mediterranean and Sea of Marmora.   We shall discuss this question below in more detail.

[32] Dorn-Kunik, *Caspia*, p. 321 (German ed.); 373 (Russian ed.).   See also J. Steenstrup, *Normannerne*, I (Copenhagen, 1876), p. 122.   Steenstrup follows Kunik.

[33] C. de Boor, 'Der Angriff der Rhos auf Byzanz,' *Byzantinische Zeitschrift*, IV (1895), 464.

[34] G. Laehr, *Die Anfänge des russischen Reiches. Politische Geschichte im 9. und 10. Jahrhundert* (Berlin, 1930), p. 94.

Next to Johannes Diaconus comes Saxo Grammaticus, the author of a *Danish History* (*Gesta Danorum*) in sixteen books. We know very little about his life and derive our information from his own work. A Dane by birth, he was born about 1150; he was closely connected with the Archbishop of Lund, Absalon (Axel), the founder of Copenhagen, as his domestic chaplain and secretary, and died after the year 1216. He did not have time enough to give the last touches to his historical work. We know now that Saxo first compiled the last seven books of his *History* (x–xvi), and then, probably between 1202 and 1216, he compiled the first nine books.[35] The best edition of Saxo's History belongs to Alfred Holder.[36]

Almost all scholars divide the *History* of Saxo into two sections of unequal value. Whereas the last seven books, dealing with the later period of Danish history, have great historical significance, the first nine, dealing with its early period and crowded with sagas, songs, and oral traditions, have none. The passage which interests us particularly belongs to the end of this part and is to be found in book ix. I entirely share the opinion that the two sections of Saxo's *History* are unequal in their historical value; but I find it necessary to disagree radically with those who, on the basis of the material which Saxo used for his first nine books, deny them any historical value at all. Sagas, songs, and oral traditions often possess a kernel of historical facts which have not survived in other more reliable sources. Moreover, in considering our particular passage, we may note that book ix, where it is to be found, is the last book of the earlier and less valuable section and thus, being to some degree transitional, may be regarded with more respect than the first eight.

The passage follows: 'After the victorious Regnerus had spent a year in the same country, he summoned his sons to help him and went to Ireland (*Hiberniam*); after having killed its King, Melbricus,[37] he besieged, stormed and captured Dublin (*Duflinam*), which was filled with barbarous (= Irish) treasures. He stayed there a year in a cantonment, and then,

---

[35] On Saxo's biography see Paul Herrmann, *Erläuterungen zu den ersten neun Büchern der Dänischen Geschichte des Saxo Grammaticus*, i, Uebersetzung (Leipzig, 1901), 468–470; ii (Leipzig, 1922), 1–2. M. Manitius, *Geschichte der lateinischen Literatur des Mittelalters*, iii (Munich, 1931), 502–507. Manitius follows Herrmann's study. Danish, English, and German translations of Saxo's work are listed in P. Herrmann, *op. cit.*, i, pp. vii–viii; add also the latter's German translation of the first nine books, i, 1–435.

[36] *Saxonis Grammatici Gesta Danorum*, herausgegeben von Alfred Holder (Strassburg, 1886). I use this edition. Manitius, *op. cit.*, iii, 507, gives the wrong date for this edition: Strassburg, 1858. The previous edition, *Saxonis Grammatici Historia Danica*, ed. by P. E. Müller and J. M. Velschow in two volumes (Copenhagen, 1839–1858) will be also sometimes quoted in this study. So far I have not seen Saxo's recent edition by J. Olrik and H. Raeder (Copenhagen, 1931), 2 vols.

[37] See P. Herrmann, *Erläuterungen* . . . ii, 648: 'A petty Irish king, Melbridge, was captured by the Northmen in 831 . . . Melbrik is an Irish royal name.'

sailing through the Mediterranean Sea (*mediterraneum fretum*) he reached the Hellespont, traversing the countries which lay on his way with most brilliant victories, no mishap interfering anywhere with the course of his continuously successful expedition.'[38]   Then Saxo says that Harald, with the aid of some Danes who were rather unwilling servants of Regnerus, began again to foment uprisings and usurped kingly power.   But Regnerus, *who was returning from the Hellespont*, attacked and defeated him.[39]

It would be quite out of my province to discuss here the question of the identity of the semi-mythical leader Regnerus mentioned by Saxo.   According to P. Herrmann, who has made a special study of Saxo, the historical prototype of Ragnar Lodbrok (Regnerus Lodbrog) or, more correctly, one of the historical prototypes of the Saga king Ragnar Lodbrok, is Ragneri, who belonged to the Danish royal family, but seems to have originated from Frisland; he is mentioned as a leader of the Normans (in the ninth century).[40]   His sons were carrying out raids in Spain and the Mediterranean, in England, Scotland, and Ireland, in 855 and subsequent years.[41]

Now another interesting and rather confusing question arises: What did Saxo mean by the name Hellespont?   In his work Saxo uses several times the names *Hellespontici, Hellespontus, Hellesponticus.*[42]   First of all he means the alleged sea route which links the East Sea with the Black Sea.   In his time the east trade route from the East Sea by boat along the Dvina and Dnieper Rivers to the Black Sea was imagined to be a real sea route, and Saxo, a well-read priest, identified it with the classical Hellespont.   He thought the inhabitants of the Hellespont (*Hellespontici*) could sail across the East Sea to Denmark; they were neighbors of the Livonians and their chief city was Dunaburg.   The King of the Hellespontians, Dian, killed Regnerus Lodbrog.[43]   This is one interpretation of

[38] 'Cumque ibidem Regnerus annum victor explesset, excitis in opem filiis, Hiberniam petit, occisoque ejus rege Melbrico, Duflinam barbaris opibus refertissimam obsedit, oppugnavit, accepit; ibique annuo stativis habitis, mediterraneum fretum pernavigans ad Hellesponticum penetravit, interiecta regionum spacia clarissimis emensus victoriis, continue felicitatis progressum nusquam interpellante fortuna,' Saxonis Grammatici *Gesta Danorum*, liber ix, ed. A. Holder, pp. 312–313 (=ed. Müller-Velschow, p. 459).   In *mediterraneum fretum*, the word *fretum* is used by Saxo not in its original sense *strait, channel*, but in the rather poetical sense of *sea*, like *fretum Euxinum, fretum Lybicum*.   See a German translation of this passage in Paul Herrmann, *Erläuterungen* . . . i, Uebersetzung (Leipzig, 1901), 422; then one of the Danish translations: Saxo Grammaticus, *Danmarks Kronike* oversat af Dr. Fr. W. Horn (Copenhagen-Kristiania, 1898), p. 369.

[39] 'Qui Regneri ab Hellesponto redeuntis armis exceptus . . . ,' ed. A. Holder, p. 313 (=ed. Müller-Velschow, p. 459).   In German by P. Herrmann, pp. 422–423.

[40] P. Herrmann, *Erläuterungen* . . . , ii (1922), 614.   On Regnerus Lodbrog (Lothbrog), in connection with book ix of Saxo's *Danish History*, in general see *ibidem*, pp. 613–661.

[41] *Ibidem*, ii, 662 (Anhang I, Zeittafel).

[42] See index to A. Holder's edition of his *Gesta Danorum*, p. 696.

[43] *Saxo*, ed. Holder, book i, p. 24.   See Hermann, *op. cit.*, ii, 92, note 3.

the names derived from the Hellespont, and with this we have nothing to do.   The other meaning assigned to Hellespont in Saxo's work is, on the contrary, of great value for us.   We have already met this second meaning in the passage from book ix which has been quoted above.   Saxo says that Regnerus, sailing through the Mediterranean Sea (*mediterraneum fretum*) reached the straits of Hellespont (*Hellesponticum*).   By this he means the real straits of Hellespont.   And when some lines below he says that Regnerus was returning from Hellespont he meant also the real Hellespont.[44]   Here is new evidence on the Norman raids in the western, central and eastern sections of the Mediterranean about the year 860.   This evidence is supported by Arab and Latin sources and cannot be disregarded; on the contrary, it is clearly a very important indication of the Norman approach to Constantinople from the south about 860.   Evidently Saxo employed two different sources about the term Hellespont.   His story of Regnerus' successful raid in the Mediterranean as far east as the Hellespont comes from another source than his semi-fabulous stories about the Hellespontians in the north, in Livonia, with their chief city of Dunaburg.[45]   Saxo's report of the raid in the Mediterranean must be regarded as a very essential and valuable addition to our scanty evidence on the subject.

The next Latin source to be considered in our study comes from the pen of the Venetian doge Andrea Dandolo.   He headed the Republic of St Mark from 1348 to 1354, and in his leisure hours applied himself to the compilation of the Venetian *Chronicon*.   It was of course necessary for a Doge of Venice to devote most of his time, during the six years of his administration, to state affairs.   Born between 1307 and 1310, he died in 1354.   It is surprising that Andrea, even if he started writing his chronicle before taking office, had time enough to compile his work, which is extremely long.   We are using the old and defective edition of Dandolo's *Chronicle* which was printed by Muratori in 1728.[46]   A new and much better manuscript has been discovered, *Codex Zanetti, 400, Bibl. Marciana* (at Venice); but unfortunately no new edition on the basis of this *Codex* has yet been published.[47]

---

[44] In connection with this, A. Holder's index (p. 696) is incorrect: 'Hellespontus [circa Düna fluvium],' ix, p. 313, l. 10.   [45] See Hermann, op. cit., ii, 648.

[46] Andreae Danduli Venetorum Ducis *Chronicon Venetum* a pontificatu Sancti Marci ad annum usque mcccxxxix, Muratori, *Rerum italicarum scriptores*, xii (Milan, 1728), coll. 13–416.

[47] The best special study on the historical work of Andrea Dandolo is still an old monograph by H. Simonsfeld, *Andreas Dandolo und seine Geschichtswerke* (Munich, 1876).   An Italian translation of this monograph appeared in *Archivio Storico Veneto*, xiv (1877), 49–149.   In another article H. Simonsfeld has given the variants from the text of *Cod. Zanetti*, comparing them with the Muratori edition: H. Simonsfeld, 'Textvarianten zu Andreas Dandolo,' *Neues Archiv der Gesellschaft für ältere deutsche Geschichtskunde*, xviii (1893), 336–346.   For the passage which interests us in this study, the variants give nothing new.   See also W. Lenel, *Zur Kritik Andrea Dandolos* (Strassburg, 1897).

Dandolo's *Chronicle* begins with the origin of Venice and carries events down to the year 1339, according to Muratori,[48] or, according to more recent writers, to the year 1280, when a new doge, Giovanni Dandolo, was elected.[49] With some exaggeration, I believe, a British historian says that Dandolo's *Chronicle* in narrative is fully as dry and discursive as its prototypes; but in point of precision and accuracy it has deservedly placed its author in the first rank of mediaeval historians.[50]

The passage which is particularly interesting to us runs as follows: At that time the Normans (*Normannorum gentes*) on 360 ships, attacked (*aggressi sunt*) Constantinople; and they attack the suburbs, kill many and return with glory.[51]

The source of Dandolo's record is absolutely clear: it is Johannes Diaconus in an abridged form.[52] Dandolo exactly reproduces *Normannorum gentes, trecentis sexaginta navibus, suburbanum*; for Johannes Diaconus' words *quamplurimos ibi occidere non pepercerunt* Dandolo gives *multosque occidunt*, and for *cum triumpho ad propriam regressi sunt* Dandolo writes *cum gloria redeunt*. In my English rendering of Dandolo's record, which I have given a few lines above, I have translated Dandolo's words *aggressi sunt Constantinopolim* by *they attacked Constantinople*. Here he has changed Johannes Diaconus' words *Constantinopolitanam urbem adire ausi sunt*. I translated Diaconus' verb *adire* by *to approach, to come near*. The original meaning of the Latin verb *aggredior* is also *to go to, to come near, to approach*. In the fourteenth century when Dandolo compiled his chronicle, he had no specific knowledge whatever about the Norman raids, which had occurred in the middle of the ninth century, in other words five centuries before. I presume that Dandolo really meant an attack on Constantinople; therefore in my rendering above I have translated *aggressi sunt* by *they attacked*. But Dandolo's wording can give no valid evidence to change our original conviction that about 860 the Normans approached Constantinople but, seeing that the city was too strong to be taken, contented themselves with devastating its suburbs and returned home in triumph.

Andrea Dandolo gives no exact chronological date for the raid; and the

---

[48] The same date in Potthast, *Bibliotheca medii aevi*, 2nd ed., I, 362. See also Kruse, *Chronicon Nortmannorum*, p. 261, no. VII.

[49] See H. Kretchmayr, *Geschichte von Venedig*, I (Gotha, 1905), 391; II (Gotha, 1920), 536–537.

[50] W. C. Hazlitt, *The Venetian Republic. Its Rise, its Growth, and its Fall A.D. 409–1797*, I (London, 1915), 595.

[51] 'Per haec tempora Normannorum gentes CCCLX navibus aggressi sunt Constantinopolim, et suburbana impugnant, multosque occidunt et cum gloria redeunt,' Muratori, *Rerum italicarum scriptores*, XII (Milan, 1728), col. 181 (Lib. VIII, cap. IV, pars XLI).

[52] See Kruse, *Chronicon Nortmannorum*, p. 261, note. Dorn-Kunik, *Caspia*, p. 231 (German ed.); 374 (Russian ed.). Kunik says: 'Among other things Dandolo borrowed from J. Diaconus the evidence of the expedition of Askold.'

events which he lists just before (col. 181, pars XL) and immediately after (col. 181, pars XLII) fail to help us in this respect. But he says nothing to contradict the fact that this raid occurred about the year 860.

The first scholar who used Andrea Dandolo's story of the Norman raid was the French orientalist Saint-Martin, in 1832. But he of course naturally thought it referred to the Russian attack on Constantinople in 865. The text of Johannes Diaconus was unknown to Saint-Martin.[53]

In conclusion, it is to be noted that Andrea Dandolo's text is not an independent source, but is entirely based on Johannes Diaconus' *Chronicle*; the Doge of Venice has no proof to make us change our conviction that about the year 860 and most probably in 861, the Normans came to Constantinople, but failed to attack the capital and only devastated its environs.

Another Venetian writer is next to be dealt with in this study. This is Flavius Blondus (Biondo) Forliviensis, who belonged to the epoch of Italian humanism and to the opening of humanistic Venetian historiography. Born in 1392, he spent most of his official life and literary activities at the Curia Romana during the pontificate of Popes Eugenius IV (1433–1447) and Nicholas V (1447–1455). He died on June 4, 1463.[54]

Blondus was the author of several historical works. The one in which we are interested is entitled *Historiarum Romanarum decades tres*. There is no recent edition of this book.[55]

The passage with which we are concerned runs as follows: 'At that time when, as we have said, Charles the Bald assumed the Roman imperial power, the Normans, glutted with the booty taken in Aquitania and other regions of France, took a fleet of 360 vessels to Constantinople, and after having pillaged and burned its suburbs, returned to the Britannic Sea.

---

[53] See Lebeau, *Histoire du Bas-Empire*, nouvelle édition par Saint-Martin et Brosset, XIII (Paris, 1832), 228, n. 5. See also E. Kunik, *Die Berufung der schwedischen Rodsen durch die Finnen und Slawen*, II (St Petersburg, 1845), 379. Dorn-Kunik, *Caspia*, p. 233 (Germ. ed.); 377 (Russ. ed.).

[54] See the recent detailed and well documented biography of Biondo by Bartolomeo Nogara, *Scritti inediti e rari di Biondo Flavio* con introduzione di B. N. (Rome, 1927), pp. XIX–CLXXXIII (*Studi e testi*, 48). See also Ed. Fueter, *Geschichte der neueren Historiographie*, 3d ed. (Munich-Berlin, 1936), p. 30 and 106–110.

[55] I have used the Venetian edition of 1483: Blondus Flavius, *Historiarum Romanarum Decades tres* (Venice, 1483). In this edition the pagination is not ordinary. At the bottom of the last page of the volume *Decadis Tertiae liber XL* we read: 'Finis historiarum Blondi quas morte preventus non complevit . . . impressarum Venetiis per Octavianum Scotum Modoetiensem anno salutis MCCCCLXXXIII. Kalendas augusti Joanne Mocenico Inclyto Venetiarum Duce.' Kunik used another edition: *Blondi Flavii Forliviensis Historiarum ab inclinato Romano imperio Decades III* (Basel, 1559). *Caspia*, p. 231 (Germ. ed.); 375 (Russ. ed.). I have also used an old Italian translation of the work. *Le Historie del Biondo, de la Declinatione de l'imperio di Roma, insino al tempo suo*. Ridotte in compendio de Papa Pio, e tradotte per Lucio Fauno in buona lingua volgare (1547).

And almost at the same time the Saracens attacked the island of Crete and took entire possession of it.'[56]

Undoubtedly Blondus' passage reflects the Venetian historical tradition which goes back to the chronicles of Johannes Diaconus and Andrea Dandolo; this is absolutely clear if we note his statement of the number of the vessels, 360, the sailing of the fleet to Constantinople, and the devastation of its suburbs. But Blondus' additions of the coronation of Charles the Bald, the raids in Aquitania and France, and, specially, the striking mention of the return of the Norman fleet from Constantinople to the Britannic Sea, plainly show that he did not depend directly upon Johannes Diaconus or Andrea Dandolo. Evidently he had at his disposal other written Venetian evidence which has not survived or which has not yet been discovered. He could not have invented these additions. Kunik knew this passage; but he was firmly convinced that Blondus' story referred to the Russian attack on Constantinople, which he ascribed to the year 865; accordingly he tried to explain the words 'in Britannicum mare' as a modification of Johannes Diaconus' words *ad propriam* and added that this was probably only a speculation of the author, 'which could not cost him much. Blondus could not have known that the pirates of 865 were for the most part headed by Norman Rhos.'[57] Kunik's speculations, however interesting they may have been for his own epoch, have no value now in the light of our later knowledge.

Blondus' report is extremely interesting for our study, because it confirms once more the evidence of other Western sources, both Arabian and Latin, that the Normans in the Mediterranean extended their raids east as far as Constantinople and returned from the Sea of Marmora, through the Mediterranean and the Straits of Gibraltar, to the Atlantic and then northwards to the Britannic Sea or the North Sea, in other words towards England. This is the most natural and most plausible interpretation of Blondus' mention of the Britannic Sea, which is without doubt based on an older written source and is in full accord with other historical evidence.

---

[56] 'Per ea tempora, in quibus Carolum Calvum diximus Romanum imperium assumpsisse, Normanni praeda in Aquitania et caeteris Galliarum regionibus facta satiati, classem trecentarum sexaginta navium Constantinopolim duxere, suburbanisque illius spoliatis atque incensis in Britannicum mare sunt reversi; et fere per eadem tempora Saraceni Cretam insulam aggressi ea omni sunt potiti,' Blondus, *Historiarum Romanarum decades tres* (Venetiis, 1483), foll. ovii^v–oviii^r (these figures are not indicated in the book). See the Italian translation of this passage with a few omissions by Lucio Fauno (1547), p. 89 verso. For *Britannicum mare* of the Latin text the translation gives *nel mare di Bertagna (sic!)*, and then proceeds: 'Poco avanti a questi tempi s'erano i Saraceni insignoriti de l'isola di Candia.' A rather inaccurate title of Blondus' work, 'a later Venetian story of about 1450 by Blondus or Biondo,' is given in G. B. Ravndal, *Stories of the East-Vikings*, p. 188.

[57] Dorn-Kunik, *Caspia*, pp. 231–232 (Germ. ed.); 375 (Russ. ed.).

The chronological data which Blondus gives in his book in connection with the Norman raid on Constantinople differ in their value.   His reference to the destructive raids on Aquitaine which preceded the raid on Constantinople is chronologically correct, because Aquitaine was attacked and devastated by the Normans in the years 843, 849, and 857,[58] in other words before the years 860 or 861, when the Constantinopolitan raid took place.   On the other hand, his reference to the coronation of Charles the Bald is quite erroneous: Charles the Bald reached Rome and was crowned by Pope John VIII on Christmas Day, 875.   Moreover, Blondus' statement that the raid was made almost at the time of the conquest of the island of Crete by the Arabs is not correct, for this conquest of Crete was achieved in the 'twenties of the ninth century (about 826–827).[59]   But we have the correct date for the Norman raid, 860 or 861, as we know from other sources.   Another work of Blondus, *On the Origin and Deeds of the Venetians*, contains no mention of this Norman raid.[60]

It is to be noted that Blondus' tale attracted the critical attention of one of the Italian humanists, Sabellicus.   Marcus Antonius Coccius Sabellicus was born in 1436 and died at Venice in 1506.   Sabellicus collected a vast store of material from ancient sources and from more recent historical works, like Blondus, on history in the broad sense, and compiled in a readable form a world history from the creation of the world down to the year 1504.[61]   Sabellicus is interesting to us as the author of an historical work *Rapsodiae historiarum Enneadum*, which, beginning with the end of the fifteenth century, passed in the sixteenth century through several editions.[62]

Sabellicus expresses surprise that when Blondus describes the Norman expedition against Byzantium in 300 ships[63] he says that the Normans returned to the Britannic Sea.   Sabellicus believes it impossible for a

---

[58] See *Annales Bertiniani* under these years.

[59] The Italian translation of Blondus' *Decadus* which I have used says that the Saracens captured Crete *a little before* the raid under review.

[60] Biondi Flavii Forliviensis *De origine et gestis Venetorum*.   Joannes Georgius Graevius, *Thesaurus antiquitatum et historiarum Italiae* (Leyden, 1722), pp. 26.   Some other historical works of Blondus which deal with later periods have now been published by Bartolomeo Nogara, 'Scritti inediti e rari di Biondo Flavio' (Rome, 1927), pp. 3–89 (*Studi e testi*, 48).

[61] On Sabellicus see, for instance, Ed. Fueter, *Geschichte der neueren Historiographie*, 3d ed. (Munich-Berlin, 1936), pp. 30–35.   A. Prost, 'Les chroniques vénitiennes,' *Revue des questions historiques*, XXXI (1882), 525.

[62] *Rapsodiae historiarum Enneadum* Marci Antonii Cocci Sabellici, Ab urbe condita.   Pars secunda sex posteriores complectens Enneades.   Here I am using two editions of this work, Venice, 1535, and Basel, 1538.   Kunik also used this work.   See *Caspia*, p. 232 (German ed.); 375 (Russian ed.).   His reference is: Basileae, in fol. col. 630; he does not indicate the year of the edition of the book.   Since his *col. 630* does not correspond to the pages of the two editions which I am using, I think that Kunik used Sabellicus' edition, *Basel*, 1560.

[63] As we know, following his sources Blondus gives 360 ships.

Norman fleet to have made such an expedition 'per interna maria per totam Europae oram et immensos anfractus littorum.' He thinks that Blondus, through usually very circumspect, has made a mistake because of his ignorance of geography, thinking that navigation was possible from the Britannic Sea through Germany and Sarmatia to the Maeotis and Bosphorus and then, from there, to the Pontic Sea. Nor could the Normans descend by the Ister (i.e., the Danube), because the Normans possessed no territory close to that river and the river itself fails to touch the Britannic Sea, to which the fleet returned.[64] As I understand Sabellicus' speculation, he doubts the Norman raid through the Mediterranean and believes that Blondus was confusing information about the Norman attack on Constantinople from the north. In another book by Sabellicus, *Venetian Histories*, there is no mention of the raid on Constantinople.[65]

There is also some unpublished Italian material which may concern our study. Many years ago Kunik wrote: 'In his *Chroniques gréco-romanes* (Berlin, 1873, p. 014 and 015) Hopf mentions an unpublished *Cronica* and *Annali veneti* by Magno (+1572), from which we shall hardly learn anything new about the *Normannorum gentes* of 865.'[66] This note is very puzzling, because in all the copies of Hopf's book which I have consulted, there is no such pagination as p. 014 and 015. Kunik may have used a special copy which has not come into my hands. As far as I know, this *Venetian Cronaca Magno*, which was probably compiled in the sixteenth century, has not yet been published. The manuscript of the *Chronicle of Stefano Magno* is preserved at Venice in *Museo Civico Cicogna 3530*, and it is identical with the *Chronicle of Stefano Magno* in the *Marciana it. VII*,

---

[64] It might be helpful to give here Sabellicus' Latin text in extenso: 'Miror Blondum hoc loco, quum normanicos motus perstringeret, scriptum reliquisse, ab ea gente petitum esse hostiliter Byzantium trecentarum navium classe, vastatisque suburbanis locis in Britannicum mare reversos, qua sane expeditione oportuisset totam Europam tumultuari, si tam longo terrarum circumjactu ut per Gallicum oceanum, Hibericum et Atlanticum evecta classis inde per interna maria per totam Europae oram et immensos anfractus littorum, Constantinopolim pervenisset; suspicor itaque deceptum virum alioqui prudentissimum locorum ignoratione, ut ita rem digerat, quasi pervia sit navigatio ex Britannico per Germanicum et Sarmaticum, in Meotim et Bosphorum, et mox inde in Ponticum mare, quod quidam Graecorum persuasum habuere, et in his Orpheus, cui opinioni Geographiae peritissimi quique non accedunt; neque per Histrum descenderunt potest intelligi, quando circa id flumen nihil Normani possiderent, nec ad Britannicum mare Hister attinet, quo normanicam, ait, classem reversam, sed ut in ejusmodi expeditione aegre illi accedo, sic libens sequor in iis, quae de Saracenis eodem loco prodidit,' Sabellicus, *Rapsodiae historiarum Enneadum*. Pars secunda sex posteriores complectens Enneades (Venice, 1535), p. 327 (Enneadis IX Liber I); Basel (1538), pp. 473–474. This text is also reproduced by Kunik, *Caspia*, p. 232 (Germ. ed.); 375 (Russ. ed.).

[65] Sabellicus, *Le istorie veneziane latinamente scritte*. Degl' istorici delle cose Veneziane, I (Venice, 1718). I have consulted this Italian version of the book. See also R. Bersi, 'Le fonti della prima decade delle Historiae rerum venetarum di Marcantonio Sabellico,' *Nuovo archivio veneto*. Nuova serie, Anno X (1910), t. XIX, 422–460; XX, 115–162.

[66] Kunik, *Caspia*, p. 385 (Germ. ed.); 374, note (Russ. ed.). By misprint Kunik gives the incorrect title of Hopf's book: *Chroniques gréco-remaines* for *Chroniques gréco-remanes inédites ou peu connues*.

513–518. Apparently the *Chronicle of Stefano Magno* is an important source.[67] I do not know what period his chronicle covers, or, if it deals with the ninth century, whether it mentions the Norman activities in the Mediterranean.

Among other unpublished Venetian chronicles I may mention here the work of a Venetian historian, diplomatist, and secretary to the Council of Ten at the end of the fifteenth and in the early part of the sixteenth century, Giovanni Giacome Caroldo, who compiled a *History of Venice* (*Istoria Veneta*) from the time of the origin of the city and Attila down to the year 1383. Although this historian is obviously a late writer, I mention him here because those who have used him for later periods than the ninth century, as it happens, have a very high opinion of his work. I myself employed this source in the Vatican Library for my study on the voyage of the Byzantine Emperor John V Palaiologos to Italy in 1369–1371.[68] A German scholar, Zahn, calling Caroldo *Alvise* Caroldo, writes that class VII of the *Marciana* at Venice contains a great number of chronicles of the fifteenth century. Among unpublished chronicles, he says, that of Alvise Caroldo is a real pearl. Caroldo apparently took from cases the documents which were at his disposal, made excerpts from them, and combined these excerpts. Caroldo's official position increases the value of his chronicle.[69] Of course it is hardly to be expected that Caroldo could give much new information on the ninth century. It is surprising that his chronicle has not been published, for instance by the *Società Veneta di storia patria*. It certainly merits investigation. When circumstances permit us to resume our work in European libraries, it would be extremely interesting to consult a considerable number of unpublished Venetian chronicles and find whether or not they record the Norman attack on Constantinople in the ninth century. If they do, it will be interesting to find the relationship of their records to the text of Johannes Diaconus, or even to an alleged more ancient text, which served as the basis for his narrative.[70]

[67] See, for instance, H. Kretschmayr, *Geschichte von Venedig*, II (Gotha, 1920), 542, 549. I am unable to find Magno's name in A. Prost, 'Repertoire of Venetian Chronicles,' *Revue des questions historiques*, XXXI (1882), 541–555.

[68] A. Vasiliev, 'Il viaggio di Giovanni V Paleologo in Italia e l'unione di Roma,' *Studi Bizantini e Neoellenici*, III (Rome, 1931), 151–193; see pp. 172–173. Following A. Potthast, *Bibliotheca historica medii aevi*, 2 ed. I (Berlin, 1896), p. 192, who calls the chronicler *Alvise* Caroldo (saec. XIV), I assigned him to the fourteenth century. Caroldo was also used by a Polish historian, Oscar Halecki, who published a detailed monograph on the same subject. O. Halecki, *Un Empereur de Byzance à Rome* (Warsaw, 1930), p. 134, n. 1; 320; 340–342, 385–386 (the name of Caroldo is omitted in the index). A few words on Caroldo and his chronicle in F. Hodgson, *Venice in the thirteenth and fourteenth centuries* (London, 1910), pp. 202–203. H. Kretschmayr, *Geschichte von Venedig*, II (Gotha, 1920), 545, 547.

[69] J. v. Zahn, *Fontes rerum austriacarum*, II, vol. XL (Vienna, 1877), p. XXI. Zahn's opinion is repeated by O. Lorenz, *Deutschlands Geschichtsquellen im Mittelalter*, 3 ed. II (Berlin, 1887), 282. I do not yet know why Zahn called Caroldo *Alvise*.

[70] For this purpose see Aug. Prost, *loc. cit.*, XXXI (1882), 512–555; on Caroldo, p. 545, no. 49; 551, no. 137.

LITERATURE OF THE NINETEENTH AND TWENTIETH CENTURIES ON NINTH-CENTURY NORMAN RAIDS IN THE MEDITERRANEAN

PIRATIC activities of the Normans in the Mediterranean in the ninth century have been many times described in more or less detail by historians from the beginning of the nineteenth century. I give here some examples which review the period from the famous year 844, when the Normans captured Seville, down to the years 860–861, when they completed their piratic operations in the Eastern Mediterranean and returned west. In 1826 the French historian Depping wrote of the Norman invasion of Spain and the capture of Seville that this armed encounter in Spain was a strange accident, the meeting of two piratic and conquering peoples, one from boreal ices, the other from the burning sands of Africa, who had perhaps never heard of each other. After having pillaged and attacked the coast of Spain and of Mauretania, the Normans passed into the Mediterranean, ravaged the Balearic islands, and reached Italy, where they entered the port of Luna, which they mistook for Rome. This adventure, Depping notes, seems so extraordinary that it has been called in question by modern historians.[1]

In 1837 a German scholar, K. Zeuss, in a short passage says that the Danish Normans made inroads into almost all the Mediterranean, and quotes the statement mentioned above of Sebastian of Salamanca that the Normans reached Greece.[2] In 1844, a Russian historian, A. Chertkov, referring to Depping's book, writes that after the capture of Seville in 844 the Normans devastated and pillaged the shores of Spain and Northern Africa, captured the Balearic islands, and took possession of the cities of Pisa (860) and Lucca in Northern Italy. On their return from Italy, their leader Hastings lost in a storm half of his ships.[3] Another Russian scholar, E. Kunik, in 1845 wrote a long chapter on the capture of Seville by the Swedish *Rhos* in 844, and later, in his notes to Dorn's *Caspia*, mentioned and discussed from his own point of view the Venetian sources on the Norman attack on Constantinople. Still later, in 1878, he once

---

[1] G. B. Depping, *Histoire des expéditions maritimes des Normands, et de leur établissement en France au dixième siècle*, I (Paris, 1826), 134–135, 164–167. In the new edition entirely recast which came out in one volume in 1844 (Paris), pp. 85–86, 111–115.

[2] K. Zeuss, *Die Deutschen und die Nachbarstämme* (Munich, 1837), p. 532.

[3] A. Chertkov, 'On the number of the Russian troops who conquered Bulgaria and fought against the Greeks in Thrace and Macedonia in the years 967–971,' *Zapiski of the Odessa Society of History and Antiquities*, I (Odessa, 1844), 175–177 (in Russian).

more brought up the question of the Norman raids in the Mediterranean.[4] But Kunik, who was prejudiced by his idea of the exclusively Swedish founding of the Russian state and failed to conceive the possibility of the Norman approach to Constantinople from the South, was entirely wrong in calling the Normans who captured Seville, Swedish Russians (*die schwedischen Rodsen*). As has been noted several times above, the Normans who captured Seville were Danes and, to some extent, Norwegians. Kunik was also irrevocably attached to the year 865 as the date of the first Russian attack on Constantinople. It is not to be forgotten that when Kunik wrote in the forties about the 'Summoning' (*Berufung*) of the Swedish Russians, he was not well informed on Arabian sources. He himself was not familiar with oriental languages, and only later, when he worked with two eminent Russian orientalists, B. Dorn and Baron V. Rosen, did he become acquainted with oriental sources in translation and begin to employ them.

In 1849 the Dutch orientalist and historian R. Dozy, whose significance for the history of mediaeval Muhammedan Spain we have already pointed out, published in French two volumes of his remarkable study, *Researches on the history and literature of Spain during the Middle Ages.*[5] In this work Dozy, on the basis of Arab texts and Latin sources, drew for the first time an accurate picture of the Norman raids in the Mediterranean in the ninth century. One chapter is devoted to the invasion of 844, which resulted in the capture of Seville (pp. 252–267); another to the invasions of 858–861 (pp. 279–296). This is the first realization of the importance Arabian historians have for the question under consideration, particularly from the point of view of chronology. Nor should it be forgotten that one of them, Ibn-al-Kutiya, mentions that the Normans, in their advance, east, reached the country of *Rum*, as the Arabs always call the Byzantine Empire, and Alexandria as well.[6]

---

[4] E. Kunik, *Die Berufung der schwedischen Rodsen durch die Finnen und Slawen*, II (St Petersburg, 1845), 285–320. B. Dorn, *Caspia, Mémoires de l'Académie des Sciences de Saint-Pétersbourg*, VIIe série, t. XXIII (1877); this edition in German. The same study in Russian, in the Supplement (*Priloženie*) to the vol. XXVI (1875) of the same Memoires. Kunik discusses Venetian sources in many places. See above. *Accounts of al-Bekri and other authors on Russia and the Slavs* I, by A. Kunik and Baron V. Rosen (St Petersburg), 1878, *supplement* (*Priloženie*) to vol. XXXII of the *Zapiski* of the Ac. of Sciences of St Petersburg. See also part II of the same study (St Petersburg, 1903). Both parts in Russian.

[5] R. Dozy, *Recherches sur l'histoire et la littérature en Espagne pendant le moyen âge* (Leyden, 1849). In 1859–1860 and in 1881 the second and third editions of this work came out, revised and augmented. I am using the third edition.

[6] In his general history of the Moslems in Spain Dozy omits the story of Norman expeditions in Spain, because they are studied in detail in his *Recherches*, 3d ed. II, 250–286. R. Dozy, *Histoire des musulmans d'Espagne*. Nouvelle édition revue et mise à jour par E. Lévi-Provençal, I (Leyden,

In 1851 a very important book in Latin was published by Fr. Kruse, a professor of the University of Dorpat-Yuryev (which was at that time in Russia), which gives a rich collection of very well documented evidence from Latin, Greek, and Old-Russian sources on the Normans for the period from 777 to 879 in the east, the west, and the south.[7] Kruse gives various excerpts from Latin sources as to the raid of the Norman leader Hastings on Italy, the capture of Luna and Pisa and, on the authority of Sebastian of Salamanca, writes that in 858–859 the Normans reached Greece.[8] Evidently Kruse had not seen the first edition of Dozy's book, *Recherches sur l'histoire et la littérature de l'Espagne pendant le moyen âge*, which came out in 1849. Kruse also used some Arabic sources which were available at his time, and Depping's book on the Norman invasions, which I have mentioned above.[9]

In 1859 a Russian scholar, especially well known in the field of Slavonic history and literature, V. Lamanski, published a very interesting and even now important book on the Slavs in Asia Minor, Africa, and Spain. In this book he briefly tells the story of the Norman raids in Spain and the Mediterranean in the ninth century. His sources were an Arab writer of the seventeenth century al-Maqqari (for Spain only), Sebastian of Salamanca, *Annales Bertiniani*, and another Arab geographer of the eleventh century, al-Bekri. Without entering into details, Lamanski mentions that the Normans reached Italy and Greece and attacked Pisa.[10] In the historical notes to his book Lamanski rightly corrects Kunik's opinion that the Normans who pillaged Seville in 844 were Swedes. As we have noted above, they were mostly Danes.[11]

In 1876 and 1878 respectively a Danish historian, Johannes Steenstrup, published in Danish the first two volumes of his four volume general work *The Normans*. For our study the first two volumes have special value as written by a Danish scholar, who must have been particularly interested

---

1932), the last page 362 and the last note 2. The editor refers the reader to Dozy's *Recherches* and to the article *Madjus* in the *Encyclopaedia of Islam*.

[7] Fr. C. H. Kruse, *Chronicon Nortmannorum, Wariago-Russorum, necnon Danorum, Sveonum, Norwegorum inde ab a.* DCCLXXVII *usque ad a.* DCCCLXXIX (Hamburg and Gotha, 1851).

[8] Kruse, *op. cit.*, pp. 240–243, 255–256, 259. Later we shall return to Kruse's work.

[9] Kruse, *op. cit.*, introduction, p. x and xvi.

[10] V. I. Lamansky, *On the Slavs in Asia Minor, Africa, and Spain* (St Petersburg, 1859), pp. 315–316 (in Russian).

[11] V. Lamanski, *Historical notes to the study on the Slavs in Asia Minor, Africa, and Spain* (St Petersburg, 1859), p. 48 (in Russian). This second part of Lamanski's study, an immediate continuation of the book mentioned in the preceding note, has a separate pagination. Both parts were originally published in *Učenija Zapiski* of the Second Section of the Academy of Sciences of St Petersburg, book v (1859).

in the activities of his compatriots in Western Europe and in the Mediterranean.[12]   Steenstrup uses all material available at his time, Arab sources through Dozy's work *Recherches* and Russian information from Dorn-Kunik's *Caspia*, in its German edition.   He points out the very remarkable coincidence that the Norman expedition to Scythia, by which he means one of the Norman raids in the north, happened just at the time of the expedition of Lodbrog's sons to Greece in the south (I, 126).   Then, Steenstrup adds that, according to Saxo Grammaticus, Regner, a Scandinavian leader, also went once to the Hellespont from the Straits of Gibraltar by the Mediterranean.   Steenstrup poses the question whether the Normans in the ninth century during the Viking expedition into the Mediterranean reached the Dardanelles.   There is hardly proof enough for this, he answers his own question, but there are some sources which speak of it.   Here Steenstrup refers to Ibn-al-Kutiya and Sebastian of Salamanca.   The rumor of Northmen's pillagings in the eastern part of the Mediterranean precisely at the same time has led historians unto uniting into one the separate expeditions in the Mediterranean from the east and west.   According to one writer of the fifteenth century, the Normans, who made an expedition on Constantinople in 866, were the same Normans who pillaged France (I, 127).[13]   If I understand correctly Steenstrup's rather vague statement about the pillagings by a northern people in the eastern basin of the Mediterranean, he means the Russian raid on Constantinople, which, in his opinion, might have extended as far south as the Mediterranean.   As a matter of fact, the Norman raids in the Mediterranean from the west hardly reached the Dardanelles.   But the remarkable chronological coincidence of these two raids misled some historians into considering the two raids as one.   The second volume of Steenstrup's work has the subtitle *Viking Expeditions against the West in the Ninth Century* (*Vikingetogene mod vest i det 9-de Aarhundrede*).   The eleventh chapter of this volume deals with the Viking expedition to Spain, Africa, and Italy (II, 287–302).   Here Steenstrup mentions the Norman attack on the Balearic Islands and on the Italian cities Luna and Pisa. As to Greece, Steenstrup confines himself in the second volume of his work to a note only, in which he says that some (though not good) sources

---

[12] Johannes C. H. R. Steenstrup, *Normannerne*, I (Copenhagen, 1876); II (Copenhagen, 1878). The first volume, which has a special subtitle, *Indledning i Normannertiden* (*Introduction to the Norman Period*), was translated by the author into French and was printed, with the introduction of E. de Beaurepaire, under the title 'Études préliminaires pour servir à l'histoire des Normands,' *Bulletin de la Société des Antiquaires de Normandie* (Caen, 1880), pp. 240.

[13] In his last statement Steenstrup refers to Kunik's notes in Dorn's *Caspia*, p. 231. The writer of the fifteenth century, whose name Steenstrup fails to give, is the Italian historian Blondus (Biondo), whose work has already been discussed above.

record the Normans as going farther, to Greece (II, 301, n. 1, with a reference to his volume one, p. 127). In Steenstrup's opinion, in the Mediterranean the Normans barely reached the Hellespont, that is, the Dardanelles.

An English book, *The Vikings in Western Christendom A.D. 789 to A.D. 888,* by C. F. Keary, gives little for our question. The author began this book in 1882 and published it in 1891.[14] The writing of the book, he says, was due more than anything else to the publication of the first two volumes of Professor Steenstrup's important work, *Normannerne* (preface, London, p. IX). Mediterranean activities of the Normans are treated in the first section of chapter XII, *The Great Army* (London, pp. 320–326; New York, pp. 358–365). Besides several places raided by the Normans in Spain and Mauritania, Keary mentions Pisa and Luna in Italy. After the Luna expedition, Keary says, we do not quite know the next movement of the Norman fleet. In 862 we find the leaders of this expedition back again in the west, in Brittany (London, pp. 325–326; New York, pp. 363–364). He gives no mention of Greece.

In 1906 a German scholar, W. Vogel, published a very accurate monograph, *The Normans and the Frankish State down to the founding of Normandy (799–911).*[15] Although his chief subject is the relations between the Frankish State and the Normans, he pays some attention to Norman activities in the Mediterranean as well. But for this he depends in general on Steenstrup's work. He writes that in 859 the Vikings began their great expedition in the Mediterranean and reached Italy, where they captured Pisa and Luna (pp. 171–173). Vogel tells the story of the capture of Luna in great detail (pp. 174–178). Then he says that the Vikings in 861 sailed back from the Italian coast to Spain; and here he notes, with reference to Steenstrup, that many not very reliable sources have the Normans advance at that time as far as Greece; but this theory is based on confusion with the Swedish Varangians, who, nearly at the same time, came through Russia as far as Constantinople (pp. 173–174; 178). So Vogel gives nothing new as to the Norman activities in the Eastern Mediterranean, basing his presentation almost exclusively on Steenstrup's work.

In 1915 in his very well known book *The Normans in European History,* C. H. Haskins confines himself to the following few words about the Normans in the Mediterranean in the ninth century. 'One band more venture-

---

[14] There are two editions of this book in the same year, 1891, in London and New York. Pagination differs.

[15] W. Vogel, *Die Normannen und des fränkische Reich bis zur Gründung der Normandie (799–911)* (Heidelberg, 1906), *Heidelberger Abhandlungen zur mittleren und neueren Geschichte,* no. 14 (1900).

some than the rest entered the Mediterranean and reached Marseilles, whence under their leader Hastings they sacked the Italian town of Luna, apparently in the belief that it was Rome.'[16]

In 1929 a Russian scholar, N. T. Beliaev, in his very important study *Rorik of Jutland and Rurik of the original (Russian) Annals* gives a brief list of the Norman raids in the Mediterranean after the capture of Seville in 844, mentions the episode of Luna, near Pisa, and incorrectly remarks that according to al-Bekri, part of the Normans reached Greece.[17] We have noticed above that the information about Greece derives not from al-Bekri, but from Ibn-al-Kutiya.

In 1938 G. B. Ravndall, in his interesting book on the East Vikings, points out the geographical vision as well as the political insight of the 'savage' Northmen who in 859 entered the Mediterranean through Gibraltar and projected their warlike expeditions even into Italy, Greece, and perhaps Egypt, as did Geiseric's Vandals in earlier days.[18]

The general opinion of these different historians, to sum up, is that the attack of the Normans on Italy was an historical attack; but they seem to be rather doubtful as to their farther advance east as far as Greece. Steenstrup called the sources which mention Greece unreliable, 'not good' (*ikke gode*); and some later historians follow him in this opinion. Let us see what sources are, according to him, 'not good,' unreliable. Had Greece been mentioned in only one source, in this case we should be obliged to estimate the reliability of that unique source, which is very often difficult and not very convincing. But for this particular fact we have at our disposal three absolutely independent sources. The first is Sebastian of Salamanca, who lived at the end of the ninth and at the outset of the tenth century, in other words almost a contemporary of the event in review; he plainly states: 'postea Graeciam advecti.' Then comes an Arab historian, Ibn-al-Kutiya, who lived in the tenth century; he writes that the *Madjus*, i.e., the Normans, reached the land of Rum, i.e., that of the Greeks, as Arab writers call the Byzantine Empire, and Alexandria as well. Finally, the third and later source is Saxo Grammaticus, who lived in the second half of the twelfth and at the beginning of the thirteenth century. It is true that, generally speaking, he is less reliable than the others, especially in the first nine books of his historical compilation. As I have pointed out above, from his record we may conclude that the Normans in the Mediterranean reached the Hellespont;

---

[16] C. H. Haskins, *The Normans in European History* (Boston-New York, 1915), p. 33.

[17] N. T. Beliaev, 'Rorik of Jutland and Rurik of the original (Russian) annals,' *Seminarium Kondakovianum*, III (1929), 241 (in Russian).

[18] G. Bie Ravndal, *Stories of the East-Vikings* (Minneapolis, Minnesota, 1938), pp. 190–191.

and I have tried to show that Saxo used the name of the Hellespont in two senses, which may be explained by the fact that he himself employed two different sources. Undoubtedly, had we at our disposal Saxo's record alone, not enough material would be available for us to accept the conclusion. But since his record has been confirmed by two independent and reliable sources, Saxo's information cannot be dismissed and must be seriously considered with our other material. I am convinced that from objective study of our evidence we have the right to say that in the ninth century the Normans in their steady advance east actually reached the Byzantine Empire. But where and when this took place is a different question, to which I plan to return later.

NORMAN RAIDS IN THE MEDITERRANEAN IN THE NINTH CENTURY

A. NORMAN RAIDS IN THE WESTERN MEDITERRANEAN

THE Norman piratic raids in the Mediterranean, of course, are closely connected with their raids on Spain. As we have already pointed out, the Northmen who raided France and Spain were mostly Danes and only partly Norwegians. From the Baltic Sea, through the North Sea and the English Channel, they embarked on the Atlantic Ocean and then, through the Straits of Gibraltar, entered the Mediterranean. In this connection we discover some interesting information among Arabian writers to which clings some legendary tradition. The Arab historian and geographer of the tenth century, Maṣ'udi, telling about the Norman raids on 'al-Andalus,' as the Arabs call the Iberian Peninsula, writes that the inhabitants of al-Andalus thought that there was a people of *Madjus* (i.e., a pagan people), who appeared on that sea every two hundred years; they came to al-Andalus through the straits which open out of the sea — Okiyanus, but not through the straits on which stand the brazen lighthouses (i.e., Gibraltar). 'But I think,' Maṣ'udi continues, ' — God knows best — that these straits are linked up with the sea Maiotas and Naitas, and that that people are the *Rus*, of whom we have spoken above in this book; for no one but they sail on that sea, which is connected with the Sea — Okiyanos.'[1] In Maṣ'udi's text the names Maiotas and Naitas should be read Bontas and Maiotas, i.e., Pontus, the Black Sea, and Maiotis, the Sea of Azov. Here we have the widespread belief of that period that the Baltic Sea or the North Sea in general was connected with the Black Sea. The sea on which no one but the Russians sail means not the Black Sea, as often has been assumed, but the Baltic Sea.[2] It is interesting to point out Maṣ'udi's puzzling remark that the *Madjus* come to al-Andalus every two hundred years. Al-Bekri took this legendary detail from Masudi.

Now let us see what picture of Norman raids in the Mediterranean in the middle of the ninth century we may draw on the basis of the evidence which has been discussed above, and some other minor sources.

---

[1] Maçoudi, *Les Prairies d'or*, ed. Barbier de Meynard, I (Paris, 1861), 364–365. See also A. Harkavi, *Accounts of the Mohammedan writers on the Slavs and Russians* (St Petersburg, 1870), p. 129 (in Russian). *Accounts of al-Bekri and other authors on Russia and the Slavs*, by A. Kunik and Baron V. Rosen, I (St Petersburg, 1878), pp. 30–31 (Arab text); 11 (Russian translation).

[2] F. Westberg, 'On the Analysis of Oriental Sources in Eastern Europe,' *Journal of the Ministry of Public Instruction*, 1908, February, pp. 379–380 (in Russian). See also J. Marquart, *Osteuropäische und ostasiatische Streifzüge* (Leipzig, 1903), pp. 151–152.

The first warning to Spain and through Spain to the Mediterranean took place in 844, when the Normans, whom the anonymous Latin *Chronicon Albeldense* calls *Lordomani*, for the first time reached the north of Spain, the little kingdom of the Asturias, which lay between the sea, the Pyrenees, and the Arab Amirate in the south. The King of the Asturias, Ramiro I (842–850), collected an army, gained a victory and burnt no less than seventy Viking ships; whereupon the raiders withdrew from his kingdom,[3] and sailed south. After an unsuccessful raid on Lisbon, where an Arab fleet drove them off, they continued their voyage southwards and through the straits of Gibraltar entered the Mediterranean, where they plundered Cadiz, Medina Sidonia, and finally, sailing up the Guadalquivir, they attacked Seville and held it for a short while (end of September and beginning of October 844). Meanwhile the Arabs were reinforced and gained the victory; many of the Viking ships were burnt. For the time being this action put an end to the hopes of the Normans, who put out to sea and sailed north. For fourteen years they were heard of no more.[4]

The Norman failure of 844 resulted in a very interesting and rather unexpected episode. Friendly relations were established between the Umayyad emir of Cordova, Abd-al-Rahman II (822–852), and the King of the Normans. The latter, after 844, sent an ambassador to Abd-al-Rahman asking for peace, and the Spanish Umayyad, in his turn, sent an embassy to the Norman King. The story of this embassy is told by an Arab writer, Abu-l-Kattab-Umar-Ibn-al-Hasan-Ibn-Dihya (Dahya is also correct), who was born in Valencia, in Spain, about 1159, and died, almost an octogenarian, in Cairo, in 1235.[5] Ibn-Dihya's source for this

---

[3] *Chronicon Albeldense*, §59. Flores, *España Sagrada*, XIII (Madrid, 1756), 452; Migne, *P. L.*, CXXIX, col. 1438. *Chronicon Albeldense* was compiled about 883 and continued by Vigila down to 976 (according to the Spanish era, the years 921 and 1014). See inexact information by A. J. Toynbee, who writes that the first of the Transpyrenaean marauding expeditions from France to the Iberic Peninsula was made in A.D. 1018 by a Norman war-band under the leadership of Roger de Toeni. A. J. Toynbee, *A Study of History*, V (London, 1939), 243, note; also p. 291. In the six volumes of his work Toynbee fails to mention the Norman activities in Spain and the Mediterranean in the ninth century.

[4] The best story of the Norman invasion of Spain in 844 is R. Dozy, *Recherches sur l'histoire et la littérature de l'Espagne*, 3d ed., II (Paris-Leyden, 1881), 252–267 (especially as to the Arab sources). See also a special chapter on the capture of Seville by the Swedish Rodsen in 844, in E. Kunik, *Die Berufung der schwedischen Rodsen durch die Finnen und Slawen*, II (St Petersburg, 1845), 285–320 (Kunik was not very familiar with Arab sources, which at his time were still not very abundant). Arab sources in an English version (from Dozy's book) in Jón Stefansson, *The Vikings in Spain*, Saga Book of the Viking Club, VI, 1 (London, Jan. 1909), 32–37.

[5] The only manuscript of Ibn-Dihya's work, *Al-mutrib min ashar ahli'l Maghrib* (i.e., *An Amusing Book from Poetical Works of the Maghrib*) was purchased by the British Museum in 1868 and is preserved there. The Arab text of the story of this embassy was first published by R. Dozy, *Recherches*, 3d ed., II, appendix, pp. LXXXI–LXXXVIII; then by A. Seippel, *Rerum normannicarum fontes arabici*

story is Tammam-ibn-Alqama, vizier under the three consecutive sultans of Spain in the ninth century, who died in 896.   He heard the story directly, from the envoy al-Ghazal and his companions.[6]

As his chief envoy, Abd-al-Rahman chose al-Ghazal, a highly cultivated man, a fine diplomat and a talented poet, who a few years previously, at the beginning of the year 840, had been sent to Constantinople to the court of the Emperor Theophilus.   After his defeat by the Arabs at Amorium in Asia Minor in 838 Theophilus sought for aid and alliances in Western Europe.   Al-Ghazal was cordially welcomed in Constantinople, and was invited to the Imperial table.   But his mission ended in failure because, on account of the internal troubles in Spain and the Norman invasion in 844, Abd-al-Rahman was unable to help Theophilus in his struggle against the Oriental caliph.[7]

Abd-al-Rahman's embassy to the far-off north left Spain probably in 845.   After a long and stormy voyage al-Ghazal, with his companions, including the Norman envoy to Cordova, arrived at a large island, where al-Ghazal was well received by the Norman king and even recited poetry before the beautiful queen.   Al-Ghazal returned safely to Cordova after a voyage of twenty months.   It is not easy to define where the meeting between the Norman King and the Moslem ambassador took place, or the identity of the Norman King.   Since the embassy is attributed to the year 845, the northern king might have been Horic (Eric) I of Jutland, who died a violent death in 854.[8]   Moreover, since the Arabs use the same

---

(Oslo, 1896), pp. 13–20.   A French translation by Dozy, *op. cit.*, ii, 269–278; reprinted by A. Fabricius, *Akten des Stockholmer Orientalisten-Kongresses* (Leyden, 1891), 121.   A German translation by Georg Jacob, *Arabische Berichte von Gesandten an germanische Fürstenhöfe aus dem 9. und 10. Jahrhundert* (Berlin-Leipzig, 1927), pp. 37–42 (Quellen zur deutschen Volkskunde herausgeg. von V. v. Geramb und L. Mackensen, Erstes Heft).   On Ibn-Dihya himself see Dozy, *op. cit.*, ii, 267–269. Seippel, *op. cit.*, p. 32, no. xxxi.   C. Brockelmann, *Geschichte der arabischen Litteratur*, i (Weimar, 1898), 310–311.   *Idem*, Erster Supplementband (Leyden, 1937), 544–545 (some additional bibliography).   F. Pons Boigues, *Ensayo bio-bibliográfico sobre los historiaedores y geógrafos arábigo-españoles* (Madrid, 1898), pp. 281–283, no. 238 (not very much information).   If I am not mistaken, Ibn-Dihya is not included in the *Encyclopaedia of Islam*.   Before Dozy's work, only excerpts from Ibn-Dihya on this embassy in a very incomplete shape, had been known from the Arab writer of the seventeenth century, al-Makkari.   *Analectes sur l'histoire et la littérature des Arabes d'Espagne par Al-Maqqari*, publiés par R. Dozy, G. Dugat, L. Krehl et W. Wright, i (Leyden, 1855–1860).   P. de Gayangos, *The History of the Mohammedan Dynasties in Spain by . . . Al-Makkari*, ii (London, 1843), 114–116.   In English Ibn-Dihya's story of the embassy to the King of the Normans is given by Jón Stefansson, *The Vikings in Spain*, Saga Book of the Viking Club, vi, 1 (London, January, 1909), 37–39.

   [6] Dozy, *Recherches*, ii, 268, 274.   Jacob, *op. cit.*, 40.

   [7] See A. Vasiliev, *Byzance et les Arabes*, i (Brussels, 1935), 186–187; Russian ed. (St Petersburg, 1900), pp. 148–149.

   [8] *Annales Bertiniani*, under 854 (at the end of the year).   See G. Jacob, *op. cit.*, p. 38, n. 5.   Steenstrup, *Normannerne*, ii (Copenhagen, 1878), 151–157.

word both for island and for peninsula, and since Horic (Eric) I was King of Jutland, the interview between the King of the Normans and Abd-al-Rahman's envoy most probably took place in Jutland.

This friendly exchange of embassies between the Normans and the Spanish Moslems probably delayed for some years the resumption of Norman raids on Spain. A new Norman raid took place in 858, in other words after the death of Horic (Eric) I, who was assassinated in 854.[9]

Thus the second Viking invasion of Spain occurred in 858. It is extremely important for our study, because it was not confined to the Iberian peninsula, or even to North Africa, the so-called Maghrebin coastland, but extended far eastward, to the easternmost confines of the Mediterranean.[10]

Two contemporary Spanish chronicles are very brief in their statements on this invasion, and fail to give us a precise year. The *Chronicle of Albelda* writes that under the King of the Asturias, Ordoño I (850–866), the Normans (*Lordomani*) appeared again on the coast of Galicia (*in Gallaeciae maritimis*), but were thoroughly defeated by the *comes* Peter.[11] In his chronicle Sebastian of Salamanca (or the alternative author, Alphonsus III), under the same king Ordoño I, says that at that time the Norman (*Nordemani*) pirates arrived again at our coasts, i.e., at the coasts of Leon and the Asturias; then they came to Spain (*in Hispaniam perrexerunt*) as the north Iberian chroniclers call Arab Spain; 'ravaging with sword and fire,' they devastated the whole coast of the Peninsula.[12]

The exact year of the second Norman raid on the Iberian peninsula is supplied by two Arab historians, Ibn-al-Kutiya,[13] who lived in the tenth

---

[9] Brockelmann believes that Gazzal (*sic*) was sent in 844 or 845 to the court of the Normans, in one of the Danish islands. He died in 860. Brockelman, *op. cit.*, Erster Supplementband (Leyden, 1937), 148.

[10] The best sketch of the Norman raids in the Mediterranean during the years 858–861 is to be found in Dozy, *Recherches*, 3d ed., pp. 279–286; also p. 262. But of course his chief attention is concentrated on the Iberian peninsula, so that he simply mentions the Norman activities in other sections of the Mediterranean, without giving them any special consideration. A brief general summary of the Norman raids in the Mediterranean, with some chronological confusion, in Kunik-Rosen, *Accounts of al-Bekri and other writers on Russia and the Slavs*, I (St Petersburg, 1878), 164–167 (in Russian). In English, the story of the Viking raids in the Mediterranean in 858–861 based on Dozy's sketch, with an English translation of Arab texts referring to the subject, is given by Jón Stefansson, *The Vikings in Spain, from Arabic (Moorish) and Spanish sources*, Saga Book of the Viking Club, VI, 1 (London, January, 1909), 40–42 (hereafter quoted as Stefansson).

[11] *Chronicon Albeldense*, c. 60. *España Sagrada*, XIII (Madrid, 1756), 453; Migne, *P. L.*, CXXIX, col. 1138. This anonymous chronicle was compiled about 883.

[12] *Chronicon Sebastiani Salmaticensis episcopi sub nomine Alphonsi tercii vulgatum*, c. 26. *España Sagrada*, XIII (Madrid, 1756), 489; in the edition of 1782, p. 492. Migne, *P. L.*, CXXIX, col. 1124. On this chronicle see above.

[13] The Arab text in Dozy, *Recherches*, 3d ed., II (1881), appendix, p. LXXXI, l. 11. Seippel, *Rerum normannicarum Fontes arabici* (Oslo, 1896), p. 5. *Historia de la conquista de España por Abenalcotia*

century, and al-Bekri,[14] who lived in the eleventh century. They give the year 244 according to the Moslem era (of the hegira). The year 244 corresponds to the period from April 19, 858 to April 7, 859 of our era. But all the Viking raids were carried out during the spring and summer season, before the stormy autumn and winter time set in; so that undoubtedly the second Norman invasion on the Iberian peninsula took place in the spring and summer of 858.

A third Arab historian, Ibn-Idhari, who lived in the thirteenth century and simply compiled or abridged older chronicles, evidently united under one year, 245 of the hegira (April 8, 859–March 27, 860) the Norman raids which were carried out in the three years 858, 859, and 860, so that he cannot be used as to the chronology of events and must be rectified by other sources.[15] In all likelihood his chief source was the Arab historian of the tenth century and the continuator of the Annals of Tabari, Arib, whom I have mentioned above.[16]

The Norman raids in the Mediterranean in the years 858–859 were confined to its western basin, and may be regarded as a preparatory stage to their further advance east. During those two years the Normans entered the mouth of the Guadalquivir and once more drew near Seville; but, facing stiff resistance from Muhammedan troops, they left Seville and captured and ravaged Algeciras; then sailing south, they crossed the Straits and captured and devastated the North African city of Nachor (Nekur, Nekor).[17] Afterwards they returned to Spain and sailing north, along the eastern coast of the Peninsula, landed in the province of Tadmir and took possession of the fortress of Orihuela. The Balearic Islands, Majorca, Minorca and Formentera, were attacked and pillaged. Prob-

---

el-Cordobés, ed. Don Julian Ribera (Madrid, 1926), 65. *Colección de obras arábigas de historia y geografía que publica la Real Academia de la Historia,* vol. ii. Ribera reprinted the Arab text, with some corrections, from its old Madrid edition in 1868. See above. In French, Dozy, *Recherches,* ii, 263; in Spanish, Ribera, *op. cit.,* p. 53.

[14] The Arab text by Baron de Slane, *Description de l'Afrique septentrionale par Abou Obaid al-Bekri* (Alger, 1857), p. 92. Seippel, *op. cit.,* 7–8. In French, by Mac Guckin de Slane, *Description de l'Afrique septentrionale par el-Bekri* (Paris, 1859), 213; a new revised and corrected edition (Alger, 1913), 184. Dozy, *Recherches,* ii, 281.

[15] Ibn-Idhari (Adhari), ed. R. Dozy, ii, 99. A. Seippel, *op. cit.,* 29–30. French translation, Dozy, *Recherches,* ii, 279–283. E. Fagnan, *Histoire de l'Afrique et de l'Espagne intitulée al-Bayano 'l-Mogrib,* traduite et annotée par E. F., ii (Alger, 1904), 157–158. In English, Stefansson, *op. cit.,* pp. 40–41. The Arab historian al-Nuwairi, who lived in the fourteenth century, also ascribes the second Norman invasion on Spain to the year 245 of the hegira. Dozy, *Recherches,* ii, 283 (French translation); appendix, no. xxxiv, p. lxxviii (Arab text). In English, Stefansson, p. 41. On al-Nuwairi, see A. Vasiliev, *Byzance et les Arabes,* i (Brussels, 1935), 378–379.

[16] Dozy, *Recherches,* ii, 283. On Arib see above, p. 19.

[17] In present day Morocco. Later this city received the name of *Mezemma.* Dozy, *Recherches,* ii, 279, n. 2. Cf. C. Keary, *The Vikings in Western Christendom* (London, 1891), p. 323; n. 1: the place still called Nekor.

ably the Normans spent the winters of 858–859 and 859–860 at the delta of the Rhone, on the low island, which is now called the Camargue (Camaria). At any rate, Prudentius, under the year 859, says that the Danish pirates, after having navigated between Spain and Africa, entered the Rhone and, after they had devastated some cities and monasteries, took up their abode in the island Camaria,[18] which was very rich in many respects and where some churches and monasteries were located.[19] The island was not an unknown place. It had already for some time been a favorite haunt of the Arab corsairs, the Mediterranean counterparts of the Vikings.[20] In addition to Prudentius' record it may be desirable to cite here a text from hagiographic literature. A monk and abbot Ermentarius, *ca* 863, narrated the miracles of St Philibertus, who in the seventh century founded monasteries at Jumièges (Gemmeticensis) and in the island of Noirmoutier (Herio) in France; in addition to the miracles, Ermentarius also tells the story of the translation of St Philibertus' relic from the monastery of Noirmoutier, which was raided by the Normans in 836. In this hagiographic text we read also that the Normans invaded Spain and entered the Rhone.[21] Ibn-Idhari also mentions that the *Madjus* spent the winter of 859–860 in France.[22]

A little earlier, I have noted that the Normans probably spent two winters (858–859 and 859–860) at the delta of the Rhone. This assumption becomes almost a certainty if we consider what the Normans achieved after their first settlement in the Camargue. From the mouth of the Rhone they went up the river and devastated the country on a large scale; they reached Nîmes and Arles. Afterwards they ravaged the country down to Valence, and perhaps reached the Isère. They returned safely to the Camargue. Only then did Girard de Roussillon, the Count of Provence, inflict upon them a defeat after which they decided to quit the Rhone and try their luck elsewhere. The abbot of Ferrières, in the dio-

---

[18] 'Piratae Danorum longo maris circuitu, inter Hispanias videlicet et Africam navigantes, Rhodanum ingrediuntur, depopulatisque quibusdam civitatibus ac monasteriis in insula quae Camaria dicitur sedes ponunt,' *Annales Bertiniani*, s.a. 859. Pertz, *Mon. Germ. Hist., Scriptores*, I, 453; ed. Dechaisnes, p. 98. *Chronicon de gestis Normannorum in Francia*, Pertz, I, 633 (22).

[19] See *Ann. Bertiniani*, a. 869: 'in insula Camaria nimis undecumque ditissima, et in qua res ipsius abbatiae plurimae conjacent. . . . '

[20] Keary, *The Vikings in Western Christendom* (London, 1891), p. 323.

[21] '(Nortmanni) Hispanias insuper adeunt, Rhodanum intrant fluvium,' *Miracula et Translatio S. Philiberti ex Herisiensi monasterio ob Normannorum irruptiones a. 836 in varia loca auctore Ermentario monacho, dein abbate Tornusiensi (ca 863), Libri duo. Acta Sanctorum*, Augustus, IV, Liber secundus, praefatio, p. 92, §54. Excerpts ed. by Holder-Egger, *Ex Ermentarii miraculis S. Filiberti*, in Pertz, *M. G. H., Scriptores*, XV, 1, p. 302 (ex libro II Miraculorum). See *Bibliotheca hagiographica latina antiquae et mediae aetatis*, II (Brussels, 1900–1901), 989–990. He is commemorated on Aug. 24. Cf. *Acta Sanctorum, ibid.*, p. 67, 9; on Aug. 20.

[22] Ibn-Idhari, ed. Dozy, II, 99. Seippel, *op. cit.*, 29–30. Dozy, *Recherches*, II, 280, 282.

cese of Sens in France, Servatus Lupus, in his letter to the Count Girard, which is attributed to the year 860, felicitates him upon his victory over the Normans.[23] All these raids could not have been achieved within a few months. The Normans, with headquarters at the mouth of the Rhone, must have made these raids in the spring, summer, and autumn of 859; and then, probably at the end of 859 or at the beginning of 860, they were defeated by Girard de Roussillon. The French historian R. Poupardin, author of a special monograph on the Kingdom of Provence, even believes that these Norman raids must have occupied more than the span of one year.[24] Prudentius clearly says that after their raid on Valence, the Normans returned to the Camargue in 860.[25] Prudentius fails to mention the Norman defeat by Girard de Roussillon. But probably the Normans had already returned to the Camargue after their reverse, because this time they did not tarry long there and left the mouth of the Rhone in the same year, 860, as Prudentius states.[26]

Thus, after their defeat in Provence, the Normans in 860 undertook their first raid east of Spain, on Italy. At the head of their expedition were two Viking leaders very well known at that time, Björn Ironside and Hasting. Arab sources are absolutely silent as to the Norman raid on Italy, so that for this we must depend entirely on the Latin evidence, which is rather varied, sometimes not free from the taint of legend, but which in general allows us to trace the most important movements of this amazing piratic undertaking. As has been pointed out a few lines above, the exact date of the Norman raid on Italy, the year 860, is supplied by Prudentius. Doubtless from the mouth of the Rhone the Normans sailed along the shore towards Italy.

What was the chief object of their expedition? Of course pillaging and booty. For booty it was Rome, the papal residence with its limitless wealth, that particularly attracted their attention and stimulated their

---

[23] *Lettres de Servat Loup abbé de Ferrières*, Texte, notes et introduction par G. Desdevises du Dezert (Paris, 1888), epistola CXXV (122), p. 209: 'Illi laudes, illi gratiae, illi exquisita praeconia, quo auctore hostes molestissimos partim peremistis, partim fugastis.' Also in D. M. Bouquet, *Recueil des historiens des Gaules et de la France*, V, nouvelle édition (Paris, 1870), 516, LXIII, an. 860.

[24] R. Poupardin, *Le royaume de Provence sous les Carolingiens* (Paris, 1901), 23–24. Poupardin attributes the second Norman invasion on Spain not to the year 858, which is correct, but to 859. According to him, the Norman raid on Valence and Isere took place probably in April or May 860, and the Norman defeat by the Count Girard in the summer or at the outset of the autumn of the same year. See also A. Longnon, 'Girard de Roussillon dans l'histoire,' *Revue historique*, VIII (1878), 253: the Norman pirates settled in the Camargue in 859.

[25] 'Revertentes ad insulam in qua sedes posuerant redeunt,' *Annales Bertiniani*, a. 860. Pertz, I, 454 = *Chronicon de gestis normannorum in Francia*, *ib.*, 633 (23); ed. Dehaisnes, pp. 102–103.

[26] 'Dani qui in Rhodano fuerant, Italiam petunt,' a. 860. The same references as in the preceding note.

greed.[27] They had already had some experience in attacking and pillaging large cities in the West, such as Cologne, Paris, Bordeaux. Rome had already been several times attacked and devastated. To say nothing of the attacks of the Visigoths in 410, the Vandals in 455, and the Ostrogoths, under Justinian I, in the sixth century, Rome had suffered an Arab attack in 846, i.e., a few years before the Norman expedition. The basilicas of St Peter and St Paul, which were located outside the city walls, were taken and pillaged by the Arabs; we do not know whether the city itself was attacked. Probably not, because this was not a real military expedition, but a piratic raid, a razzia, only organized on a larger scale;[28] and the city itself had powerful walls.

The Normans sailing from the mouth of the Rhone east along the coast, reached the Italian bay of Spezia, in Liguria, and captured and pillaged some maritime cities. Our sources mention Luna, Pisa and 'some other cities.'[29] But the central event of this raid was the siege, capture and pillaging of the city of Luna, 'one of the most celebrated exploits in the history of the Normans.'[30] Luna, an old Etruscan city, famous under the Roman Empire for its white marble, lay about thirty miles north of Pisa, quite close to the famous marble quarries of Carrara. This was not the

[27] Some historians are evidently doubtful as to the raid on Rome. L. M. Hartmann mentions Pisa and fails to mention Rome. *Geschichte Italiens im Mittelalter*, III, 1 (Gotha, 1908), 249. K. Gjerset, *History of the Norwegian People*, Two volumes in one (New York, 1932), p. 49: 'a new Viking expedition was fitted out . . . possibly also for the purpose of attacking Rome itself.' On the contrary, A. Mawler, *The Vikings* (Cambridge, 1913), p. 47, writes that the real aim of the Vikings in this campaign was the capture of Rome with its mighty treasures. In his very well known *History of the city of Rome in the Middle Ages* (*Geschichte der Stadt Rom im Mittelalter*), F. Gregorovius fails to mention at all the episode of Luna and Rome.

[28] See A. Vasiliev, *Byzance et les Arabes*, I (Brussels, 1935), 210–211; Russian edition (St Petersburg, 1900), pp. 166–167. To the evidence given in this book I may add a mention of an Arab traveller of the end of the ninth century, Harun-ibn-Yahya, whose journey is included in the geographical work of the Arab geographer Ibn-Rostah, who wrote about 903 A.D. Harun-ibn-Yahya writes: 'Against the inhabitants of Rome, the Berbers of Andalus and Tahert undertake by sea piratic raids from the country of the Idrisids and from Upper-Tahert,' Ibn-Rostah, ed. by M. J. de Goeje, *Bibliotheca geographorum arabicorum*, VII (Leyden, 1892), 129 (Arab text). German translation, J. Marquart, *Osteuropäische und ostasiatische Streifzüge* (Leipzig, 1903), p. 261. The Arab dynasty of the Idrisids ruled in Morocco from 788 to 985 A.D. Tahert, in modern Algeria, was, from 761 to 908, the residence of a small state of the Rostemids.

[29] *Ann. Bert. an.* 860: 'Dani qui in Rhodano fuerant, Italiam petunt, et Pisas civitatem aliasque capiunt, depraedantur atque devastant,' Pertz, *Scr.*, I, 454 = *Chr. de gestis Normannorum in Francia*, ib. p. 633 (23); ed. Dedaisnes, p. 103. *Miracula et translatio S. Philiberti* mentions only the devastation of Italy: '(Nortmanni) Italiam populantur.' *Acta Sanctorum*, Aug. IV, p. 92, §54. Pertz, *M. G. H., SS.*, XV, 1, p. 302. The editor of the *Miracula* erroneously believes that this statement about the Normans is to be probably referred to the Arab attacks in 845–852. *Ex fragmento Historiae Franciae*: 'Alstagnus (Hasting) a Francorum terra per Oceanum pelagus Italiam tendens, Lunae portum attigit, et ipsam urbem continuo cepit.' (*Recueil des historiens des Gaules et de la France*, nouvelle édition sous la direction de M. L. Delisle, VII [Paris, 1870], 224.)

[30] Steenstrup, *Normannerne*, II (Copenhagen, 1878), 298.

first time Luna had suffered a piratic raid.   In 849 it had been plundered by Saracen pirates.[31]   Our most important source for the siege and capture of Luna by Hasting is Dudo of St Quentin, the oldest historian of the Normans, who wrote at the beginning of the eleventh century, the author of a book on the first Norman Dukes.   Totally lacking in historical criticism, Dudo was an unabashed glorifier of the Normans and their rulers, and often closely followed legendary traditions.   But in spite of these very essential defects, Dudo's information is interesting and important.[32] At any rate, the siege, capture and devastation of Luna by Hasting and his Normans is an historical fact, which took place in 860.   Dudo gives a detailed story of this event, filled with legendary elements, which has often been used by various historians and therefore is very well known.

According to our sources, Hasting's fleet was sailing towards Rome in order to capture the city by a sudden unexpected attack; but a violent storm carried the vessels out of their course and brought them to the city of Luna.[33]   This unexpected deviation apparently was not realized at once by Hastings and his companions, who seem to have taken Luna for Rome.   In an abridged form Dudo's account runs as follows:

Seeing that the city was very well fortified, Hasting devised a trick in order to let his companions find their way into the city.   He sent to say that he and his followers had not come to make war upon Christians; that they had been driven by their fellow-countrymen from France, and that he himself being desperately ill had only one desire, to be baptized.   The Bishop of Luna came out with due procession of priests and choir to visit the sick Hasting to perform the rite of his conversion.   On the following day it was announced that the Viking leader was dead, but before his death he had claimed Christian burial in Christian ground. Accordingly the governor of Luna and its Bishop admitted into the city a cortege of mourners round the bier of the deceased Viking.   In solemn procession, it was conducted to the monastery in the middle of the city, and the mass for the dead was sung.   Then preparations for the burial were made.   Suddenly the north-

---

[31] *Ann. Bert.*, an. 849: 'Mauri et Sarraceni Lunam italiae civitatem adpraedantes, nullo obsistente maritima omnia usque ad Provinciam devastant.'

[32] On Dudo see, among recent writers, M. Manitius, *Geschichte der lateinischen Literatur des Mittelalters*, II (Munich, 1923), 257–265 (bibliography is given).

[33] Dudo super congregationem S. Quintini decani *De moribus et actis primorum Normanniae ducum Libri tres*, liber primus: 'Altis, namque longe lateque fluctibus factis, terrisque cis citraque littora sibi lateque fluctibus factis, terrisque cis citraque littora sibi vindicatis, Romam, dominam gentium volentes clam adipisci, Lunxe urbem (Lux urbem), quae Luna dicitur, navigio sunt congressi,' *Historiae Normannorum Scriptores antiqui*, ed. A. Duchesne (Paris, 1619), p. 64; Migne, *P. L.*, CXLI, col. 622.   For a paraphrase of this story of Dudo about the storm, see Willelmi (Guielelmi) Calculi Gemmeticensis monachi *Historiae Normannorum Libri VIII*, Liber I, c. IX; ed. Duchesne, p. 220; Migne, *P. L.*, CXLIX, col. 786.   A brief but very clear note on Willelmus in J. Calmette, *Le monde féodal* (Paris, *s.s.*), p. 349.   Calmette indicates a new edition of the chronicle of Willelmus (Guillaume), ed. Jean Marx (Rouen, 1914).   Société de l'histoire de Normandie.

men round the coffin raised a shout of refusal.   The governor, the clergy, and the chief men of the city stood astonished, not knowing what this meant.   At this moment the body of the dead Hasting sprang up.   Only then they understood that they had been cheated, and that Hasting had feigned death.   He and the mourners drew their swords, cut down all who stood in their way, and opened the city gates, near which the Normans had set an ambush.   In a few minutes, the town was taken, the citizens were massacred, an immense booty fell into the hands of the invaders, the city walls were pulled down.   Such is the story told by Dudo and repeated later by other writers with some additional imaginary details.[34]

It is rather strange that Hasting and his Vikings mistook Luna for Rome, so that after they had discovered their mistake they treated the city with extreme cruelty and savagery.   But after all the mistake may be explained by their elementary knowledge of Italian geography and the violent storm which had driven them off their original course.

The trick of Hasting's pretended death and his resurrection was a legend which became widespread in the West during the Middle Ages.   In various sources we have other accounts of the pretended death and burial of prominent persons.   A very well known example is that of Bohemond of Tarentum, who after the First Crusade simulated death, was put into a coffin, and thus accomplished his crossing from Syria to Italy.[35]

As has been noted above, the Italian raid took place in 860, and most probably early in the summer, in June.[36]   How long Norman activities

---

[34] Dudo, *op. cit.*, I, 5–7; ed. Duchesne, p. 64; Migne, *P. L.*, CXLI, coll. 622–625.   Willelmus (Guilelmus) Gemmeticensis, *op. cit.*, I, c. IX–X; ed. Duchesne, p. 220–221; Migne, *P. L.*, CXLIX, coll. 786–787.   Following these two writers, an Anglo-Norman trouvère of the twelfth century, Benoit de Sainte-Maur, set the Luna episode to verse: *Chronique des ducs de Normandie par Benoit, trouvère Anglo-Normand du 12ᵉ siècle*, publiée pour la première fois par Fr. Michel (Paris, 1836), I, 49–67, verse 1289 foll., *Collection de documents inédits sur l'histoire de France*.   The principal passages of Benoit's story on the siege and capture of Luna are printed also in M. Depping, *Histoire des expéditions maritimes des Normands*, sec. ed. (Paris, 1844), pp. 399–411.   In the first edition of his book (1826), Depping inserted the complete text.   The Anglo-Norman chronicler Robert Wace, also of the twelfth century, described in verse the same episode in his metrical chronicle, the *Roman de Rou*. *Maistre Wace's Roman de Rou et des Ducs de Normandie*, ed. H. Andresen, vol. I (Heilbronn, 1877), 27–55, v. 476–753.   A mere mention of the capture of Luna in *Chronicon Turonense*: 'Hastingus, per pelagus Italiam rediens, Lunam civitatem cepit, et ibi remansit,' Ed. Duchesne, *Hist. Normannorum scriptores antiqui* (Paris, 1619), p. 25.   *Veterum scriptorum et monumentorum amplissima collectio*, ed. Edm. Martene, V (Paris, 1729), col. 967.

[35] See F. Chalandon, *Essai sur le règne d'Alexis 1-er Comnène* (Paris, 1900), p. 236, n. 6.   R. B. Yewdale, *Bohemond I, prince of Antioch* (Princeton, 1924), p. 102, n. 99.   A. Vasiliev, *History of the Byzantine Empire*, II (Madison, 1929), 58; French ed. II (Paris, 1932), 47.   Some other examples of the same sort see in V. Vasilievski, *Works*, I (St Petersburg, 1908), 234–235 (in Russian).

[36] Prudentius, *s.a.* 860, places the plundering of Pisa a few lines after mentioning the meeting of the three kings, Lewis, Charles, and Lothair, which was held on the first of June (Kalendas Junias). Without giving any ground, Amari ascribes the sack of Luna (Luni) to 859 and the attack on Pisa to 860, M. Amari, *Storia dei musulmani di Sicilia*, sec. ed., III, 1 (Catania, 1937), 19.   Confused chron-

around Luna lasted we do not know; but we are sure it was not a short raid.[37]   The Luna raid apparently brought to a close the Viking expedition to Italy.   According to one source, the *Pagani* realized that they had not captured Rome, and were doubtful of their success in doing so, because the rumor of their atrocities at Luna had already reached Rome, which evidently was making adequate preparations to repel the invaders; accordingly the 'pagans' decided to leave Italy.[38]   It is to be borne in mind that some erection and repairing of fortifications had already been undertaken in Rome after the Saracen raid in 846.   At the time of the Norman attack on Italy the papal throne was occupied by a very talented and energetic Pope, Nicholas I (858–867), who was undoubtedly well informed about the Norman danger in general and was much concerned as to the Norman plans for raiding Rome in particular.   Probably with some exaggeration, Kunik wrote in 1878 that Nicholas I, who could equip against the Normans neither fleet nor foot, trembled on his throne with fear of the Normans.[39]   In November 861, in other words, after the Norman danger had been averted, the Pope wrote with dignity to Unifred, the bishop of Therouanne in Western France, whose town had been ravaged by the Normans, the Bishop himself having left his diocese: 'Know, dearest brother, that it is pernicious for a pilot to desert the ship when the sea is calm; but it is more pernicious to do so in a storm.   It would be more advisable not to run away before treacheries of persecutors, and particularly the "pagans" (i.e. Normans), when in their own time they vent their rage on us and, on account of the great number of our sins, by divine providence, succeed in harming us.'[40]

It is interesting to point out that the Luna raid left a deep impression, probably deeper than that of any other Norman exploit, in the far North, in Scandinavian sagas.   In *Ragnar Lodbrok's Saga*, originally written in

---

ology in Fr. Kruse, *Chronicon Nortmannorum* (Hamburg et Gotha, 1851), pp. 240–243, 259.   In the eighteenth century Muratori attributed the capture of Luna to 857 and the devastation of Pisa and other Italian cities to 860, L. A. Muratori, *Antiquitates Italiae medii aevi*, I (Milan, 1738), col. 25.

[37] The story of the siege and capture of Luna, especially on the basis of Dudo's presentation, has been often told by modern writers. See, for example, J. Steenstrup, *Normannerne*, II, 298–301. W. Vogel, *Die Normannen und das fränkische Reich* (Heidelberg, 1906), pp. 174–178; C. F. Keary, *The Vikings in Western Christendom* (London, 1891), pp. 324–326; (New York, 1891), pp. 363–365.

[38] Willelmi Gemmeticensis *Historiae Normannorum liber I*, c. XI: 'comperientes Pagani se Romam nullatenus cepisse, veriti ne ulterius quicquam proficerent (quippe cum Romanas aures fama volante eorum profana opera iam occupassent) inito consilio de regressu disponunt,' Ed. Duchesne (Paris, 1619), p. 221; Migne, *P. L.* CXLIX, coll. 787–788.

[39] Kunik and Rosen, *Accounts of al-Bekri and other authors on Russia and Slavs*, I (St Petersburg, 1878), 164 (in Russian).

[40] Nicolai I Papae *Epistola ad Unifredum Morinensem episcopum. Mon. Germ. Hist., Epistolae,* VI (Berlin, 1925), ep. 104, p. 613.   Migne, *P. L.*, CXIX, col. 782.   *Morinensis episcopus* is the Bishop of Therouanne.   *Moriensis seu Tarvannensis episcopus, an.* 856–870. See *Ann. Bert., an.* 861: 'Dani qui pridem Morinum civitatem incenderant.'

Icelandic, we read that the Normans reached the fortress of Luna, destroyed all the forts and castles in the whole Southern Empire, and were then so celebrated over all the world that even the smallest child knew their name.   They had intended not to abandon their enterprise before they reached Rome (*Romaborgar, Romaborg*), because they had been told so much of the size of that city, its vast population, splendor, and wealth. However, they did not know exactly how far away the city was; and they had so numerous an army that they ran short of food.   So they stayed in the city of Luna and deliberated about their expedition.   Then follows an episode with a traveler who explained to the Normans that Rome was too far away.   After that they realized that they would be unable to carry out their projected attack on Rome.   They departed with their troops and conquered many forts which had never been taken before; even today traces remain of their successes.[41]   An Icelandic geographer, the learned abbot of the Benedictine monastery of Thingeyrar, in northern Iceland, Nicolaus, who lived in the twelfth century, made a pilgrimage to Rome and the Holy Land (1151–1154), and compiled an itinerary to the Holy Land.   Nicolaus mentions Luna among other Italian cities without referring to the Norman raid.[42]

In Italy itself a story has survived connected with the destruction of Luna, which reminds us rather of the romance of Romeo and Juliet than of Hasting's military actions.   The prince of Luna and a young empress travelling with her husband fell in love with each other.   She pretended to be fatally ill and finally dead; her burial was carried out, but she managed to escape and joined her lover.   In a fit of fury, the Emperor destroyed the city of his rival.[43]

I have probably devoted too much time to the story of the capture and destruction of Luna.   A real historical fact which has been told by Dudo and his followers and given rise to many legends, the Luna episode has

[41] Icelandic text in *Volsunga Saga ok Ragnars Saga Lodbrokar*, ed. Magnus Olsen (Copenhagen, 1906–1908), ch. 14 (13), pp. 152–153 (Rome is called *Romaborgar*).   Not being familiar with the Icelandic language, I have used Danish and German translations of the saga. *Ragnar Lodbroks Saga*, transl. from Icelandic to Danish by C. Ch. Rafn (Copenhagen, 1822), ch. 14, pp. 50–52 (Rome is *Romaborg*); see also p. 147 (another saga).   *Volsunga- und- Ragnars-Saga*, German transl. by Anton Edzardi, 2d ed. (Stuttgart, 1880), ch. 13, pp. 300–302 (*Altdeutsche und altnordische Helden-Sagen* transl. by F. R. von der Hagen, III).

[42] Icelandic text with a Latin translation by E. Ch. Werlauff, *Symbolae ad geographiam medii aevi ex monumentis islandicis* (Copenhagen, 1821), p. 20.   In the abridged text of Nicolaus' *Itinerarium* which was published in *Antiquités Russes*, II (Copenhagen, 1852), 394–415, the lines on Luna are lacking.   On Nicolaus of Thingeyrar see P. Riant, *Expéditions et pèlerinages des Scandinaves en Terre Sainte* (Paris, 1865), pp. 80–85.   In the Middle Ages, those pilgrims from the north who came to Rome after having carried out the pilgrimage to Santiago de Compostela, in north-western Spain, usually disembarked at Luna.

[43] This story is told from an old Italian book by M. Depping, *Histoire des expéditions maritimes des Normands*, new ed. (Paris, 1844), pp. 114–115.

left a deep impression in many countries, and the story has been told and revised as far north as Iceland, as well as in Italy itself.

The Normans, then, finally abandoned their plan to raid Rome and decided to quit Italy. On their way thence, they ran into a violent storm and lost many ships. Where the storm fell upon them, whether they were still in the Mediterranean or beyond the Straits of Gibraltar, is not very clear.[44] A little later we shall return to this question in connection with Norman activities in the eastern basin of the Mediterranean.

About 867, at any rate before the death of Pope Nicholas I on November 13, 867, the King of Lorraine, Lothair II who, because of his family affairs and divorce, had much trouble with this pontiff, wrote him a letter in which we have an interesting hint of the Norman raid on Italy. Lothair II first emphasizes that his kingdom granted to him by divine providence has so far remained entirely safe from any infestations by the pagans or plundering by other enemies, being protected by the power of omnipotent God, by the help of the blessed Apostle Peter and by the prayers of the Pope. Then Lothair proceeds: 'If any incursion of the *pagani* attempts to assault the confines of the Blessed Peter, which have been granted to you from heaven, or perhaps dares to invade the territory of the most august Emperor, our much beloved brother, Lewis, as we have learned from a very recent and most disastrous account, we require that you let us know about this as soon as possible, without any delay. . . . We are ready to consign to death and peril ourselves and our faithful servants.'[45] The exact date of Lothair's letter is unknown, although it is placed by Baronius under the year 867. Lothair twice mentions the word *pagani*, which in the ninth century meant *Normans*. Then he indicates that the territory of the Pope and of the Emperor Lewis, his brother, who lived in Italy, had been very recently ('nuperrima . . . relatione') invaded by the pagans, i.e.,

[44] Willelmi Gemmeticensis, *op. cit.*, I, c. XI: 'Nam Bier (=Björn) totius excidii signifer, exercituumque Rex, dum nativum solum repeteret, naufragium passus, vix apud Anglos portum obtinuit, quampluribus de suis navibus submersis, 'Ed. Duchesne, p. 221; Migne, *P. L.*, CXLIX, coll. 787–788. Benoit de Sainte-Maur, *Chronique des ducs de Normandie*, ed. Fr. Michel, I (Paris, 1836), 68–69; 'plusurs de lur nefs i perirent' (p. 69, verse 1870); Depping, *op. cit.*, p. 410 (last line). Dudo fails to mention the storm; Dudo, *op. cit.*, I, ed. Duchesne, p. 64; Migne, *P. L.*, CXLI, col. 625: 'jam vertunt proras ad Francigenae gentis regnum ducendas. Permeant mare Mediterraneum, revertentes ad Franciae regnum.' I believe that Dozy was wrong in referring the above-mentioned statement of Benoit de Sainge-Maur to the passage of Ibn-Idhari who, under the year 859, says that the Normans lost more than forty ships somewhere between France and Spain. Dozy, *Recherches*, sec. ed., II (1860), 292, 294; 3d ed. (1881), 280, 282. Ibn-Idhari mentions neither storm nor Italy.

[45] Baronii *Annales ecclesiasticus*, XV (Bar-le-Duc, 1868), an. 867, §§120–124, pp. 107–108. §123, p. 108: 'Inter ista vere ratum esse duximus inserendum, quod si aliqua incursio paganorum fines beati Petri vobis coelitus commissos, adire tentaverit, aut forte terminos augustissimi imperatoris, atque amantissimi germani nostri Hludovici, prout nuperrima atque infausta relatione comperimus, irrumpere praesumpserit, illud nobis absque ulla dilatione ocius significari deposcimus . . . nos ac fideles nostros morti ac periculo tradere parati sumus.'

by the Normans.   He undoubtedly refers here to the Norman raid on Italy in 860, which has just been discussed.   *Nuperrima* indicates that the letter was written before 867.   Kunik, who in 1878, if I am not mistaken, was the first among scholars to point out the connection of Lothair's letter with the Norman raid on Italy, ascribes the letter to the year 860 or 861.[46]   Of course since Kunik's study was written in Russian and dealt according to its title with an Arabian writer and with Russia, it has remained unknown to West European historians who were not orientalists.   The orientalists have sometimes cited Kunik — Rosen's study.   Therefore Kunik's reference to Lothair's letter as one of our sources for the Norman raids on Italy has passed unnoticed.   Lothair's letter has not yet been attentively studied by the West-European historians treating the ninth century.[47]

B. Norman Raids in the Eastern Mediterranean

Let us now turn to the Norman activities in the eastern basin of the Mediterranean.   In this section of the sea they were carried out in two directions, north-east and south-east.   In the north-east, our evidence, both Latin and Arab, indicates that the Normans reached Greece, the Land of Rum, the Hellespont, and finally the suburbs of Constantinople. In the southeast the Normans reached Alexandria in Egypt.

The general situation in the eastern basin of the Mediterranean, *ca* 860, was very complicated.   At this time the Byzantines and Arabs were engaged in a continuous struggle over Sicily and South Italy, and the Cretan Arab pirates were making devastating raids in the Aegean and even in the Sea of Marmora.   Sicily, which was assaulted by the Aghlabids of Qayrawan in North Africa (now Tunisia) in 827, was gradually passing into their hands.   The Byzantine Empire, whose vital forces had been exhausted by the terrific civil war against Thomas the Slavonian in Asia Minor and the Balkans, which had ended in 823, was unable to protect effectively its western possessions in Sicily and South Italy.   For our purpose, of course, the period about 860 is particularly interesting.   In the summer of 858, a Byzantine fleet was probably defeated off the shores of Apulia.   At the very beginning of 859, the almost impregnable fortress in Sicilia, Castrogiovanni, surrendered to the Arabs.   A powerful Byzantine fleet of three hundred ships, which had been hurriedly sent by the Constantinopolitan government to Syracuse to save the situation, suf-

---

[45] Kunik and Rosen, *Accounts of al-Bekri and other authors on Russia and the Slavs* (St Petersburg, 1878), pp. 165, 167–168 (in Russian).

[47] For instance, I could find nothing on this subject in the second edition of E. Dümmler, *Geschichte des ostfränkischen Reiches* (Leipzig, 1887–1888) or in R. Parisot, *Le royaume de Lorraine sous les Carolingiens* (Paris, 1899).

fered a severe blow and lost a hundred vessels. In 860 Byzantine troops
were defeated at Cefalù and retreated to Syracuse. In South Italy, from
849 to 866, during more than sixteen years, Apulia was occupied by the
Saracens. Bari became their capital and was strongly fortified under the
Arab commander who declared himself a 'sultan,' independent of the emir
of Palermo. A few years before 860 the envoys of the sultan of Bari were
received with great honors at Salerno and, to the great scandal of the local
bishop, who fled to Rome, were lodged in his palace. About 859, the
prince of Benevento paid a tribute to the sultan and gave him hostages.

Almost simultaneously with the Arab invasion of Sicily, Arab adventur-
ers from Spain, after sojourning for a time in Egypt, captured Crete (in
827 or 828) and established there a terrible pirate nest. Their raids devastated the islands of the Aegean and, about 860, extended through the
Hellespont as far as the Proconnesian islands in the Sea of Marmora.
An Arab commander, Fadl-ibn-Qarin, in the same year, 860, ravaged the
south coast of Asia Minor and captured the fortress of Attalia.[1] The
conquests of Sicily and Crete taught the Byzantine government the necessity of increasing the fleet and carrying out more active operations. In
853 the Byzantine fleet appeared at the mouth of the Nile before Damietta, and without opposition plundered and burned this undefended city
which the inhabitants hastily deserted. In 859 a Byzantine fleet probably reappeared before Damietta and Pelusium (al-Farama).[2] Just as
the conquests of Sicily and Crete by the Saracens had taught the Empire
the necessity of a stronger navy, the Byzantine descent on Damietta led
to the establishment of the Egyptian navy, which a century later was so
powerful under the dynasty of the Fatimids.

Such was the complicated situation in the central and eastern basin of
the Mediterranean, when the Normans made their first appearance in
this section of the Mediterranean world. It is not to be forgotten that at
that time the Byzantine Empire could not expend all its energy on the
Mediterranean, since it was permanently occupied with its wars with the

---

[1] On the events in Sicily and Crete see A. Vasiliev, *Byzance et les Arabes*, I (Brussels, 1935), 49–88,
204–212, 219–222; Russian edition (St Petersburg, 1901), pp. 43–75, 162–168, 174–177. M. Amari,
Storia dei Musulmani di Sicilia, sec. ed., I (Catania, 1933), libro secondo, 382–530. On South Italy,
J. Gay, *L'Italie Méridionale et l'Empire Byzantin* (Paris, 1904), pp. 64–67.

[2] On two Damietta episodes see A. Vasiliev, *op. cit.*, I, 217, 389, 394; Russ. ed., pp. 168–172; supplement, p. 126. E. W. Brooks, 'The Relations between the Empire and Egypt from a new Arabic
source,' *Byzantinische Zeitschrift*, XXII (1913), 381–385, 390–391. Maqrizi, *Description topographique
et historique de l'Egypte*, traduite en français par U. Bouriant (Paris, 1900), p. 634 (*Mémoires publiés
par les membres de la Mission Archéologique Française au Caire*, Tome XVII). On the expedition of
853 see H. Grégoire, 'L'expédition de Damiette. Études sur le neuvième siècle,' *Byzantion*, VIII
(1933), 515–517.

Arabs in the east and became unexpectedly threatened by a new danger from the north, from the Russians.

The year of the Norman raids in the eastern basin of the Mediterranean is to be fixed on the basis of the two Arabian historians, Ibn-al-Kutiya and al-Bekri, and the Latin chronicle of Sebastian of Salamanca. The Arabs, as we have pointed out above, fix the year of the beginning of the Norman expedition into the Mediterranean, viz., 858;[3] and the contemporary chronicler Sebastian of Salamanca informs us that the duration of the expedition was three years, i.e., from 858 to 861.[4] Sebastian's information must be regarded as most reliable evidence, because the author was not only a contemporary of the events which he recorded, but also because he lived in the Christian region of the Iberian Peninsula, i.e., quite near the place of the Norman activities, and he must have been personally relieved at the end of the Norman expedition, which had so cruelly devastated his country at its beginning in 858. We have already seen what the Normans did in 859 and 860; in the latter year they invaded, raided, and left Italy. So for their expedition east of Italy remains only the year 861.

It is not easy to decide who was the chief leader of the eastern expedition. I do not think that its leader was either Hasting or Björn, who both together in 860 headed the raid on Italy. As we have mentioned above, they had left Italy to return directly to their own country. Saxo Grammaticus calls the leader Regnerus. But we have already discussed the question of this semi-mythical Viking, and it is clear that his name fails to help us in identifying the leader of the eastern Norman Mediterranean

---

[3] Ibn-al-Kutiya, *Tarih iftitah al-Andalus*, ed. Ribera (Madrid, 1926), p. 65; Dozy, *Recherches*, 3d ed., II, appendix, p. LXXXI; Seippel, *Rerum Normannicarum Fontes Arabici* (Oslo, 1896), p. 5. French translation, Dozy, *op. cit.*, p. 263, Spanish by Don J. Ribera, *Historia de la conquista de España por Abenalcotia el Cordobés* (Madrid, 1926), pp. 52–53. al-Bekri, *Description de l'Afrique septentrionale par Abou Obaid al Bekri*, texte arabe par le baron de Slane (Algiers, 1857), p. 92; Seippel, *op. cit.*, pp. 7–8. French transl. by Mac Guckin de Slane, *Description de l'Afrique septentrionale par el-Bekri*, éd. revue et corrigée (Algiers, 1913), p. 184; first ed. (Paris, 1859), p. 213; Dozy, *Recherches*, II, 281. The year of the Hegira given by these historians is 244=April 19, 858–April 7, 859. On these historians in general see above.

[4] 'Post triennium in patriam suam reversi,' *Chronicon* Sebastiani Salmaticensis episcopi sub nomine Alphonsi tercii vulgatum, c. 26; E. Flores, *España Sagrada*, XIII (Madrid, 1782), 492; Migne, *P. L.*, CXXIX, col. 1124. On Sebastian of Salamanca see above. Following the latter, F. Kruse also accepts the year 861 as that of the Norman departure from the Mediterranean. F. Kruse, *Chronicon Nortmannorum* (Hamburg et Gota, 1851), pp. 255–256, n. 3. Ibn-al-Kutiya writes: 'during this expedition which lasted fourteen years,' Dozy, *Recherches*, II, 262. The duration of fourteen years for the Mediterranean expedition is incredible. A fragment of a *History of France* mentions that, after the conquest of Luna, Hasting (Alstagnus) 'per numerosa annorum curricula ibidem deguit,' *Recueil des historiens des Gaules et de la France*, VII (Paris, 1870), 224. Dozy is also inclined to believe that the expedition which had begun in 858 lasted many years ('plusieurs années') (II, 281).

expedition. Regnerus' sons might have been raiding in the Mediterranean at that time. But the fact of their participation has not been established.[5] But for our study this question is only of secondary significance. For us the most important deduction is that the Norman expedition in the eastern basin of the Mediterranean did take place, that it is an historical fact.

Two of our sources give some very important but rather vague information that the Normans, in their advance eastwards, reached the territory of the Byzantine Empire. The contemporary Latin chronicler, Sebastian of Salamanca, says that the Norman pirates reached Greece.[6] By Greece the chronicler meant merely the Byzantine Empire; other west European mediaeval writers use this word to designate the Byzantine Empire. A German writer of the second half of the eleventh century and the beginning of the twelfth, Adam of Bremen, wrote: 'The capital of Russia is Kiev (Chive), vying with the power of Constantinople and the most famous ornament of Greece.'[7] Also the Arabian historian of the tenth century, Ibn-al-Kutiya, writes that the *Madjus* (Normans) reached the Land of Rum.[8] Arabian historians of that epoch always call the Byzantines *Rum*, i.e., Romans, Romaioi, their land or empire *bilad al-Rum* or *mulk al-Rum*, and the Byzantine emperor *malik al-Rum*. So, when Ibn-al-Kutiya wrote that the Normans reached the Land of Rum, he undoubtedly meant the Byzantine Empire. A few modern historians who have translated the passage of Ibn-al-Kiutiya just quoted have interpreted it in complete accordance with me.[9] So on the basis of Sebastian of Sala-

---

[5] The evidence referring to Regnerus and his sons has been already given and briefly discussed above.

[6] 'Nordemani piratae . . . postea Graeciam advecti,' *Chronicon Sebastiani Salmaticensis episcopi*, c. 26, *España sagrada*, xiii (1782), 492; Migne, *P. L.*, cxxix, col. 1124.

[7] Adami *Gesta Hammaburgensis Ecclesiae Pontificum*, ii, 19. Without trying to give any interpretation, several modern writers simply quote Sebastian's statement about Greece. For instance, Kruse, *Chronicon Normannorum* (1851), pp. 255–256. Kunik-Rosen, *Accounts of al-Bekri*, i (1878), 167 (in Russian). Dozy, *Recherches*, 3d ed. ii (1881), 279. B. Ravndal, *Stories of the East-Vikings* (1938), 191. Steenstrup, *Normannerne*, i (1876), 127. Beliaev, as we have noted above, erroneously writes that according to al-Bekri a part of the Normans reached Greece. N. Beliaev, 'Rorik of Jutland and Rurik of the original (*Russian*) annals, *Sem. Kondak.*, iii (1929), 241. Al-Bekri does not mention Greece.

[8] Ibn-al-Kutiya, Dozy, *Recherches*, ii, appendix, p. lxxx (Arabic); 262 (French); Seippel, *Rerum Normannicarum Fontes Arabici*, i (1896), 4, lines 15–18 (Arabic); ed. Ribera, i (1926), 65, line 9 (Arabic); ii, 52 (Spanish).

[9] See for instance J. Marquart, *Osteuropäische und ostasiatische Streifzüge* (Leipzig, 1903), p. 387: 'ins Land der Römäer,' J. Ribera, *loc. cit.*, 'a los paises de los bizantinos.' Erroneous is Stefansson's interpretation, who sees in Ibn-al-Kutiya's Rumland Rome-land, Italy, i.e., Rome. J. Stefansson, *The Vikings in Spain. From Arabic (Morrish) and Spanish Sources, Saga-Book of the Viking Club*, vi (London, 1909), p. 41. Ph. Hitti is rather inexact when he translates *Bilad al-Rum* by "the territory of the Romans, Asia Minor," referring to the seventh century, P. K. Hitti, *History of the Arabs* (London, 1937), p. 199. In the seventh century these words meant the Byzantine Empire in general.

manca and Ibn-al-Kutiya we clearly conclude that in 861 the Normans in their steadfast advance east in the Mediterranean, reached the shores of the Byzantine Empire.

Now let us try to find out how far they went and what parts of the Empire they raided. According to Saxo Grammaticus, whose work with its value has already been discussed above, the Normans under Regnerus sailing through the Mediterranean, reached the Hellespont and, after a brilliantly successful expedition, returned from the Hellespont, apparently again through the Mediterranean, northwards to their homes.[10] For our study the question of whom Saxo Grammaticus meant by Regnerus is not essential (see above). But one statement of Saxo, which cannot be dismissed, is of extreme importance for us; that in 861, as we have pointed out above, the Normans, in their raid in the eastern basin of the Mediterranean, reached the real Hellespont (the Dardanelles), which is quite different from the other Hellespont which Saxo also mentions and places somewhere in the north, east of the East Sea (see above).[11]

We know now that in 861 the Normans reached the Hellespont. Other Latin sources testify beyond a doubt that the Normans passed through the Hellespont, entered the Sea of Marmora, and reached the suburbs of Constantinople. The basic text for this raid is the passage in the Chronicle of Johannes Diaconus, which has been discussed above. It can refer in no way to the Russian attack on Constantinople in 860. First, the invaders are called not Russians but Normans ('*Normannorum gentes*'); secondly, the number he gives for the Norman ships is 360 and not 200, as is stated in Greek and Russian sources; finally, Johannes Diaconus' chronicle tells of a Norman victory ('cum triumpho ad propriam regressi sunt'), whereas Greek and Russian sources tell of Russian defeat. In his chronicle, Andreas Dandolo, who abridged Johannes Diaconus, gives the same story and says that the Normans returned with glory ('cum gloria redeunt'). Finally, the Italian writer of the fifteenth century, Flavius Blondus (Biondo), also giving the number of Norman ships as 360 and mentioning the devastation of the suburbs of Constantinople, makes an extremely interesting and important addition, that from Constantinople the Normans returned to the Britannic Sea ('in Britannicum mare sunt

---

[10] 'Regnerus . . . mediterraneum fretum pernavigans ad Hellespontum penetravit, interiecta regionum spacia clarissimis emensus victoriis, continue felicitatis progressum nusquam interpellante fortuna . . . (Haraldus) Regneri ab Hellesponto redeuntis armis exceptus . . . ,' Saxonis Grammatici *Gesta Danorum*, liber IX, ed. A. Holder, p. 313 (=ed. Müller-Velschow, p. 459); in German by P. Herrmann, pp. 422–423.

[11] Quoting this passage of Saxo, Steenstrup (*Normannerne*, I, 127) writes: 'Did the Normans, in their Viking expedition in the Mediterranean, in the ninth century, reach the Dardanelles? There is hardly enough proof for this, but not a few sources speak of it.' See above, pp. 37–39.

reversi).[12]   This last statement is so unexpected that the Italian humanist Sabellicus, who died in 1506, accused Blondus of a mistake due to his ignorance of geography (see above).

All these texts have been known for a long time.   But they have always been connected with the first Russian attack on Constantinople and therefore misinterpreted.   Kunik, who has devoted more attention to these writers than any one else, felt that their statements disagreed with his cherished idea of a Russian attack in 865, and tried to reconcile their statements with Greek and Russian sources by ascribing errors to the Italian authors, especially the later ones, like, for instance, Blondus, and calling them ignorant of eastern conditions.   But now we know that all three Italian writers, Johannes Diaconus, Andreas Dandolo, and Blondus (Biondo), go back for their information to an earlier written source or more probably several written sources, which have not survived or, to speak more cautiously, have not yet been published.   I am certain that their statements have no connection with the Russian attack on Constantinople in 860.   The Norman raid of which they tell took place in 861 and resulted in the invaders' breaking into the Hellespont, entering the Sea of Marmora, and pillaging and devastating its islands and shores, extending their ravages, according to those writers, as far as the suburbs of Constantinople.   After that they returned 'in triumph' ('con triumpho'). The fact that they passed through the Hellespont is not extraordinary, especially if we consider the large number of Norman vessels.   It should not be forgotten either that, probably in 861, a fleet of Cretan Arabs consisting of some thirty or forty ships devastated the Cyclades in the Aegean, passed through the Hellespont and reached the Proconnesian islands in the Sea of Marmora.[13]   It is clear that the Byzantine fortifications on the shores of the Hellespont were not strong enough to prevent piratic raiders, both the Cretan Arabs and the Normans, from pillaging the islands and shores of the Sea of Marmora.   The Aegean Sea was at the mercy of the Cretan Arabs.   In the years 862–866, they devastated the island of Mytilene and twice raided the Holy Mountain of Athos and an island lying not far from its shore; they burnt a church and captured many monks.   The remnant of the terrorized inhabitants of Mount Athos fled from the place, and Mount Athos became a desert.[14]   I have

---

[12] Johannes Diaconus, *Chronicon*.   Pertz, *Scriptores*, VII, 18; Migne, *P. L.*, CXXXIX, col. 905; ed. Monticolo, pp. 116–117.   Andreas Dandolo, *Chronicon*, Muratori, *Rerum italicarum scriptores*, XII, col. 181 (Lib. VIII, cap. IV, pars XLI).   Blondus, *Historiarum Romanarum Decades tres* (Venice, 1483), foll. OVIIᵛ–OVIIIʳ.   All the original texts of these three writers referring to our question have been given above in the appropriate places.

[13] *Cont. Theoph.*, p. 196, c. 34 (Cedr., II, 173).   Zonaras, XVI, 5; ed. Dindorf, IV, 15; Bonn, III, 404.   See Vasiliev, *Byzance et les Arabes*, I, 246; Russian ed., p. 196.

[14] Our chief source for these raids is the *Life of St Euthymius the Younger*, L. Petit, 'Vie et office de

intentionally mentioned here the raids of the Cretan Arabs, although they took place after the years 860 and 861.   Since the Greco-Byzantine sources on the Russian attack in 860, especially such priceless contemporary sources as the Patriarch Photius and Nicetas Paphlagon, fail to mention any Norman incursion from the south, their silence may indirectly confirm our opinion that the Normans penetrated into the Sea of Marmora not in 860 but in 861.   At first sight, it is strange that Byzantine sources omit to mention the Norman raid from the south.   But this might have been included among the successive raids of the Cretan Arabs, of which we have spoken above, which are mentioned in Byzantine evidence.   The sources may have mistaken the Norman raid into the Sea of Marmora for one of the usual Cretan raids.   I am thinking particularly of the raid of 861, when a fleet of Cretans[15] devastated the Cyclades, passed through the Hellespont and reached the Proconnesian islands in the Sea of Marmora.   At all events, the Cretan raids clearly show that at that time the Hellespont was not an impenetrable barrier into the Propontis.   Byzantine sources, oddly enough, sometimes pass over in silence important events known to us exclusively from foreign evidence; for instance, a very successful attack by the Byzantine navy on Damietta, in Egypt, in 853, which we have mentioned above; the expedition of the Russian Prince Oleg against Constantinople at the beginning of the tenth century; and the conversion of the Russians under Vladimir in 988–989, one of the most brilliant pages in the history of Byzantine diplomacy. Moreover, the Norman operation of 861, like the piratical operations of the Cretan Arabs, was a brief raid, whereas the Russian campaign of 860 was a real expedition, which lasted almost a year.   Therefore there is nothing in the silence of the Byzantine sources inconsistent with our theory.

In connection with these Viking expeditions it is very interesting to quote a passage from the letter of Pope Nicholas I to the Emperor Michael III.   The papal letter was written on September 28, 865, and addressed to 'our most pious and most beloved son, conqueror of nations and the most serene Emperor Michael, the august one always protected by God.' The passage runs as follows: 'Finally it is not we who, after having massacred many men, have burnt churches of the Saints and the suburbs of Constantinople, which are almost adjacent to its walls.   And indeed, there is no punishment whatever inflicted on those who are pagans, who are of another faith, who are the enemies of Christ, who continually oppose

---

saint Euthyme le Jeune,' *Revue de l'Orient Chrétien*, viii (1903), 189–190.   See A. Vasiliev, *Byzance et les Arabes*, i, 258; Russian edition, 204.

[15] Theoph. Cont., p. 196, ch. 34, and Cedrenus who follows him, (ii, 173) fail to mention the Arabs and tell of ὁ τῆς Κρήτης στόλος. But Zonaras, xvi, 5, gives complete indication: οἱ ἐκ Κρήτης Ἀγαρηνοί.

the ministers of the truth. And on us who, by the grace of God, are Christians . . . warnings are tried, terrors are imposed, even some molestations are inflicted.'[16]   First it is very interesting to point out the similarity of the Pope's words 'suburbana Constantinopoleos' with 'suburbana' of Johannes Diaconus and his followers. Owing to his official position, Nicholas undoubtedly was well informed as to the Russian attack on Constantinople in 860 and was familiar as well with the Norman activities in the Mediterranean. Five years before his letter to Michael III was written, he himself had been menaced by the Normans in 860. Nicholas certainly meant the Normans who threatened Constantinople, and probably he was considering both actions, the Russian attack of 860 and the Norman raid of 861. The Latin word *suburbana* applies equally well to both inroads. In their attack in 860 the Russians, i.e., the Northmen (Normans), were unable to capture the city itself, and confined themselves to pillaging its suburbs — *suburbana*.[17]

To sum up, the records of Johannes Diaconus and his followers have no reference to the Russian attack on Constantinople in 860 and reflect the Norman activities in the Mediterranean Sea, the Aegean Sea, and the Sea of Marmora. In 861 the Normans, through the Hellespont, entered the Propontis or the Sea of Marmora, and pillaged its shores and islands, reaching in their advance north the outskirts of Constantinople. Such is the conclusion derived from our study of the Norman activities in the Mediterranean in 858–861. I repeat that, as soon as it is possible, scholars should go to Venice and look over a great number of unpublished Venetian chronicles, which may reveal to us some new essential data, which may confirm the result of our study.

Probably in the same year, 861, when the Normans entered the Sea of Marmora, another group of their compatriots reached Alexandria in Egypt.[18] We have already seen that the Byzantine fleet had attacked

---

[16] 'Postremo non ecclesias sanctorum, interfectis numerosis hominibus, ac suburbana Constantinopoleos, quae et muris ejus pene contigua sunt, incendimus. Et vere de istis nulla fit ultio, qui pagani sunt, qui alterius fidei sunt, qui inimici Christi sunt, qui veritatis ministris jugiter adversantur; et nobis qui per gratiam Dei Christiani sumus . . . minae praetenduntur, terrores promittuntur, etiam et nonnullae molestiae irrogantur.' 'Nicolai I Papae epistolae et decreta,' *M. G. H.*, *Epistolae*, vi (Berlin, 1925), 479–480. Migne, *P. L.*, cxix, col. 954. Baronii *Annales Ecclesiastici*, xv (Bar-le-Duc, 1865), 41, no. 92. See Ph. Jaffé, *Regesta pontificum romanorum*, ed. secunda, i (Leipzig, 1885), 358, no. 2796 (2111) (circa Novembrem, 865). As for the exact date of the letter see *M. G. H.*, Ep. vi, 454, note 1. (Bibliography also given.)

[17] De Boor, absolutely erroneously, is inclined to connect Nicholas' passage quoted above not with the Normans but with the Cretan Arabs, C. de Boor, 'Der Angriff der Rhos auf Byzanz,' *Byzantinische Zeitschrift*, iv (1895) 460–461.

[18] A mere mention of this fact is supplied by Ibn-al-Kutiya: (the *Madjus*) reached Alexandria Ibn-al-Kutiya, Dozy, *Recherches*, ii, appendix, p. lxxx (Arabic); 262 (French). Seippel, *Rer. Normann. Fontes Arabici*, i (1896), 4, lines 15–18 (Arabic); ed. Ribera, i (1926), 65, line 9 (Arabic); ii, 52 (Spanish). Steenstrup, *Normannerne*, i (1876), 127 (from Dozy's translation).

Damietta and Pelusium (al-Farama) in 853 and perhaps again in 859 and had withdrawn, so that in 861 there was no danger for the Normans from the Byzantine navy in this south-east corner of the Mediterranean. On the other hand, Egypt, as has been noted above, at that time had only begun to build a strong new navy, which became powerful later under the Fatimids (909–1171). No doubt this was an ordinary Norman raid without serious consequences; but the fact itself cannot be denied.[19] Marquart thinks that the Arab geographer of the ninth century, Yaqubi, learned about this raid on Alexandria when he was in Egypt, and already knowing of the Russian attack on Constantinople in 860 identified the Normans who had pillaged Seville in 844 with the Russians: 'Madjus who are called Rus.'[20]

The raids on the shores of the Sea of Marmora and the outskirts of Constantinople and on Alexandria as well which were carried out in 861 were the last events of the Norman Mediterranean campaign from 858 to 861. In the latter year they definitely quitted the Mediterranean and through the Straits of Gibraltar returned north to the Britannic Sea, according to Blondus' (Biondo's) statement, i.e., to the North Sea, and then home. It is not clear whether the Norman expedition which raided the east Mediterranean was the same which, a year before, had invaded Italy. My impression is that there were two different groups of Normans. The first had departed from Italy in 860 to return directly home; this group, on its way home, suffered the terrible storm mentioned in the sources. Where this storm struck the Normans, whether in the Mediterranean or in the Atlantic, we do not know. The other group, after having raided the shores of the Sea of Marmora and Alexandria, retraced their way home in 861.

---

[19] Ravndal hesitates to accept this raid on Alexandria, saying that the 'savage' Northmen projected their warlike expeditions even into Italy, Greece, and perhaps Egypt. Bie Ravndal, *Stories of the East-Vikings* (1938), p. 191.

[20] Marquart, *Osteuropäische und ostasiatische Streifzüge* (Leipzig, 1903), 387. See my interpretation above.

THE QUESTION OF THE ORIGIN OF THE
RUSSIAN STATE

W E know accurately that the Russians appeared before Constantinople and began their famous raid on the capital and its vicinity on June 18, 860.[1] Of course this raid, as has been noted above, is not to be recorded and studied as an independent separate fact, but in connection with Norman aggression and pillage all over Western Europe, including the Mediterranean. Some Russian historians who have written special books on the history of Russia have closely followed this approach and pointed out that the Norman activities in Western Europe help us to explain events on the Dnieper and the Volkhov. Klyuchevski wrote that nothing in this expedition need be looked upon as unusual or remarkable or peculiar to our country alone, for it belongs to a category of phenomena common enough at that time in the other, the Western half of Europe.[2]

The wealth, luxury and refinement of Constantinople, which the Scandinavians of that time called Miklagard (Micklegard), the Great City, were widely known, so that it is not surprising that the Northmen were strongly drawn to that great center. They knew much more about it than about other points in Western Europe which they raided in the same century. In their imagination they were much more familiar with the New Rome than with the Old Papal Rome, which, as we have pointed out above, they had intended to raid in 860, in other words in the same year that another group of their compatriots attacked Constantinople for the first time. As we know, the Swedes took the preponderant part in the expeditions south, towards Constantinople; the Danes and some Norwegians raided Western Europe, entered the Mediterranean, and in their steadfast drive east threatened Constantinople in 861 from the south. The lure of Constantinople — Miklagard — was very strong. The attraction of the capital of the Byzantine Empire to the Northmen or Varangians has many times been emphasized by many writers. The founder of Marxism himself, Karl Marx, wrote: 'The same magic charm which attracted other northern barbarians to the Rome of the West at-

---

[1] I do not clearly understand what Shakhmatov means when he mentions a Russian campaign on Constantinople which took place before 860. He writes: "Seemingly the first incursion of Rus failed to produce any great impression in Constantinople, because Byzantine historians do not mention it." A. Shakhmatov, 'Survey of the Oldest Period of the History of the Russian Language,' *Encyclopedia of Slavic Philology*, vol. II, 1 (Petrograd, 1915), p. xxvii. Shakhmatov may refer here to the story of a Russian attack on Amastris, mentioned in the *Life* of St George of Amastris.

[2] V. O. Klyuchevski, *A History of Russia*, transl. by C. J. Hogarth, 1 (London-New York, 1911), 66. See also a contemporary German historian, G. Laehr, *Die Anfänge des russischen Reiches. Politische Geschichte im 9. und 10. Jahrhundert* (Berlin, 1930), p. 25.

tracted the Varangians to the Rome of the East.'[3] I wish here to insert a passage written by P. Riant concerning the charm of the East for the Northmen. He wrote: 'One of the principal facts which strike the reader in the study of various sources of the history of the North, is the peculiar attraction which the Orient seems to have exercised upon the spirit of the Scandinavians from remotest times, and the persistence, through all national traditions, of a mystical idea attached to the distant countries where the sun rises.'[4]

The more we study the old Russian Annals concerning the first pages of Russian history and consider data from all other available sources, the more plausible and, in my opinion decisive, seems this conclusion: the chronology of the Russian Annals as to the ninth century is often incorrect; but the sequence of facts, beginning with Rurik, Askold and Dir, Oleg, etc. corresponds to historical reality, and these facts may be accepted as historical factual landmarks in the primitive history of the Russian State. If the Annals sometimes contain legendary stories, like, for instance, Oleg's death from the bite of a serpent which crawled forth from the skull of his dead horse, such stories in no way diminish the great historical value of the Annals, which has been so many times unjustly assailed.

The Russian Annals, then, give us the best general picture of the political situation in the territory of present-day Russia in the first half of the ninth century. Under the year 6367 (859) we read: 'The Varangians from beyond the sea imposed tribute upon the Chuds, the Slavs, the Merians, the Ves, and the Krivichians. But the Khazars imposed it upon the Polyanians, the Severians, and the Vyatichians, and collected a squirrel-skin and a beaver-skin from each hearth.'[5] In other words in the first half of the ninth century the northern tribes were under Varangian domination and paid tribute to them; the southern tribes were under Khazar domination and paid tribute to them. But about this time some important changes described by the Russian Annals occurred in political relations. The best studies on this subject are those of A. Shakhmatov; they have most satisfactorily clarified the process of the formation of the Russian State, which is of extreme importance for our particular study on the attack of Constantinople in 860. I have already briefly discussed the

---

[3] K. Marx, *Secret diplomatic history of the eighteenth century* (London, 1891), p. 76. This passage in Russian is also given in M. Levchenko, *A History of Byzantium* (Moscow-Leningrad, 1940), p. 159.

[4] Paul Riant, *Expéditions et pèlerinages des Scandinaves en Terre Sainte au temps des Croisades* (Paris, 1865), p. 14.

[5] I give here the English translation by S. H. Cross, *The Russian Primary Chronicle* (Cambridge, 1930), p. 144.

most important results of Shakhmatov's studies in connection with the first appearance of the Russians in 839.   Here I wish to enlarge upon the subject, because it has fundamental significance for the event of 860, and, in addition, the results of Shakhmatov's investigations on this point are not sufficiently well known outside Russia, for his works are written in the Russian vernacular.

There is no doubt that, in the ninth century and perhaps even already in the eighth, the Scandinavians had raided Russia and also at the same time carried on trading operations there.   Spreading over Russia in the ninth century to pillage and trade, the Varangians had a different significance for local life in the south from that they had in the north.   In both places they met the Slavic population; but the living conditions of the northern Slavs and Krivichians and of their nearest neighbors, the Finns, as well, were different from those of the Severians, Polyanians, Uluchians and other southern tribes.   A culture of long duration in South Russia going back to the epoch of the first Greek colonies, the nearness of Byzantium, the neighborhood of the Khazars, and the dependence upon this people with a developed state organization, all this gave southern life a different structure from that of the forested and swampy north.   The southern tribes, among whom the Varangians settled, were organized in towns and provinces, whereas the northern tribes, composed of fishermen and hunters, continued to live under tribal conditions, unified by the same language, customs, and occupations.   The role of the Varangians in the north was confined to collecting tribute from the conquered Slavs and Finns; there the Varangians were bandits and robbers.   They failed to mix with the local population and associate with them in daily life.   The Varangians must have played quite a different role in the south where town and provincial life was developed.   In the south the Varangians were not exactors of tribute and bandits, but warriors and merchants who took the power into their own hands.   In this way probably Askold and Dir established themselves at Kiev, and they liberated the Polyanians from paying tribute to the Khazars.   The chief arena of Varangian action in the south, as well as in their fatherland, was the sea: they soon became masters of the Black Sea, which received from local inhabitants the name of the Russian Sea, as the Baltic Sea was called the Varangian Sea.[5a]   On the banks of the Dnieper foundations for a Slavonic state were established; elements for the foundation of a state had long existed there; they had been prepared by town life, which had developed under the influence of Byzantium and its Crimean colonies, and by the old civilization which, for a long time, had accumulated on the northern shores of the Black Sea.

[5a] As we shall see later, some scholars assert that the name 'Russian Sea' was applied to the Baltic Sea instead of the Black.

First Iranians, then Greeks, later Romans, Goths, and finally the most highly cultured of the Turkish or Hunno-Bulgar tribes, the Khazars,[6] were the bearers of higher forms of customs and manners. There was lacking only a force which might have united and revived all these elements of culture and civilization. Such a force appeared in the Russes (*Rus'*), whose name was applied both to the state which they created and to the tribes which they conquered. Thus, according to Shakhmatov, the first Varango-Russian State at Kiev, on the banks of the Dnieper, was established about 840, or more probably (I believe) before this date, since the Russian envoys from Kiev, as we have seen above, came to Constantinople in 838 and were at Ingelheim in 839. There is no doubt whatever that the daring Russian expedition on Constantinople in 860 definitely proves that a political organization north of the Black Sea must have existed before 860. The young Russian state on the Dnieper could not be indifferent to the political growth of the north, because the importance of Kiev was based on the condition that the whole trade route from the north to Constantinople, this great route 'from the Varangian land to the Greeks,' should belong to one state. Many years ago a Russian historian, Bestuzhev-Ryumin, wrote that whoever possessed Kiev must also hold Novgorod. The north began to feel danger from the south. Accordingly the northern tribes appealed to the Varangians overseas, in Scandinavia. At their invitation Rurik came to Novgorod and became the founder of the Russian state in the north. Thus the Varangians who came with Rurik were no longer bandits and robbers, but a mercenary company, a military force, invited to defend the northern tribes against the southern Russian state. Rurik laid a solid foundation for a firm political organization in the north by putting an end to the civil wars and rivalry among various towns, and he unified the tribes under the domination of Novgorod. Conflict between the south and north became unavoidable. The victory of the northern prince Oleg, Rurik's successor, unified the north and south of Russia under one ruler. So there were, according to Shakhmatov, three Russian states: the first at Kiev, founded before 840, the second at Novgorod in the middle of the ninth century, and the third at the end of that century, that under Oleg, who captured Kiev and united both north and south.[7]

[6] Recently Brutzkus has laid special stress on the political and cultural influence of the Khazars on the Slavonic tribes in the ninth century. Y. Brutzkus, 'The Khazars and Kievan Rus,' in the Russian magazine *Novosely'e*, which is published in New York City, no. 6 (1943), pp. 74–81. M. Artamonov asserts that the Khazars were not Turks, but a Hunno-Bulgar tribe. M. I. Artamonov, *Sketches in the Ancient History of the Khazars* (Leningrad, 1936), p. 87, 134 (in Russian).

[7] A. Shakhmatov, 'The Tale of the Calling of the Varangians,' *Sbornik Otdelenija Russkago Jazika i Slovesnosti*, IX, book 4 (St Petersburg, 1904), 337–346. *Idem, The Earliest Fortunes of the Russian Nation* (Petrograd, 1919), p. 58, 60, 61–62. Both in Russian.

This is the outline of the development of the Russian State which has been elaborated by Shakhmatov. Of course it is open to criticism, but it is very plausible and greatly contributes to our better understanding of the attack of 860.

For our study the two first stages in the formation of the Russian state are of utmost importance; information about these two stages can be factually substantiated by data in the Primary Russian Annals. The first Russian state was established at Kiev before 840, for, as has been noted above, the Russian envoys, who were Swedes by origin, appeared in 838–839 at Constantinople and then at Ingelheim, in Germany. The opening lines of the so-called Laurentian Text of the Russian Primary Chronicle may refer to this period. We read: 'These are the narratives of bygone years regarding the origin of the land of Rus, who first began to rule in Kiev, and from what source the land of Rus had its beginning.'[8] The Russians, who established themselves at Kiev about 840, must have overcome the Khazars who at that time were dominating Kiev and the middle course of the Dnieper; in other words, the Russians found a very well organized Khazar political and administrative organization, so that they did not have to start from the beginning; and this situation explains to us why the Russians were able in such a short time not only to control the situation in Kiev and the territory south, down to the Black Sea, which also had been under Khazar domination, but also to send envoys to Constantinople to open friendly relations with the Byzantine Empire. In his speculations Shakhmatov fails to emphasize the very essential fact that in the first half of the ninth century the Khazar Empire or the Khazar Khaganate, extending from the Caucasus and the mouths of the Volga, where their capital Itil was situated, as far west as, and probably beyond, the Dnieper, and south as far as the Tauric Peninsula, was in a state of decline. The heyday of the Khaganate belonged to the eighth century. But evidently the Slavs around Kiev continued to pay tribute to the Khagan. In the ninth century the Khazars were hard pressed on their eastern frontier by the Pechenegs (Patzinaks), a savage people of Turkish origin, who possessed a wide dominion between the Volga and the Ural. To hold them in check the Khazars allowed the Magyars (Hungarians) to enter their territory, and these rapidly spread in the steppes of present-day Russia. It was the Magyars who in 838–839 prevented the Russian envoys from returning home to Kiev by the same way by which they had come to Constantinople. Our sources say that the Magyars made their first appearance in Western Europe in 862; in this year they invaded the

---

[8] I use throughout Cross's English translation of the Russian Primary Chronicle.

Frankish Empire.[9]   This Hungarian wave evidently was not very strong in the steppes of present-day Russia, because in 860 the Russians from Kiev managed to go down the Dnieper to the Black Sea and attack Constantinople.[10]   Vernadsky supposes that in the ninth century even the actual control of Kiev was taken over by the Magyars.[11]

Returning to the Russian Annals, we learn that very important events occurred in the north.   The tributaries of the Varangians drove them back beyond the sea and refusing them further tribute set out to govern themselves.   But discord ensued among them, and they began to war one against another.   Then they appealed beyond the sea to the Varangian Russians (Rus).   Three brothers, with their kinsfolk, came to the warring tribes.   The oldest brother Rurik settled in Novgorod and after the death of his brothers assumed sole authority, and had dominion over many northern districts.   So parallel to the first Russian state in the south, with its capital in Kiev, which had been organized about 840, the second Russian state in the north, with its capital in Novgorod, was established.

According to the Russian Annals there were two men with Rurik, Askold (Oskold) and Dir, who were not his kin, but were boyars (nobles). They obtained permission to go to Tsargrad (Constantinople) with their families.   They sailed down the Dnieper, and in the course of their journey they saw a small city on a hill.   Upon inquiry as to whose town it was, they were informed that three brothers, Kii, Shchek, and Khoriv, had once built the city, but that since their death, their descendants were living there as tributaries of the Khazars.   Askold (Oskold) and Dir remained in this city, and after gathering together many Varangians, they established their domination over the country of the Polyanians at the same time that Rurik was ruling at Novgorod.   All these events, begin-

[9] *Ann. Bert.* (Hincmar), *an.* 862: sed et hostes antea illis populis inexperti, qui Ungri vocantur, regnum ejusdem populantur.

[10] Recently Prof. H. Grégoire has come to the conclusion that the Magyars spent in South Russia not three years, as is indicated by Constantine Porphyrogenitus, but three hundred years; if so they must have come there about 588 A.D.   H. Grégoire, 'L'habitat primitif des Magyars et les Σαβαρτ-οιάσφαλοι,' *Byzantion*, XIII (1938), 267.   Grégoire's theory has been fully accepted by G. Vernadsky. See Vernadsky, 'Lebedia.   Studies on the Magyar Background of Kievan Russia,' *Byzantion*, XIV (1939), 180, 186; *Idem, Ancient Russia* (New Haven, 1943), p. 240.   But already at the end of the eighteenth century, a German scholar (Thunmann, 1774), had supposed that the Magyars spent in South Russia not three years but 203 years.   See K. Grot, *Moravia and the Magyars from the middle of the ninth to the beginning of the tenth century* (St Petersburg, 1881), pp. 204–205 (in Russian). Grot himself believes that there is no ground whatever to suppose that the sojourn of the Magyars in the south steppes of Russia was long.

[11] Vernadsky, *Ancient Russia*, p. 332: 'Since the Magyars themselves were Khazar vassals, there is no contradiction in the sources when some of them mention the Khazars and others the Magyars as rulers of Kiev.'

ning with driving the Varangians back beyond the sea, are narrated in the Russian Annals under the years 6368–6370 (860–862).[12]   If we discard some rather legendary details as to the calling in of Rurik and as to the story of the foundation of Kiev, the fact remains that the general presentation of the Russian Annals has a real historical background and corresponds to historical reality.   There is no ground whatever for questioning the authenticity of Rurik and his activities at Novgorod, and in the north in general.   Of course the dating is incorrect.[13]   In all likelihood, Rurik's rule at Novgorod began in the opening years of the fifth decade of the ninth century at least, because in 860 Askold and Dir appeared under the walls of Constantinople.

Rurik's establishment at Novgorod, the organization of his new principality, the departure of Askold and Dir from Novgorod south, their establishment at Kiev and finally the organization of the raid against Constantinople in 860 required no doubt several years of strenuous work.   Suppose we construct a table of the stages in the formation of the Russian state which interest us in this study.   About 840 or better a little before this year, the first Varangian-Norman-Russian state was founded at Kiev; then about 850 the Varangian-Norman-Russian state was founded in the north at Novgorod by Rurik; after that about 855 Askold and Dir departed south from Novgorod and established themselves at Kiev, which apparently, according to the Russian Chronicle, they occupied without meeting much resistance;[14] and finally they undertook an expedition across the Black Sea against Constantinople in 860.   The last stage in the formation of the Russian state, that is to say the capture of Kiev by Oleg at the end of the ninth century, goes beyond the chronological limits of this study.   In 860 there was no danger as yet from the Pechenegs (Patzinaks), who burst from the east into the southern steppes only at the end of the ninth century and then began to menace the Kievan state.

---

[12] Cross, *op. cit.*, pp. 144–145.

[13] Fortunately we have now a satisfactory explanation of the initial error in the chronology of the *Russian Primary Chronicle.*   See Shakhmatov, 'Ischodnaja točka letoščislenija Povesti Vremennych Let,' *Journal of the Ministry of Public Instruction,* 1897, March, 217–222 (in Russian).   A brief and clear presentation of Shakhmatov's study in Cross, Introduction to his translation of the Russian Primary Chronicle, p. 109.   It would be out of place here to enlarge on this question.

[14] Kunik following the chronology of the Russian Chronicle wrote that in 860 Askold and Dir begged Rurik to let them go to Byzantium to enter the Greek army.   In the south they had to pass by the Slavonic regions which had already been occupied for a long time by the Khazars.   The two leaders gave up their original plan and preferred to take Kiev from the Khazars and dominate the Polyanians in their stead; *Accounts of al-Bekri and other authors on Russia and the Slavs,* II (St Petersburg, 1903), 107 (in Russian).   Cf. below, p. 235.

THE LIFE OF GEORGE OF AMASTRIS AND THE LIFE OF STEPHEN OF SUROZH

WE come now to the question of the Russian raids in the Black Sea, both in Asia Minor and in the Crimea, which are supposed to have taken place before 860. This question has been discussed and interpreted in one way or another for about a hundred years, and has an almost inexhaustible literature. Only now in our own day, in my opinion are we nearing the final solution of the question. Of course all scholars interested in the first pages of the history of Russia and in the history of the Byzantine Empire in the ninth century know that I have in view here the *Life of St George of Amastris* and the *Life of St Stephen of Surozh*. For this study it is very essential to reach a definite conclusion as to whether or not raids on the territory of the Byzantine Empire were carried out by the Russians before 860.

In 1844 appeared a brief article signed by Pogodin but in reality written by A. Gorski, 'On the expedition of the Russians upon Surozh.'[1] It was the first introduction of the two *Lives* into the history of Russia. At that time the *Life of George of Amastris* was known only in its Latin translation printed in the *Acta Sanctorum*, and the *Life of Stephen of Surozh* in a Slavo-Russian manuscript of the Rumyantzev Museum in Moscow. Gorski failed to deal with the dating of the Russian raids. Next Vasilievski published the complete Greek text of the *Life of George of Amastris*, an old Slavo-Russian version of the *Life of Stephen of Surozh*, and added a brief Greek text of the latter preserved in a *Synaxarium*.[2] I omit here various opinions of Russian historians who worked on these *Lives* before the publication of Vasilievski's first study in 1878, and tried to interpret their data according to their own varying and conflicting standpoints.[3]

---

[1] In the *Zapiski* of the Odessa Society of History and Antiquities, I (Odessa, 1844), 191–196 Later it was revealed that the article was only presented by Pogodin to the Odessa Society; but the actual author was a learned Russian priest, A. V. Gorski, see Vasilievski, *Works*, III (Petrograd, 1915), p. IV.

[2] Vasilievski published his first study on the *Life of George of Amastris* in 1878, and a revised and augmented form with a complete Greek text and its Russian translation, appeared in 1893; this work was posthumously revised and republished in 1915 (Vasilievski died in 1899), in the third volume of Vasilevski's *Works*. His study on the *Life of Stephen of Surozh* has also passed through three stages: the first study came out in 1889; then a revised and augmented form, containing a brief Greek text from a *Synaxarium*, accompanied with a Russian translation, and an old Slavo-Russian version, was published in 1893 in the same volume in which the *Life of George of Amastris* was printed; and finally in 1915 this study was included in the third volume of Vasilievski's *Works*.

[3] On this question see Vasilievski, *Works*, III, pp. I–XI and CXLII–CLVI. To his exhaustive information I may add Fr. Kruse, *Chronicon Normannorum, Wariago-Russorum* . . . (Hamburg Gotha, 1851), pp. 208–214, where the author tentatively attributes the data in the *Lives* to the years 851–852.

Briefly, in his investigation Vasilievski came to the conclusion that according to the story of miracles which occurred after the death of George of Amastris, the Russians raided the city of Amastris on the northern shore of Asia Minor in Paphlagonia earlier than 842 A.D., and according to the *Life of Stephen of Surozh*, a Russian prince Bravlin invaded the Crimea in the first quarter of the ninth century. Vasilievski's monographs were written with so deep a knowledge of sources and literature, with so much skill and brilliancy, and his authority in the field of Byzantine studies was so overwhelming, that most historians, both within and without Russia, fully accepted his conclusions. Klyuchevski, one of the best Russian historians, wrote that the researches of Vasilievski into the biographies of Saint George of Amastris and Saint Stephen of Surozh proved beyond all practical doubt that the first half of the ninth century saw the Rus already raiding the coasts — even the southern coasts — of the Black Sea.[4] In 1903 J. Marquart, who knew Vasilievski's two studies only from V. Jagić's review in the *Archiv für slavische Philologie*, xvi (1894), pp. 215–224, accepted the conclusions of the Russian scholar and regarded the appearance of the Russians in the Black Sea in the first half of the ninth century as an established fact.[5] In 1912 J. B. Bury, unable to procure Vasilevski's edition of the *Lives*, 1893, like Marquart derived some idea of his conclusions from Jagić's review. Bury remarks: 'Vasilievski seems to have shown that the whole legend of George of Amastris was compiled before A.D. 843.'[6] In 1913 there came out in Russia two studies which are almost entirely unknown outside that country and which refer to the question under review. In an article written in German Jos. Marquart says that the oldest mention of the people *Ros* is found in the *Life of Stephen of Surozh*.[7] In the same year, 1913, V. Parkhomenko devotes several pages to the *Life of Stephen of Surozh* and the *Life of*

Probably it would be not amiss to mention here that very recently the Oriental Institute of Chicago, during its archaeological work in Persepolis and its environs, discovered a remarkable inscription containing the autobiography of the Persian-Sasanian King Shapur I, who ruled from 241 (finally crowned in 242) to 272 A.D. It was this king who defeated and captured the Roman Emperor Valerian. In the Greek section of the inscription, among the regions represented in Valerian's army during his expedition against Shapur, is mentioned Amastris. M. Sprengling, 'Shahpuhr I the Great or the Kaabah of Zoroaster,' *The American Journal of Semitic Languages and Literatures*, LVII, no. 4 (October, 1940), 374; also 379.

[4] V. Klyuchevski, *A History of Russia*, transl. by C. J. Hogarth, I (London-New York, 1911), 72. From Klyuchevski, an English writer, A. J. Toynbee, recently inserted this information in his book; A. J. Toynbee, *A Study of History*, v (London, 1939), 289, note 3.

[5] J. Marquart, *Osteuropäische und ostasiatische Streifzüge* (Leipzig, 1903), p. 389.

[6] J. B. Bury, *A History of the Eastern Roman Empire from the Fall of Irene to the Accession of Basil* I (London, 1912), p. 417, n. 3 and 4.

[7] Jos. Marquart, 'Ueber die Herkunft und den Namen der Russen,' *Baltische Monatsschrift*, Jahrgang 35 (Riga, October, 1913), p. 265; the entire article, pp. 264–277.

George of Amastris which tell of the first cases known in history of a contact of Russia with the Christian faith.[8] In 1917, Miss Polonskaya, in her study on Christianity in Russia before Vladimir, fully accepting Vasilievski's chronological conclusions, is inclined to believe that the Russians of the *Life of George of Amastris* and the *Life of Stephen of Surozh* were Slavs.[9] After the first World War (1914–1918) several historians referred to the two *Lives* and were in accordance with Vasilievski's conclusions. In 1925 F. Braun wrote that the Northern 'guests' had already traveled in the first half of the ninth century all over European Russia and reached the Black Sea and even penetrated beyond. 'The *Lives of George of Amastris* and *Stephen of Surozh* know them already as *Rus*, not as merchants but as Vikings.'[10] In 1929 N. Beliaev not only accepted the existence of the Prince Bravlin, who is mentioned in the *Life of Stephen of Surozh*, but even connected his name, following Kunik, with the battle famous in Northern tradition at Bravalla in Sweden, probably close to Norrköping in Östergötland, which was fought about the middle of the eighth century (about 750 or 770) when the young Swedish King Sigurd vanquished his elderly relative Harald Hilditönn (Wartooth),[11] and put an abrupt end to the Danish supremacy over one or more of the northern states in Sweden. In 1930 an American scholar, S. H. Cross, asserts that the Greek *Life of St. George of Amastris*, written prior to 842, provides the earliest Byzantine record of the Rus, and the Slavic *Life of St Stephen of Surozh* gives the account of a Russian raid from Novgorod to the Crimea which took place early in the ninth century.[12] In the same year a German historian, G. Laehr, remarks of the two *Lives:* 'They are legends. But they show that the Normans soon made their name dreaded in the Black Sea'; in another passage he writes that the Russian raids before 842 have been convincingly proved by Vasilievski.[13] In 1931 a Russian historian, V. Mošin, who following Golubinski's theory adhered to the existence of the so-called Tmutorokan Russia on the Taman Peninsula, on the northern shore of the Black Sea, believes that the Prince of Bravalla devastated the Crimean coast at the end of the eighth or the outset of the ninth century, and that from the Taman Peninsula the Russians

[8] V. Parkhomenko, *The Origin of Christianity in Russia. An Essay from the History of Russia in the ninth-tenth centuries* (Poltava, 1913), pp. 12–16 (in Russian).

[9] N. Polonskaya, 'On the question of Christianity in Russia before Vladimir,' *Journal of the Ministry of Public Instruction*, 1917, September, pp. 36–42, 76–77 (in Russian).

[10] F. A. Braun, 'Varangians in Russia,' *Beseda*, nos. 6–7 (Berlin, 1925), p. 317 (in Russian).

[11] N. Beliaev, 'Rorik of Jutland and Rurik of Original (Russian) Annals,' *Seminarium Kondakovianum*, III (Prague, 1929), 220–223 (in Russian).

[12] S. H. Cross, *The Russian Primary Chronicle* (Cambridge, 1930), p. 131.

[13] G. Laehr, *Die Anfänge des russischen Reiches, Politische Geschichte im 9. und 10. Jahrhundert* (Berlin, 1930), pp. 19–20, 23, 94–95.

raided Amastris in the first half of the ninth century.[14]   In 1933 a Czech scholar, Fr. Dvorník, considers the *Lives* an historical source for the Russian raids in the first half of the ninth century.[15] Quite recently (in 1941) G. Vernadsky, following Golubinski and Mošin, continues to assert that apparently from Tmutorokan the Russians set forth for their raids on Sugdaia (Surozh), at the end of the eighth or the beginning of the ninth century, and on Amastris some time before 842.[16]

Before the publication of Vasilievski's first study in 1878, Kunik, who in 1845 knew the *Life of George of Amastris* only in a Latin translation (*Acta Sanctorum*, Febr., III, 269–279), supposed that the anonymous author of the *Life* was a contemporary of Askold and Dir, and that his account referred to the first Russian attack on Constantinople which Kunik attributed to the year 866.[17]   Thirty-three years later, in 1878, when Kunik was familiar with the original Greek text of the *Life of George of Amastris*, he was inclined to hold to his previous opinion and continued to refer the data of the *Life* to the first Russian attack on Constantinople.   Kunik wrote that after their retreat from Constantinople, the Russians 'seem to have rushed to the northern coasts of Asia Minor, where the heavy Byzantine ships could not pursue them rapidly.   The compiler of the *Life of George of Amastris*, who borrowed the characterization of the Russians in part literally from the circular letter of Photius, says that their devastations began in the Propontis and ended in Amastris.'[18]   In the twentieth century a few scholars expressed doubts concerning the Russian invasions in the first half of the ninth century.   In 1903–1904, V. Lamanski wrote: 'The invasions of the Russians on Amastris and Surozh must have taken place from the upper and middle Dnieper, if they took place at all.'[19]   In 1914 F. Uspenski hesitates to accept Vasilievski's conclusions.   He emphasizes especially the fact that

[14] V. Mošin, 'The Origin of Russia. The Normans in Eastern Europe,' *Byzantinoslavica*, III, 2 (1931), 295–296 (in Russian). The same account is given by Mošin in 1939, in his article 'Christianity in Russia before St Vladimir,' *Vladimirski Sbornik* 988–1938 (Belgrade, 1939), pp. 8–9 (in Russian).

[15] Fr. Dvorník, *Les légendes de Constantin et de Méthode vues de Byzance* (Prague, 1933), p. 173.

[16] G. Vernadsky, 'Byzantium and Southern Russia,' *Byzantion*, XV (Boston, 1940–1941), 73. In 1943, mentioning the Russian raid on Amastris in or around the year 840, the same author adds: 'if we admit that such a raid actually took place' (*Ancient Russia*, p. 343). In this work Vernadsky is hesitant about acknowledging the historical importance of the *Life of Stephen of Surozh* (pp. 280–281).

[17] E. Kunik, *Die Berufung der schwedischen Rodsen durch die Finnen und Slawen*, II (St Petersburg, 1845), 343–348.

[18] A. Kunik and Baron V. Rosen, *Accounts of al-Bekri and other authors on Russia and the Slavs*, I (St Petersburg, 1878), 175, note 7 (in Russian).

[19] V. Lamanski, *The Slavonic Life of St Cyril as a Religious and Epic Work as well as an Historical Source* (Petrograd, 1915), p. 59 (in Russian). This is a separate posthumous edition of Lamanski's articles under the same title, which originally were printed in the *Journal of the Ministry of Public Instruction*, years 1903–1904.

the passage about the *Rus*, in the *Life of George of Amastris*, occurs not in the story of the Saint's life, but in the narrative of the miracles after his death, so that the period of the life and the period of the posthumous miracles signify two separate periods which are not close to each other chronologically. Uspenski finds our information on the *Life of Stephen of Surozh* so vague and incomplete that he feels unable to use it for historical information.[20] In 1938, G. Bie Ravndal in his book on the East-Vikings devotes three pages to the two *Lives*, and seems to vaccillate when he says: 'Unfortunately legendary biographies of saints are not first-rate historical material. Basically they are intended to revive and stimulate religious feeling. While the salient features of these particular legends may be accepted as facts, doubt has arisen as to their chronology.' But finally he follows the majority of scholars by saying: 'Vasilievski, Marquart, Bury, Vasiliev, and other excellent authorities fix Amastria's visitation and Prince Bravalin's exploits in the Crimea as certainly having occurred prior to 850, which view is shared by the compiler of the present chronicles.'[21]

Now I wish to say a few words as to my own position. For a very long time I was influenced by Vasilievski's studies on these two *Lives*, and accepted his conclusions as a whole, without examining the question.[22] But in 1936 for the first time I wrote that the question deserved further investigation.[23] The immediate cause of this statement of mine was that the editors of the French version of my work *Byzantium and the Arabs* had inserted an interesting note on the work of Miss Louillet, which I shall discuss fully later. She suggested that the attack on Amastris took place not prior to 842 but in 860; and my editors themselves accepted her view, 'in spite of Vasilievski and Loparev.'[24] The more I considered the question, the more I became convinced that a thorough revision of the evidence was urgently needed. In May, 1939, when I was delivering a series of lectures in the Collège de France, in Paris, on the subject *Byzantium and Old Russia*, I told my audience this, when we reached the question of these two *Lives:* 'After having carefully considered the ques-

---

[20] F. Uspenski, 'The First Pages of the Russian Chronicle and Byzantine Vagrant Legends (*Vizantijkija Perechožija Skazanija*), *Zapiski* of the Odessa *Society of History and Antiquities*, xxxii (1914), 199–228. I cite here a separate offprint with special pagination, pp. 13–14.

[21] G. Bie Ravndal, *Stories of the East-Vikings* (Minneapolis, Minnesota, 1938), pp. 114–116. Here it would not be amiss to point out once more that neither Marquart nor Bury was acquainted with Vasilievski's work itself, but took their information from Jagić's review.

[22] See A. Vasiliev, 'La Russie primitive et Byzance,' *L'Art byzantin chez les Slaves*, i, dédié à la mémoire de Th. Uspenski (Paris, 1930), 16. *The Goths in the Crimea* (Cambridge, Massachusetts, 1936), pp. 111–112.

[23] A. Vasiliev, *The Goths in the Crimea*, p. 112, n. 2.

[24] A. Vasiliev, *Byzance et les Arabes*, i (Brussels, 1935), 242, n. 1; 243.

tion, I think that Vasilievski's thesis on St Stephen of Surozh and George of Amastris urgently requires a serious and detailed reconsideration. I admit that I myself in my previous works have accepted Vasilievski's deductions, sometimes with hesitation. And finally I no longer believe that the Russian raids which are dealt with in those two *Lives* occurred before 860, the year of the first Russian attack on Constantinople, which we are going to discuss now and which is an indisputable fact.'

Almost simultaneously with my lectures in the Collège de France I became acquainted with a French monograph by N. de Baumgarten, *On the Origin of Russia*.[25] I must put aside here the author's too sweeping statements that true Russian history begins only with the year 941, the date of the expedition of the Grand Prince of Kiev, Igor, against Constantinople, and that all preceding this date is mere legend and tradition mixed with fable (p. 5), and that Oleg's exploits are but a fabulous and fantastic tale, a popular ballad intended to flatter the national *amour propre* (p. 39). In these statements Baumgarten is influenced by hypercritical tendencies concerning the opening pages of Russian history which can sometimes be noted in the historiography of our own day. Here I wish to dwell on Baumgarten's discussion of the *Life of Stephen of Surozh* and the *Life of George of Amastris*. He devoted to the *Lives* the second chapter of his monograph (pp. 24–35). He wrote under the influence of Miss Louillet's opinion that the data of the *Life of George of Amastris* deal not with an event prior to 842, as Vasilievski tried to prove, but with the first Russian attack on Constantinople in 860. Baumgarten knew Miss Louillet's opinion from the French version of the first volume of my book *Byzantium and the Arabs*, where one of the editors, H. Grégoire, inserted a note (p. 242, n. 1), saying that Miss Louillet had quite recently attributed the devastation of Amastris in the *Life* of George to the year 860; H. Grégoire then on p. 243 included the following statement: 'We also believe in spite of Vasilievski and Loparev that the pillaging of Amastris in Paphlagonia by the Russians which is recounted in the *Life of George of Amastris* is an episode of the same expedition (in 860). According to a hagiographer who wrote about 865, the Russians who pillaged Amastris came from the Propontis.' Baumgarten attributed this passage to me, which was quite natural, because in the text of the French edition there is no indication that this statement was added by Grégoire. 'This testimony,' Baumgarten continues, 'is especially interesting because the same scholar (i.e. Vasiliev) some years before adhered to a contrary opinion and accepted Vasilievski's deductions.[26] Vasiliev himself has thus recognized the

---

[25] N. de Baumgarten, 'Aux origines de la Russie,' *Orientalia Christiana Analecta*, no. 119 (Rome, 1939), pp. 88.

[26] Here Baumgarten refers to the Russian edition of my study *The Goths in the Crimea*.

impossibility of Russian raids against Byzantium before 860' (p. 25). I have no objection whatever to these lines because from the year 1936 on I have felt increasingly that a thorough revision of Vasilievski's thesis was urgently needed.

I wish to give here in an English version some statements of Baumgarten about Vasilievski's studies on the *Lives*. According to Baumgarten, 'Vasilievski's treatise (433 pages) on St George of Amastris and St Stephen of Surozh is, in fact, nothing but the magnificent speech of a brilliant barrister (*avocat*) endeavoring to exculpate his client by establishing an alibi for him. The great name of the erudite Byzantinist and eminent scholar was so impressive that even his adversaries, for example Kunik, consider themselves defeated and lay down their arms. The existence of the Russians on the shores of the Black Sea prior to 842 seems to them to be definitely established, and if even feeble doubts arise, they pay no attention whatever to them. A serious scholar, like Lamanski, for instance, absolutely denies in his *Life of St Cyril* the possibility of Russian expeditions to Amastris and Surozh at the epoch indicated by Vasilievski, but without scrutinizing the question thoroughly. Father Peeters has also voiced some doubts about Vasilievski's chronology. But it is only quite recently that Miss Louillet recognized that the pillaging of Amastris by the Russians took place in 860, not at the epoch attributed to it by Vasilievski (pp. 26–27). . . . The researches and arguments of Miss Louillet which Vasiliev and Grégoire mention are unfortunately inaccessible to me' (p. 27). As a matter of fact, at the time when Baumgarten was writing his monograph, Miss Louillet's study was not yet published, and when later it was, she herself, as we shall see below, had changed her original opinion on the connection of the *Life of St George* with the attack of 860.[27] Baumgarten submits Vasilievski's work to serious criticism; but he contributes almost nothing new because all the weak points of Vasilievski's study had already been pointed out by several previous Russian historians and critics. But his new approach, which has once more revived interest in these two *Lives*, to the study of Vasilievski's method and point of view is not devoid of significance. He emphasizes Vasilievski's rather far-fetched interpretation of the name of the Propontis, from which the Russians supposedly attacked Amastris, not in its usual meaning of the Sea of Marmora, but as the Strait of the Bosphorus.[28] Vasilievski's principal if not unique argument, is a negative argument. Discovering no mention of the icons in the *Life of St George*,

----

[27] Baumgarten's passage just quoted has been reproduced in its original French by H. Grégoire in *Byzantion* (xv, 1940–1941, p. 232), as his introductory remark to Mrs Costa-Louillet's article, which we shall discuss below.

[28] See many references to this question in Vasilievski, *Works*, iii, pp. cxxix–cxxxii.

he decided that the *Life* must have been compiled at the time of an iconoclastic emperor, namely under the Emperor Theophilus, who died in 842
(p. 27).   On the whole, Baumgarten rejects Vasilievski's chronology that
the incursion on Amastris took place before 842, and accepts Miss Louillet's view, which he knew, as we have noted above, only from Grégoire's
mere mention in the French version of the first volume of my book
Byzantium and the Arabs, that the story must be attributed to the attack
of 860.

Let us turn now to Miss G. Louillet or, as she later became, Mrs Germaine da Costa-Louillet, of whom I have already spoken above.   I
learned first of her attribution of the pillaging of Amastris, which is told
in the *Life of George*, to the attack of 860, from the French version of my
own book *Byzantium and the Arabs*.   There as I have already noted, one
of the editors of my book, H. Grégoire, in note 1 to p. 242, made the following addition: 'Quite recently Miss Louillet has recognized that the
pillaging of Amastris by the Russians which was dated by Vasilievski
from 825–830 is instead (the episode) of 860; this was already Kunik's
opinion.'   Then, on p. 243 Grégoire inserted in the text itself the following statement: 'We think also in spite of Vasilievski and Loparev that the
pillaging of Amastris in Paphlagonia by the Russians, which is told in the
Life of St George of Amastris, is an episode of the same expedition (i.e.,
860).   According to a hagiographer who wrote about 865, the Russians
who ravaged Amastris came from Paphlagonia.'   This was the material
which, as we have seen above, Baumgarten used as the foundation for his
point of view, entirely in accordance with Miss Louillet.   But Miss
Louillet failed to hold her opinion long.   The French version of my book
came out in 1935 and in September 1936 at the International Congress of
Byzantine Studies in Rome, Mrs. da Costa-Louillet read a paper under
the title *Were there Russian Invasions in the Byzantine Empire before 860?*
in which, after announcing that history knows only two Russian attacks
on Constantinople, one in 860 and one by the Russian Prince Igor in 941,
and that the so-called expedition of Oleg is not an historical fact,[29] she
attributed the passage in the *Life of George of Amastris* to the expedition
of the Russian Prince Igor in 941, because chroniclers say that the Russians, after they had been repulsed from Constantinople, infested Paphlagonia.   At the session where Mrs da Costa-Louillet read her paper,
Grégoire confirmed her thesis.[30]   Vernadsky, who knew only the resumé

[29] Mrs de Costa-Louillet has forgotten the Russian attack on Constantinople in 1043.

[30] The resumé of Mrs da Costa-Louillet's paper is published in the *Atti del V Congresso Inter-
nazionale di Studi bizantini.   Studi Bizantini e Neoellenici*, v (Rome, 1939), 85.   By misprint Igor's
expedition is attributed there to 914 instead of 941.   The title of the paper: 'Y eut-il des invasions
russes dans l'Empire Byzantin avant 860?'

of the paper just quoted, wrote that Mrs da Costa-Louillet's argument did not seem convincing to him.[31]   Mrs da Costa-Louillet's article has since been printed under the same title as her paper at the Congress, 'Were there Russian Invasions in the Byzantine Empire before 860?,' with an introduction by H. Grégoire.[32]

The introductory remarks written by Grégoire consist of two sections. In the first (p. 231) Grégoire deals with the article of Mrs da Costa-Louillet, who is his pupil.   He says that, by definitely rejecting Vasilievski's theories, her discovery has simplified the problem of Russian origins; and he accompanies these words with the rather sweeping statement that 'to tell the truth, there is no problem whatever' ('A vrai dire, il n'y a pas de problème du tout').   In accordance with Mrs da Costa-Louillet's opinion, which is also his own, he regards only two attacks on Constantinople as historical facts: one in 860 and one in 941.   Mrs da Costa-Louillet, he says, seems to have hesitated to identify the raid on Amastris with either of these two attacks.   He writes: 'Finally she has accepted my identification, the sole possible one; in this case, the expedition is that of Igor, because we know that in 941 and 941 only, the Russians sacked Paphlagonia. As to the *Life of Stephen of Surozh*, it is but a late imitation of the *Life of George.*'   And Grégoire concludes: 'Such are the realities by which Mrs da Costa-Louillet has replaced Vasilievski's chimeras.'   In the second section of his introductory remarks, Grégoire gives a long passage from Baumgarten's monograph (p. 232), which we have discussed above, and ends his remarks with the following words: 'This quotation fully justifies, we believe, the publication of Mrs da Costa-Louillet's meritorious critical work.'

Let us turn now to da Costa-Louillet's article itself.   We have already briefly discussed her general ideas about the opening pages of Russian history when we took up the paper she delivered in 1936 at the Congress in Rome.   At this point it is the second part of her article which interests us, in which she deals with the two *Lives*.   She fails to attribute much historical value to the *Life of Stephen of Surozh* and is right in saying that the Slavonic text of the *Life* does not provide us with any precise chronological indication,[33] and that the episode of the conversion of the Russian

---

[31] G. Vernadsky, 'Byzantium and Southern Russia' *Byzantion*, xv (1940–1941), 73. n. 29.   Probably by misprint, his reference to *Studi Bizantini* is inexact; instead of 1936, pp. 21–22, it should read 1939, p. 85.

[32] Germaine da Costa-Louillet, 'Y eut-il des invasions russes dans l'Empire Byzantin avant 860?, *Byzantion*, xv (1940–1941), 231–248; Grégoire's introductory remarks, pp. 231–232.

[33] Here Mrs da Costa-Louillet makes a blunder in her text.   She says that Bravalin's attack, according to the *Life*, took place '*many* years after the death of the saint' ('plusieurs années après la mort du saint'), whereas the Slavonic text reads '*a few* years after the death of the saint' (Vasilievski,

Prince Bravlin to Christianity is obviously a memory (*souvenir*) of the conversion of Vladimir. According to Vasilievski, the *Life of George of Amastris* was compiled during the iconoclastic period, before 842, under Michael II (820–829) or Theophilus (829–842). Mrs da Costa-Louillet is inclined to believe that the text of the *Life* which we now possess, which lacks a well established plan and has no chronological order of events, was not compiled in the ninth century; we have the text as it was remodeled by Symeon Metaphrastes, at the end of the tenth century. It is he who added the Russian episode, and this may explain the fact that such an important event is told at the very end of the *Life*. For her final deduction, Mrs da Costa-Louillet refers to the *Life of Basil the Younger*, the compiler of which, speaking of the expedition of Igor in 941 against Constantinople, mentions that the Russians attack Paphlagonia. The result of her article, then, is that the Russian episode in the *Life of George of Amastris* is to be referred to Igor's expedition in 941. Mrs da Costa-Louillet concludes this section of her article as follows: 'However this may be, it will not henceforth be permitted to invoke hagiography or the authority of the man whom we must not cease to admire (for the *Russo-Byzantine Researches* of Vasilievski will eternally remain classical), in order to introduce into history Russian invasions previous to the year 860. In the final lines of her article Mrs da Costa-Louillet says: 'We believe with the majority of scholars that the installation of Rurik and his brothers in Novgorod and afterwards in Kiev cannot have taken place before about 856. . . . In fact, the results of our researches confirm on the whole the narrative of the old Russian Chronicle, called that of Nestor.'

The results of Mrs da Costa-Louillet's article, which was very carefully written under H. Grégoire's guidance, are not strikingly new. About a hundred years ago, in 1849, the Archbishop of Kharkov, Philaret, in his *History of the Russian Church*, believed that the Russian episode in the *Life of George of Amastris* referred to the expedition of Igor. In 1876 a Russian historian, D. Ilovaiski, in his book *Studies on the Origin of Russia*, discussing the raid on Amastris, thought of Igor's expedition, and wrote that it was not surprising if during this invasion the Rus managed to pay a visit also to Amastris.[34] In passing, in a mere note, Mrs. da Costa-Louillet mentions that in 1881 W. von Gutzeit also attributed the attack on Amastris to the year 941 (p. 248, n. 51). I do not know whether she read Gutzeit's article itself or not.[35] It deserves much more attention

---

p. CCLXIX; also CCLXXII). Of course my correction fails to make the chronology of the *Life* more precise.

[34] See Vasilievski, *Works*, III, pp. VI-VII. Vasilievski quotes the second edition of Ilovaiski's book, which was printed in 1882.

[35] Her reference to the article is incorrect; vol. XXXVII should read vol. XXVII, and p. 338, 337.

than dismissal in a note.   Gutzeit very carefully discusses Vasilievski's argument, with which he disagrees, concludes that the attack on Amastris is to be referred to Igor's expedition in 941, and writes that this assumption receives final confirmation from the statement found in §46 of the *Life*, that the Russians after Igor's campaign never appeared as enemies in those regions (i.e., in Bithynia, Paphlogonia, and Nicomedia).   For Igor's campaign was the first and last.[36]

Mrs da Costa-Louillet is highly to be commended for having reconsidered the question which once had occupied the minds of Russian scholars regarding the Russian attack on Amastris.   But her article produced nothing new, and her 'discovery' had already been made over sixty years before.

As I have noted above, in several previous writings of mine I worked under the spell of Vasilievski's amazing knowledge and brilliant presentation of the subjects with which he dealt.   But during the last years I have begun to question the decisive value of his deductions from these two *Lives*, especially on the *Life of Stephen of Surozh*.   The very fullness of information gathered by Vasilievski to prove his thesis helps us to come to opposite conclusions from his.   Of many of his own statements Vasilievski is himself not certain.   The complete *Life of Stephen* has been preserved only in a Slavo-Russian version of a very late date.   The manuscript belongs to the sixteenth century, and our version is the work of a Russian writer of the fifteenth century (p. ccxxiii and cclxiii).   Vasilievski himself acknowledges that the text has very little historical value (p. cclxiii), and the chronology of the *Life* is full of inconsistencies and contradictions (p. ccxxxvii).   The Slavonic version may go back to a complete Greek original; but this is only an hypothesis; such a text may never have existed.   The saint lived in the eighth century under the first iconoclastic emperors, Leo III the Isaurian and Constantine V Copronymus; under the latter he suffered a martyr's death in 767 (p. ccviii and ccxxxix).   Vasilievski supposes that the miracles which occurred after the Saint's death are connected with the *Life* itself and were not added later.   But this is only a conjecture which cannot be definitely proved. The miracle which interests us particularly is connected with the attack on Surozh, a city in the Crimea, by a Russian prince Bravlin.   The *Life* tells us: 'A few years after the death of the Saint a huge Russian army

---

[36] W. von Gutzeit, 'Ueber die Lebensgeschichte des heil.   Georgios von Amastris und die Zeit ihrer Abfassung,' *Bulletin de l'Académie Impériale des Sciences de St Pétersbourg*, xxvii (1881), p. 337. The whole article, pp. 333–338.   Reproduced also in *Mélanges russes, tirés du Bulletin de l'Académie des Sciences de St Pétersbourg*, vol. v.   See also W. von Gutzeit, *Legenden von Amastris und Surosh* (Riga, 1893).   Pamphlet of 20 pages.

under the powerful prince Bravlin came from Novgorod,' *etc.* (III, p. 95). Here everything is doubtful. The name of the Prince is not certain: the manuscripts give us various forms, *Bravlin, Bravalin,* sometimes not even a proper name but an adjective *branliv* meaning *quarrelsome;* some writers think that this name is connected with a place *Bravalla* in Scandinavian where the famous battle took place (see p. CCLXXII). The miracle of the healing of Queen Anna of Kherson in the Crimea is told in the *Life.* But in some other manuscripts this name is not given, and we read 'another empress' or simply 'the empress.' Vasilievski himself wonders uncertainty of these two names 'if they were in the Russian version at all from the very beginning' (p. CCLXXII). The name of the city of Novgorod in connection with events of the end of the eighth century is absolutely impossible. Vasilievski himself conjectures, 'the indication of Novgorod may have been added by copyists of the text' (p. CCLXXII). To support his thesis that the Russians might have appeared in the Crimea at the end of the eighth or at the beginning of the ninth century Vasilievski resorts to the *Life of George of Amastris* in which he says the Russians also are mentioned before 842. But this episode, which is told in the latter *Life,* is now also subject to reconsideration.[37]

Before coming to a final conclusion as to the *Life of Stephen of Surozh,* I wish to point out here that one of Vasilievski's points in his commentary on this *Life* must be definitely discarded. Writing on the Tauroscythians who, in the ninth and tenth centuries, were very often identified with the Russians (*Ros*), Vasilievski makes the following conjecture. 'The very sounds of the word Tauroscythians include elements from which in spoken Greek, which is so inclined to contractions, the name *Ros* might have been formed.' To support this hypothesis, Vasilievski refers to the remark of Leo Diaconus (p. 63), that *Ros* is a popular word which designates the people who, in fact, are named Tauroscythians (p. CCLXXXII–CCLXXXIII). The reaction which this unexpected conjecture aroused outside Russia was tremendous and indeed harsh. In his review of Vasilievski's work, V. Jagić wrote, 'I could hardly believe my eyes when I discovered this statement signed by the author; I would perhaps have expected it from a Gedeonov, Ilovaïski, or other Russian historians who are on bad terms with philology, but never from Vasilievski.'[38] Krumbacher said, 'The laws of the "distortions" of spoken Greek (*des Vulgärgriechischen*) are sufficiently clarified so that the idea of deriving *Ros* from *Tau-ros-cyten,* an idea whose monstrosity surpasses the boldest tricks of antescientific (*vorsprachwissenschaftlichen*) etymology, should not even be conceived,

---

[37] On p. CCLXXIV, evidently by misprint, the attack on Surozh is attributed to the first half of the tenth century. This error is not corrected in the list of *errata* (p. 122).

[38] *Archiv für slavische Philologie,* XVI (1894), 222.

far less expressed. How poor Modern Greek would have looked had the Greek vernacular ever possessed such an unrestrained predilection for distortion as Vasilievski attributes to it.'[39] In 1912 J. B. Bury remarked, 'The theory propounded by Vasilievski in his old age 'Ρώς is a corruption of ταυ-ροσ-κύθαι may be mentioned as a curiosity.'[40]

An identical negative reaction may be noted from the same three writers concerning another conjecture of Vasilievski that the Russians who raided Amastris and Surozh might have been the Tauric (Crimean) Goths.[41] Vasilievski himself, however, regarded this theory as one of three which he believed more or less plausible. Of course now all idea of the Crimean Goths must be rejected and the dating of the events involved must be reconsidered.

After rereading Vasilievski's monograph on the *Life of Stephen of Surozh* and reconsidering his often indecisive theories, I conclude that we cannot use its text for any historical purpose. As an historical source, the *Life of Stephen of Surozh* must be eliminated; its text may have some interest for the history of old Russian literature. The discovery of the complete Greek text of the *Life*, if such a one exists, could hardly increase the historical value of the late Slavo-Russian version. A very vague recollection of the conversion of the Russian Prince Vladimir and his marriage to the Byzantine Princess Anna may occur in the names of Bravlin and Anna in some old Russian manuscripts; but this recollection is not certain, and if it were certain, it would not help us to clarify the question of the Russian military activities at the end of the eighth or the beginning of the ninth century.[42]

Vasilievski's foundation was much stronger when he was working on the *Life of George of Amastris*. The complete Greek text of the *Life* was at his disposal. The Parisian manuscript, which contains, among many other *Lives*, the *Life of George*, according to the opinion of such a first class scholar as the famous French philologist Charles-Benoit Hase (1780–1864), the first editor of the History of Leo the Deacon, was written in the tenth century (p. XVIII; XX). According to Vasilievski, the whole text of the *Life of George* was compiled by the same anonymous author and, including the posthumous miracles of the Saint, represents one continuous whole (p. CIX).[43] Having reread the text of the *Life*, I must distinguish

---

[39] *Byzantinische Zeitschrift*, IV (1895), 210.

[40] J. B. Bury, *A History of the Eastern Roman Empire* (London, 1912), 412, n. 1. In 1893, when the second edition of the *Lives* under review came out, Vasilievski was fifty-five. He died in 1899, at the age of sixty-one.

[41] Jagic, Krumbacher, Bury. The same references. Bury uses the same words: 'The theory . . . that the Russians were (Crimean) Goths . . . may be mentioned as a curiosity' (p. 412, n. 1).

[42] See a very useful article of Fr. Westberg, 'On the Life of St Stephen of Surozh,' *Viz. Vremennik*, XIV (1907), 227–236 (in Russian).   [43] Cf. da Costa-Louillet, *Byzantion*, XV, 246.

it as one of the most bombastic, rhetorical, and unnecessarily lengthy texts ever written. Vasilievski himself called it 'a very lengthy glorification of a miracle filled with unbearable declamation' (p. XXXVII). I must emphasize Vasilievski's wonderful knowledge of the Russian language and command of a style suitable to the text, because his Russian translation of the *Life* is a real masterpiece. In opposition to Kunik's opinion that the text of the *Life* contained some borrowings from the Circular Letter of the Patriarch Photius, Vasilievski considers the text absolutely independent of him.

George of Amastris died at the beginning of the ninth century, between 802 and 807 (p. LXXVI), and since in the *Life* no direct mention of icons occurs, Vasilevski concludes that the *Life* was compiled during the second period of iconoclasm in 820–842, in any case before 842 (843) when iconveneration was restored (p. LXXXVI; CIX). No doubt this is a very ingenious hypothesis; but it is only an hypothesis, not a fact. Vasilievski tries to identify the anonymous author of the *Life*, and comes to the conclusion that its probable author is Ignatius the Deacon, later the Metropolitan of Nicaea, a younger contemporary of George (p. LXXXVII), who was born about 770–774 (p. XCIII) and died about the middle of the ninth century (p. XCVIII). Ignatius the Deacon is a fairly well-known writer in the history of Byzantine literature: he composed the Lives of the Patriarchs Tarasius and Nicephorus, and also wrote a Life of Gregory Dekapolites, and a canon to celebrate the Forty-two Martyrs of Amorion, those 'stars in the holy firmament of the Church'; in addition, he wrote several poetical works.'[44] There are indeed some striking resemblances in the style of the Deacon Ignatius and that of the author of the *Life of George of Amastris;* but this is not a definite solution of the authorship of the *Life*, and Vasilievski's hypothesis has not been accepted by scholars in general. Jagić considered the authorship of the Deacon Ignatius not well established and admitted only 'a certain degree of probability.'[45] Loparev rejected Ignatius' authorship.[46] P. Nikitin is very doubtful on the question. He writes: 'May the new trait of the similarity of the Life of George with the Lives of Ignatius which we have indicated, be regarded as a proof in favor of Vasilievski's supposition that Ignatius was the com-

[44] On the Deacon Ignatius, Krumbacher, *Geschichte der byzantinischen Litteratur* (1897), p. 73, no. 6; 716–720. G. Montelatici, *Storia della Letteratura Bizantina* (Milan, 1916), pp. 136–138 (Gregory Dekapolites is not mentioned). V. Vasilievski and P. Nikitin, 'Tales (Skazanija) of the Forty-two Martyrs of Amorion and the Church Service to them' (St Petersburg, 1905), p. 79 and 272 (Greek and Russian), *Zapiski (Mémoires)* of the Academy of Sciences of St Petersburg, *VIII*° sér. *VII*, 2.

[45] Jagić, in *Archiv für slavische Philologie*, XVI (1894), 219.

[46] Ch. Loparev, 'Byzantine Lives of the Saints of the eighth-ninth centuries,' *Viz. Vremennik*, XVIII (1911–1913), 16–35 (in Russian).

piler of the Life of George? Not, of course, by itself alone.' And then, a few lines below, Nikitin remarks: 'It is to be recognized that, if the three Lives belong to the same author, the Life of George must be the earliest, the Life of Tarasius the latest.'[47] Dvorník only sums up the facts and writes that this delicate problem deserves special study.[48] So the author of the *Life of George* is still unknown. The question has naturally arisen whether the author of the *Life* may not have been Symeon Metaphrastes, the famous compiler of a vast collection of Lives of Saints, who lived at the end of the tenth century and at the beginning of the eleventh. The Parisian manuscript which contains the *Life of George* was still catalogued in 1589 under the title *Symeon Metaphrastes, mensis Februarius* (p. XIII). But this designation was founded on a misunderstanding, and the Lives which this codex contains, according to Vasilievski, mostly appear there in their original form, not in their later version by Symeon Metaphrastes (p. XIII; XVIII). Recently Mrs da Costa-Louillet turned back to this question, and wrote that it would be possible and even probable to attribute the actual version to Symeon Metaphrastes or one of his contemporaries (p. 246). But obviously the authorship of Symeon Metaphrastes is also only problematical. At any rate the attribution of the undated Parisian manuscript to the tenth century does not contradict the idea.

To support his thesis about the Russian invasion on Amastris before 842, Vasilievski referred among other proofs to the very well known evidence of the Arabic geographer of the ninth century, Ibn-Khurdadhbah (Khordadhbeh) on Russo-Byzantine trade relations. According to the editor and translator of his work, the celebrated Dutch orientalist, M. J. de Goeje, the work had two editions: the first version belongs to the year 846–847 and the second edition was written by the author about 885–886 A.D. The record of the Russian merchants who transacted their business with Byzantium occurred already in the first original version of 846–847, so that Vasilievski found in this Arabic text new support for the possibility of the Russian attack on Amastris prior to 842 (p. CXIX–CXXIII). But de Goeje's theory concerning Ibn-Khurdadhbah's two versions was later questioned. In 1903, for example, Marquart, who had previously adopted this theory himself, finally rejected it and decidedly stated that Ibn-Khurdadhbah published only one edition of his work, and that he

---

[47] P. Nikitin, *On some Greek texts of the Lives of Saints* (St Petersburg, 1895), pp. 48–49; also 21 (in Russian). *Zapiski* (Mémoires) of the Academy of Sciences of St Petersburg, Cl. historico-philologique, *VIIIe* série, *I* (St Petersburg, 1897).

[48] F. Dvorník, *La Vie de Saint Grégoire le Décapolite et les Slaves Macédoniens au IXe siècle* (Paris, 1926), p. 15, n. 1.

finished it not earlier than 885–886 A.D.[49]   It is known that in the story of the Russian attack on Amastris as it is related in the *Life of George*, the Russians came to Amastris from the Propontis, i.e., from the Sea of Marmora (p. 64, §43).   In order to make more probable the Russian attack on Amastris and explain the otherwise inexplicable silence in the text about the city of Constantinople by which the Russians should have passed on their way from the Sea of Marmora to Paphlagonia, where Amastris was situated, Vasilievski, very ingeniously too, tried to prove that the compiler of the *Life* might have used the name of the Propontis not in its usual meaning, but in the meaning of the Straits of the Bosphorus, and even in the sense of the coastland of Asia Minor from the river of Sangarius to Amastris (p. CXXVII–CXXXII). Vasilievski's far-fetched interpretation of the name of the Propontis was pointed out by several scholars; he did not succeed in proving his point. The Propontis must mean the Sea of Marmora; and granting this, the tale of the *Life* of George cannot be interpreted as a simple local episode referring only to the shores of Paphlagonia and to its center, Amastris.[50]

In my opinion, the strongest evidence against Vasilievski's theory is to be found in the text of the *Life of George of Amastris*, where the compiler asserts that at the time of the attack on Amastris the Russians were a very well-known people. We read: 'There was an invasion of barbarians, of Rus, a people, as all men know (ὡς πάντες ἴσασιν), extremely savage and harsh, who possess no traces whatever of humanity,' etc. (p. 64, §43). Vasilievski is perfectly right in calling our attention to the desperate penury of evidence in Byzantine chronicles of the ninth and tenth centuries, so that several events of great importance, which have come down to us in other sources, are not listed there.   It is true that such a local episode as a Russian attack on Amastris might easily have escaped mention in the chronicles.   But it is absolutely impossible to justify the statement that in the first half of the ninth century before 842 the name of *Ros* ('Ρῶς) was widely known, a people furnished with such a deplorable character, full of savagery, cruelty, and devoid of any trace of humanity, as they are described in the *Life*.   For this statement there is no historical ground whatever.   The Russian envoys who visited Constantinople in 838 *amicitiae causa* and appeared in 839 at Ingelheim at the court of

---

[49] J. Marquart, *Osteuropäische und ostasiatische Streifzüge* (Leipzig, 1903), p. 390; cf. pp. 202–203. F. Westberg, 'On the Analysis of Oriental Sources on Eastern Europe,' *Journal of the Ministry of Public Instruction*, February, 1908, p. 374 (in Russian).

[50] F. Dvorník, evidently adhering to the opinion of scholars like Golubinski, Mošin, and Vernadsky, who believe that the raid on Amastris was made from Tmutorokan or from the Crimea by the so-called southern Russians, considers the Propontis of the *Life* the banks of the channel which separates the peninsulas of Kerch and Taman; F. Dvorník, *Les Légendes de Constantin et de Méthode vues de Byzance* (Prague, 1933), p. 173.

Lewis the Pious, or the Russian merchants and traders who transacted business in the ninth century with the Byzantine Empire, provide no justification whatever for such a disgraceful characterization. The attitude which we find in the *Life* would have arisen only after the experiences which the Empire had in 860, when the Russians for the first time attacked Constantinople, and in 907, when the Russian prince Oleg reached the capital and made his famous treaty with the Byzantine Emperors. Everyone who is familiar with Byzantine history knows that an analogous description of the Russians was given by the Patriarch Photius just after the attack of 860.

One of the very essential reasons for referring the Amastris episode to the expedition of Igor has been that our sources on the latter expedition mention Paphlagonia, where Amastris was located, which was raided in 941. But we have something more to add to confirm this opinion. According to the *Life of George*, the Russians reached Amastris coming from the Propontis, i.e., from the Sea of Marmora. Our sources on Igor's expedition give us the entire route of the Russians. They ravaged the whole Asiatic side of the Bosphorus, beginning with its mouth where Hieron, a Byzantine toll-house, was situated, pillaged Chrysopolis, facing Constantinople (Scutari at present), and laid waste the entire region surrounding Nicomedia, the metropolis of Bithynia lying in the basin of the Sea of Marmora. On the other side, the Russians, along the northern coast of Asia Minor, reached and invaded Heraclea Pontica and Paphlagonia, where the prosperous city of Amastris was situated. So on the basis of our Greek and Old Slavonic evidence, we have an absolutely exact idea of the extent of the Russian operation in 941: from Nicomedia, in other words from the Propontis or the Sea of Marmora in the south to Paphlagonia in the north. There is no need whatever to explain the Propontis in any but its original meaning. I am now absolutely convinced that the story told in the *Life of George of Amastris* deals with Igor's expedition of 941. If the undated Parisian manuscript really belongs to the tenth century, the story itself must have been compiled and included in the manuscript not many years after the expedition. An Arab Christian historian, who lived and wrote in Egypt and Syria in the eleventh century, Yahya of Antioch (died about 1066) wrote a few very interesting words on Igor's expedition, which have never been properly appreciated by Russian or other historians. He wrote: 'In this year (Oct. 6–Sept. 25, 941) the Russians made an attack on Constantinople and reached the gate of Aqrubuli (Aqroobooli) in the Khazar Sea; the Greeks fought them, drove them back, and vanquished them.' In Akrubuli I recognize the Acropolis, the northern point of mediaeval Constantinople, at the very mouth of the Golden Horn, Seraglio Point at present. The gate mentioned by Yahya was one of the gates in the wall which surrounded the Acropolis. Yahya erroneously placed the Acropolis in the Khazar Sea, i.e., in the Black Sea; but this confusion is very natural in a writer who was writing far from Constantinople. This detail supplies us with the very interesting information that in 941 the Russians did not confine themselves to devastating the Asiatic coast but also made an unsuccessful attempt to raid Constantinople itself on the European side.[51]

Lastly, I wish to call attention to a source which, if I am not mistaken, has not been seriously enough considered in connection with the *Life of George of Amastris*. I refer to the *Eulogy on St Hyacinth of Amastris*, compiled by Nicetas Paphlagon after the Russian invasion of 860–861. From this Eulogy we learn that the city of Amastris, 'which lacks little of being the eye of the Universe,' had powerful walls, a fine harbor, and was a busy commercial center (ἐμπόριον), where the Scythians from the northern shores of the Euxine, i.e., the Russians, and the people from the south of the city assembled together to transact commercial business.[52] In my opinion, even if we remember that we are dealing with a *Eulogy* such a passage would have been impossible had Amastris been pillaged by the Russians either before 842, as Vasilievski asserted, or during the campaign of 860–861. The complete silence of the *Eulogy* as to any previous devastations of Amastris, and its prosperous state after 860–861, clearly show that the Russian attack on Amastris mentioned in the *Life of St George* must refer to a later period, namely to Igor's campaign of 941.

My criticism of Vasilievski's work on the *Lives* of Stephen of Surozh and George of Amastris in no way minimizes or belittles the admirable work in general of the founder of Byzantine studies in Russia. Many of his works will remain forever informative and standard. We must not forget that Vasilievski was writing his monographs on the two *Lives* in the heat of the struggle between Normanists and Antinormanists which was raging at that time in Russia. The crucial problem was who founded

---

[51] Arab text and French translation in 'Histoire de Yahya-ibn-Said d'Antioche' editée et traduite par I. Kratchkovsky et A. Vasiliev, *Patrologia Orientalis*, XVIII (1924), 727 (29). Arab text only by R. P. L. Cheikho (Beyrouth-Paris, 1909), p. 98 (*Corpus Scriptorum Orientalium, Scriptores Arabici*, Series III, tome VII). Russian translation of the passage, Baron V. Rosen, *The Emperor Basil Bulgaroctonus* (St Petersburg, 1883). p. 059. A. Vasiliev, *Byzantium and the Arabs. The political relations between Byzantium and the Arabs in the Time of the Macedonian Dynasty* (St Petersburg, 1902), sec. section, p. 61.

[52] Nicetae Paphlagonis *Oratio* XIX. In laudem S. Hyacinthi Amastreni. Migne, *P. G.*, CV, col. 421, §4. The Greek text of this passage is given below (p. 233) when we deal with the results of the invasion of 860–861. Vasilievski mentions the *Eulogy* in his study several times (*Works*, III, index, p. 105), without paying special attention to its information.

the Russian state, the Normans, i.e., Scandinavians, or the Slavs. At that time it was extremely difficult, almost impossible, to be absolutely objective in the stormy process of clarifying this question, when nationalistic interests and nationalistic excitement were intermingled with historical interests and historical views, and very often got the upper hand. Now when a span of about eighty years separates us from that turbulent but eventually fruitful period, we may see more clearly and discuss problems more objectively. But of course, when we have to deal with a scholar of the first water and of high caliber like Vasilievski, we criticize his works slowly and gradually, since we have been for so long under the spell of his personality, his amazing knowledge, and his exceptional gift of historical penetration. Perhaps it has taken me longer than it has other scholars to criticize Vasilievski's works because he was the professor, teacher, and friend who initiated me into Byzantine studies. I wish to conclude this section of my study with the words which I wrote in Russian in my recollections of Vasilievski on the occasion of the centennial of his birth in 1938: 'Vasilievski and Baron Rosen[53] have made my life. On my desk, in St Petersburg, in Yuryev (Dorpat, in Estonia), where I was professor at the University from 1904 to 1912, and now at Madison, Wisconsin, in America, their pictures have always stood. In moments of doubt and hesitation I look at them, gain new strength and courage, and feel how boundlessly I esteem them and how cordially I love them.'[54]

[53] Baron Victor Rosen was one of the most eminent orientalists not only in Russia but also in Europe. He was professor of Arabic at the University of St Petersburg and taught me Arabic.

[54] *Annales de l'Institut Kondakov (Seminarium Kondakovianum)*, xi (Belgrade, 1940), 214. I have added to this quotation the reference to Madison, Wisconsin. In the same year, 1940, Ostrogorsky, referring to the two *Lives*, wrote: 'The correctness of the central and, so to speak, most sensational conclusion does not seem to me personally indubitable. But in any event Vasilievski's studies as a whole on the Lives must be regarded as a model of critical and scholarly talent,' G. Ostrogorsky, 'V. G. Vasilievski as a Byzantologist and Creator of Modern Russian Byzantology. *Annales de l'Institut Kondakov (Seminarium Kondakovianum)*, xi (1940), 231 (in Russian).

GREEK SOURCES ON THE ATTACK ON CONSTANTINOPLE IN 860

L ET us turn now to the attack of 860. First of all, we must make a brief survey of our sources: Greek, Latin, and Old Russian. In 1878 Dr W. von Gutzeit in his critical remarks on the first edition of Vasiliev-ski's study on the *Life of St George of Amastris* pointed out that all our sources fail to breathe a word on the supposed Russian raid before 842, whereas the devastating expedition of 865 'set all pens in motion.'[1] We shall begin with Greek sources. There are at our disposal only two contemporary writers, the Patriarch Photius, and Nicetas of Paphlagonia (Nicetas Paphlagon).

Photius, not only a contemporary but even an eyewitness of the attack, speaks of it in two sermons, *On the Incursion of the Russians*. The first edition of the text with a Russian translation was made in 1864 by the Archimandrite (later Archbishop) Porphyrius Uspenski who in 1858, during one of his voyages to Mount Athos, discovered among other sermons of Photius a manuscript of the two sermons just mentioned in the Iberian (Georgian) monastery or Iviron. Porphyrius Uspenski's edition of the Greek text and a Russian translation came out under the title *Four Homilies of Photius, the Most Holy Archbishop of Constantinople, and a discussion on them*, by the Archimandrite Porphyrius Uspenski (St Petersburg, 1864). The edition unfortunately was rather unsatisfactory, and its deficiencies gave rise to a very important and regrettably long-lived blunder, of which we shall speak later. P. Uspenski informed Peter Sevastyanov, a Russian philologist, of his discovery, and the latter made a photographic copy of the sermons, brought it in 1861 to St Petersburg, and transmitted it to Kunik, who in his turn gave it for study and publication to a member of the Academy of Sciences of St Petersburg, August Nauck. Nauck published the text in 1867 in book form under the title *Lexicon Vindobonense, recensuit et adnotatione critica instruxit Augustus Nauck* (Petropoli, 1867). The sermons were printed in the Appendix, *Photii in Rossorum incursionem Homilia* I, pp. 201–215, and *Homilia* II, pp. 216–232. Nauck's edition was the second edition of the sermons and at the same time their first critical edition. In his *proemium* Nauck mentions that there were two more manuscripts of the sermons, one in Mos-

---

[1] W. von Gutzeit, 'Ueber die Lebensgeschichte des heil. Georgios von Amastris und die Zeit ihrer Abfassung,' *Bulletin de l'Académie Impériale des Sciences et St Pétersbourg*, XXVII (1881), 337: 'während der Verwüstungszug von 865 alle Federn in Bewegung setzte.' Reproduced also in *Mélanges russes*, tirés du Bulletin de l'Académie des Sciences de St Pétersbourg, v, 6, and by Vasilievski, *Works*, III, p. CXI, n. 2.

cow, the other in Spain, in the *Bibliotheca Escorialensis*.   But both these
manuscripts seem to have been destroyed by fire (*proemium*, p. xxiii).
The third edition, made by a very well known German classicist, C.
Müller, was published in 1870 in his *Fragmenta Historicorum Graecorum.
Volumen quintum, pars prior* (Paris, 1870), pp. 162–173 (*Homilia* i,
pp. 162–167; *Homilia* ii, pp. 167–173).   C. Müller prepared the edition
of the text on the basis of Sevastyanov's photographic copy which had
been sent to him in Paris.   He praises Nauck's edition highly (p. 162,
note), and in his *Prolegomena* (p. xvi) gives a passage from Nauck's *proemium* concerning the codices of the sermons.   The fourth edition of the
sermons came out in Constantinople in the Greek newspaper Ἀλήθεια
(1881, nos. 9 and 13), on the basis of a new copy from the same Athonian
manuscript.   I have not seen this edition.[2]   The fifth, and, for the time
being, the last, edition of Photius' two sermons, with many other addresses
and sermons, eighty-three all together, came out in 1900 in Constantinople, the work of a Greek scholar, S. Aristarkhes: Τοῦ ἐν ἁγίοις πατρὸς ἡμῶν
Φωτίου πατριάρχου Κωνσταντίνου πόλεως Λόγοι καὶ Ὁμιλίαι ὀγδοήκοντα τρεῖς,
ἐκδιδόντος Σ. Ἀριστάρχου, in two volumes (Constantinople, 1900).   The
first sermon on the Russian attack in vol. ii, pp. 5–27, no. 51; the second,
vol. ii, pp. 30–57, no. 52; many explanatory notes on Photius' life and
sermons in the general introduction, pp. α'-ρνδ' (1–194) and in the special
introductions to the sermons (ii, 1–5 and 28–30).[3]

There are two Russian translations of the two sermons.   The first was
made by the Archbishop Porphyrius Uspenski in his edition of the sermons in 1864, and is not very satisfactory.   The best translation belongs
to E. Lovyagin, in *Khristianskoe Chtenie*, 1882, September–October, pp.
414–443.   Lovyagin based his translation on the edition in the Greek
Constantinopolitan newspaper Ἀλήθεια (1881, nos. 9 and 13), which he
carefully collated with the editions of Porphyrius Uspenski, Nauck,
Müller, and with Sevastyanov's photographic copy as well (p. 419).
Lovyagin's translation is very accurate and exact.   I do not know any
complete translation into any other language of Photius' two sermons on
the Russian attack.

The first sermon was delivered by Photius in St Sophia during the
Russian attack itself; the second some time after the Russian retreat.
That is, the first was delivered in the second half of June, 860, because
the attack started on 18 June.   The approximate dating of the second

----

[2] My information is derived from the introduction to the Russian translation of the sermons made
in 1882 by E. Lovyagin, in *Khristianskoe Chtenie*, 1882, September-October, p. 419.   We shall speak
of this translation later.

[3] In 1930 G. Laehr was wrong in stating that C. Müller's edition of Photius' two sermons was the
last one: G. Laehr, *Die Anfänge des russischen Reiches* (Berlin, 1930), p. 92.

sermon depends on the question of the duration of the invasion, which we shall discuss later. Photius' sermons are historical evidence of the first class. It is to be remembered that this source is not a brief drab chronicle, nor an historian's presentation of fact. The sermons represent a special form of literature. They were sermons publicly delivered from the pulpit of St Sophia and addressed to the masses of Constantinople. They are characterized by a declamatory oratorical style, by many references to the books of the Old Testament, and by some exaggeration and high coloring of the event. They are tinged with a moral implication, implying that calamity has befallen the people on account of their sins and transgressions. All these elements are amply represented in these two homilies. But, with all their rhetorical embellishments, they give a contemporary description of the savage and cruel pagan Russian people of the ninth century, a description which, even allowing for some very natural exaggeration, differs in no way from accounts of Scandinavian savagery and cruelty in Western Europe. As given in the sermons, the picture of ruin and devastation in the suburbs and vicinity of the capital, which was revealed after the withdrawal of the Russian vessels, must be very close to reality. Once more we must always keep in mind West European analogies of the ninth century. In Photius' sermons the Russian incursion serves as a warning from God to people who have deviated from the path of virtue and embraced sin, and also as a stimulus for their moral regeneration.

Since we have now eliminated the data of the *Life of George of Amastris* and the *Life of Stephen of Surozh* on Russian raids before 842, Photius' homilies give the first appearance in Greek sources of the Russian people under their own name. The Emperor Theophilus, in 839, in his letter to Lewis the Pious, may also have called the Russian envoys by their own name *Ros* (*Rhos*). But, as we have seen above, Theophilus' letter has not survived in its own vernacular. It must be admitted that the priceless historical authenticity of Photius' homilies is often clouded by his rhetorical ornamentation and by numberless quotations from various books of the Old Testament; yet in spite of this their historical significance is unquestioned and illuminating.

A French writer, A Chassang, remarked in 1871, in his brief note on Photius' homilies: 'It is fortunate that the title of the Homilies indicates the event which was their occasion; for it would perhaps be difficult to disentangle it from the rather vague amplifications of Photius, who may have thought he was insulting his *beau langage* by pronouncing the barbarous name οἱ ʽΡῶς.'[4] Chassang's statement is of course strikingly exaggerated.

[4] A. Chassang, 'Deux homélies de Photius au sujet de la première expédition des Russes contre

It seems clear that, if Photius' sermons were delivered in St Sophia in the form which we now possess, they could only have been understood and adequately appreciated by the most educated of his congregation, that is, by a minority.[5]   It is possible that the sermons were preached in St Sophia in a simpler and probably briefer form, and were later remodeled by Photius to acquire that elaborate Byzantine style which marks homilies of many other Byzantine preachers.[6]

It may not be irrelevant to give here a few lines of appreciation of Photius' two sermons by their first editor, the Archbishop Porphyrius Uspenski, the more so as this book is absolutely unknown outside Russia. He wrote: 'They are the first pages of our history, the first brief accounts of the faith and people of our remotest ancestors, of their military strength on land and at sea, of their plans, courage, fame, and relations with Tsargrad, the accounts of a contemporary, who saw the Russians face to face and heard their insulting cries.'[7]   In 1867 in the first volume of his fundamental work on Photius, J. Hergenröther was not exact when, after mentioning that Photius delivered two addresses on the occasion of the Russian invasion, he added, 'Unfortunately these addresses (*Reden*) are not yet printed.'   In 1867 Porphyrius Uspenski's edition was already available.[8]

Among Photius' writings is another interesting text directly referring to the attack of 860.   His circular letter to the Oriental Patriarchs, which was sent in the spring or summer of 867,[9] contains a brief character-

---

Constantinople (865), *Annuaire de l'Association pour l'encouragement des études grecques en France*, v (1871), 79, n. 2.   This statement receives support from the famous authoress Anna Comnena, who apologized to her readers when she chanced to give the barbarian names of the western or *Russian (Scythian)* leaders, which 'deform the loftiness and subject of history,' Anna Comnena, x, 8 and vi, 12.   In another passage, Chassang criticizes Photius' homilies rather vaguely: 'What shocks us most in those two Homilies is not the vagueness and lack of relief of his pictures; it is not the banality, perhaps inevitable, of his moral reflections, it is the lack of elevation of general conception at the basis of his two discourses' (p. 85).

[5] See Bury, *A History of the Eastern Roman Empire*, p. 420.

[6] Photius' sermons may call to mind the brilliant inaugural oration delivered by the archbishop of Athens, Michael Acominatus, in the twelfth century, who realized that his speech, being beyond the understanding of the Athenians of the twelfth century, remained incomprehensible and dark to his hearers.   But it is not to be forgotten that in the twelfth century Athens was a second-rate and rather backward city.

[7] Porphyrius Uspenski, *The Four Homilies of Photius, the Most Holy Constantinopolitan Patriarch, and Discussion of them* (St Petersburg, 1864), introduction (in Russian).   These lines are also reproduced by Th. Uspenski, *The First Pages of the Russian Annals* (Odessa, 1914), p. 16 (pagination of an offprint); *Zapiski* of the Odessa Society of History and Antiquities, vol. xxxii (1914).

[8] J. Hergenröther, *Photius*, i (Regensburg, 1867), 533.   Later he became familiar with A. Nauck's edition (1867).   See *Photius*, iii (Regensburg, 1869), p. viii.   But cf. his article 'Der erste Russenzug gegen Byzanz,' *Chilianeum*. Neue Folge, 3 Heft (Würzburg, 1869), 210–224, where he still failed to use the printed text of the two sermons.

[9] See V. Grumel, *Les regestes des actes du Patriarcat de Constantinople*, Fasc. ii *Les regestes de 715 à 1043* (Socii Assumptionistae Chalcedonenses, 1936), pp. 88–90, no. 481 (printed in Turkey).

ization of the Russian people analogous to that given in his homilies, mentions the Russian conquest of their neighbors and the succeeding expedition against the Byzantine Empire, and finally gives extremely interesting information about the conversion of the Russians to Christianity.[10]   This text, which has been frequently discussed by scholars, will be reconsidered also later in this study.

I do not know why the very well-known Russian antinormanist, S. Gedeonov, announced in 1867 that the real characterization of the Russia of 865 should be sought not in the circular letter, which was written under political influence, but in the Patriarch's homilies, which were delivered immediately after the withdrawal of the barbarians from the walls of Tsargrad.[11]   In both documents the characteristics ascribed to the Russian people are identical; but in the circular letter the subject is confined to a few words compared with long passages in the homilies.

In the course of this study we shall return several times to Photius' works and his activities.

The second contemporary source is Nicetas of Paphlagonia or Nicetas Paphlagon.   Nicetas David, the bishop of Dadybra in Paphlagonia, died at the end of the ninth century.[12]   He bore the surnames of Philosophus, Rhetor, and Paphlagon and, along with Photius, was the most eminent panegyrist of the ninth century.   For our study his biography of the Patriarch Ignatius is very valuable.[13]   The deposed Ignatius was his hero, so that we are not surprised to find in his biography a very sharp criticism of Photius, whom Nicetas regarded as the fundamental cause of all Ignatius' miseries and tribulations; and no doubt the imposing figure of Photius did overshadow Ignatius.   We cannot, accordingly, use Nicetas' biography for the presentation of the history of Photius without thorough critical investigation.   Recently, when the historical study of Photius' manifold activities entered a new phase, criticism of Nicetas, both as a man and as a writer, became once more exceedingly sharp.   I say 'once more' because this trend goes back a long time.   Many years ago Laman-

---

[10] Photii *Epistolae*, ed. Montakutius (London, 1651), p. 58, ep. 2. Migne, *P. G.*, cii, coll. 736–737, ep. 13 (in the text τορῶς; in a note τὸ 'Ρῶς); Φωτίου 'Επιστολαί, ed. Valetta (London, 1864), p. 178, ep. 4 (τὸ 'Ρῶς).

[11] S. Gedeonov, *Varangians and Rus'*, ii (St Petersburg, 1876), 470.   Gedeonov has forgotten that the first homily was delivered during the attack itself.

[12] See Krumbacher, *Gesch. der byz. Litteratur*, pp. 167–168: Nicetas died in 890 (Ehrhard); p. 679: in 880 (Krumbacher).

[13] Papadopoulos Kerameus' view that the *Vita Ignatii* was not written by Nicetas, but at a much later time by a Greek Unionist, has not been accepted: Papadopoulos-Kerameus, Ψευδονικήτας ὁ Παφλαγὼν καὶ ὁ νόθος βίος τοῦ πατριάρχου 'Ιγνατίου, *Viz. Vremennik*, vi (1899), 13–38.   Also his article 'Η ψευδωνυμία τοῦ ἐπ' ὀνόματι Νικήτα Παφλαγόνος βίου τοῦ πατριάρχου 'Ιγνατίου, which was printed in the Greek newspaper Νέα 'Ημέρα (1899).   Vasilievski has flatly refuted Papadopoulos-Kerameus' opinion in *Viz. Vremennik*, vi (1899), 39–56.

ski called Nicetas 'this obtuse and slightly educated bigot.'[14]   In another
place, referring to Ignatius' biography, the same scholar asked if it were
possible to rely on Ignatius' information.   Then he answered his own
question: 'Ignatius wrote more than twenty years after (the Russian attack), and in his hazy and entirely uncritical head he might have confused
many things.   Exactness is not to be expected from such obtuse and
stubborn fanatics, who are, in addition, old.'[15]   In 1933 Dvorník remarks that sometimes 'the illustrious biographer of Ignatius' takes liber-
ties for which an historian cannot excuse him, and he gives information
which has contributed to discredit Photius in the eyes of posterity.[16]
Finally, in 1934, H. Grégoire called the *Life of the Patriarch Ignatius* an
odious pamphlet and added that Nicetas might be a contemporary, but
nevertheless he deserves an even stronger condemnation than the characterization which the editor of Photius' letters (Valetta) bestowed upon
him: 'Rhapsodus omnium mendaciorum, fons et origo omnium calum-
narum, quibus Photium καταπλύνει cardinalis Baronius.'[17]

Luckily for us, in spite of all these disparaging opinions about Nicetas'
work and personality, his Biography of Ignatius remains a very valuable
source for the first Russian attack on Constantinople.   He wrote the
biography about 880, at the end of his life, in any case after Ignatius'
death on October 23, 877.   He mentions twice the Russian attack of 860
on the Islands of the Princes, in the Sea of Marmora, near Constantinople.
At that time Ignatius was living in exile in one of the small islands of that
group, Terebinthos (now Anderovithos), where he had founded a monastery.   In fact Ignatius *alone* gives us the complete extent of the Russian
raid: from the Black Sea (διὰ τοῦ Εὐξίνου πόντου) through the Bosphorus
(τὸ Στενόν), into the upper part of the Sea of Marmora, where the Islands
of the Princes are situated.   In 813 the young Ignatius, a son of the deposed Emperor Michael I (811–813), was mutilated, tonsured, and exiled
to the Islands of the Princes; he founded thereafter three monasteries in
three islands of this group, over which he presided as abbot.   All these
islands were raided by the Russians, and the monasteries were despoiled.[18]
We shall speak of these events in more detail later.   Other sources tell

---

[14] V. Lamanski, *The Slavonic Life of St Cyril* . . . (Petrograd, 1915), p. 110 (in Russian).   Originally
this chapter of the work was printed in 1903–1904.   [15] Lamanski, *op. cit.*, p. 117.

[16] F. Dvorník, *Les Légendes de Constantin et de Méthode vues de Byzance* (Prague, 1933), p. 137.

[17] H. Grégoire, 'Du nouveau sur le Patriarche Photius,' *Bulletin de la classe des lettres* . . . *de l'Académie royale de Belgique*, 5-e série, xx (1934), no. 3, p. 53.   The verb καταπλύνειν means *to asperse,
to bespatter* (with calumnies).

[18] Nicetae Paphlagonis *Vita S. Ignatii archiepiscopi Constantinopolitani*. Migne, *P. G.*, cv,
col. 516–517; also Mansi, *Conciliorum Collectio*, xvi, col. 236.   See J. Pargoire, 'Les monastères de
saint Ignace et les cinq plus petits îlots de l'Archipel des Princes.'   *Izvestiya* of the Russian Archaeological Institute in Constantinople, vii (1902), 56.

about Russian pillaging of the neighborhood of the capital and about the siege of the city itself, but they fail to mention the raid in the Sea of Marmora.   In the other reference Nicetas mentions that Ignatius restored a communion table in one of his chapels in the island of Plati, which had been hurled down and damaged by the Russians.[19]   In addition in his *Eulogy of S. Hyacinthus of Amastris*, which has already been mentioned above, Nicetas furnishes extremely interesting information on the Russians.   We may discount the excessive praise of the city of Amastris, which, according to him, "lacked little of being the eye of the universe," but we read that the Scythians from the northern shores of the Euxine, i.e., the Russians, came to Amastris to transact commercial business.[20] This important record may be explained by the fact that the Russian danger of 860–861 was already over and forgotten, and normal relations were re-established between the Russians and the Empire.

Had we not so long and so stubbornly adhered to the traditional date of the Russian attack indicated in the Russian Annals as 865, we should long ago definitely have discarded this year on account of the data which the *Life of Ignatius* supplies. Several scholars, as early as the eighteenth century, realized the importance of the *Life* in this respect and concluded that the Russian attack took place not in 865 but in 860–861.[21] Vasilievski himself, referring to the data of the *Life of Ignatius*, wrote that the Russian attack on the Islands of the Princes, as it is told in the *Life*, falls within the year 861, and perhaps it is only the traditional doctrine of the origin of the Russian name that makes the majority of scholars insist that this attack is to be linked with the expedition of Askold and Dir attributed to the year 865. 'After all,' Vasilievski adds, 'it is not impossible that daring raiding incursions on the shores of Asia Minor — certain reconnoitring expeditions — may have preceded the siege of Constantinople by the Russians.'[22] Here Vasilievski is inclined to distinguish the incursion told in the *Life of Ignatius* from the real attack on Constantinople. This view cannot be justified, but, as we shall see later, it was shared by Kruse and Hergenröther.

To sum up, though, as I myself believe, the *Life of Ignatius* is a very dubious and biased source for the authentic history of Photius, yet for the history of the first Russian attack on Constantinople it is evidence of the first class, like Photius' homilies.

---

[19] *Ibidem*, col. 532; also Mansi, xvi, col. 252.

[20] Nicetae Paphlagonis *Oratio* xix.   *In laudem S. Hyacinthi Amastreni*, Migne, *P. Gr.*, xv, col. 421, 3–4.

[21] In 1755 an Italian orientalist, Assemani, ascribed the attack to the end of 859 or to the beginning of 860. A Russian historian, Golubinski, favored 860 or the beginning of 861. See A. Vasiliev, *Byzance et les Arabes*, i (Brussels, 1935), 241–242; Russian edition (St Petersburg, 1900), pp. 190–192.   [22] Vasilievski, *Works*, iii, p. cxxviii.

Along with these two pieces of evidence which are indubitably contemporary, Photius and Nicetas Paphlagon, there is a source which is potentially contemporary and may have been composed by Photius himself. I refer here to the church hymn, widely known in the Greek Orthodox Church, composed in honor of the Holy Virgin, 'the Champion Leader' (Στρατηγὸς Ὑπέρμαχος) the so-called *Akathistos* ('Ακάθιστος). In this hymn the Holy Virgin, as the specific protectress of Constantinople, is glorified for having saved the city from the enemies who besieged it. Various opinions have been expressed on the chronology of the hymn; some have attributed it to the liberation of Constantinople from the Arabs in 677; others, and I must admit the majority, to the famous siege of the capital by Avars and Persians in 626; in addition there have been other opinions. Krumbacher declared that, for the time being, the question was not decided.[23]

In 1903, in his study *The Akathistos of the Mother of God, Russia, and the Patriarch Photius*, Papadopoulos-Kerameus gave it as his decided opinion that the hymn referred to the event of 860 and that its author was probably Photius, the hymnographer, church poet, and founder of a religious festival 'at which every year on a fixed day this hymn has been sung.'[24] Papadopoulos-Kerameus, in fact, considers this hymn a reflection of Photius' first sermon on the Russian invasion; and in his second sermon, he says, we even discover the words and expressions of the hymn itself and direct similarities to it. To prove this thesis the author brings forward some examples (pp. 396–397). After thoroughly considering all his arguments, I believe his attribution of this hymn to the year 860, though not definitely proved, is very plausible. More problematic is the authorship of Photius. Mošin wholly accepts Papadopoulos-Kermeus' conclusion as to the year 860.[25] Jean B. Papadopoulos, in 1928, also attributed the hymn to the Russian attack. He wrote: 'The hymn was not merely a religious chant; it was a paean, a song of triumph, which, as such, has become a part of all the hymns of triumph and victory, which has been sung on every occasion and especially at the triumphal feasts of victorious emperors. It is at once a martial and religious chant.'[26]

But even today the hymn is still very often attributed to the Patriarch

[23] Krumbacher, *Gesch. der byz. Litteratur*, p. 672.   [24] *Vizantisky Vremennik*, x (1903), 357–401.

[25] V. Mošin, 'Study of the first conversion of Russia,' in Serbian magazine *Bogoslovle*, v, 2 (Belgrade, 1930), 56–57 (in Serbian).

[26] Jean B. Papadopoulos, *Les palais et les églises des Blachernes* (Thessalonica, 1928), p. 41. He gives the Greek text of the opening lines of the hymn and their French translation (pp. 41–42). The last words of the fragment of the hymn printed by Papadopoulos are χαῖρε Νύμφη ἀνύμφευτε. He translates them *Salut, ô Vierge, Mère de Dieu*, which is, of course, incorrect. But translation into any language would not be very easy. In English the words may be rendered — very lamely — as 'Rejoice, oh unwedded Bride!' The words have a beautiful sound in Church Slavic: 'Raduisja, Nevěsta Nenevěstnaja!'

Sergius, a contemporary of the siege of 626.[27]   The *Akathistos* is a very long hymn, consisting of twenty-four stanzas (οἶκοι) with many refrains.[28] In the ritual the Hymn Akathistos (ὁ ἀκάθιστος ὕμνος) meaning 'all standing' (or rather, to be precise, 'standing all through the night') is the service of the Holy Virgin, partly read and partly sung, which is held every year on the Saturday of the fifth week in Lent, in commemoration of the liberation of Constantinople from the barbarians who besieged the city. None of the twenty-four stanzas allude to any particular fact; such statements as 'Rejoice, who, like thunder, hast struck down thine enemies' or 'Rejoice, through whom enemies fall down' do not refer to any specific event.[29]   But I shall try to show later, especially in connection with the day on which the hymn is to be read and sung every year in the Greek Orthodox Church, that the hymn refers to the Russian invasion and can be used as very essential material for definition of the duration of the invasion.

Then follows another source, which may be with some probability dated at the beginning of the tenth century, and may be connected with the attack of 860.   I refer here to Constantine Cephalas (Kephalas) who, at the outset of the tenth century, compiled a collection of epigrams, short poems, which have been preserved in a unique copy of the famous codex of the *Bibliotheca Palatina*, at Heidelberg, from which this collection is usually called *Anthologia Palatina*.   In the collection are two iambic poems on the Church of Blachernae, which deal with enemies who attacked Constantinople and were defeated by the miraculous intercession of the Holy Virgin.   Chassang and Bury, with most probability, refer the poems to the Russian attack,[30] but P. Waltz, after carefully comparing the poems with the text of the *Bellum Avaricum* by the poet of the seventh century, George of Pisidia, finally concludes that the poems are written by George of Pisidia and, without any doubt, deal with the siege of Constantinople by the Avars and the Persians in 626.[31]   I must admit that the similarity between these texts is striking.

[27] See, for instance, a special monograph on the reign of Heraclius by A. Pernice, *L'Imperatore Eraclio* (Florence, 1905), p. 148.

[28] The complete Greek text in W. Christ and M. Paranikas, *Anthologia graeca carminum christianorum* (Leipzig, 1871), pp. 140–147; also in Cardinal Pitra, *Analecta Sacra Spicilegio Solesmensi parata*, I (Paris, 1876), 250–262.   Papadopoulos-Kerameus points out that there is no critical edition of the text.   *Viz. Vremennik*, x (1903), 358–359.

[29] χαῖρε, ὡς βροντὴ τοὺς ἐχθροὺς καταπλήττουσα (line 255, Christ-Paranikas, p. 146). χαῖρε, δι'ῆς ἐχθροὶ καταπίπτουσι (line 285, *ib.*, p. 147).

[30] A. Chassang, 'Deux homélies de Photius au sujet de la première expédition des Russes contre Constantinople,' *Annuaire de l'Association pour l'encouragement des études grecques en France*, v (1871), 79 (he refers the second poem particularly to the Russian attack).   Bury, *A History of the Eastern Roman Empire* (London, 1912), p. 421, n. 2 (the poems refer to the rout of the Russians).

[31] P. Waltz, 'Notes sur les epigrammes chrétiennes de l'Anthologie Grecque,' *Byzantion*, II (1925), 317–328; especially p. 323.

These two iambic poems on the Church of Blachernae are short, so that I will give the complete text of them here in an English version for a better understanding of their data.   They are published in the section called *Christian epigrams*, nos. 120 and 121, and both are entitled *On Blachernae* ('Ἐν Βλαχέρναις).

Here is the first iambic poem, no. 120:

'If thou seekest the dread throne of God on Earth, marvel as thou gazest on the house of the Virgin.   For She who bears God in her arms, bears Him to the glory of this place.   Here they who are set up to rule over the Earth believe that their sceptres are rendered victorious.   Here the Patriarch, ever wakeful, averts many catastrophes in the world.   The barbarians, who attacked the city, on only seeing Her at the head of the army bent at once their stubborn necks.'[32]

The second iambic poem is no. 121:

'The house of the Virgin, like her Son, was destined to become a second gate of God.   An ark has appeared holier than that of old, not containing the tables written by God's hand but having received within it God Himself.   Here are fountains of purification from flesh, here is redemption of errors of the soul.   No matter how many are evil circumstances, from Her gushes a miraculous gift to cure them.   Here, when She overthrew the foe, She destroyed them by water, not by the spear.   She has not one method of defeat alone, who bore Christ and puts the barbarians to flight.'[33]

The second part of both poems contains historical hints.   In the first poem, no. 120, we have 'a wakeful Patriarch' and the barbarians, who were routed by divine intercession of the Holy Virgin.   This 'wakeful Patriarch' may be either Sergius, a contemporary of the Avar siege in 626, or Photius, because Byzantine tradition relates that the Holy Virgin saved her city in both cases.   In the second poem, no. 121, we read that the Holy Virgin overthrew the foe and destroyed them by water, not by the spear.   We know that in both sieges the fleet of the invaders was destroyed.   But I believe that the words that the Holy Virgin destroyed boats by water, not by the spear, stress the word *water*, reminding us of the dipping of the garment of the Holy Virgin into the water in 860–861 when a sudden violent storm arose from a dead calm and destroyed the enemy's ships.   This poem then, I believe, refers to the attack in 860;

---

[32] *Anthologia Graeca epigrammatum Palatina cum Planudea*, ed. H. Stadtmueller, ɪ (Leipzig, 1894), 33–34.   *The Greek Anthology*, with an English transaltion by W. R. Paton, ɪ (London-New York, 1916), 52–53.   With a slight modification I have used Paton's translation.

[33] Ed. Stadtmueller, ɪ, 34–35; ed. Paton, ɪ, 54–55.   The Greek text reads: ἀνεῖλεν αὐτοὺς ἀντὶ λόγχης εἰς ὕδωρ (verse 11).   Stadtmueller evidently failed to understand the real meaning of the sentence and missed the point by proposing εἰσόδῳ for εἰς ὕδωρ (p. 34, note: εἰς ὕδωρ corrupt, perhaps εἰσόδῳ).

and since it would not be logical to assume that the two poems refer to two different sieges, one to 626 and the other to 860, I think that both were composed in reference to the more recent Russian attack of 860.   Of course the similarity between the poems and the work of George of Pisidia, *Bellum Avaricum*, remains to be explained; and I have not sufficient material in my hands to solve the question whether the similarity arises from the likeness of the events described, or whether the anonymous author of the poems consciously imitated the writing of George of Pisidia.   It should be noted that in the descriptions of the siege of 626 several later sources list Russians also among the allies of the Avar Khagan who besieged Constantinople.   This is evidently the application by later writers of the name of Russians to the Scythians, who, according to evidence contemporary with the siege of 626, participated in this siege, and in the ninth and tenth centuries, were identified with the Russians.

At first sight, the tenth century is unusually rich in chroniclers who record the Russian attack.   Their accounts are very brief.   It must be pointed out that the historian of the tenth century, Joseph Genesius, who belonged to the circle of literary and scholarly men around the Emperor Constantine Porphyrogenitus, and who wrote a history extending from 813 to 886, fails to mention the Russian attack.   The chroniclers who mention it may be divided into two groups: the first one is represented by one chronicler, the so-called Continuator of Theophanes (Theophanes Continuatus); the second group may be designated as that of Symeon Logothete with a number of his copyists, abbreviators, and revisers.   The best record, but unfortunately a too brief one, belongs to the anonymous author of the continuation of Theophanes' *Chronicle*, who has not yet been identified; the attempt to identify him with another historian of the tenth century, Theodore Daphnopates, cannot be regarded as a final solution of the question.   His story, which is entirely devoid of any miraculous element, is entirely credible.   The Continuator of Theophanes tells that the Russians devastated the shores of the Euxine and surrounded Constantinople, that the Emperor was at that time out of the city, at war with the Arabs, that Photius 'appeased God' (τὸ θεῖον ἐξιλεωσαμένου), and the Russians 'left for home' (οἴκαδε ἐκπεπόρευντο).   Soon after that a Russian embassy came to Constantinople and asked for Christian baptism, which was granted (ὃ καὶ γέγονεν).[34]   This is a very sober brief account.   There is no miraculous interference by the Holy Virgin, such as we find in the other group of our evidence.   In presentation of fact, the Continuator of Theophanes is in complete accordance with the contemporary evidence of the Patriarch Photius.

[34] Theoph. Cont., ed. Bonn., p. 196, c. 33.

The second group of the chroniclers of the tenth century who deal with the Russian attack is usually represented by four names: Leo the Grammarian, Theodosius of Melitene, the anonymous Continuator of George Hamartolus, and Symeon Magister and Logothete, the so-called Pseudo-Symeon Magister. But these are not original writers; they are all of them copyists, abbreviators, or revisers of the Chronicle of Symeon Logothete, whose complete original Greek text has not yet been published, but is fairly well known from many printed excerpts, especially from the two manuscripts, *Paris 854* and *Vatican 1807*. The *Chronicle* of Symeon Logothete has also survived in an Old Slavonic version, which was published by V. Sreznevski in 1905. This complicated problem was elucidated for the first time by Vasilievski in 1895 and recently in greater detail discussed and clearly explained by Ostrogorski.[35] Since the original text of the Chronicle of Symeon Logothete has not been published, we can have the best idea of his own work by combining the texts of Theodosius of Melitene and the Slavonic version of Logothete.[36]

I have not seen the record of the Russian attack in the unpublished Greek text of Symeon Logothete. But all the printed texts, which are merely copies, abbreviations, or revisions of his work, including the Old Slavonic version of his *Chronicle*, tell the identical story of how the Russians, in two hundred boats, entered the Bosphorus (ἔνδοθεν τοῦ ἱεροῦ), devastated its banks and surrounded the capital, and how the Emperor, informed of the invasion, hurriedly returned from Mauropotamon in Asia Minor to the city. All these texts introduce the miraculous element. The Emperor and Photius took from the Church of Blachernae the precious garment of the Virgin Mother, bore it in solemn procession to the seashore, and dipped it in the water. At this time the sea was dead calm. But the garment had hardly been dipped when a violent storm arose and scattered the Russian ships, and the defeated invaders, smarting under their losses, returned home.[37] It is to be pointed out that in the text of

---

[35] V. Vasilievski, 'The Chronicle of Logothete in Slavonic and Greek,' *Viz. Vremennik*, II (1895), 78–151. G. Ostrogorsky, 'A Slavonic Version of the Chronicle of Symeon Logothete,' *Seminarium Kondakovianum*, V (Prague, 1932), 17–36. Both in Russian. See also a brief but very clear summary of this question by Ostrogorsky in his study, 'L'Expédition du Prince Oleg contre Constantinople en 907,' *Annales de l'Institut Kondakov (Seminarium Kondakovianum)*, XI (1839), 50.

[36] Ostrogorsky, 'A Slavonic Version,' p. 36.

[37] Leo Grammaticus, ed. Bonn, pp. 240–241 (no dating). Th. Tafel, *Theodosii Meliteni Chronographia, Monumenta Saecularia*, III, Classe 1 (Munich, 1859), p. 168. Georgii Hamartoli Continuator, ed. Muralt (1859), pp. 736–737; ed. V. Istrin (Petrograd, 1922), pp. 10–11. An Old Slavonic Version of the chronicle, ed. V. Istrin (Petrograd, 1920), p. 511 (no dating). Symeon Magister (Pseudo-Symeon), ed. Bonn., p. 674, c. 37–38. A Slavonic version of the *Chronicle* of Symeon Logothete, *Simeona Metafrasta i Logotheta Spisanie mira ot bytiya* . . . ed. A. Kunik, V. Vasilievski, V. Sreznevski (St Petersburg, 1905), p. 106, ll. 1–14 (no dating). The text of the Old Slavonic Symeon Logothete on the Russian attack is also reproduced in M. Weingart, *Byzantské kroniky v literatuře*

Symeon Logothete or Pseudo-Symeon, as we have it now in printed form, the story of the Russian campaign is told under two years of Michael's reign, the ninth and tenth. Of course the chronology is incorrect; but the two years assigned to the campaign should be taken into account when we discuss the question of the duration of the Russian invasion.

So, for the Russian attack of 860, among the Greek chronicles of the tenth century, we have only two brief accounts: the Continuator of Theophanes and the still unpublished original Symeon Logothete, occurring with his modifications in the four chroniclers mentioned above, and in the Old Slavonic version of his complete work published in 1905.

If we pass to the eleventh century and if the dating of the Chronicle to be discussed is correct, we definitely solve one of the most debatable questions connected with the Russian attack. I mean the exact year of the invasion. I remember very well our excitement and surprise when we became familiar with the publication of the noted Belgian scholar, Franz Cumont, who, in 1894, on the basis of a manuscript of the Bibliothèque Royale de Bruxelles, printed a brief anonymous Byzantine chronicle which contained the exact date (year, month, and day) of the Russian incursion. The year is even indicated in three ways: by indiction, by the year of the reign of the Emperor Michael, and by the Byzantine era from the creation of the world; and all these three datings are in complete accordance with each other. The date was 18 June, 860. The brief note of the chronicle announces that at that date the Russians arrived in two hundred ships but through intercession of the Mother of God were overcome, severely defeated, and destroyed.[38] According to Cumont, the Chronicle was probably compiled in the eleventh century, by a clergyman of Constantinople, perhaps a monk of the monastery of Studion. No special study on this Chronicle has yet been made. In addition to the exact date of the invasion, the brief record of the Chronicle belongs to the group of sources which tell of the crushing defeat of the Russians.

The Brussels Chronicle definitely settled the crucial question of the date of the invasion. But Kunik, the stubborn veteran defender of the year 865 (866), wrote in 1894 to Carl de Boor that the new Chronicle failed to convince him and did not make him abandon his point of view.[39] The year 860 is now accepted by all scholars, with the exception of those few of

---

církevněslovanské, ii, 1 (Bratislava, 1923), 135–136. The Old Slavonic version of George Hamartolus with the anonymous continuation was made in Russia between 1040 and 1050, under the Russian Prince Yaroslav the Wise. Istrin, *The Chronicle of George Hamartolus in Old Slavo-Russian Version*, ii (Petrograd, 1922), 309, 410 (in Russian).

[38] *Anecdota Bruxellensia. i. Chroniques Byzantines du Manuscrit 11370* par Franz Cumont (Ghent, 1894), in *Recueil de Travaux publiés par la Faculté de philosophie et lettres*, 9e fascicule, p. 33. Vasilievski immediately made a special mention of Cumont's discovery in *Viz. Vremennik*, i (1894), 258.

[39] See C. de Boor, 'Der Angriff der Rhos auf Byzanz,' *Byz. Zeitschrift*, iv (1895), 465–466.

whom we shall speak later, who evidently are not familiar with Cumont's Chronicle and the vast literature which after 1894 has dealt with the question.

To the second half of the eleventh century belongs a chronicler, John Scylitzes, whose narrative, beginning with 811, was almost entirely incorporated in the chronicle of George Cedrenus, who lived under Alexius Comnenus (1081–1118). The chronicler John Zonaras lived in the twelfth century. The chronicles of Scylitzes-Cedrenus and Zonaras contain brief records of the Russian invasion. They mention the devastation of the shores of the Black Sea and the raid on the capital; they call the Russians *Ros*, a Scythian people who live near the northern Tauros (περὶ τὸν ἀρκτῷον Ταῦρον; περὶ τὸν Ταῦρον), i.e., in the Crimea. Here, of course, the chroniclers are reproducing in this form the name Tauroscythians (Ταυροσκύθαι), as Russians were very often called in Byzantine texts in the tenth and eleventh centuries. Cedrenus and Zonaras regard a celestial interference as the cause of the Russian retreat without defining it exactly. Cedrenus' report is very close to the text of the Continuator of Theophanes, but is abridged.[40]

From the thirteenth century we have an interesting and very little known text which may or may not be connected with the attack of 860. The author was the young, highly educated, and enlightened Emperor of the Empire of Nicaea, Theodore II Lascaris (1245–1258), who was much more interested in literature and writing than in state affairs. It is his *Discourse on the Very Holy Lady Mother of God, which is to be read on the day of the Acathistus (Akathistos).*[41] Since this *Discourse* is almost unknown in historical literature, I give here in an English version its most important parts. The *Discourse* begins as follows:

'Today the barbarians have been destroyed (τὸ βαρβαρικὸν ἐσκυθίσθη); today the Christians have been raised up on high; today the people of the pious have been liberated and the troops of the impious have been plunged into the sea like that of the Pharaoh (φαραωνιτικῶς) . . . and that numerous unconquerable gathering of boats has been sent to the bottom, into the sea. . . . Who does not know the happening? The Russians (ὁ 'Ρῶς) who had once sailed against the Byzantis (ὁ 'Ρῶς ὁ τὸν ῥοῦν κατὰ Βυζαντίδος κινήσας ποτέ), who placed their hopes upon naval

---

[40] We shall speak below, in the section on Slavonic sources, of Slavonic versions of Zonaras.

[41] Αὐτοκράτορος Θεοδώρου[Δούκα τοῦ Λασκάρεως] λόγος εἰς τὴν ὑπεραγίαν δέσποιναν Θεοτόκον, ὀφείλων ἀναγινώσκεσθαι ἐν τῇ ἑορτῇ τῆς 'Ακαθίστου, published from a manuscript of the fourteenth century of the Public Library of Athens in the Greek magazine Σωτήρ, XVI (Athens, 1894), 186–192. A brief fragment of the text, where the name 'Ρῶς is mentioned, was also published in *Viz. Vremennik*, III (1896), 206–207. This *Discourse* is mentioned neither in the list of Theodore's works in the special monograph on his reign by Jean B. Pappadopoulos, *Théodore II Lascaris Empereur de Nicée* (Paris, 1908), pp. IX–XII, nor in the more recent work by M. A. Andreyeva, *Essays on the culture of the Byzantine court in the thirteenth century* (Prague, 1927), pp. 13–15 (in Russian).

battle, were immediately drowned, and the pious in their weakness were saved by the strong hand of God, for His Mother is their guardian. And what slave can oppose the powerful Mother of the Lord? That well known host, dog-like, greedy, fond of pleasure, looking only for pleasure and not recognizing God, was speedily drowned . . . as by the might of a very great army sent down from a very high citadel (ἔκ τινος ἀκροπόλεως). Her girdle (zone) which was most piously carried by the priest and which encircled the sea as by a plumbline and rope, aroused an agitation in the water, though the air continued calm and the winds were not blowing at all, so that the powerful fleet of the impious which was stationed in the harbor, suddenly became a great and strange spectacle of destruction. The stirring was not from the air, but the wind was rising from the bottom; rudders were twisted; sails torn up; prows of boats sunk; and the enemies who were close to the shore, not knowing what had happened, hurriedly tried to escape only to be drowned. Seeing confusion they failed to realize that an angel of the Lord, through the power of the Queen (the Mother of God? δυνάμει τῆς βασιλίδος), had stirred up the water and sent to destruction through drowning the imitators of the Egyptian army . . . and their grave was billowy depth; the sea ate up their corpses. . . . The girdle (zone) of the Very Holy and Immaculate (Mother of God) has achieved victory . . . (pp. 187–188). . . . Rejoice, oh famous pride of Christians (p. 190). . . . Was not the assault of the fleet terrible? Was not its number immeasurable? . . . Who drowned the innumerable army? Who stirred up the calm? Who delivered (us) from the danger? . . . Only the Protectress of all has saved her flock alive and sent to the bottom a great number of boats (p. 192).'

This rhetorical description of the miraculous defeat of the barbarian Russian fleet under the walls of Constantinople applies equally well to the two sieges of the capital, both in 626 and in 860. The name *Russian* in 626 need not trouble us, because in several later sources on this siege, as we know, this name replaces *Scythian* which is given in earlier evidence. In this text, the miraculous element in the story is represented not by icons of the Mother of God (τὰς ἱερὰς εἰκόνας τῆς Θεομήτορος) nor by her garment (τὴν τῆς παναγίου τιμίαν ἐσθῆτα or μαφόριον)[42] but by her zone (girdle). Comparing this text with the corresponding verses of the *Bellum Avaricum* of George of Pisidia, who described the siege of 626, I have discovered many analogies in phraseology and vocabulary.[43] As a result I am inclined to ascribe Theodore Lascaris' *Discourse* rather to the Avar invasion of 626 than to the Russian invaison of 860.[44] I have given the

---

[42] See for instance, Διήγησις ὠφέλιμος, in Migne, *P. G.*, cvi, coll. 1337 and 1340. Symeon Magister, ed. Bonn., p. 674, c. 37. *Slavonic Version of Simeon Logothete*, ed. Sreznevski, p. 106. Weingart, *Byzantské Kroniky*, ii, 1 (Bratislava, 1923), 136. See also Leo Sternbach, *Analecta Avarica* (Cracow, 1900), pp. 311–313 (Rozprawy Akademii Umiejętnošci, Wydział fiłołogiczny, ser. ii, vol. xv).

[43] Georgii Pisidae *BellumAvaricum*, vv. 348–541 (ed. Bonn., pp. 371–373).

[44] Papadopoulos-Kerameus attributes this text to the event of 860. Papadopoulos-Kerameus, 'The Akathistos of the Mother of God, Russia, and the Patriarch Photius,' *Viz. Vremennik*, x (1903), 394.

English version in this study, nevertheless, because this text is very little known, since it came out in a rather inaccessible Greek magazine, and I wish to make it available so that scholars may use it, even in an English version, and come to their own conclusions.   It is not to be forgotten that such events as the sieges of 626 and 860 have so much common material for legend that often it is not easy to decide whether the text is to be referred to the earlier or later siege.   Such stories furnish little historical material, in addition to our evidence from historical and very often from hagiographic sources.   The question may be raised which of the two events, 626 or 860, more deeply affected the imagination of the masses of the population.   In both cases, of course, the Holy Virgin as the specific champion of Constantinople plays the central part.   'The humble monk of Studion,' Antonius Tripsychus, referring to the Holy Virgin, remarks, "One may cross the Atlantic Sea more easily than grasp in one's mind Thy miracles on the sea coast.'[45]

Later Byzantine chroniclers, Constantine Manasses (in the first half of the twelfth century), Michael Glycas (in the twelfth century), Sathas' Ἀνωνύμου Σύνοψις Χρονική (in the thirteenth century), Joel (probably in the thirteenth century), and Ephraim (in the fourteenth century), fail to mention the Russian incursion of 860.   Only two of them, Glycas and Ephraim, narrate how the Russians besought Constantinople that they might be converted to the Christian faith, and mention sending a bishop to them, which, it is known, occurred shortly after the attack of 860.[46]

In concluding the survey of the Greek sources connected with the incursion of 860 I wish to say a few words on the Russian article of Ch. Loparev which came out in 1895 under the title, 'Old Evidence on the placing of the garment of the Mother of God in Blachernae, in a new interpretation in relation to the incursion of the Russians upon Byzantium in 860.'[47] Loparev considered an old Greek text which was published in 1648 by Fr. Combefis,[48] collated it with various Greek and Old-Slavonic versions, and has given a new revised edition of the story.   He concludes that the story refers to the Russian incursion of 860, and that its author is George, the *Chartophylax* of St Sophia and later the Archbishop of Nicomedia. But in the following year (1896) Vasilievski in his article *Avars not Russians, Theodore not George* has definitely proved that Loparev was wrong in his conclusions; the text under consideration deals with the first siege

---

[45] εὐκολώτερον γὰρ ἄν τις διαπεραιώσαιτο τὸ Ἀτλαντικὸν πέλαγος ἢ τῇ τῶν σῶν θαυματουργημάτων παραλίῳ ἀκτῇ ποσὶ νοὸς ἐπιθίξειε. Λόγος ἀναγνωσθεὶς ἐν Βλαχέρναις παρὰ τοῦ ταπεινοῦ Στουδίτου μοναχοῦ Ἀντωνίου τοῦ Τριψύχου.   Sternbach, *Analecta Avarica*, p. 339, lines 36–38.

[46] Michaeli Glycae *Annales*, IV (ed. Bonn.,) p. 553. Ephraemius, vv. 2593–2604 (ed. Bonn.) p. 114.   [47] *Viz. Vremennik*, II (1895), 581–628.

[48] Fr. Combefis, *Graeco-Latinae Patrum Bibliothecae Novum Auctarium*, II (Paris, 1648), 806–826; reprinted in Migne, *P. G.*, XCII, coll. 1348–1372.

of Constantinople by the Avars, which took place in 619, and its author
was Theodore Syncellus, who also wrote a detailed story of the siege of
the capital by the Avars in 626.[49]   In connection with this study I have
reread both articles, and I find Vasilievski's refutation of Loparev's thesis
absolutely convincing; clearly we must eliminate Loparev's study from
our sources on the incursion of 860.[50]

Latin sources have already been discussed above, in connection with
the Norman danger to Constantinople from the south, from the Mediterranean and Aegean.   In my opinion, they have no relation to the Russian attack in 860 from the north.   However, the letter of Pope Nicholas
I, written in 865, might have referred to either raid on Constantinople,
that from the north in 860 or from the south in 861.   Arab historians fail
to mention the Russian attack of 860.

Let us turn now to Slavic sources.

[49] Vasilievski, in *Viz. Vremennik*, III (1896), 83–95.   The detailed story of the Avar siege in 626,
which has been mentioned in the text, was first published in 1853 by Angelo Mai, *Nova Patrum
Bibliotheca*, VI, 2 (Rome, 1853), 423–437; a more complete and revised edition by Leo Sternbach,
Analecta Avarica (Cracow, 1900), pp. 298–320; on the author, p. 333.

[50] It is to be noted that in 1919 Shakhmatov, without mentioning Vasilievski's criticism, accepted
Loparev's conclusions and wrote: 'Loparev has managed to prove that this expedition ended not at
all as Symeon Logothete (Hamartolus' Continuator) tells; it ended in an honorable peace for the
Russians which was concluded under the walls of Tsargrad; after that, on the twenty-fifth of June
they withdrew from the city.'   A. Shakhmatov, *The Earliest Fortunes of the Russian Nation* (Petrograd, 1919), p. 60 (in Russian).   On the end of the Russian expedition we shall speak later.   In any
case, Shakhmatov's absolute approval of Loparev's conclusions is rather surprising.

RUSSIAN OR OLD SLAVONIC SOURCES

THE Russian Annals or the Russian *Letopisi* give little new material for the invasion of 860 because in their earlier part they depend on the Byzantine Chronicles, especially on the *Continuator* of George Hamartolus.[1] They supply us with only one essential addition as to the attack of 860; they give us the names of the two Russian leaders who attacked Constantinople, Askold and Dir. This detail comes from a local tradition.

It is unnecessary here to discuss the brilliant but sometimes rather debatable results of Shakhmatov's studies on the Russian chronicles in general which form at present the starting point for any critical examination of these sources. In our study we are interested only in one episode of the attack of 860, which, as has been noted just above, is based on George Hamartolus' *Continuator*.[2]

We begin with the so-called Laurentian text of the Russian Primary Chronicles.[3] The Laurentian text tells the story of the attack in two places, under the years 6360 (852) and 6374 (866). In the first story we have only a brief mention that under the Emperor Michael III, the Rus' went against Tsargrad, 'as is written in the Greek Chronicle,' In its second story the Laurentian text gives a detailed narrative of the attack as we have it in George Hamartolus' Continuator, with the addition of the names of the two Russian leaders Askold and Dir. The name of the Bosphorus, which in the Greek text is called *Hieron*, is given in the Slavonic text as *Sud*, of which we shall speak below. The chronology of the Slavonic text is, of course, incorrect.[4] The so-called Hypatian (Ipatian)

---

[1] See a list of the subjects borrowed by the Russian chronicler from George Hamartolus and his Continuator in S. H. Cross. *The Russian Primary Chronicle* (Cambridge, 1930), p. 100.

[2] According to Shakhmatov, the story of the Russian attack on Constantinople failed to occur in the original text of the Russian Primary Chronicle, but was taken by its later compiler from a certain Chronograph. A. A. Shakhmatov, *Studies on the oldest Russian Chronicles* (St Petersburg, 1908), pp. 97–98 (in Russian).

[3] The most recent edition of this *Chronicle* by E. F. Karski, 2d ed. (Leningrad, 1926), in *Complete Collection of Russian Annals*, vol. 1 (in Russian, *Polnoe Sobranie Russkich Letopisei*. I shall quote this collection as *PSRL*). We have a very fine English translation of this chronicle by Samuel H. Cross, *The Russian Primary Chronicle* (Cambridge, 1930), provided with a very important introduction by the author (pp. 77–135) and three appendices (pp. 299–300). Cross' work was published in *Harvard Studies and Notes in Philology and Literature*, vol. XII, pp. 75–320. A French translation came out in 1884, *Chronique dite de Nestor*, trad. par Louis Leger (Paris, 1884). *Publications de l'Ecole des Langues Orientales Vivantes*, IIe serie, vol. XIII. A German translation by R. Trautmann, *Die altrussische Nestorchronik: Povest vremennych let* (Leipzig, 1931). On some other translations of the Laurentian text see Cross, *op. cit.*, p. 80.

[4] *PSRL*, I (sec. ed., Leningrad, 1926), 17 and 21–22. Shakhmatov, *The Tale of Bygone Years*, I. Introduction, text, notes (Petrograd, 1916), 21–22. Cross, p. 144 and 145–146. The name of this version comes from the monk Lawrence (Lavrenti) who copied the manuscript in 1377.

text of the Russian Chronicle reproduces literally the Laurentian text.[5]
The four Novgorod chronicles begin their narrative later than 860 (with
the years 1016, 911, 988, and 1113).   There are two Pskov Chronicles.

The first, beginning with the year 859, tells briefly under the year 6374
(866) how Askold got permission from Rurik in Novgorod to go to Tsar-
grad, how he settled in Kiev, then went with two hundred boats to fight
Tsargrad, and made much devastation; but finally the sea drowned the
Russians, so that only a few of them survived.[6]   The second Pskov
Chronicle, although beginning with the year 851, fails to mention the
Russian attack on Tsargrad.[7]

The usual story of the Russian attack as it was told in the Laurentian
and Hypatian texts with some abridgments has been reproduced in several
other later chronicles: the *Chronicle of Avraamka*;[8] the *Simeonovskaya
Letopis'*, compiled at the beginning of the fifteenth century;[9] the *Chronicle
of Lvov (Lvovskaya Letopis')*;[10] the *Ermolinskaya Letopis'*, compiled in the
second half of the fifteenth century;[11] *Tipografskaya Letopis'*.[12]   The same
story has been incorporated in the *Voskresenskaya Letopis'*, which was
compiled in the sixteenth century.[13]   The so-called West Russian Chronicles (*Letopisi*) fail to mention the invasion of 860.[14]

The Nikonovski Chronicle (*Nikonovskaya Letopis'*) which is sometimes
also called the Patriarchal Chronicle (*Patriarshaya Letopis'*), compiled in
the middle of the sixteenth century, like other Russian chronicles is a
digest of earlier Greek chronographies and Russian chronicles, but contains some new material.   This new material comes from the so-called
Paralipomena of Zonaras.

Here I wish to say a few words about this interesting text.   In spite
of its great length, the Greek Chronicle of Zonaras was very popular
among the Slavs.   As we know, John Zonaras wrote in the twelfth century not the usual dry chronicle, but, according to Krumbacher, 'a manual
of world history evidently intended to meet higher requirements.'[15]   A
complete translation of Zonaras' Greek text into Slavonic was most prob-

---

[5] *PSRL*, II (sec. ed., St Petersburg, 1908), 12 and 15.   The name of this version comes from the
name of the Hypatian (*Ipatevski*) Monastery at Kostroma, where the manuscript was discovered.
This redaction dates from the middle of the fifteenth century.

[6] *PSRL*, IV (St Petersburg, 1848), 174.   [7] *PSRL*, V (St Petersburg, 1851).

[8] *PSRL*, XVI (St Petersburg, 1889), col. 35.

[9] *PSRL*, XVIII (St Petersburg, 1913), 8.   This volume gives also some fragments preserved from
the beginning of the *Troitskaya Letopis*, which was burned in 1812 during the fire of Moscow.

[10] *PSRL*, XX (St Petersburg, 1910), 44.   The prefect of Constantinople Ooryphas is called *Ory-
thant*, and the Patriarch Photius, *Thatiy*.

[11] *PSRL*, XXIII (St Petersburg, 1910), 3.   [12] *PSRL*, XXIV (St Petersburg, 1921), 7.

[13] *PSRL*, VII (St Petersburg, 1856), 269 (under the year 6374–866); see also pp. 7–9.

[14] *PSRL*, XVII (St Petersburg, 1907).

[15] Krumbacher, *Geschichte der byzantinischen Litteratur*, p. 371.

ably made in the same twelfth century, in 1170, in Bulgaria.   The
Paralipomena is an abridgment of the text of the complete Slavonic
translation, where almost the whole history of the Jewish people and many
other sections and episodes from other parts were excluded.   The original
abridged text may go back to the epoch of Stephen Dushan (1331–1355),
King of Serbia.   The text of the *Paralipomena* which we now possess
was executed probably in 1383.   Since the names of Askold, Dir, and
Oleg are mentioned in the *Paralipomena*, it is clear that it was made by a
Russian scribe.   Such are the results of recent studies on Zonaras'
Paralipomena.[16]

The *Nikonovski Chronicle* gives several versions of the story of the attack on Constantinople by Askold and Dir.   The first is entitled *On the
aggression of Rus' upon Tsargrad*.   In it the chronicler writes that the
Russian princes Oskold and Dir once sent forth from Kiev upon Tsargrad, in the reign of the Emperor Michael and his mother Theodora, who
proclaimed veneration of holy icons in the first week of Lent, and they
carried out much slaughter.   Then follows the usual story of how the
Emperor Michael and the Patriarch Photius after performing a night
service in the church of the Mother of God at Blachernae, dipped her
precious garment in the sea; a storm arose; the boats of the impious
Russians were driven to shore, and all the men were massacred.[17]   This
story, of course, is based on Greek sources.   The year of the attack is
not indicated, and the mention of Theodora is incorrect, because the
attack took place after her deposition.

A little below, the *Nikonovski Chronicle* gives a very brief item entitled
On the aggression of Agarenes upon Tsargrad.   We read that the masses
of Agarenes, i.e., Arabs, went against Tsargard and made devastation.
And then we have an extremely interesting statement: 'Hearing this, the
Kievan princes Askold and Dir went on Tsargrad and did much evil.'[18]
Here we have, if I am not mistaken, the only mention in all our evidence
on the attack that the Russians knew beforehand that the Arabs were invading the territory of the Byzantine Empire, and therefore the Emperor
and his army must have left the capital and its surroundings to campaign

---

[16] See P. O. Potapov, 'Destiny of Zonaras' Chronicle in Slavo-Russian Literature,' *Izvestiya* (Accounts) of the Section of Russian Language and Literature at the Academy of Sciences of St Petersburg, xxii, 2 (1917–1918), pp. 141–186 (in Russian).   A very good presentation of the question in
M. Weingart, *Byzantské Kroniky v literatuře církevněslovanské,* i (Bratislava, 1922), 125–159.   When
Weingart was writing the first part of his work, he was not yet aware of Potapov's study.   See Weingart's additional note in his part ii, 2 (Bratislava, 1923), p. 522 (in Czech).   The text of the Slavo-
Russian *Paralipomena* was published by O. Bodyanski in *Chteniya of the Moscow Society of Russian
History and Antiquities*, 1847, no. 1.   On Bodyanski's edition see V. Jagić, 'Ein Beitrag zur ser-
bischen Annalistik mit literaturgeschichtlicher Einleitung,' *Archiv für slavische Philologie*, ii (1877),
pp. 14–17.   [17] *PSRL*, ix (St Petersburg, 1862), 7.   [18] *PSRL*, ix, 8.

against them.   Although he did not know the *Nikonovski Chronicle*, Bury wrote, 'The Russians must have known beforehand that the Emperor had made preparations for a campaign in full force against the Saracens.'[19] Of course in the title given in the *Nikonovski Chronicle*, 'On the aggressions of Agarenes upon Tsargrad,' the word *Tsargrad* means not Constantinople itself, but the Byzantine Empire in general.[20]

Then a little farther on the *Nikonvski Chronicle* repeats under two years, 6374 (866) and 6375 (867), the usual story of the attack, taken from the earlier Russian chronicles, which are based originally on Hamartolus' Continuator.   Under 6374 (866) we read that Askold and Dir went upon the Greeks, when the Emperor Michael and Basil had marched against the Agarenes.   Then follows the generally known story about the Black River, the message of the eparch of the city, the Emperor's return, the solemn procession with Photius, the storm, and the destruction of the Russian vessels.   In this version a detail is to be noted which has not been given in any other evidence, that on his campaign against the Arabs Michael was accompanied by his new favorite Basil, destined to be emperor and his future assassin.   Under the following year 6375 (867) the *Nikonovski Chronicle* briefly says, 'Askold and Dir returned from Tsargrad with a small force (*druzhina*), and there was in Kiev great weeping.'[21] I should like to point out that in the *Nikonovski Chronicle* the Russian campaign against Byzantium is told under two successive years, as in Symeon Logothete's (Pseudo-Symeon's) *Chronicle*.

All three of these stories are based through the earlier Russian chronicles, on Greek sources.   But the *Nikonovski Chronicle*, in addition, contains more information which comes from the *Paralipomena* of Zonaras.[22] Under the year 6384 (876), in other words, in the reign of Michael's successor, Basil I (867–886), we have a story entitled *On the Rus' prince Oskold* (*O knjaze Rustem Oskolde*).   We read: 'The race called Russians, who are also Cumans, live in Euxinopontus; they began to capture the Roman country and wished to go to Constantinople (*Konstantingrad*); but supreme providence prevented them; and divine anger fell upon them, and their princes Askold and Dir returned unsuccessful.'   Then follows the very well known story about the miracle of the gospel which cast into the fire failed to burn.[23]

[19] Bury, *op. cit.*, p. 421.

[20] Cf. Zonaras, XVI, 5: οἱ ἐκ τῆς Ἄγαρ ταῖς χώραις τῶν Ῥωμαίων εἰσβάλλοντες (ed. Dindorf, IV, 16; Bonn, III, 405).   [21] *PSRL*, IX, 9.

[22] Ed. O. Bodyanski (Moscow, 1847), p. 101.   For complete reference see above.   See also A. Popov, *Survey of the Russian chronographs of Russian version*, I (Moscow, 1866), 169–170 (in Russian).

[23] *Russian Letopis* according to the Nikonovski version, I (St Petersburg, 1767), 21.   *PSRL*, IX, 13.   A. Popov, *Collection (Izbornik)* of Slavonic and Russian works and articles, inserted in the Chronographs of Russian version (Moscow, 1869), pp. 4–5; 136.

This story of the unsuccessful attack on Byzantium in the *Nikonovski Chronicle*, through the Slavonic *Paralipomena* of Zonaras, goes back to the original Greek text of Zonaras, which runs as follows: 'The Scythian race of Russians, who live around Taurus, overran with a fleet the regions of the Euxine and intended to attack Byzantis herself; but their intention was not executed, because they were prevented by supreme providence, which made them, against their will, retreat unsuccessful, after they had undergone divine anger.'[24]

We see at once that in the Slavonic version the original Greek text has submitted to several alterations. The Greek text places this undated event in the time of Michael III and ascribes it to the Russian attack of 860. Then 'the Scythian race' of the Greek original is replaced by the Cumans, who were much better known to the translator of the twelfth century than the vague 'Scythians.' The Slavonic version distorts the Russians 'who live around Taurus and overran the regions of the Euxine' of the Greek text to 'they live in Euxinopontus.' The *Nikonovski Chronicle* reads, 'The race called Russians, *who are also Cumans.*' We have just indicated that here the term *Cumans* is but the translator's interpretation of *Scythians*, so that his words would mean 'the race called Russians, who are also Scythians.' Therefore Mošin's statement, which is based on the Serbian version of the *Paralipomena*, that 'there was even an attempt to identify Rus with the Turks-Cumans' is to be discarded.[25] About a hundred years ago F. Kruse wrote that to translate the words of the *Nikonovski Chronicle* by 'the Russians who are also Cumans' would be unwise.[26] But Kruse failed to refer to Zonaras' original Greek text. Had he done this, he would have understood at once that the identification of Russians with Cumans in the *Nikonovski Letopis* is but the translator's interpretation of the term 'Scythian' in the Greek original. So with all these reservations I have preserved in my own translation 'the Russians who are also Cumans.' It is not irrelevant to note that if we consider the text of the *Nikonovski Chronicle* by itself, without going back to its original Greek source, it might be supposed to refer to another unsuccessful Russian attack, on a smaller scale than in 860, under Basil I, in the seventies of the ninth century. On the possibility of other Russian attacks in the ninth century on Byzantium after 860, we shall speak later.

---

[24] Zonaras, XVI, 5: τὸ δ'ἔθνος τῶν ῾Ρὼς Σκυθικὸν ὂν τῶν περὶ τὸν Ταῦρον ἐθνῶν στόλῳ τὰ τοῦ Εὐξείνου πόντου κατέτρεχε καὶ αὐτῇ τῇ Βυζαντίδι ἐπιέναι διεμελέτα. ἀλλ' οὐκ εἰς ἔργον ἤχθη σφίσι τὸ βούλευμα, κωλυσάσης τούτο τῆς προνοίας τῆς ἄνωθεν, ἣ καὶ ἄκοντας αὐτοὺς ἀπράκτους, μᾶλλον δὲ καὶ θείου πειραθέντας μηνίματος, ἀπελθεῖν ᾠκονόμησεν (ed. Dindorf, IV, 15; Bonn, III, 404).

[25] V. Mošin, 'The Varangian-Russian Question,' *Slavia*, x (1931), 120.

[26] 'Russi, qui et Kumani, insania esset,' F. Kruse, *Chronicon Normannorum* (Hamburg-Gotha 1851), p. 408, n. 2, *Idem*, 'The Two First Invasions of the Russians into Byzantium,' *Journal of the Ministry of Public Instruction*, 1840, December, p. 158 (in Russian).

I have spent so long on the data of the *Nikonovski Chronicle* because they differ greatly from other Russian sources, and supply us with new material from Zonaras' *Paralipomena*.

This material from Zonaras' *Paralipomena* has also been incorporated in a book on the genealogy of the Russian Tsars of the dynasty of Rurik, which was compiled in the sixteenth century under the title *Stepennaya Kniga Tsarskago Rodosloviya (Book of Steps of the Imperial Genealogy)*.[27] We read here: 'The Kievan princes Oskold and Dir captured the Roman country; with them there were the people called Rus, who are also Cumans; they lived in Euxinopontus.   And the Emperor Basil made with them peaceable agreement; he converted them to Christianity; they promised to accept baptism and asked him for an archbishop.'[28]

The distorted traditon of the 'Euxinopontic Russians,' which, from Zonaras' *Paralipomena*, was taken over by the *Nikonovski Chronicle* and *Stepennaya Kniga*, has become an essential proof for those scholars who advocated the theory that the Russian invasion of 860 was carried out not from Kiev but by the Black Sea Russians from the Crimea.   In 1847 the editor of the Russian version of Zonaras' *Paralipomena*, O. Bodyanski, wrote, 'From Zonaras' *Paralipomena*, then passed into the *Stepennaya Kniga* and the *Nikonovski Letopis* the mention of the Euxinopontic Russiaus, who were called Cumans, who attacked Constantinople under the leadership of Askold and Dir, and about whom scholars of Russian history since Schlözer have so long been uncertain.'[29]   Literature on the so-called Black Sea Russians is enormous.[30]

After the fifteenth century, along with the Chronicles or *Letopisi*, historical works of a different type made their appearance, the so-called chronographs, where presentation of the events of Russian history is preceded by a brief rudimentary sketch of universal history compiled on the basis of the Bible and Greco-Roman and Byzantine sources as well. I wish to mention the *Chronograph* of the redaction of the year 1512, and the *Chronograph* of West-Russian redaction, which was compiled approximately at the beginning of the second half of the sixteenth century. In both books, as in the *Nikonovski Chronicle*, we have the usual story of the invasion of the Russians in 860, taken over from earlier Russian

[27] The final redaction of this work was done in March-December 1563, under John the Terrible. See P. Vasenko, *Stepennaja Kniga Tsarskago Rodosloviya* and its significance in old Russian historical literature, I (St Petersburg, 1904), p. 244; also p. 125 (in Russian).

[28] *Stepennaya Kniga, PSRL*, xxi, 1 (St Petersburg, 1908), p. 35.

[29] O. Bodyanski, introduction to Zonaras' *Paralipomena* (Moscow, 1847), p. iv.   See V. Ikonnikov, *Essay on the Cultural Importance of Byzantium in the History of Russia* (Kiev, 1869), p. 529 (in Russian).

[30] We shall briefly discuss this problem later in connection with the question from where the Russian invasion of 860 was carried out.

chronicles, and then the story based on Zonaras' *Paralipomena*, which has been told above.[31]

The old Slavonic version of the *Chronicle* of Simeon Logothete, whose original Greek, as we know, has not yet been published, reproduces the story told by the Greek chroniclers of Simeon Logothete's group.[32]

An old Slavonic version of George Hamartolus' Continuator reproduces the Greek text faithfully with the addition of the names of Askold and Dir and the introduction of the term *Sud* to designate the Bosphorus instead of the Greek *Hieron*.[33] The names of the two Russian leaders, Askold and Dir, were taken by the Russian translator of George Hamartolus' *Continuator* from Russian sources.[34]

Zonaras' *Paralipomena* has already been discussed above.

[31] *Chronograph* of 1512. *PSRL*, xxii, 1 (St Petersburg, 1911), 348 and 352. *Chronograph* of West-Russian redaction, *ibid.*, xxii, 2 (St Petersburg, 1914), 150, 153, 154.

[32] *Simeona Metafrasta i Logotheta Spisanie mira ot bytija* . . . ed. A. Kunik, V. Vasilievski, V. Sreznevski (St Petersburg, 1905), p. 106.   M. Weingart, *Byzantské Kroniky v Literatuře Cirkovněslovanské*, ii, 1 (Bratislava, 1923),135–136.

[33] M. Istrin, *An Old Slavonic Version of George Hamartolus and His Continuator*, i (Petrograd, 1920), 511.

[34] See Istrin, *op. cit.*, ii (Petrograd, 1922), 294. The question has not been definitely settled. Cf. V. Ikonnikov, *Essay in Russian Historiography*, ii, 1 (Kiev, 1908), 121.

THE RUSSIAN EXPEDITION OF 860 IN
RUSSIAN LITERATURE

IN this section of my study I wish to examine how Russian historians have described and interpreted the first Russian attack on Constantinople. Such a survey, however incomplete it may prove to be, has never been even attempted. By Russian literature I mean studies written by Russian scholars in Russian, and I shall include the works of a few foreigners who lived and worked in Russia and wrote either in Latin, like G. Bayer and occasionally F. Kruse, or in German, like A. Schlözer and to some extent E. Kunik. I shall examine first general histories of Russia, then general histories of the Byzantine Empire, and lastly some special studies dealing with various questions connected with the early history of Russia.

It is interesting that only one monograph on the attack of 860 has been written in Russia. This monograph was written in Latin by G. Bayer over two hundred years ago and published in 1738. To this fine piece of work I shall return later.

The first attempt at a brief presentation of Russian history in chronological sequence was compiled in the Ukraine at the end of the seventeenth century and is known under the title of *Synopsis*. This compendium, of which the first edition came out in 1674, covers the history of Russia from earliest times to the reign of Tsar Fyodor Alekseyevich (1676–1682) and was the most popular textbook in Russia during the eighteenth century; it ran into over twenty editions. This *Synopsis*, which is based mostly on the work of Polish compilers, has often been attributed to Innocent Gisel, a Prussian by origin, who emigrated to Kiev, adopted the Greek-Orthodox faith, and became the archimandrite of the famous Crypt Monastery in Kiev. But his authorship of the *Synopsis* is not certain, and it is sometimes stated that the compiler of this work is unknown.[1]

We find in the *Synopsis* only a few words on the attack on Constantinople. These are as follows: 'And Oleg, hearing that Oskold and Dir who

---

[1] See for example V. Ikonnikov, *Essay of Russian Historiography*, II (Kiev, 1908), 1554–1556. Ikonnikov usually refers to Gisel's *Synopsis* (66, n. 3; 104; 1377; 1425; 1547, n. 1; 1590); but on p. 1554 he writes, 'The *Synopsis* attributed to the Archimandrite of the Crypt Monastery in Kiev, Innocentius Gisel.' See also vol. I, 1 (Kiev, 1891), 203; additions to this page, p. XIII. Milyukov says plainly that the compiler of the *Synopsis* is unknown. P. N. Milyukov, *Main Currents of Russian Historical Thought*, I, sec. ed. (Moscow, 1898), 10. But the Ukrainian historian Doroshenko in his book *Survey of Ukrainian Historiography* (Prague, 1923, p. 22), positively considers Gisel the author of the *Synopsis*. For this information I am greatly indebted to Professor G. V. Vernadsky of Yale University.

had made war on Tsargrad, had returned to Kiev in defeat (literally *ashamed*) with a small *druzhina* (company), took with him Igor Rurikovich and went towards Kiev . . . .' Then follows the story of Oleg's murder of Oskold and Dir.[2]

Under Peter the Great, at the beginning of the eighteenth century, A. I. Mankiev wished to correct the essential defects of the *Synopsis*, especially its disproportionate use of Polish sources and its predominant interest in Kiev. As secretary, he accompanied to Sweden the Russian ambassador, Prince A. Khilkov; along with him he was arrested by the King of Sweden, Charles XII, and held in captivity eighteen years. He died in 1723. During his detention he wrote a *Summary* (*Yadro*) of *Russian History*. But, since his compilation was not approved by Peter the Great, it was not printed till many years after the author's death in 1770; it had four editions (1770, 1784, 1791, and 1799). Mankiev's *Yadro* is sometimes attributed to Khilkov, the ambassador whose secretary Mankiev was.[3]

Mankiev's description of the attack on Constantinople is much more detailed and substantial than that in the *Synopsis*. 'At the same time,' we read in the *Yadro*, 'in southern Russia Oskold and Dir, the heirs and descendants of Kiev, magnificently ruled over the Principality of Kiev; having gathered a vast Russian army, they in boats (*lodiyakh*) and other sea vessels had gone from the Dnieper into the Black Sea, and, crossing the sea, drawn near Constantinople. But, through the prayer to God of the Greeks who then despaired of any other aid to beat off the Russian force, or, as others write, because the Patriarch of Constantinople, Sergius, dipped in the sea the precious garment (*riza*) of the Mother of God, the stormy sea destroyed all Russian vessels and sank the men, so that the princes Oskold and Dir themselves barely escaped with a few people and returned to Kiev. Aware of Oskold and Dir's failure, Oleg, taking with him the young prince Igor, and gathering a vast army, drew near Kiev, killed Oskold and Dir, and captured the city.'[4]

In this text Mankiev has accurately preserved the usual traditional story. The only error is that instead of the Patriarch Photius he named the Patriarch Sergius, who is connected with the famous siege of Constantinople by the Avars and Slavs in 626.

The first serious study on the attack of 860 was made in 1738 by a German scholar, Gottlieb Siegfried Bayer, a member of the newly organ-

[2] I use here the edition of 1810, *Synopsis or a Brief Description of the Origin of the Slavonic People from various annalists* . . . (St Petersburg, 1810), p. 28.

[3] I use here the print of 1770, *Yadro of Russian History*, compiled by the *blizhni stolnik* and former resident in Sweden, Prince Andrey Yakovlevich Khilkov (Moscow, 1770). *Blizhni stolnik* was one of the court titles of the epoch.   [4] *Yadro*, ch. ii, pp. 28–29.

ized Academy of Sciences in St Petersburg, which was opened in 1726. His study was written in Latin and entitled *De Russorum prima expeditione Constantinopolitana*; his German name *Gottlieb*, in the Latin version, is rendered *Theophilus*.[5] In his study Bayer gives a detailed description of the attack which was carried out from Kiev (pp. 371–391). He knows all the Greek sources available at his time, including Photius' *Circular letter*, which he attributes to the year 866 (pp. 381–384 and 387), and which he uses as authority for the conversion of Russia to Christianity in the time of that Patriarch (pp. 387–388). As far as Russian sources are concerned, he uses the *Stepennaya Kniga*, whose author 'Russorum in locum Cumanos substituit' (pp. 387–388; also p. 366). After mentioning that the year of the attack is uncertain (pp. 365–368) and that Symeon Logothete tells the story of the attack under the ninth and tenth years of Michael's reign, Bayer concludes that the Russian expedition is to be ascribed to the years 864 and 865, 'quibus annis expeditio Russorum inserenda est' (p. 368; see also p. 371). A little below he writes more specifically, 'We have proved that the Russian war was waged in 865' ('bellum Rossicum A.C. 865 gestum esse demonstravimus,' p. 387). Bayer knew that, according to Nicetas Paphlagon's *Life of Ignatius*, the Russians in 860 devastated the island of Terebinthus, where the Patriarch was living in exile (p. 368), but he thinks that Nicetas was in error here ('vitio laborat,' p. 370). In another place he makes the same statement: 'Si Nicetam conferas cum Ignatii Patriarchae de causa sua ad Nicolaum P.R. epistola, eum in temporum rationibus rebusque ipsis aberasse senties. Nicetas per errorem in superiorem aetatem rejecit, quae tum (864 et 865) gesta fuerunt' (p. 371). Bayer locates the river Mauropotamus in Thrace, west of the Chersonesus of Thrace; it emptied into the Aegean Sea (p. 373). Bayer recognizes Oskold as the sole leader and thinks the word *Dir* a title of dignity. He begins his discussion on this subject with the following statement: 'Whereas the Greek writers give only one king or prince who at that time possessed Kiev, the Russians (Rutheni) name two, Oskold and Dir; in another place I shall show that the Greeks were right, for the Russians, perplexed by an obsolete word, have erroneously taken the title of dignity, *Diar*, which was attributed to Oskold, as the name of another prince' (p. 391). I am puzzled by Bayer's statement that the Greek writers mention only one king or prince of Kiev, for the Greek sources which deal with the first attack on Constantinople, as we

---

[5] T. S. Bayer, 'De Russorum prima expeditione Constantinopolitana,' *Commentarii Academiae Scientiarum Petropolitanae*, VI (1732 et 1733), 365–391 (editum Petropoli 1738). Later Bayer's Varangian studies were collected and republished under the title *Theophili Sigefridi Bayeri opuscula ad historiam antiquam, chronologiam, geographiam, et rem numariam spectantia*, ed. Ch. A. Klotzius (Halle, 1770), pp. XXXVIII+572. I use the original edition of 1738.

have seen above, say that the Russians attacked Constantinople (οἱ 'Ρώς, οἱ 'Ρῶς); but they fail to mention their leader by name. Bayer may have had in mind the famous passage in the *Chronicle of Symeon Magister* (p. 707 and 746) about 'Ρῶς τινος σφοδροῦ. But this passage has no connection with the attack of 860.

I wish also to emphasize that chronologically Bayer is inclined to attribute the Russian attack not to the years 864 *or* 865, but to 864 *and* 865; in other words he seems inclined to believe that the Russian expedition may have lasted over a year.[6] But as I have already noted above, in another place in the same study, Bayer claims to have proved that the Russian expedition was carried out in 865 (p. 387).

Bayer's study has become the foundation for the work of some later writers who have been particularly interested in the Russian attack of 860.

Also in the eighteenth century, one of Russia's geniuses, M. V. Lomonosov (1711–1765), among his numerous works wrote *A History of Old Russia down to the year 1054*, which is even now regarded as one of the most eminent historical works of the eighteenth century.[7] Under the year 865 Lomonosov gives accurately the usual story of the Russian expedition on Constantinople under Oskold and Dir in the time of the Byzantine Tsar Michael. He mentions the Black River (Mauropotamus), two hundred ships, the Church of *Lakherna*, the Patriarch Photius, the miracle of the precious garment of the Holy Virgin, and finally the defeat of the Russians, and their pitiful return to Kiev.[8] In another place, Lomonosov refutes the opinion of the noted explorer of Siberia, G. F. Müller (1705–1782), a naturalized German, who asserted that Oskold and Dir were not two men, but one, Oskold by name and by title Diar (i.e., in Gothic a *judge*). And here Lomonosov adds, Müller 'has taken all this from Bayer's dissertation in order to derive (the name of) Rus from the Goths.'[9] Lomonosov was the first to refute the Norman origin of the name *Rus'* (Russia).

---

[6] In his other study Bayer writes: 'Russicum nomen fuisse Rurico antiquius ex eo colligo, quod, cum A. 864, 865, Kiouienses, qui tum sub Rurico non erant, *Constantinopolitanam expeditionem susciperent*, iam ita pervulgatum nomen fuit ut Constantinopoli haud aliter, quam Russi discerentur,' T. S. Bayer, 'Origines Russicae,' Commentarii Academiae Scientiarum Petropolitanae, T. VIII, ad annum MDCCXXXVI (Petropoli, 1741), p. 408. In 1840 F. Kruse wrote: Bayer has exactly fixed the time of Oskold and Dir's expedition; he refers it to the years 864 and 865. F. Kruse, 'The Two First Invasions of the Russians into Byzantium,' *Journal of the Ministry of Public Instruction*, 1840, December, p. 157 (in Russian).

[7] See Iv. Tikhomirov, 'On the Works of M. V. Lomonosov on Russian History,' *Journal of the Ministry of Public Instruction*, 1912, September, p. 64 (in Russian).

[8] M. Lomonosov, *Ancient Russian History from the Beginning of the Russian people to the Death of the Grand Prince Yaroslav the First or to the year 1054* (St Petersburg, 1766), p. 60 (in Russian).

[9] Lomonosov's opinion on Müller's speech on the origin of the Russian people and name is pub-

Under Catherine the Great (1762–1796) was published the voluminous *Russian History from the Most Ancient Times* compiled by V. N. Tatishchev (1686–1750).   Tatishchev in his youth was one of the collaborators of Peter the Great and later governor of Astrakhan.   He was not a professional historian; but gradually he grew much interested in Russian history, became very well acquainted with its sources, and wrote his *Russian History*, which has given him the right to be regarded as an eminent historian.   Among his sources he used the *Chronicle of Joakim, a bishop of Novgorod*, a source entirely unknown otherwise.   Russian historians have sometimes been doubtful, therefore, of its authenticity.   I am not myself a specialist in Russian history, but I am extremely loath to accuse Tatishchev of forgery; he was a very conscientious writer, and his *History*, according to the opinion of specialists, is a very valuable acquisition in the study of Russian history in the eighteenth century.   Very recently (in 1943) the noted Russian historian, G. Vernadsky, fully acknowledged the importance of Tatishchev's work, especially since it contains fragments from chronicles which have since been lost, and uses 'the so-called *Joakim's Chronicle*' without raising any question as to its authenticity.[10] The question of *Joakim's Chronicle* is especially interesting for my study, because, according to Tatishchev, it deals with the Russian expedition on Constantinople.   Tatishchev died before the appearance of his work, which was published after his death by the academician mentioned above, G. F. Müller.[11]

Tatishchev speaks of the Russian expedition in two places.   First he gives a few lines from the *History* of the Bishop of Novgorod, Joakim (I, 1, p. 35).   They read, 'Afterwards (Oskold) goes in boats towards Tsargrad; but a storm destroyed the boats at sea; and he returned (and) sent to Tsargrad, to the Emperor (Tsar). . . .'   Tatishchev notes at this point, 'Here on the margin (of the manuscript) was written: Two sheets in the Chronicle are lost.'   Then we read, 'Michael thanked God (and) marched on the Bulgarians.'   Here Tatishchev remarks, 'Therefore I presume that (the story) of Oskold's baptism has been lost' (I. 1, p. 35).

Tatishchev tells the story of the expedition a second time on the basis of other Russian annals and the Greek sources which were accessible to him (Cedrenus, Zonaras, the Circular Letter of Photius, Leo Grammati-

---

lished in P. Pekarski, *History of the Academy of Sciences*, II (St Petersburg, 1873), 897–907 (in Russian).   On Bayer's study see above.

   [10] George Vernadsky, *Ancient Russia* (New Haven, 1943), p. 265, 335, 340.

   [11] V. N. Tatishchev, *Russian History from the Most Ancient Times*, I, part 1 (Moscow, 1768), and II (Moscow, 1773).   These two volumes contain references to the story of the Russian expedition. On the *Joakim Chronicle* see vol. I, 1, pp. 29–51.   Tatishchev writes, 'Joakim, the first bishop of Novgorod, is a writer unknown to Nestor and a forgotten historian' (I, 1, p. 29).

cus); he also refers to Boronius' *Annales* (ii, 12–13, and note 54, p. 364).

Under the year 6374 = 865 Tatishchev tells the usual story (ii, 12–13): 'Oskold went against the Greeks by sea in the fourteenth year of the Tsar Michael.' The Emperor on his expedition against the Saracens had reached the Black River; the eparch sent him word that the Russians were approaching. 'Oskold, with the Polyanians, upon arriving inside the *sud* (strait) made a great massacre of the Christian Greeks, and attacked Tsargrad in two hundred boats.' Then comes the very well known story about Photius, the sacred vestment at the Church in Blachernae (in Lachernae), the storm, and the destruction of the Russian boats. 'And few returned to their native land. And there was great weeping among the Polyanians in all the country.'

To this story Tatishchev refers in his note 56 (ii, 364). In this note he says that Cedrenus and Zonaras call Oskold *Ros'*. In the same note he also mentions Baronius (under the year 867), the *Joakim Chronicle*, and Photius' *Circular Letter*. Then he remarks that Cedrenus narrates that Oskold, after leaving ambassadors in Tsargrad, was baptized; with this information Leo Grammaticus, in his *Chronography*, agrees. It is shown that Oskold's baptism was fully described by Joakim; but this part of the manuscript is missing.

This note clearly shows how far Tatishchev (who died in 1750) penetrated not only into Slavic sources but also into Byzantine and West European evidence. We observe that Tatishchev has overlooked the chronicle of Theophanes Continuatus, which in his time was accessible in the Parisian edition, and was the original source for Cedrenus and Zonaras. It is not irrelevant to note Tatishchev's statement that those two Byzantine chroniclers call Oskold *Ros'*. In this case, of course, he has erroneously taken the name of the people *Ros'* for the name of a single man.[12] Tatishchev then states that Cedrenus speaks of the baptism of Oskold, who left ambassadors in Tsargrad and was converted to Christianity.[13] In mentioning Leo Grammaticus Tatishchev refers to Strykowski, 463.[14] As we have seen Tatishchev fails to mention Dir.

In the middle of the eighteenth century a prominent Russian writer, V. Tredyakovski (1703–1769) believed that in 864 'the Christians of Kiev went upon Constantinople; though living in the time of Rurik they were not under his power.' He gives a few lines from the *Circular Letter* of

---

[12] *Cedrenus* ii, 173: ὁ τῶν Ῥῶς . . . στόλος. *Zonaras*, xvi, 5 (Bonn, iii, 404): τὸ δ' ἔθνος τῶν Ῥῶς.

[13] Cf. *Cedrenus*, ii, 173: οἱ μετ'οὐ πολὺ τῆς θείας πειραθέντες ὁρμῆς οἴκαδε ὑπενόστησαν, πρεσβεία τε αὐτῶν τὴν βασιλίδα καταλαμβάνει, τοῦ θείου μεταλαχεῖν βαπτίσματος λιτανεύουσα, ὃ καὶ γέγονε.

[14] Here of course he has in view M. Stryjkowski, *Kronika Polska, Litewska, Żmódzka i wszystkiéy Rusi* (Królewiec Königsberg 1582). A reprint of this work in two volumes came out in Warsaw in 1846.

Photius. 'The Russians who had conquered numberless peoples and become, on that account, very arrogant, raised their hands against the
Roman (Greco-Roman) empire.'[15]

In the time of Catherine the Great, and under her patronage and with
her assistance, N. Novikov published in twenty volumes the *Ancient
Russian Library* (*Drevnyaya Rossiskaya Vivliofika*), a collection of ancient
Russian documents. In volume XVI we have *A Most Detailed History
of the Russian Rulers*, which contains only forty-four pages (42–86). In
this sketch the Russian attack on Constantinople is briefly told: 'And in
the year 6374 (866) (Oskold and Dir) went to make war on the Greeks
in two hundred boats, and massacred many people; and they were vanquished by the prayers of the Immaculate Mother of God; only they,
themselves, i.e., Oskold and Dir, returned. The Tsar Michael and the
Patriarch Photius performed in the Lakherna a night service (*vsenosh-
chnoye nesedalno*).[16]

In 1770 came out the first volume of Prince M. M. Shcherbatov's
Russian History from the Most Ancient Times, which contains the story
of the Russian expedition on Constantinople.[17] Shcherbatov (1733–
1790), to whom the Empress Catherine the Second threw open the state
archives, wrote a very voluminous work which tells the history of Russia
down to the beginning of the seventeenth century. His work was a very
important contribution to the history of Russia, and exerted great influence on Karamzin, the leading Russian historian of the first half of the
nineteenth century.

Shcherbatov's description of the Russian expedition does not differ
much from the usual presentation (I, coll. 275–276). The expedition of
Oskold and Dir upon Tsargrad took place in 866, in the fourteenth year
of Michael and his associate Basil. The Emperor, who was on his campaign against the Saracens, was informed by the Patriarch of the Russian
approach. On his return to the capital the Emperor Basil with the
Patriarch, trusting mainly to divine protection, dipped in the sea the
sacred vestment of the Holy Virgin from the Church in Lachernae.[18]
Then follows the usual story of a storm, the destruction of the Russian
boats, and the painful escape of Oskold and Dir with the remnants of their

---

[15] V. Tredyakovski, *Three discussions on three most important Russian Antiquities.* III. *On Varangians-Russians of Slavonic name, origin, and language* (St Petersburg, 1773), p. 274. Tredyakovski
is among those who regard Varangians-Russians as Slavs by origin.

[16] N. Novikov, *Drevnyaya Rossiskaya Vivliotfika*, sec. ed., XVI (Moscow, 1791), 53. The first edition of this work came out in 1773–1775.

[17] I use the new edition of the first volume, published by Prince B. S. Shcherbatov (St Petersburg,
1901). This edition is merely a reprint of the first, which was published during the author's life-
time (1770).

[18] Here in parentheses, with an interrogation mark, Shcherbatov puts *Blachernae?* (col. 276).

troops.   From Shcherbatov's narrative we see that, contrary to G. Müller and Tatishchev, he mentions two leaders, Oskold and Dir instead of one, Oskold; also he names not only the Emperor Michael but also his associate Basil, and even makes the latter, under the title of *Emperor*, take the principal part along with the Patriarch in the procession with the sacred vestment which saved the city; the name of Photius is not given; but it was the Patriarch who informed the absent Emperor of the Russian approach, not the eparch of the city, as it stands in our sources.   In a note to his narrative Shcherbatov refers to Novikov's *Russian Library*, to the *Nikonovski* and *Tipographski Annals* (the latter in manuscript), and to the old but still useful voluminous French *Ecclesiastical History* by the Abbot Fleury.[19]

Considerable interest for our study is presented by two volumes of comment written by I. N. Boltin (1735–1792) on the French work of Leclerc, *Histoire physique, morale, civile et politique de la Russie ancienne et moderne* (Paris, 1783–1784).   Boltin, an official of the War Collegium, sometimes called 'the first Slavophile,' was one of the first who, under the influence of Montesquieu, attempted to consider Russian history as a gradual, integral process of development in accordance with definite laws directing the history of all mankind.   In the preface to the first volume of his *Notes* Boltin says that Leclerc, Frenchman by origin, physician by profession, member of many academies, etc., spent ten years in Russia. Boltin was indignant because of the lies and prejudices displayed in this work.[20]

Since Leclerc (Le Clerc) in his work devotes a fair amount of attention to the Russian expedition on Constantinople, Boltin in his turn deals with this question in his *Notes* with much detail.   As much criticism of a foreign work by a Russian writer of the eighteenth century is rather an unusual phenomenon, I think it would repay attention to examine both the French original and Boltin's comments.

I give the description of the Russian attack as it stands in Leclerc's book:

Oskold and Dir began their reign in Kiof by gaining control of the Russians (*par discipliner les Russes*), and soon became masters of the Khazars, and began to conquer Poland (*la Pologne*).[21]   Those first successes inspired them with audacity, and their temerity went very far, if the narrative of Byzantine historians is trustworthy, and if Nikon who confirms this by an ancient Russian chronicle,

[19] M. l'Abbé C. Fleury, *Histoire ecclésiastique*, xi (Brussels, 1722), 23–24.   Fleury tells the story of the Russian expedition only on the basis of Nicetas' *Vita Ignatii*, under the year 861.

[20] *Notes to the history of ancient and modern Russia of M. Leclerc*, compiled by the Major-General Ivan Boltin, vol. i (St Petersburg, 1788).

[21] Here we recognize the Slavic tribe of Polyanians (Polyane).

was not misled by Greek anachronisms. They report an incursion of the Russians on Constantinople in 851, in the reign of Michael III, after which, they say,
Oskold, the chief of the enterprise, demanded peace and baptism, and returned
to Kiof. How can we reconcile this tradition with the arrival of the Varangians
(*des Vareges*) at Novgorod in 862? Others assert that this expedition took place
only in 866, and that Oskold and Dir assembled a great number of vessels, embarked with an army, and laid siege to Constantinople, after having ravaged all
the neighboring countries . . . (here follows the usual story of the Russian attack
and retreat). As for this story told above about the beginning of the tenth
century, it is for our readers to judge whether it is probable that Oskold and Dir,
who were far from well established as princes, and who had deep reason to fear
the vengeance of the Khazars, would have defied the forces of Greece, eighteen
months after their installation in Kiof. Before going to combat a distant enemy,
through a thousand dangers, it is necessary to have no fear of one's neighbors;
and the Russians of Kiof were far from being in a state of such security.[22]

In his criticism of Le Clerc's presentation, Boltin, first of all, objects to
his doubts of the Byzantine historians. 'It is impossible,' Boltin writes,
'that the Greek writers, agreeing moreover in this case with the Russian
annals, should write what had not occurred.'[23] Then Boltin gives the
story of the Russian attack as it stands in Nestor (pp. 60–61). Then he
writes, evidently following Tatishchev's work, that the Greek writers
Cedrenus and Zonaras, as well as Baronius, under 867 in their writings
agree with Nestor's story, and quotes Tatishchev's passage (II, 364).
'This attack and devastation so badly affected the Greeks that in his
circular letter to the Oriental Patriarchs, the Patriarch Photius declared
that the Russians, a strong people, had come and done much devastation.
Le Clerc, mentioning this event,' Boltin continues, 'says that it is not con-
sistent with Byzantine writers, who believe that Oskold's enterprise
against Constantinople took place eleven years before the reign of
Rurik, which is confirmed also by an ancient Russian chronicle, and he
refers here in the margin to the name of Nikon. On this I will say,'
Boltin continues, 'that the chronicle of Nikon is recent not ancient; among
the oldest (Russian annals) we recognize those of Ioakim and Nestor;
and had Le Clerc consulted them, he would have seen that this event was
set under the year 865. Le Clerc was unable to consult Russian annals
because of his want of knowledge of the language, or he did not have them

---

[22] Le Clerc, *Histoire physique, morale, civile et politique de la Russie ancienne*, I (Paris, 1783),100–
101. We may compare Le Clerc's presentation with an interesting and somewhat similar description
of Oskold's campaign by another French writer of the eighteenth century, P. Levesque, who was
unknown to Boltin. Pierre-Charles Levesque, *Histoire de Russie*. New edition, I (Hamburg and
Brunswick, 1800), 65–66. The first edition came out in 1781.
[23] Boltin, *Notes*, I, 60.

available.   There is no doubt whatever concerning the authenticity of this event.'[24]

I think Boltin was perhaps hasty in saying that Le Clerc regarded Nikon's chronicle as an old source.   If we examine the text closely we will see that Le Clerc writes that Nikon confirms the event by an ancient Russian chronicle: 'Nikon qui le confirme par une ancienne chronique Russe.'   Le Clerc obviously means that when Nikon told the story of the Russian attack he based his narrative on an ancient Russian chronicle.

At any rate Boltin's notes to Le Clerc's work present a very interesting page in the development of Russian historiography of the epoch of Catherine the Great.   As we have noted above, Boltin accepted the year 865 as the date of the first Russian attack on Constantinople.

The Empress Catherine the Great (1762–1796) not only inspired others to study the history of her adopted country, i.e., Russia, but also herself devoted one of her own writings to Russian history.   In her *Accounts concerning Russian History* she gives a rather detailed story of the Russian expedition.   Her presentation is largely based on Tatishchev's *History*. Owing to the unusually high position of the authoress, I pay her the compliment of a complete translation of the story which she wrote originally in Russian.[25]   Before starting the description of the Russian expedition, Catherine mentions that the name of *Rus* was known among the Greeks long before Rurik (p. 14).   Here is the story as it stands in her *Zapiski*. 'In 865 Oskold went against the Greeks.   He descended the Dnieper in boats, canoes (*na lodiyakh*), and other vessels, about two hundred in number, then crossed the Black Sea to Tsargrad, in the fourteenth year of the Greek Tsar Michael.   The Greek Tsar with his troops was then making war on the Saracens and had reached the Black River.   The eparch (governor) who was left in Tsargrad sent a message to the Tsar that the Russi were approaching Tsargrad; hearing this, the Tsar returned.   But Oskold with the Polyanians, entering inside the straits from the Black Sea into the Mediterranean, which is called the Thracian Bosphorus, surrounded Tsargrad with ships.   On his return the Tsar had great difficulty in entering the city.   The Greeks then did not expect any help for their defense, and they addressed their prayers entirely to God. Towards morning a storm arose . . . .[26]   A small number returned home.' Then Catherine remarks that the Greek writers called Oskold the Prince Ros (p. 27), and adds that Oleg, aware of Oskold's failure in the campaign

[24] Boltin, *op. cit.*, I, 61–62.

[25] Catherine the Second, *Accounts (Zapiski) concerning Russian History. Works of the Empress Catherine the Second*, edited by A. N. Pypin, VIII (St Petersburg, 1901), 26–27.

[26] Here follows the usual story of the Russian failure.

on Tsargrad and of the loss of many men and ships, went himself to Kiev (p. 31).

From Catherine's text we see that, following Tatishchev, she dates the Russian expedition in the year 865 and mentions Oskold with the Poly-anians as its only leader. Instead of the *sud*, as Tatishchev calls the Bosphorus, she gives the Thracian Bosphorus, which is much more easily understood by the general reader. From Tatishchev's note 56 Catherine asserts that Greek writers called Oskold the Prince Ros.

Now from the eighteenth century we pass to the nineteenth, which opens with a very important contribution to the study of the first pages of Russian history. A German scholar, August Ludwig Schlözer (1735–1809), who arrived in Russia to study the Russian Chronicles and spent several years there, laid the first solid foundation for critical analysis of the Russian annals. In his classical work *Nestor* he deals also with the first Russian expedition against Constantinople.[27] For his time Schlözer gives a very clear and detailed description of the expedition and uses all available sources. Slavonic texts are accompanied by a German translation. Byzantine sources, also with a German translation, are used from Stritter's *Memoriae populorum*. The chief foundation for his chapter on the Russian expedition is the above mentioned Latin dissertation of T. S. Bayer.

Schlözer's main results may be briefly pointed out. Oskold and Dir are doubtless (*unstreitig*) two different persons (p. 213). The *Nikonovski Chronicle* errs when it states that the invasion took place under Michael's mother, Theodora, and that at that time Basil was already co-emperor. Following Bayer, Schlözer believes that the author of *Vita Ignatii* was mistaken in ascribing the expedition to the time of Ignatius' second exile to the island of Terebinthus. According to Schlözer, the Russian expedition must have taken place in 866 (pp. 228–229). He identifies the River Mauropotamus with the river of the same name in the Thracian Penin-sula, and says that it is unthinkable to identify it with another Black River in Pamphylia (p. 231). But in a special chapter Schlözer asserts that 'the Russians, who in 866 made their appearance before Constanti-nople, were a people entirely different from the Russians of the present time, and consequently do not belong to Russian history. It is impossible that the Russians ('Ρῶς) who in 866 alarmed Constantinople could have been Oskold's Russians' (II, 247–263; esp. 258). On pp. 266–268, re-ferring to Bayer, Schlözer discusses the question of Dir-Diar as a title of dignity, not as a proper name, and disagrees with Bayer's speculations.

---

[27] *Nestor. Russische Annalen in ihrer slavonischen Grundsprache verglichen, übersetzt und erklärt von August Ludwig Schlözer.* Zweiter Teil (Gottingen, 1802), 150, 213, 221–236. A Russian translation of Schlözer's work came out later in 1809.

In 1814 a professor of the University of Dorpat in Russia, J. F. G. Ewers, published in German a book entitled *Critical Preliminary Studies on the History of the Russians*, in which he deals with the Russian expedition on Constantinople in 866.[28]   'As seafarers,' Ewers writes, 'Constantinople might have known something of the Russians before the year 866, for they suddenly terrified the capital with a fleet of two hundred sailboats, and under the leadership of Oskold and Dir horribly devastated the beautiful surroundings of the canal of Pera' (p. 247).   Ewers points out that there are two contemporary sources on the event: Photius in his Pastoral Letter, and Nicetas, who took the name of David on taking orders, the bishop of Paphlagonia in 878 (pp. 247–249).   Ewers says that after their expedition the Russians received a bishop and shepherd from Constantinople, which indicates that after the clash Russians and Greeks came into closer association, and some Greeks visited the Russian country (p. 249).[29]   The invasion had been planned by Russians beforehand, which presupposes their knowledge of the city (p. 250).   They came from the northern or eastern shore of the Black Sea, where they had already navigated (p. 251).   Then Ewers raises the question how Nestor knew that Oskold and Dir were their leaders, a detail which, as we know well, is not indicated by Greek evidence, and he answers, Nestor might have drawn his information from two sources: either from a local tradition or from a Greek historical source which is unknown to us, or perhaps from both (pp. 251–252).   But it remains beyond doubt (*unläugbar*) that Oskold and Dir led the Russians in 866 to Constantinople (p. 252).

The leading Russian historian in the first half of the nineteenth century and a brilliant man of letters, N. M. Karamzin who, according to Pushkin, discovered ancient Russia as Columbus discovered America,[30] in his voluminous work *History of the Russian Empire*, deals with the first Russian expedition against Constantinople.   In picturesque language Karamzin tells the usual story of the Russian campaign which must have taken place in 866.   'Askold and Dir dared proclaim themselves the enemies of Greece.   The navigable Dneiper favored their intention . . . .   For the first time the capital pronounced with horror the name of Russians,

---

[28] Johann Filipp Gustav Ewers, *Kritische Vorarbeiten zur Geschichte der Russen.* Erstes und zweites Buch (Dorpat, 1814), pp. 247–255 (VII, Russen vor Konstantinopel, 866 n. Chr.).   I have not seen his later work *Geschichte der Russen*, I (Dorpat, 1816).

[29] Here Ewers remarks that Schlözer has overlooked the information that Photius sent a bishop to the Russians.

[30] Pushkin's statement is of course an exaggeration.   G. Vernadsky rightly says that the Russian past was "discovered" long before Karamzin, by Tatishchev, Shcherbatov, and by generations of earlier scholars, beginning with the compiler of the *Primary Chronicle*.   "It would be more to the point to call Karamzin the Russian Gibbon," G. Vernadsky, *Ancient Russia* (New Haven, 1943), p. 265.

'Ῥῶς. Popular tradition announced them Scyths, the inhabitants of the fabulous mountain Taurus, who had won victory over many surrounding peoples. Michael III, the Nero of his time, was then reigning in Constantinople . . . . Some Byzantine historians add that the pagan Russians, terrified by celestial ire, immediately sent envoys to Constantinople and demanded holy baptism.'[31] Referring to Photius' *Circular Letter* and mentioning that in our sources there is information of two Russian conversions, one under Photius and the other under Ignatius, Karamzin believes that these two versions are not contradictory. Photius might have sent missionaries to Kiev in 866 and Ignatius later on might have done the same thing (p. 139). In note 279 to this story Karamzin refers to Stritter's *Memoriae populorum*, II, 958, to Bayer's dissertation and the *Annales Baronii*. Then he writes, 'In vain the cruel hater of Photius, the learned Assemani, proves to us that this great Patriarch wished to deceive contemporaries and posterity, and had already compiled his *spurious* Letter when Ignatius ruled again over the Church (*Kalendaria Eccl. Univ.*, II, 254, 256). The true ancient tradition that Christianity entered Russia under Photius led later chroniclers into a great error: not taking into account the element of time, they say that Photius baptized Olga, and that the same Photius sent bishops to Vladimir!'

For our study Karamzin's note 283 is of interest. Here, refuting Schlözer's opinion that the Russians who attacked Constantinople could not have come from Kiev, Karamzin firmly asserts that Askold and Dir did come from Kiev. He writes: 'Where the truth presents itself to the eyes of an historian there is no need to resort to strange hypotheses and invent other Russians, who, according to Schlözer's opinion, in 866 came in two hundred vessels to Tsargrad, nobody knows whence, *only not from Kiev*: they were called thus (i.e., Russians), nobody knows why; and they departed nobody knows where, and later entirely disappeared in history yielding their name and place to the Kievan Russians!' And then Karamzin adds, 'Peoples do not fall from heaven nor hide in the earth like the dead, according to superstitious fairy tales.' In the same note Karamzin admits that Schlözer has proved that Bayer made an error in saying that *Diar* (*Dir*) was not a proper name but a title, a dignity. But at the same time Karamzin mentions Bayer's supposition that the word *Dijar* (*Diar*) may be an Arabic word meaning *a number of houses, country, region*, and rightly says, 'but a *region* is not a *ruler*.' Of course Bayer's conjecture must be discarded.

---

[31] N. M. Karamzin, *History of the Russian Empire*, I, 3d ed. (St Petersburg, 1830), 136–138. Karamzin's work has been translated into French and German but has, if I am not mistaken, no English version.

In 1838 in Moscow came out the first volume of *The History of Russia* (*Povestvovanie o Rossii*), compiled by N. S. Artsybashev (1773–1841), whose work as a collection of historical materials has not lost its significance even down to our own day.   Under the year 866 Artsybashev gives the usual story of the Russian expedition under the command of Askold and Dir (p. 18).   Following Schlözer, he places the River Mauropotamus in the western part of the Thracian Peninsula, flowing into the Aegean Sea (p. 18, n. 72).   Greek historians confirm Nestor's tale, failing, however, to name Askold and Dir.   But whether by Rossi ('Pῶs) they mean the Kievan Russians remains very doubtful.   To this statement Artsybashev refers in his own note 73, which is not devoid of interest.   He says: 'Schlözer also shares my doubt' (see above).   Karamzin (i, n. 283) refutes Schlözer's arguments.   'But,' Artsybashev remarks, 'one cannot dismiss them because (1) even some of our own (i.e., Russian) annals fail to call the Russians who were besieging Constantinople in 866 the Kievan Russians; (2) Greek historians say that the *Rossi* are a Scythian people who dwell near the Northern Taurus; see *Cedr.*, ii, 50, and *Zonoaras*, ii, 162, in Stritter's *Memoriae Populorum*, ii, 958; therefore besides the Baltic Russians there were also other (Russians).   The Arab writers call the latter Turks.   Frähn, 41, 42; (3) *Continuator Constantini* and *Cedrenus* write that the Russians on their return home sent envoys to Tsargrad seeking for baptism and received it; and Photius' *Circular Letter* written at the end of 866 testifies that they had a bishop and priest, which is confirmed by Constantine Porphyrogenitus (*Vita Constantini*) and Codinus (in *Notitiae Graecorum Episcopatuum*, c. 380, see Stritter, iii, 155).'   Probably by oversight Artsybashev names *Continuator Constantini* for *Continuator Theophanis* and *Vita Constantini* for *Vita Basilii*; the author of this was of course Constantine Porphyrogenitus.

In the first half of the nineteenth century came out also *A History of the Russian People* by Nicholas Polevoi (1796–1846).[32]   His most essential source for the history of Byzantium is 'the immortal work of Gibbon in its new French edition with notes by Guizot.'   Polevoi merely compared Gibbon's sources with recent discoveries. He also used Schlözer's *Nestor*.

Polevoi reproduces the usual story of the expedition led by Askold and Dir, but in a rather elevated style.   I give here some examples.

The enemy unheard of heretofore!   The Greeks had known Bulgars, Avars, Danubian Slavs, Arabs; but the name of Russians struck their ears for the first time.   They heard with horror that the Russians had come from the north, in boats, by sea: a new phenomenon, unheard of, because the Greeks expected

---

[32] I use the second edition of Polevoi's work (Moscow, 1830), vol. i, pp. 89–91.

enemies by land from the Danube or from Asia. It was told in Tsargrad that the Russians were Scythians, inhabitants of the mountain Taurus; they (the Greeks) were terrified on hearing that (the Russians) already had devastated the islands of the Sea of Marmora . . . . Considering previous experiences, the Greeks might have supposed that the barbarians whom they saw were only the forerunners of numerous enemies; they thought that as had occurred after the first detachments of Goths, Avars, Arabs, in the wake of the Russians thousands of boats were on the way; it was thought that Tsargrad would be besieged, and the dispirited people shivering at their fate horrified Michael: a tyrant is always dastard and merciless! Forgetting his profanation of religion, he took part in a solemn procession . . . . The results of this campaign were important. Askold and Dir returned to Kiev, and undertook no more campaigns on Greece: this seems inconsistent with the character of the Varangians. The cause of this was probably that Askold and Dir's companies (*druzhiny*) were very small and they perished under the walls of Constantinople; and the new companies of Scandinavian emigrants must have gone through the dominions of northern Russians who, themselves, wanted to seize Kiev (pp. 89–91).

In his *History of Christianity in Russia before the Isoapostolic Prince Vladimir*, the first edition of which came out in St Petersburg in 1846, the Archbishop of Kharkov, Macarius (Makari, 1816–1882), enlarges on the first Russian expedition against Constantinople.[33] 'It is a fact,' Macarius writes, 'that in the reign of Michael III the Russians attacked Byzantium because twelve Byzantine writers, and among them two contemporaries (Nicetas Paphlagon and Photius) speak of the attack' (p. 215). Here are the names of the other ten Byzantine writers mentioned by Macarius: (1) the Continuator of George Hamartolus or Symeon Logothete; (2) Leo Grammaticus; (3) George the Monk; (4) the Abridger of Symeon Logothete who lived in the eleventh century (*Bonn Corpus* XXI, 333);[34] (5) Zonaras; (6) Theophanis Continuator; (7) Cedrenus; (8) Constantine Porphyrogenitus; (9) Scylitzes; (10) Michael Glycas. This list clearly shows how imperfect at Macarius' time was the knowledge of interrelations between Byzantine sources, especially those connected with the *Chronicle of Symeon Logothete*. Michael Glycas, as we know, fails to mention the Russian expedition at all; he gives only a few lines on the first conversion of the Russians to Christianity under Basil I (p. 553).[35] Then Macarius proceeds, 'Second, it is absolutely authentic — the miraculous defeat of the Russians under the walls of Byzantium, which is also confirmed by eight Greek writers and one contemporary (p. 215). The inva-

---

[33] I am using here the second corrected edition of Macarius' work which appeared in 1868.

[34] I do not know exactly whom Macarius means here. In vol. XXI of the Bonn Collection the later Byzantine chronicler Ducas is given.

[35] We have the same information in Ephraim's *Chronicle* (p. 114, verses 2593–2604), which is omitted from Macarius' list.

sion of the Russians upon Byzantium took place when Askold and Dir were ruling in Kiev, and ended, according to Constantine Porphyrogenitus (*Vita Basilii*, p. 157, *Venet.*), in the conclusion of an alliance between Russians and Greeks. These events refer to us Russians; otherwise we should not understand the reference to the amity and love which had existed many years between Christians and Russians, of which the envoys of Oleg spoke at the conclusion of a treaty with the Byzantines in 911' (p. 220). Macarius writes that 'according to Symeon Logothete, or rather his abridger, the Russian attack upon Constantinople occurred from 864 to 865, i.e., in the last days of the former and at the outset of the latter (c. 221). The Russian conversion could in no way have occurred before 866; on the other hand, we cannot say either that it happened after that year, because Photius' *Circular Letter* was written at the end of 866 or even at the beginning of 867; and in this *Letter* Photius writes: "The Russians . . . who only *recently* have been our enemies, have *now* become Christians, and accepted a bishop"' (pp. 222–223).

In his text book on *Russian History* which came out in the first half of the nineteenth century and has had several editions, N. Ustryalov (1805-1870) devotes a few words to the Russian attack. We read: 'Askold and Dir were determined to found an independent princedom (in Kiev) and to seek gold in Greece not by service but by arms; they went in canoes into the Black Sea, approached Byzantium and horrified the Greeks, who saw in them invincible enemies and did not dare to repel them by arms. A storm saved Byzantium: the Russian canoes perished in the waves. Askold and Dir with difficulty got back to Kiev and accepted the Christian faith, probably by conviction.'[36] Such was the picture of the first Russian attack upon Constantinople which was given the Russian youth in their schools in the first half and in the middle of the nineteenth century.

In his twenty-nine volume *History of Russia from the Most Ancient Times* the noted Russian historian, S. M. Solovyov (1820–1879), who was professor at the University of Moscow from 1851 to 1879, devotes only a few words to the Russian expedition. He writes, 'Askold and Dir decided to make an incursion upon Byzantium, to accomplish the cherished Varangian aim, with which they had started from Novgorod.' Then follows the usual story. According to Greek evidence, the Russians were defeated by the miraculous intercession of the Mother of God. Askold's campaign is usually attributed to the year 866.[37]

The Russian campaign is described in a bombastic and artificial style

---

[36] N. Ustryalov, *Russian History*, 5th ed (St Petersburg, 1855), pp. 39–40.
[37] S. Solovyov, *History of Russia*, I, 4th ed. (Moscow, 1866), p. 119.

by Michael Pogodin (1800–1875) in his *Ancient Russian History down to the Mongol Yoke*.[38]   Pogodin writes: 'In Kiev another idea came to the mind of Askold and Dir; another dream worthy of Norman blood took possession of their vivid imagination.   They determined to go upon Constantinople, of which marvels had been told in their fatherland.   Miklagard, Miklagard, Great City!   It possesses everything!   What treasures have been collected from everywhere!   Stories of gold, silver, and silk!   What wines, what food!   And defense is weak.   . . . Their brothers had gone, before and after, upon Rome, Paris, London, Seville.   Fortune favors the brave.[39]   Perhaps!   They began to make themselves ready.   Upon Tsargrad, upon Tsargrad!' (pp. 5–6).   Then comes the usual story of the attack.   'Meanwhile the Greeks doubtless opened negotiations with the attacking Rus.   A rich tribute was offered to them, provided they would raise the siege and depart . . . .   And the day of salvation came, the fifth of June, 865.   The Rus, apparently satisfied with the wealth looted in the suburbs, and the tribute received from the city, departed in their light boats as suddenly as they had appeared' (p. 7).   After giving extracts from Photius' second sermon, Pogodin says, 'Long afterwards the memories of this sudden invasion of Rus were preserved among the Greeks.   Owing to the campaign of the Russian warriors Askold and Dir the name of Rus has become known all over the world.   The (Russian) chronicle says, 'The land of Rus was first known because under this Emperor (Michael) Rus attacked Tsargrad, as is written in the Greek Chronicle' (p. 7).   Pogodin attributes Photius' *Circular Letter* to the year 865 (p. 7).

In 1872 K. N. Bestuzhev-Ryumin (1829–1897), in the first volume of his *Russian History*, merely mentions that in 865 the Kievan Princes undertook a campaign upon Constantinople, which ended in failure, and in a note says that, according to Photius, the cause of the attack was the massacre of some Russians in Constantinople (1, St Petersburg, 1872, 99).   We shall see later that this error is due to Archbishop Porphyrius' edition of Photius' sermons, which contained a number of errors.

N. Kostomarov (1817–1885) in his *Russian History in the Biographies of its most important Representatives*, writes only that 'in the middle of the ninth century, the Russians, after an unsuccessful campaign upon Byzantium, when a storm destroyed their vessels, accepted baptism; but afterwards paganism again won the upper hand in the country' (1, St Petersburg, 1873, 4).

---

[38] I (Moscow, 1871), 5–7.   See also his *Norman Period of Russian History* (Moscow, 1859).

[39] Pogodin inserts here a Russian proverb, 'Audacity takes cities,' which I translate into English by 'Fortune favors the brave.'

Now I turn to D. Ilovaiski (1832–1920) who, of the Russian historians who have written general histories of Russia, has given the most detailed story of the Russian campaign. In his earlier book *Studies on the Origin of Russia*, he briefly deals with the attack, which he places in 865.[40] We read, 'From Photius' words it may be understood that the Russian attack had been preceded by diplomatic and trade relations of Russians with Byzantium, and not only by relations but also by treaties. It is obvious that the killing of several Russians in Greece provoked the raid of the Rus upon Constantinople (pp. 278–279).' Then in another passage in the same book Ilovaiski speculates, 'If Rus in 864–865 considered herself strong enough to attack Tsargrad itself, she in all likelihood had already previously had conflicts with Greeks where their possessions bordered on the Russian lands, i.e., on the nothern shores of the Black Sea, and particularly in the Crimea' (p. 323). In the first passage once more we notice the error resulting from the Archbishop Porphyrius' defective first edition and Russian translation of Photius' sermons.

In the first volume of Ilovaiski's *History of Russia* (Moscow, 1876), we find a very detailed story of the Russian campaign written in very picturesque style with some imaginary embellishments. In the second revised and augmented edition of his work, which we are using, Ilovaiski is already acquainted with the exact chronological date of the attack given in the Brussels Chronicle, 860 (vol. I, Moscow, 1900, pp. 9–12), for he says that the event took place approximately in May, 860 (p. 9). Since, if I am not mistaken, Ilovaiski's work has not been translated into any foreign language, I give here (with some omissions) an English version of his description of the Russian attack.

The day was drawing to its close when fugitives from the hamlets situated along the shores of the Thracian Bosphorus appeared in Tsargrad and brought terrible news: numerous vessels of the barbarian people Ros had entered the Bosphorus and were going straight towards the capital. This unexpected news horrified the inhabitants of Tsargrad, who were carelessly engaging in their occupations and pleasures. In a moment all petty cares and affairs, all amusements and vain thoughts were cast away; horror and confusion spread everywhere. The barbarians evidently had exact information of the absence of the Emperor with his legions and of the almost helpless state of the capital. The fact is that some time previously the Greek government had violated its trade treaties with the Russian people and allowed many Russian traders who resided in Byzantium to be massacred; a quarrel with them had arisen on the score of an insignificant debt. In vain Rus demanded satisfaction for the offense. The Byzantines paid no attention to her demands; and now, when they expected nothing, the barbar-

---

[40] The first edition of this book came out in Moscow, 1876. I am using here the second edition (Moscow, 1882).

ians had taken advantage of a favorable time and suddenly rushed upon Byzantium, before the Greeks of Korsun or Sinope could inform the capital of their
expedition.   They certainly hoped not only to take vengeance for the death of
their comrades, but also to enrich themselves with the vast booty which the capture of such a wealthy and great city as was Constantinople promised.

Meanwhile Ooryphas and his assistants seemed to have taken adequate meas-
ures: they locked the city gates, placed in the towers the guard which was at their
disposal, and hurriedly dispatched messengers to the Emperor.   A dark and
stormy night came on, and it still more increased the anxiety and confusion in
the city.   It seemed every moment to the most timid minds that the enemies
had already scaled the walls, gained possession of the city, — and that the end of
everything had come.   But behold! darkness dispersed, the wind dropped, the
sea billows grew calm, and then the inhabitants of Byzantium saw the long line
of vessels which surrounded Constantinople from the side of the Bosphorus and
Propontis.   The barbarians, holding in their hands their unsheathed swords, menaced the city with them and uttered savage shouts.   They were in general well
built people with light blond hair and sharp gray eyes.   The noblest among
them distinguished themselves by shaven chins and long mustaches; their pointed
helmets covered their tufts of hair; above coats of mail were worn cloaks whose
corners were fastened by a buckle on the right shoulder.   The armament of that
people consisted of an arrow, a spear, an axe, and a sword with a broad double-
edged blade; their shields which grew narrower at the bottom were so long that
they covered almost the whole body.   After encircling the city from the side of
the sea, the Russians landed, and, according to their habit, began to raise a
rampart along the walls which defended the city by land, in order to seize them
more easily.   At the same time a part of them scattered in the defenseless suburbs and surroundings of Constantinople; with great savagery they set about
devastating villages and monasteries, destroying with fire and sword meadows,
dwellings, men and cattle, sparing no infants, no old men, deaf to sobs or prayers.
Among other things, they seized the islet of Terebinthus with its monastery, to
which the Patriarch Ignatius, deprived of his see, had been exiled.   The barbarians plundered there the church vessels and all furnishings; the Patriarch,
somehow, escaped; but they seized twenty-two men of his monks and servants
and dismembered them with axes on the stern of a boat.   A Te Deum and Ves-
pers were chanted.   A particularly dense crowd flowed into the Cathedral of St.
Sophia (pp. 9–10).

Then Ilovaiski speaks of Photius' sermons and gives some passages
from them (p. 11): 'The Patriarch took the sacred vestment of (the Holy
Virgin) and with prayers carried it along the walls around the city.   After
that the enemies hastily raised the siege, went on board their ships, and
left the Bosphorus enriched with the booty which they had seized on its
shores . . . .   Doubtless at that very time the news of the approaching
Byzantine legions and ships reached them; for Michael III immediately
turned back, as soon as he had heard of the Russian attack on his capital

(p. 12).   A little below Ilovaiski writes, 'The attack of 860 and its contemporary evidence undoubtedly reveal the numerous, warlike tribe of
Rus' (pp. 13–14).   In another place he says, 'When the trade treaties
between Rus and Byzantium began, we do not know exactly; at least
they were already in existence before 860, because the attack of Rus in
this year was provoked by their violation by the Greeks' (p. 18).   On pp.
675–677 Ilovaiski gives a list of the sources on the attack of 860; some of
his references are not very clear; for example, Sathas, *Bibliotheca Graeca
Medii Aevi*, vii (no page).   The chronicle printed in this volume gives
no word on the attack.

I have enlarged too much on Ilovaiski's book, which cannot be classi-
fied among the outstanding works in Russian historical literature.   But
my intention has been, first, to emphasize that Ilovaiski has given the
most detailed description of the attack which has ever appeared in general
histories of Russia, and (second) to acquaint my readers with the peculiarities of his pictorial style, which is not without an element of imagination.   I must point out, however, that Ilovaiski was very well informed
as to the relevant sources.[41]

The noted Russian church historian E. Golubinski (1834–1912) who,
even before the publication of the *Brussels Chronicle* asserted that the
Russian expedition must have taken place not in 865 or 866 but in 860
or at the very beginning of 861, believes that the Russians of that time
were not the Kievan Russians but the Azovo-Tauric or Azovo-Crimean
Russians, and that they could not have been led by Askold and Dir.   In
his work he considers all our sources on the Russian attack and gives their
Russian translation.[42]

One of the most brilliant of Russian historians, V. O. Klyuchevski
(1840–1911), says a few words on the expedition; he attributes it to the
Great Varangian Principality of Kiev, and regards it as the first Russian
enterprise undertaken for a common end — that end being the securing
of trade relations; but he, like some other historians, erroneously states
that the cause of the attack, according to Photius, was the murder of
some Russian merchants in Constantinople.[43]

---

[41] Of course the Russian attack on Constantinople was always repeated in the numberless editions
of Ilovaisky's textbook in Russian history for the Russian *gymnasia*.   I myself received my first
knowledge of Russian history and of history in general as well, from Ilovaisky's textbooks.

[42] E. Golubinski, *History of the Russian Church*, sec. ed. i, 1 (Moscow, 1901), 38, 40, 41, 42, 45;
on the sources pp. 49–51.   His speculations will be discussed below in connection with the question
whence the Russian expedition started.

[43] V. Klyuchevski, *A Course in Russian History*, i (Moscow, 1904), 170.   English translation by
C. J. Hogarth, i (London-New York, 1911), 72, 81.   We now have in English a very interesting and
important article by Michael Karpovich, 'Klyuchevski and Recent Trends in Russian Historiography,' *The Slavonic and East European Review*, vol. xxi (1943), 31–39.

Now I wish to give the names of some scholars whose activities belong to the twentieth century. The Ukrainian historian M. Hrushevski, dealing with the expedition of 860, considers the question not clear; he sees in the miracle of the sacred vestment a reflection of the Avar attack of 626, and gives a critical survey of the sources.[44] There are several historians who just mention the fact itself, such as S. F. Platonov,[45] M. K. Lyubavski,[46] D. I. Bagaley,[47] G. V. Vernadsky.[48] In his *History of Russia* (New York, 1931) M. N. Pokrovski makes no mention whatever of the Russian expedition of 860.

More attention is devoted to this expedition by one of the most talented Russian historians of the twentieth century, A. E. Presnyakov (1870–1931).[49] Presnyakov regards the expedition of 860 as an important factor in the history of the Black Sea region and Byzantium: the appearance of a new historical force. Rus thereby began to be involved in world affairs. 'This time the raid produced acute panic; but the danger was over, and preventing a repetition must be thought of' (pp. 45–46). And under the influence of the interesting speculations of V. Lamanski, Presnyakov is inclined to believe that, in order to prevent the northern danger, Byzantium opened negotiations with the Khazars; in addition, since the Khazars at that time had already been weakened by the onslaught of the Patzinaks, Byzantium resorted to the propagation of Christianity among the Russians hoping thus to make them more amenable and less hostile. 'Cultural-religious missions of Byzantium were always connected with definite political ends' (p. 47).

Recently, in 1939, B. Grekov mentions the attack of 860 in his book *Kievan Russia*. But referring to Photius' homilies of 860 and his *Circu-*

---

[44] M. Hruševśkyj, *Geschichte des ukrainischen (ruthenischen) Volkes*, i (Leipzig, 1906), 393, 412–415. In Ukrainian: *Istoriya Ukraini-Rusi*, i (Kiev, 1913), 384, 402–405, 565–566.

[45] S. F. Platonov, *Lectures in Russian History*, ed. by Iv. Blinov, 10th ed. (Petrograd, 1917), p. 67 (in Russian). *Idem, History of Russia*, translated by E. Aronsberg, ed. by F. A. Golder (New York, 1925), p.22, 24.

[46] M. K. Lyubavski, *Lectures in Ancient Russian History down to the end of the sixteenth century* (Moscow, 1915), p. 82 (the erroneous cause of the attack, the murder of some Russians, is inserted in the book).

[47] D. I. Bagaley, *Russian History*, i (Moscow, 1914), 172.

[48] G. V. Vernadsky, *A Sketch of Russian History* (Prague, 1927), p. 35: 'The expedition ended in an honorable peace for the attackers (in Russian). *Idem, A History of Russia* (New Haven, 1929), p. 17 (in English). In 1930 a revised edition came out. *Idem, An Essay on the History of Eurasia from the middle of the sixth century down to modern times* (Berlin, 1934), p. 55 (in Russian). *Idem, Political and Diplomatic History of Russia* (Boston, 1936), p. 37 (in English). In all these works Vernadsky is still inclined to attribute the attack to the Kievan Varangians; later, as we shall see below, he changed his opinion. His most recent volume (1943), *Ancient Russia*, I discuss a little later.

[49] A. E. Presnyakov, *Lectures in Russian History*, i. The *Kievan Rus* (Moscow, 1938), 45–47. This is an edition of Presnyakov's lectures which he delivered at the University of St Petersburg before 1916.

lar Letter of 866 he writes that Photius, dealing with the Russian invasion upon Byzantium had in view the southern Russians; and then Grekov adds, 'The Varangians have no connection with this.'[50]

The same year (1939) in the *History of U.S.S.R.*, published in Russia and compiled by a group of Russian historians, we find the following few words referring to the expedition of 860. 'With the Prince Dir are connected records of the first important attack of the Kievan Rus upon Tsargrad, which is dated in 860.'[51] As we see from these lines, Dir only is indicated as the leader of the expedition, though both Askold and Dir are mentioned just before as the rulers of Kiev.

Very recently in 1943 in his learned and stimulating volume *Ancient Russia*, George Vernadsky devotes much attention to the campaign of 860. In his presentation, it was a joint undertaking of the Russian Kagan, i.e., the ruler in Tmutorokan area in the south, and of Askold and Dir, the rulers of Kiev.[52] We shall discuss Vernadsky's speculation in detail later, in the section devoted to the question where the expedition of 860 originated.

Of course the expedition of 860 has been briefly discussed in general histories of the Byzantine Empire written by Russian historians who have brought the presentation of that history down to the end of the ninth century, such as F. Uspenski, A. Vasiliev, G. Ostrogorski, and M. Levchenko. I do not enlarge here upon I. Ertov's curious attempt to write a history of Byzantium. In 1837 he published in Russian his two volume *History of the Eastern Roman or Constantinopolitan Empire, Selected from General History*. This, however, has no value whatever.[53] The three-volume *History of Byzantium* of J. Kulakovski ends with the accession to the throne of Leo III, in 717. S. Shestakov's *Lectures in the History of the Byzantine Empire*, published in 1913 (a second revised and enlarged edition in 1915), ends with the coronation of Charlemagne in 800. C. Uspenski's *Sketches in Byzantine History*, which came out in 1917, goes down to the restoration of icon veneration in 843.

In the second volume of his *History of the Byzantine Empire* F. Uspenski devotes a few lines only to the usual description of the attack of 860;[54]

---

[50] B. D. Grekov, *Kievan Russia*, 3d revised and augmented edition (Moscow-Leningrad, 1939), p. 226.

[51] *Istorija SSSR*, vol. I, from most ancient times to the end of the eighteenth century, under redaction of V. I. Lebedev, B. D. Grekov, S. V. Bakhrushin (Moscow, 1939), 92.

[52] George Vernadsky, *Ancient Russia* (New Haven, Yale University Press, 1943), 342-343, 363.

[53] On Ertov's book see A. Vasiliev, *History of the Byzantine Empire*, I (Madison, 1928), 45 (French edition, I, Paris, 1932, 40). In Russian, *Lectures in the History of Byzantium*, I (Petrograd, 1917), 32-33.

[54] F. Uspenski, *History of the Byzantine Empire*, II, 1 (Leningrad, 1927), 348 (in this very brief description the names of Askold and Dir are not mentioned).

but he returns several times to the subject.   Referring to Photius' two homilies on the Russian attack, he writes: 'This is the famous expedition of Askold and Dir (860), of which we perhaps might have known nothing since it has been nowhere else recorded.   The Rus for the first time are called by their own name and for the first time are characterized by real traits.   It goes without saying how important this document is for us Russians.'[55]

In my *History of the Byzantine Empire* I mention the Russian attack of 860 stressing the fact that long before the publication of the *Brussels Chronicle*, which fixed the exact date of the event, some scholars already were inclined to ascribe it to an earlier date than 865 or 866.[56]   In 1940 G. Ostrogorski, in his *History of the Byzantine State* published in German, devotes a few lines to the event and says that the question whether the Russians who attacked Constantinople in 860 originated from the Kievan or Tmutorokan region has not been settled.[57]   Finally in the same year (1940), M. Levchenko, in his *History of Byzantium* mentions the Russian attack and adds, 'If we trust Photius, the Russians (after their failure) adopted Christianity and declared themselves subjects of the empire, promising to supply it with auxiliary troops.'[58]   The last section of this statement is inexact: Photius fails to mention any Russian pledge to supply the Empire with auxiliary troops.

To sum up the results of Russian studies concerning the Russian expedition in the field of general history of Russia and the history of Byzantium, I wish to point out the most characteristic traits which have been emphasized or discussed by historians.   (1) The year of the expedition has been given as 864, 865, or 866; only after the publication of the *Brussels Chronicle* was the year 860 generally accepted.   But it should not be forgotten that before that time Golubinski had ascribed the expedition to the year 860 or the very beginning of 861.   (2) Most Russian historians assign two leaders to the expedition, Askold and Dir; but some of them mention Askold alone, or even Dir alone.   (3) Several historians locate the River Mauropotamus in the Thracian Peninsula, i.e., in Europe, not in Asia Minor.   (4) Some historians are inclined to believe that the attack was carried out not from Kiev but from another place, preferably the Taman Peninsula.   (5) Historians are at variance concerning the first

---

[55] *Op. cit.*, 386.   See casual references to the campaign of 860 on pp. 320, n. 1; 398, 450, 456 (Letter of Pope Nicholas I to Michael III), and n. 1.   I understand Uspenski's words 'since it has been nowhere else recorded' to refer to the fact that the names of Askold and Dir have not been mentioned in Greek sources.

[56] A. Vasiliev, *op. cit.*, I, 337–338 (in French, I, 366–367); in Russian, I, 261–262.

[57] G. Ostrogorski, *Geschichte des byzantinischen Staates* (Munich, 1940), p. 159 and n. 3.

[58] M. V. Levchenko, *History of Byzantium* (Moscow-Leningrad, 1940), p. 159.

conversion of Russia: whether it took place under Photius or Ignatius, or in two stages under both.   (6) It is an historical fact that the expedition ended in failure; but the opinion is held that the Russians obtained an honorable peace, or that an alliance and treaty was made between Byzantium and the Russians.   (7) Some historians, up to the twentieth century, have continued to follow Porphyrius Uspenski's defective edition of Photius' homilies and particularly the erroneous translation and continued to affirm in spite of better editions that the cause of the expedition was the murder by the Greeks of some Russians resident in Constantinople.

Studies by Russian scholars who were especially interested in the expedition of 860 will be discussed below, so that, except for Bayer's monograph, I do not refer to them here.

THE RUSSIAN EXPEDITION OF 860 IN
FOREIGN LITERATURE

ALMOST all the scholars outside Russia who have written general histories of the Byzantine Empire, or have been particularly interested in the events of the ninth century or in the history of the Scandinavian or so-called Viking expeditions, have mentioned or briefly told of the first Russian attack on Constantinople. Since they give only the usual story of the event, it is not worth while to list them here. I have given above the names of a great number of Russian historians writing on the subject, because their works are almost inaccessible to the general reader outside Russia, and because the event itself holds special interest for the opening pages of Russian history. Among historians outside Russia I wish to give only a few names. Their writings, I believe, have special interest for various reasons which I hope to explain below.

In the eighteenth century in one of his numerous works Voltaire deals with the ninth century and, after telling the story of the restoration of icon veneration, devotes a few lines to the Russian expedition. He writes, 'The Russians embarked at the port now called Azov, on the Black Sea, and came and ravaged all the sea coast of the Pontus Euxinus.'[1] As we see, in this rather vague statement Voltaire fails to mention Constantinople as the aim of the Russian expedition. But curiously enough he mentions 'Azov on the Black Sea' as the point of departure for the Russian raid. I do not know how Voltaire came to this conclusion; but the Russian historians who believe that the Russian expedition of 860 started from Tmutorokan and was undertaken by the southern Russians, sometimes called the Azov Russians, might, of course without any serious grounds, have referred to Voltaire as the first scholar who shared this point of view.

In 1829 a German scholar, F. Wilken, the author of the very well known but now antiquated *History of the Crusades*, published a very substantial monograph *On the Relationships between the Russians and the Byzantine State from the ninth to the twelfth century*.[2] Wilken here devotes thirteen pages (77–90) to the Russian expedition. He knows all the available Greek sources, including Photius' *Encyclical Letter*, and to a great extent depends on Bayer's monograph, which I have discussed above.

---

[1] Voltaire, *Essai sur les moeurs et l'esprit des nations*, I, chapter xxix, *Oeuvres complètes de Voltaire*, xvi (Paris, 1785), 493; ed. Paris, 1819, p. 464.

[2] F. Wilken, 'Ueber die Verhältnisse der Russen zum Byzantinischen Reiche in dem Zeitraume vom neunten bis zum zwölften Jahrhundert,' *Abhandlungen der Akademie der Wissenschaften zu Berlin*, 1829, Historisch-Philologische Klasse, pp. 75–135.

Wilken writes that the Patriarch Photius, 'who lived at a period when the name of the Russians must have for the first time originated, explicitly denotes the Russians in his Encyclical Letter itself as a very well known people [Wilken gives the Greek text].   Therefore we must certainly admit that the name of the Russians had of course been in existence for some time and was already known to Byzantium' (pp. 77–78).   After mentioning that the chronological question of the attack has already been adequately settled by Bayer, who referred it to the year 864 or 865,[3] Wilken limits himself to the description of the event itself (p. 80).   He lists all the Greek sources available at that time as well as Nestor's *Chronicle* from Schlözer's study (p. 81).   Greek sources, he says, fail to mention the cause of the raid or the names of its leaders.   Oskold and Dir are to be found in Russian tradition.   Then he gives the usual story of the attack, with many corrections to the Greek text (pp. 81–83).   According to him, the Μαῦρος ποταμός is undoubtedly the Black River (*der Fluss Melas*), which, after its junction with the river Athyras and at its discharge into the Propontis, forms the Gulf of Tchekmedje, which is located six hours southwest of Constantinople (p. 83; a lengthy and out of date discussion on pp. 83–87).   Finally Wilken takes up the question of the potential cause of the attack.   He believes it was not only rapacity.   The Russians might have been taking revenge on the Greeks for an offense which was passed over by Byzantine writers in silence, for an offense of the sort that the Greeks then often indulged themselves in committing towards the peoples whom they considered rude barbarians.   All the more striking, he emphasizes, is the result: the Russians sent an embassy to Constantinople and asked for baptism (p. 89).   In his *Encyclical Letter* Photius tells the story.   It is remarkable that the Russian Chronicles fail to mention this first conversion of the Russians to Christianity (pp. 89–90).   In his speculation as to the cause of the Russian attack, Wilken seems to be foreshadowing the theory, presented by many historians many years after the publication of his study, that the murder of some Russians resident in Constantinople was the cause.   This is, of ocurse, an error stemming back to the Archbishop Porphyrius Uspenski's defective edition of the Greek text of Photius' sermon.   In spite of some unavoidable blunders which were later clarified, Wilken's monograph is the best study on the subject which has been produced by a non-Russian historian.

In 1876 a French historian, A. Couret, the author of the well-known monograph on *Palestine under the Greek Emperors* (*La Palestine sous les Empereurs Grecs*, Grenoble, 1869), published a long article *Russia in Con-*

---

[3] We have pointed out above that Bayer ascribed the Russian expedition to the years 864 *and* 865, not 864 *or* 865.

stantinople.   First Attempts of the Russians against the Greek Empire.[4]   He begins his study with the following statement: 'One may say that the capture of Constantinople is the most ancient and most cherished of all ambitions of Russia' (p. 69).   Then he gives a passage from Pogodin's book *The Norman period of Russian History* (the original Russian edition, Moscow, 1859), on the irresistible charm of Constantinople for the young Russian State and closes it with the words, 'Yes, Constantinople was the center, the capital of Russian history.'   He quotes a letter of the Russian poet Zhukovski to the Grand Duke Constantine, a brother of the Emperor Alexander II: 'This Byzantium is a fatal city' (pp. 69–70).   Of the attack, which he dates on June 865, Couret gives a lengthy and picturesque description, which he accompanies with many diversions from the subject.   His elevated and rather bombastic style reminds us of Pogodin, whom he had read, and whose peculiar style has been pointed out above. Couret is inclined to recognize only one leader of the expedition, Oskold, regarding Dir as merely his surname (pp. 79–84).   I give here one example of Couret's description.   He writes: 'The palaces of the emperors and of Byzantine nobles, the villas, the churches scattered in profusion on the enchanting shores of the Bosphorus whose aspect amazed the Norwegian crusaders in the twelfth century; the monasteries, strongholds, the country houses dispersed in the valley of Cydaris and Barbises, the woody gorges of the Mounts Strandja and the islands of the Propontis, successively become a prey to the Russians. . . .   The Emperor himself only at the cost of a thousand perils managed to return alone into his capital through the Russian boats' (pp. 81–82).   After describing the final failure of the expedition, Couret says, 'Moved by this mysterious disaster, Oskold, on his return to Kiev, sent to Constantinople to demand missionaries . . . in 867 we see already the Emperor Basil I sending to the prince of Kiev presents of gold and silver, and silk garments as well, in order to induce him to make an alliance and especially to receive a bishop from the hands of the Patriarch Saint Ignatius' (p. 83).   Couret's presentation and style may well identify him as a French Ilovaiski or Pogodin; the latter has undoubtedly influenced him.

In 1930 a German historian, G. Laehr, published his book *The Origins of the Russian State.   Political History in the ninth and tenth century*, in which he deals with the Russian attack of 860 in two sections: first he tells the story of the attack, and then he gives a substantial *excursus* on the

---

[4] A. Couret, *La Russie à Constantinople.   Premières tentatives des Russes contre l'Empire Grec, Revue des questions historiques*, 865–1116.   Vol. xix (1876), 69–129; on the attack under consideration see pp. 79–84.

sources for the attack of the Rhos on Constantinople in 860.[5]   First we
have to indicate the fact that Laehr was certain of the previous Russian
raids about 840, on Amastris and Surozh, in the Crimea, which are described in the *Lives* of George of Amastris and Stephen of Surozh, and
which, according to Laehr, have been convincingly proved by Vasilievski
(pp. 19–23; 94).   After telling the usual story of the attack, Laehr writes:
'No miracle was needed.   The Russians set before themselves not so much
the conquest of Byzantium as, first of all, the acquisition of booty.   When
this desire had been satisfied, they departed thence.   In this respect the
campaign against Constantinople did not differ from other Norman plundering expeditions of which Western Europe at that time saw so many,
and which other Greek maritime cities had already experienced' (p. 25).
Laehr's excursus on the sources of the attack is very useful.   The author
is well acquainted with Russian publications.   He begins with Photius'
two sermons, and says that the first was delivered immediately after the
appearance of the Russians, and the second after their departure.   He
knows that Porphyrius Uspenski's defective edition and translation of the
sermons has led to erroneous statements which we find in Klyuchevski
and, much later, in Lyubavski.   Laehr considers the *Vita Ignatii* by
David Nicetas Paphlagon a reliable source, and among Byzantine chroniclers he correctly gives preference to the concise report of *Theophanes
Continuatus*, whose presentation completely agrees with Photius' data,
and stands closest to the primary sources.   Then Laehr says a few words
on other Byzantine chronicles.   Surprisingly he fails to mention Cedrenus
(Scylitzes) and Zonaras.   He attributes the names of Askold and Dir to a
Kievan tradition.   There is now no doubt whatever concerning the dating, he says.   But on the basis of Joannes Diaconus, who states that the
Normans departed from Constantinople in triumph, Laehr affirms that
the destruction of the Russian fleet belongs to the realm of legend (p. 94).
He also devotes several lines to the letter of the Pope Nicholas I to
Michael III, and concludes that it is not of much importance whether in
his letter the Pope had in view Russians or Saracens (p. 94).   I shall discuss this point later.   Finally, reasoning from Vasilievski's arguments,
Laehr opposes the speculations of Loparev, who has attempted to attribute to the attack of 860 'an old text on the placing of the garment of the
Mother of God in Blachernae' (I have discussed this question above).
Laehr has devoted to the history of the attack of 860 much more attention
than any other modern writer, not only outside Russia, but inside Russia
as well.

[5] Gerhard Laehr, *Die Anfänge des russischen Reiches. Politische Geschichte im 9. und 10. Jahrhundert* (Berlin, 1930), pp. 24–25 (the story) and 91–95 (Exkurs I).

In 1938 in America an interesting book came out, G. Bie Ravndal's *Stories of the East-Vikings* (Minneapolis, Minnesota). The author uses Russian publications and seems to share N. T. Beliaev's thesis, who, going back to F. Kruse's speculations, identifies Rorik of Jutland (Friesland) with Rurik of the original Russian annals.[6] Naturally Ravndal devotes some attention to the Russian attack. To the names of Askold and Dir he gives the Scandinavian form *Höskuldr* and *Dyri* (p. 181). In his story of the attack he combines the data of Greek and Slavonic sources with the Latin chronicle of Joannes Diaconus, and regards the expedition as a purely Varangian enterprise under the headship of one leader, Askold. He writes: 'Already it has been intimated that a Varing settlement probably obtained at Kief prior to Askold's advent. The mere fact that Askold, so soon after his appearance on the Dnieper, was able to launch an expedition against impregnable Constantinople of 200–350 sail, suggests not merely audacity but also the actuality of such a stronghold at Kief. . . . Unlike Oleg and other Rus Leaders in later campaigns, Askold in his war against Byzantium of 860 was accompanied neither by Finns nor by Slavs nor by Turks: his army, which must have counted more than 10,000 men, forty to the boat, consisted only of Varings. . . . Whether this step had any connection with the embassy of 838 is uncertain. Conceivably a treaty of amity and commerce had been concluded in 838, and it may be that the 860 military endeavor was prompted by its violation by the Greeks' (p. 187). Ravndal denies the reliability of the story given by the ancient Russian chronicler. 'Against the falsehood' of Nestor's account, which 'is clearly derived from Greek annals and obviously unreliable,' Ravndal enters 'the unbiased evidence' of Joannes Diaconus, whose *Chronicon Venetum* 'unequivocally states that Normannic people about 860 approached Constantinople with 360 ships; but finding the city impregnable only plundered the countryside and returned home victorious (*cum triumpho*).' Then he turns to a later Venetian story about 1450 by Blondus or Biondo, who 'adds the intriguing bit of information that the aggressors (Normanni known from their depredations in Aquitania and other Gallic parts) returned to the Britannic Sea.' And here Ravndal questions, 'Perhaps some of Askold's men were Danes after all? Repeatedly we hear of Northmen returning from Scythia through the Black Sea and the Mediterranean, a practice not yet sufficiently explained by historians' (p. 188). From our point of view Ravndal, like most historians, is wrong in attributing Joannes Diaconus' record to Askold's expedition. For Blondus' tale we have already expressed above our own interpretation of his 'intriguing' information.

[6] N. T. Beliaev, 'Rorik of Jutland and Rurik of the Original (Russian) Annals.' *Seminarium Kondakovianum,* III (1929), 215–270 (in Russian).

In Ravndal's book much attention is paid to the Patriarch Photius and his part in the event of 860. 'In his narrative,' Ravndal writes, 'the venerable chronicler of Kief (Nestor) introduces as witness the great patriarch of orthodoxy, Photius.' Ravndal draws on his imagination for a large ransom supposedly paid by the Byzantine government; then he gives the exact date of Photius' two homilies. After saying a few words on the attack he continues: 'Photius was equal to the occasion. He at once preached his wonderful homily of June 23, 860, urging that the impending calamity was Heaven's punishment for the sins of the Byzantines. . . . The Rus (it is assumed) abandoned the siege in consideration of a large ransom, while on their part, to ease the patriarch's conscience, they promised to accept Christian teachers. Once more (early in July) Photius mounted the pulpit. . . . He made no mention of any story or of any other specific reason why the 'barbarians' struck tents and retreated. Tales, subsequently attributed to a contemporary Byzantine scribe, not only embellished the religious phase of the incident but also had the emperor return in time to assist in driving the Rus away and in scattering their vessels' (pp. 189–190).

Turning to Photius' pastoral encyclical of 866 in which the Patriarch mentions the conversion of the Rus to Christianity, Ravndal says, 'The Patriarch had done his work well. Christianity never relinquished the hold it then gained at Kief through Askold's conversion, and proud Byzantium, which never had been in direr straits since the joint attack of Avars and Persians in 626, or the Saracen assaults in the same century, once more was safe. A formal treaty had been concluded between Byzantium and Kief, perhaps confirming previous conventions, but of it we have not the text' (p. 190).

Then Ravndal gives credit to the northern 'barbarians' for their exact knowledge of the situation in Constantinople in 860, when the Emperor was absent and the capital was but poorly protected. 'Clearly the Rus were no strangers to Byzantine politics, which circumstance presupposes contacts of older date and a fertility of brain not usually credited to "barbarians" ' (p. 190).

Subsequently and evidently under the influence of Beliaev's study, Ravndal stresses the Norman expeditions in 859 in the Mediterranean into Italy, Greece, and Egypt, and wonders whether this advance had any relation to Askold's campaign. He writes, 'Time and again we are surprised at the geographical vision as well as the political insight of the "savage" northmen, and when these in 859 once more entered the Mediterranean through Gibraltar, projecting their warlike expeditions even unto Italy, Greece, and perhaps Egypt, as did Geiseric's Vandals in earlier days, one is tempted to wonder whether this advance had any relation to

Askold's venture. That Hvidserk played some part in the latter can only be conjectured but we are assured that, while infesting the Mediterranean, his brother Biorn Ironside, another of Ragnar's famous sons, only too well known all through western Europe, cherished fancies of far-reaching conquests. It would almost seem as if Vikings and Varings had planned to touch hands at Constantinople' (pp. 190–191). I shall discuss this intriguing and extremely interesting question later.

I have delayed at some length on Ravndal's book because it presents the most recent reaction of a scholar outside Russia to the most recent studies on the subject.

As a curiosity I wish to mention here the most recent study of a Brazilian professor of the University of São Paulo in Brazil, E. Simões de Paula, *Varangian commerce and the Grand Principality of Kiev*, written in Portuguese and published in 1942.[7] He devotes almost three pages to the Russian attack of 860 (pp. 42–43). Not acquainted with the Russian language, the author bases his presentation on the works of modern scholars, written mostly in French. The story of the attack itself is nothing but a literary translation of the relevant text of Ch. Diehl and G. Marçais' book *Le Monde Oriental* (p. 323); his treatment of the question of dating the attack and two quotations from Photius' homilies are merely a translation from the French edition of my *Histoire de l'Empire Byzantin* (I, 366–367); the third quotation from Photius comes from Ch. Diehl and G. Marçais (p. 324). The Brazilian historian ends his story of the Russian attack by referring to the very well known French book of J. Calmette, *Le Monde Féodal* (p. 30). The author frankly indicates his dependence on the historians mentioned, saying in his footnotes *apud Diehl e Marçais* or *apud Vasiliev* and even reproducing a misprint in Diehl's book.[8] Of course the Brazilian historian is merely repeating what two recent historians have written about the attack. But it seems to me striking that in a center so far distant from Europe as São Paulo an historian has become interested in Varangian commerce and the Grand Principality of Kiev.

---

[7] E. Simões de Paula, 'O comércio varegue e o Grão-Principado de Kiev,' Universidade de São Paulo, *Boletins* da Faculdade de Filosofia, Ciências e Letras. XXVI. História da civilização antiga e medieval. N. 3 (São Paulo, 1942), pp. 145.

[8] In Diehl's book the name of the Greek editor of Photius' homilies is, by misprint, given as *Aristerekis* for *Aristarkhes*.

DATING

THE question of the dating of the first Russian attack on Constantinople may be divided into two sections, before and after the year 1894, when Franz Cumont discovered and published a brief Byzantine chronicle which has supplied us with the exact date of the attack. In addition, the first section may be subdivided into two sections, before and after the acquaintance of Western writers with the Russian annals.

For dating, before 1894 there were three sources, two Greek, the *Life of Patriarch Ignatius* and the so-called *Symeon Magister* (*Pseudo-Symeon*), and one Slavonic, the *Russian Annals*. The most essential source is the *Vita Ignatii*, which tells us that after his deposition, November 23, 858, Ignatius was removed to the island of Terebinthos, one of the Islands of the Princes in the Sea of Marmora near Constantinople; then he was removed from there to the suburb of Promotos, on the Galata side of the Golden Horn, and later to Mytilene, where he remained six months (*circa* August 859 to February 860), and finally permitted to return to Terebinthos. During his second exile in Terebinthos, this island, like other islands in the neighborhood of the capital, was invaded and devastated by the Russians.[1] The chronology of the so-called *Symeon Magister* who attributed the Russian attack to the ninth and tenth years of the reign of Michael III, was long ago apparently proved inexact.[2] But now the question must be reconsidered. According to the Russian annals, the attack took place in 865 or 866. The *Russian Primary Chronicle* (Laurentian text) places it under the years 863–866 and ascribes it to the fourteenth year of the reign of the Emperor Michael. But we know well that the chronology of the earlier part of the Russian Chronicles is incorrect.

In the eighteenth century, when Western writers telling of the attack used Byzantine sources only, especially the *Vita Ignatii*, they were much nearer the exact date than later writers when the data of the Russian chronicles had become known. In 1743, P. A. Pagius, in his commentary on the *Ecclesiastical Annals* of Baronius, ascribed the Russian attack to 861, and in 1755 the noted orientalist Assemani to the end of 859 or the outset of 860.[3] In the first half of the nineteenth century M. Jager, un-

---

[1] On the chronology of Ignatius' wanderings after his deposition see J. Bury, *A History of the Eastern Roman Empire* (London, 1912), p. 191, n. 3. R. Janin, *Le Patriarche Ignace*, a very substantial article in *Dictionnaire de Théologie Catholique*, VII, 1, coll. 713–722. On the exact date of Ignatius' deposition, A. Vasiliev, *Byzance et les Arabes*, I (Brussels, 1935), 429–430; Russian edition, supplement, pp. 149–150. Kunik erroneously attributed Ignatius' deposition and his first exile to Terebinthos to Nov. 23, 857. A. Kunik and Baron V. Rosen, *Accounts of al-Bekri and other authors on Russia and the Slavs*, I (St Petersburg, 1878), 190 (in Russian).

[2] See F. Hirsch, *Byzantinische Studien* (Leipzig, 1876), p. 348 seq.

[3] *Baronii Annales Ecclesiastici una cum critica historicochronologica P. Antonii Pagii*, XIV (Lucca,

acquainted with Russian sources, in his monograph on Photius ascribed the Russian attack to the year 861.[4]

The Russian scholars who treated the question of the first Russian attack on Constantinople were familiar with the *Russian Annals* and were confronted with the difficulty of reconciling with their chronology the data of the *Life of Ignatius*.   Most of them gave the preference to the former and attributed the attack to 865 or 866, occasionally to 864 (Zabelin), although the *Life of Ignatius* is an almost contemporary source.[5]   In 1738 in his essay on the first Russian expedition on Constantinople, Bayer knew that Nicetas Paphlagon, the author of the *Life of Ignatius*, attributed the expedition to 860; but Nicetas, according to Bayer, *vitio laborat*, so that finally Bayer attributed the expedition to the years 864 and 865 or merely to 865.[6]   The stubborn veteran defender of the latter date was Kunik.   In 1878 he wrote, 'The Russian invasion on Tsargrad could have happened neither in 861 nor in 864 nor in 866 but only in the summer of 865.'[7]   Even after the discovery by Cumont in 1894 of the brief Byzantine chronicle which has settled the question of the year of the first attack, Kunik, as we have noted above, wrote in his letter to de Boor that the new source failed to convince him or make him abandon his point of view. The year 865 as that of the first Russian attack on Constantinople has been accepted by the majority of Russian historians.[8]   But several of them have been inclined to place the event in 866.   Among them were Schlözer, the celebrated pioneer in the investigation of the *Russian Primary Chronicle*, Karamzin, Krug, Bishop Philaret of Chernigov, and S. Solovyov.[9]   In Western Europe, basing his work on the *Russian Primary*

1743), 554, VII.   Assemani, *Kalendaria Ecclesiae Universae*, I (Rome, 1755), 240–243; II, 160–161, 231–232; IV, 9.

[4] M. l'Abbé Jager, *Histoire de Photius, patriarche de Constantinople, auteur du schisme des Grecs.* 2d ed. (Paris, 1845), pp. 44–45.

[5] A long list of the names of Russian scholars dealing with the date of the first Russian attack on Constantinople is given by Miss N. Polonskaya in her study 'On the question of Christianity in Russia before Vladimir,' *Journal of the Ministry of Public Instruction*, 1917, September, pp. 43–44 (in Russian).

[6] G. S. Bayer, 'De Russorum prima expeditione Constantinopolitana,' *Commentarii Academiae Scientiarum Imperialis Petropolitanae*, VI (1732 et 1733), 368, 370, 371.   Reprinted in *Theophili S. Bayeri Opuscula ad historiam antiquam, chronologiam, geographiam et rem nummariam spectantia*, ed. Cr. Klotzius (Hale, 1770).   On Bayer's studies see above.

[7] *Accounts of al-Bekri . . .* I, 179.   It is to be noted that Kunik in 1845 attributed this attack to 866.   Ernst Kunik, *Die Berufung der schwedischen Rodsen durch die Finnen und Slawen*, II (St Petersburg, 1845), 332–334, 347.

[8] See some examples in Vasiliev, *Byzance et les Arabes*, I, 243–244; Russ. ed., 192.

[9] Schlözer, *Nestor*, II (St Petersburg, 1816), 32 seq. (Russian edition).   Karamzin, *History of the Russian State*, I (St Petersburg, 1844), 71; see also n. 283 (in Russian).   Ph. Krug, *Forschungen in der älteren Geschichte Russlands*, II (St Petersburg, 1848), 355.   Philaret Chernigovski, *History of the Russian Church* (Chernigov, 1862), 6. S. Solovyov, *History of Russia*, 4th ed., I (Moscow, 1866), 119

Chronicle (the so-called *Nestor*), the Danish historian Steenstrup in 1876 placed the Russian attack in the year 866.[10]   In 1829 the German historian Wilken wrote that a Russian fleet of two hundred vessels attacked Constantinople in 864 or 865.[11]

Some scholars, realizing chronological contradictions between the data of the *Life of Ignatius* and the *Russian Annals*, took refuge in the theory of two different Russian expeditions, one in 860, which was mentioned in the *Life of Ignatius* and which was directed against the island of Terebinthos and other islands of the group of the Islands of the Princes, and the other, a few years later, which, under the leadership of Askold and Dir, attacked the capital itself.   Two such historians were Kruse and Hergenröther.   In 1851 Kruse, under the year 860, on the basis of *Joannis Chronicon Venetum*, Andreas Dandulus, and *Vita Ignatii* by Nicetas Paphlagon, mentions the first attack on Constantinople.   Thence we see that Kruse refers the data of the two Venetian chronicles to those of the *Life of Ignatius* and combines them.   Then later, under 866, Kruse mentions the expedition of Askold and Dir against Byzantium.   In this case, in addition to the *Russian Chronicles*, he refers to Byzantine chronicles and to the *Circular Letter* of Patriarch Photius (probably at the end of 866).[12]   Rebutting Kruse's theory of two different raids, Kunik once more emphasized that all sources presented by Kruse are connected with the Russian attack in 865 and that no other year than 865 could be admissable.[13]   The other writer who believes in two raids on Constantinople is the famous Catholic author of the fundamental monograph on Photius, Hergenröther.   According to him, the first Russian raid took place in 859; it was directed against the island of Terebinthos, where the ex-Patriarch was then living in exile.   Hergenröther writes that certainly the Russians had then already made several raids by sea in their numberless small dug-outs, μονόξυλα.   The Russian expedition of 859 is of course not identical with the direct assault on Constantinople related by the chroni-

---

(two last works in Russian).   It has been already noted that originally Kunik also accepted the year 866.

[10] J. C. Steenstrup, *Normannerne*, I (Copenhagen, 1876), 121.

[11] Wilken, 'Ueber die Verhältnisse der Russen zum Byzantinischen Reiche in dem Zeitraume vom neunten bis zum zwölften Jahrhundert, *Abh. der Akad. der Wissenschaften zu Berlin*, 1829, Historisch-Philologische Klasse, p. 80.   Wilken's authority is Bayer.

[12] Fr. C. H. Kruse, *Chronicon Nortmannorum, Wariago-Russorum nec non Danorum, Sveonum, Norwegonnum* . . . (Hamburg and Gotha, 1851), pp. 261–262 (the year 860); 318–323 (the year 866).

[13] B. Dorn (and Kunik), *Caspia* (St Petersburg, 1875), p. 377 (Russ. ed.); Germ. ed. (St Petersburg, 1877), p. 233.   See also E. Kunik, 'Ergänzende Bemerkungen zu den Untersuchungen über die Zeit der Abfassung des Lebens des h. Georg von Amastris.   Ein Beitrag zur Aufklärung der russisch-byzantinischen Chronologie des 9ten Jahrhunderts,' *Bulletin de l'Académie Impériale des Sciences de St Pétersbourg*, XXVII (1881), coll. 338–362.

clers.[14]   Later Hergenröther tells the story of the direct Russian attack on Constantinople under Askold and Dir, which, he says, seems to have occurred between 864 and 865, its chronology being uncertain.   He was familiar with the chronicle of 'the Russian monk Nestor.'[15]   Vasilievski mentioned Hergenröther's opinion of the two separate raids, but he was waiting for a special study to be written by Kunik and declined to express his own opinion on the subject.[16]

In 1939 I. Swiencicky distinguished two Russian expeditions against Constantinople, one in 860, to which two sermons of Photius testify, and the other that of the Kievan princes Askold and Dir, in 866, mentioned in Photius' *Encyclical Letter*.[16a]

In 1880 Golubinski, putting together all available sources, came to the conclusion that the Russians attacked Constantinople either in 860 or at the very beginning of 861.   According to him, there was only one raid; his chronological conclusion was based on the *Life of Ignatius*.[17]   Kunik says that Golubinski in his chronological calculations vainly builds hypotheses to define the expedition.[18]   Golubinski was the first who definitely discarded the incorrect chronology of the Russian Chronicles and ascribed the attack to the year 860, which he established on the basis of the *Life of Ignatius* by Nicetas Paphlagon.   His result was brilliantly corroborated in 1894, when Franz Cumont published the brief Byzantine chronicle which, as we know, gives the exact date of the Russian attack, June 18, 860.   The question is now definitely settled.

Since this time this date has been accepted by almost all historians and writers on the first Russian attack.   But even after 1894 there are exceptions.   In 1900 S. Aristarkhes ascribed the entrance of the Russian canoes ($\mu o\nu \delta \xi \upsilon \lambda a$) into the Bosphorus ($\epsilon i s \ \tau \delta \ \Sigma \tau \epsilon \nu \delta \nu$) to the spring of 861.[19]   Surprisingly the old year 865 was maintained in 1903 by J. Marquart, in 1915 by R. Nordenstreng, in 1928 by J. W. Thompson, in the 'thirties by E. J.

---

[14] J. Hergenröther, *Photius*, i (Regensburg, 1867), 421 and n. 12.

[15] Hergenröther, *op. cit.*, i, 531–533; also iii (Regensburg, 1869), p. viii.   His other study has been mentioned above, 'Der Erste Russenzug gegen Byzanz,' in *Chilianeum*, Neue Folge, 3 Heft (Würzburg, 1869), 210–224.

[16] Vasilievski, *Works*, iii, p. cxxviii, n. 3 (in Russian).   No special study of Kunik has ever appeared.   Vasilievski considered not only Hergenröther but also Golubinski.   Of the latter we shall speak next.

[16a] Ilarion Swiencicky, 'Die Friedensverträge der Bulgaren und der Russen mit Byzanz, *Studi Bizantini e Neoellenici*, v (Rome 1939), 324.

[17] E. Golubinski, *A History of the Russian Church*, i (Moscow, 1880), 21–22; 2d ed., corrected and supplemented, i (Moscow, 1901), 40 (in Russian).   I shall speak later on Golubinski's opinion of Askold and Dir and of the question who were the Russians who attacked Constantinople.

[18] *Accounts of al-Bekri* . . . by Kunik and Rosen, i, 183–184 (in Russian).

[19] Τοῦ ἐν ἁγίοις πατρὸς ἡμῶν Φωτίου πατριάρχου Κωνσταντίνου πόλεως Λόγοι καὶ Ὁμιλίαι ὀγδοήκοντα τρεῖς, ἐκδίδοντος Σ. Ἀριστάρχου, ι (Constantinople 1900), p. κζ.

Martin, and J. Calmette.[20]   In 1906 W. Vogel attributed the attack of
'the Swedish Russians' on Constantinople to the year 866.[21]   In 1931
Gaudefroy-Demombynes wrote, 'It was about 865 that Byzantium for the
first time heard of the Russians; but this was not the last.[22]   But we now
have the absolutely exact date of the first Russian attack on Constantinople: June 18, 860.   On that day the Russian vessels made their appearance before Constantinople.

[20] J. Marquart, *Osteuropäische und ostasiatische Streifzüge* (Leipzig, 1903), p. 202, 387, 391.
R. Nordenstreng, *Vikingafärderna* (Stockholm, 1915), p. 161, J. W. Thompson, *An Economic and
Social History of the Middle Ages* (New York-London, 1928), p. 342, J. Calmette, *Le Monde Féodal*
(Paris, s.d.), p. 30,   E. J. Martin, *A History of the Iconoclastic Controversy* (London, s.d. [1930]),
p. 216.

[21] W. Vogel, '*Die Normannen und das fränkische Reich bis zur Gründung der Normandie (799–911)*'
Heidelberg, 1906, p. 172, *Heidelberger Abhandlungen zur mittleren und neueren Geschichte*, no. 14
(1906).   In his dating Vogel follows Steenstrup's work *Normannerne*, I.

[22] Gaudefroy-Demombynes and Platonov, *Le monde musulman et byzantin jusqu'aux croisades*
(Paris, 1931), p. 459. Cf. p. 496, where Platonov, in the section he writes, gives the correct dating
(860).

GENERAL SITUATION IN BYZANTIUM
ABOUT 860

IF we wish to picture the general situation of the Empire just before 860, we shall realize at once that the capital, the real center of political and economic life, was not adequately protected. We have already described the tense and dangerous situation in the south, in the Mediterranean and the Aegean. A continuous struggle was going on with the Arabs in Sicily and South Italy, and with the Cretan Arab pirates, who across the Aegean managed to enter the Sea of Marmora, and there were frequent Norman raids in the eastern Mediterranean, which extended also as far north as the Aegean and the Sea of Marmora. Accordingly the Byzantine fleet was removed from Constantinople into southern waters, and was exceedingly occupied there with generally unsuccessful operations. In 853, and perhaps again in 859, the Byzantine fleet appeared at the mouth of the Nile, before Damietta and Pelusium (al-Farama). So in 860 Constantinople was practically devoid of any naval forces and was almost defenseless against any sea assault from the north. On land, in Asia Minor, the Empire had not yet had time enough to recover from its defeats in 838 near Ancyra and Amorium. In spite of several exchanges of war prisoners on the eastern frontier, which might have indicated some respite, hostilities went on. In 859 the young Michael III and his powerful uncle Bardas marched through Asia Minor towards Samosata in a successful campaign. In the same year Ancyra, which had been destroyed in 838, was restored. The Emperor returned to Constantinople. A new exchange of war prisoners was effected in the spring of this year, 859. But in the summer of 860 the Emperor and Bardas were already again in Asia Minor with a powerful army and a stubborn new fight was raging. The capital lacked any substantial land defense. Bury writes, 'The troops which were usually stationed in the neighbourhood of the city were far away with the Emperor and his uncle; and the fleet was absent.'[1] Only on the side of the Balkan Peninsula was the Empire in 860 free from danger. At that time peace was maintained with Bulgaria during the reign of King Boris, who before the end of the reign of Michael III, about 864, accepted Christian baptism and turned a new page in his relations with the Empire.

To sum up, in the summer of 860 the capital of the Empire seems to have been quite unprepared for any attack from the north, from the Black Sea. No doubt a garrison must have remained in the capital, and

[1] Bury, *A History of the Eastern Roman Empire*, p. 419.

this was to bear the brunt of the Russian attack. But, in spite of the lack of man power, it should not be forgotten that the powerful walls of Constantinople protected the city effectively against the Russian invaders, who had neither equipment for nor experience in surmounting such a barrier. Much more exposed to the Russian aggression were the suburbs of the capital, the coastline along the Bosphorus and the Sea of Marmora, and the islands.

MICHAEL III

AT the moment of the Russian attack on Constantinople in 860, the head of the Byzantine Empire was the last representative of the Amorian dynasty, Michael III. Born in 839, he was in 860 quite a young man, twenty-one years of age; it was the fifth year of his independent rule, since his mother Theodora, who had held the power during Michael's minority, had been deposed in March 856 and her favorite and the virtual prime minister Theoctistus assassinated in the same year. In 860 the youth had a very talented, well educated, and energetic adviser in the person of Theodora's brother, his own uncle, Bardas who, after Theodora's deposition and Theoctistus' assassination, became all-powerful. In 860 Basil, the future murderer of his benefactor, Michael III, and the future founder of the Macedonian dynasty, was already protostrator, whose duties involved frequent attendance upon the Emperor. At that time Basil was about forty-eight years of age, and his influence with the Emperor was already strong. In 859 he had been entrusted by the Emperor with the reconstruction of the walls and fortifications of the city of Ancyra, in Asia Minor, which, as we know, had been destroyed by the Arabs in 838.[1] In 860 the rivalry and competition between Bardas and Basil were beginning to be felt.

No Byzantine emperor has been so badly treated, both in Byzantine tradition and in later literature, as Michael III 'the Drunkard,' 'a Byzantine Caligula.'[2] His incredible frivolity, his fits of drunkenness, his horrible impiety and abominable scurrility have been many times described. Patriarch Photius is even represented as Michael's habitual boon companion; he once took part in a drinking contest with the Emperor and beat him; whereas Michael drank fifty cups of wine, Photius drank sixty and was not overcome.[3] A miniature in the famous Madrid

---

[1] See H. Grégoire, 'Michel III et Basile le Macédonien dans les inscriptions d'Ancyre,' *Byzantion* v (1929–1930), 342. P. Wittek, 'Zur Geschichte Angoras im Mittelalter,' *Festschrift für George Jacob zum 70 ten Geburtstag* (Leipzig, 1932), pp. 333–334. Grégoire, 'La geste d'Amorium. Une épopée byzantine de l'an 860,' *Prace Polskiego Towarzystwa dla Badań Europy Wschodniej i Bliskiego Wschodu* n. IV, (Cracow, 1933–1934), 155. Grégoire's note in A. Vasiliev, *Byzance et les Arabes*, I (Brussels, 1935), 152, n. 2.

[2] N. Iorga, *Essai de synthèse de l'histoire de l'humanité*, II, *Histoire du moyen-âge* (Paris, 1927), p. 143.

[3] *Symeon Magister*, p. 663. See E. Jeanselme, 'L'alcoolisme à Byzance.' *Communication à la Societé française d'Histoire de la médecine*, t. XVIII, nos. 9–10 (Sept.-Oct., 1924), p. 5 (pagination of an offprint). The author of the paper takes this anecdote very seriously to prove that even several Byzantine patriarchs spent a life very little edifying (*une vie peu édifiante*). A Russian scholar, Ivantsov-Platonov, calls this anecdote 'an improper fiction,' A. M. Ivantsov-Platonov, 'On the Studies on Photius, the Patriarch of Constantinople,' *Journal of the Ministry of Public Instruction*, May, 1892, p. 7 (in Russian).

Skylitzes Manuscript, which contains many precious miniatures referring to Byzantine history, represents Michael III chasing a woman who is leaving a bath.[4]   Historians have very seldom condescended to discover in his person qualities of positive merit except in his military activities. In 1895 C. de Boor wrote that Michael was not devoid of good qualities as an energetic man and soldier.[5]   In 1910 Bury remarks that the revival of the Empire's naval power was effected in the reign of Michael III, and later Basil I took the offensive on the basis of Michael's achievements.[6] In 1927 Th. Uspenski, after describing in detail all Michael's undesirable qualities, concludes: 'But the fact that, among his contemporaries and even among the men who were close to him, there are high characters and enlightened minds, may give us reason to study, not without profit, his personality from the point of view of his political and administrative activity, especially in military affairs.'[7]   Then a few pages later Uspenski writes: 'We must acknowledge that the brief period of his reign opens entirely new perspectives in the history of the Empire, and that in the decade from 856 to 867 on the historical stage appear new men well prepared for activities. . . .   It would be more correct to date a new period of history not from Basil the Macedonian, who is the executor of what was already planned and prepared, but from Michael III, under whom entirely "new men and new songs" meet the historian.'[8]

Recently H. Grégoire has opened an especially vigorous campaign to restore Michael's reputation.   He points out many facts referring to Michael's epoch, particularly his energetic and successful fighting against the eastern Arabs, and proclaims that the last sovereign of the Amorian dynasty possessing the temperament of a genius truly inaugurated the triumphant phase of Byzantine history (843–1025).[9]   In several other articles and studies Grégoire emphasizes the same idea.   Uspenski's remarks on the time of Michael III quoted above have escaped Grégoire's attention.

Since Michael III played a very important part in the repulse of the Russians in 860, we have to devote more time to his personality and to the very interesting fact that his activities against the eastern Arabs have

[4] Sp. Lambros, *Empereurs Byzantins.   Catalogue illustré de la collection de Byzance d'après les statues, les miniatures, les ivoires et les autres œuvres d'art* (Athens, 1911), p. 16, no. 171: 'Michael III poursuit une femme au sortir du bain.'

[5] C. de Boor, 'Der Angriff der Rhos auf Byzanz,' *Byz. Zeitschrift,* IV (1895), 463–464.

[6] J. B. Bury, 'The Naval Policy of the Roman Empire in relation to the Western Provinces from the 7th to the 9th Century,' *Centenario della nascita di Michele Amari,* II (Palermo, 1910), 34.

[7] Th. Uspenski, *History of the Byzantine Empire,* II, 1 (Leningrad, 1927), 345 (in Russian).

[8] Uspenski, *op. cit.,* II, 1, p. 352.

[9] H. Grégoire, 'Du nouveau sur le Patriarche Photius,' *Bulletin de la classe des lettres de l'Académie Royale de Belgique,* XX (1934), no. 3, p. 38 and 39.

left a considerable trace in popular tradition, especially in the Byzantine epic.   Now we must strongly emphasize a fact which till recent times has not been adequately appreciated — that the Byzantine disaster at Amorium which the Empire had suffered in 838 was fully revenged under Michael about 860 or perhaps in this very year, the year of the Russian attack, when Byzantine troops crossed the Euphrates.   Three years later, in 863, the Arab forces were almost annihilated in the battle of Poson, probably in the ancient Cappadocia, by the Byzantine general Petronas and their commander, Omar, the emir of Melitene, was slain.   This brilliant victory resounded in Constantinople, in the Hippodrome, and a special chant, which has survived in our sources, celebrated the death of the emir on the battlefield.   The battle of Poson was the turning point in the military history of Byzantium as regards the eastern Arabs.[10] From the year 863 we hear of no important Arab successes in the East; and from the middle of the tenth century we witness a long list of brilliant Byzantine successes, which are connected with the names of such eminent military leaders as John Kurkuas, Nicephorus Phocas, John Tzimisces, and Basil II.   The battle of Poson, in 863, put an end to the eastern Arab danger.   Much credit is to be given H. Grégoire, who not only has effectively demonstrated the capital importance of the battle of Poson, but also definitely proved that Michael's military successes against the eastern Arabs have left an indelible trace in the Byzantine epic.   The two hundred verse epic poem of Armuris, or rather of Armuropulos, the most ancient Byzantine epic which has come down to us, which mentions the crossing of the Euphrates by the Byzantine troops, is connected with the name of the city of Amorium, where the disaster of 838 had befallen the Empire.   Grégoire has shown that the young hero of the poem glorifies the real military hero of the 'sixties of the ninth century, the Emperor Michael III himself, under whom the deep-rooted and long-lived Arab danger on the eastern border was thoroughly crushed.[11]   Accordingly, the poem of Armuris is that of Amorium, and the father of the young hero of

[10] On the battle of Poson, see A. Vasiliev, *Byzance et les Arabes*, I (Brussels, 1935), pp. 249–256. The special chant on this battle in Constantine Porphyrogenitus, *De cerimoniis aulae byzantinae*, I, 69, pp. 332–333.   See also J. B. Bury, 'The Ceremonial Book of Constantine Porphyrogennetos,' *The English Historical Review*, XXII (1907), 434.

[11] To the list of Grégoire's studies on the epic of Armuris, I may add now his recent publication, in modern Greek, Ὁ Διγένης Ἀκρίτας. Ἡ βυζαντινὴ ἐποποιΐα στὴν ἱστορία καὶ στὴν ποίηση (New York, 1942), pp. 6–10; 16–19; 201–204 (on p. 204 some bibliography).   I know of four publications of the poem of Armuris: by Gabriel Destunis (St Petersburg, 1877); reproduction in *Athenaion*, VIII (1879), 385–394; by Σ. Π. Κυριακίδης, Ὁ Διγένης Ἀκρίτας (Athens, 1926), 119–129; and by Grégoire in his book just mentioned, pp. 204–212.   There is a very fine French translation of the poem by Grégoire (with the omission of verses 140–166), 'La geste d' Amorium.   Une épopée byzantine de l'an 860,' *Prace Towarzystwa dla Bodań Europy Wschodniej i Bliskiego Wschodu*, no. IV (Cracow, 1933–1934), 156–160.   A complete Russian translation was published in 1877 by G. Destunis.

the poem, the son of Armuris (Armuropulos), was probably a prisoner of war taken by the Arabs after the capture of Amorium.[12] But as Grégoire has shown, Armuropulos stands for Michael III himself. 'It is just,' Grégoire says in one of his studies, 'that the popular Muse should at last avenge the "Armuropulos" for the calumnies of historians.'[13]

Grégoire has revealed and emphasized the deep impression left in popular tradition and in popular songs by Michael's successful military activities against the eastern Arabs. I wish now to show that not only Michael's successes in the East have left their trace in popular tradition, but also — and this is extremely interesting for our study — his victory in the north, over the Ros. Here I have in view an apocryphal work known both in Byzantine and in Slavo-Russian literature, the so-called *Revelation of Methodius of Patara*. According to the best authority on this work, V. M. Istrin, there are three Greek versions of the *Revelation*, a brief Latin version, two Slavonic versions, and finally an interpolated Slavonic version.[14]

In Methodius' *Revelation* the whole history of the world, beginning with Adam and ending with the second Advent of Christ, is set within seven thousands of years. For us the most interesting period is the seventh thousand, and particularly during this period an episode of the last Emperor-Liberator, who at a moment of crisis awakes as if from sleep, and later delivers his Empire to God in Jerusalem. According to the three Greek versions of the *Revelation*, during the seventh thousand years, the Ishmaelites will come out and assemble in Gabaon, where many Greeks will fall at the point of their swords. Ishmaelite domination will be cruel. They will devastate Persia, Romania, Cilicia, Syria, and other regions, and in their pride they will say, 'No Christians will escape our hands.'[15] 'Then suddenly an Emperor of the Greeks or Romans will rise upon them with great strength; he will wake as a man from sleep, who has drunk wine, whom men regarded as dead and worthless. He will march upon them from the Ethiopian sea and will inflict sword and devastation down to Ethrimbos, that is to say down to their own father-

---

[12] To the first editor of the text of this poem, G. Destunis, and its first commentator, a famous Russian scholar, A. Veselovski, the name of Armuri was not clear. See A. Wesselofsky, 'Beiträge zur Erklärung des russischen Heldenepos,' *Archiv für slavische Philologie*, III (1879), 550: 'Der Name Armuri bleibt unklar.'

[13] Grégoire, *La geste d'Amorium, Prace* . . . IV (Cracow, 1933–1934), 160.

[14] V. Istrin, *Revelation of Methodius of Patara and Apocryphal Visions of Daniel in Byzantine and Slavo-Russian literature* (*Čtenija v Obščestve Istorii i Drevnostei Rossiskich* [Moscow, 1897]), book II, III, IV; 1898, book I, 133–162 (Vision of Daniel). There are also an Armenian and a Syrian version of the *Revelation*. Istrin calls the three Greek versions one, three, and four. No text of version two appears in Istrin's edition.

[15] See Istrin's summary of this section of the *Revelation* in Russian, *op. cit.*, 1897, II, pp. 19–22. Γαβαών — Gibeon is an ancient city of Canaan, in Palestine.

land.'[16] 'His yoke will be seven times heavier than that of the Ishmaelites. Then after his victories wonderful fertility will spread over the earth; and all men will live in peace. The Greeks will rebuild cities, and the priests will be released from violence.'[17] But during this peace a disaster will befall them. 'Then the gates of the north will open, and the forces of the peoples who have been shut within will emerge. The whole earth will be shocked by their appearance; men will be frightened and will flee away and hide themselves upon mountains, in caves and tombs. For the peoples coming from the north eat human flesh and drink blood of animals like water and eat unclean things.'[18] But after seven years, when they have captured the city of Ioppe, the Lord God will send one of his Archistrategi and smite them in a moment. Then the Greek Emperor will come to Jerusalem, and ten years and a half after his coming the Antichrist will be born.

The same story is told in the third and fourth Greek versions (1897, IV, 62–63; 72–73). But in the third version we read in addition that before marching on the Agarenes the Emperor will come out through the socalled Golden Gate,[19] and during three days he will worship and pray before the Lord God (p. 62). In the brief Latin version we have 'Surget autem rex christianorum et proeliabit cum eis (Sarracenis) et occidet eos gladio . . . ita erit adventus Gog et Magog, et cum fuerit ita pax, referabuntur portae Caspiae in lateribus aquilonis . . .' (pp. 81–82). The text of the first and second Slavonic versions is identical with that of the first Greek version (1897, IV 97–99; 112–113).

These texts fail to give the name of the Emperor-Liberator. But his characterization as a man who woke as if from sleep, who has drunk wine, and who was regarded as worthless, entirely coincides with the traditional picture of Michael III 'the Drunkard,' as it has been given in later Byzantine tradition, intentionally distorted. The story that in his

---

[16] The first Greek version: τότε αἰφνιδίως ἐπαναστήσεται ἐπ' αὐτοὺς βασιλεὺς Ἑλλήνων ἤτοι Ῥωμαίων μετὰ μεγάλου θυμοῦ καὶ ἐξυπνισθήσεται καθάπερ ἄνθρωπος ἀπὸ ὕπνου καθὼς πιὼν οἶνον, ὃν ἐλογίζοντο οἱ ἄνθρωποι ὡσεὶ νεκρὸν καὶ εἰς οὐδὲν χρησιμεύοντα. οὗτος ἐξελεύσεται ἐπ' αὐτοὺς ἐκ τῆς θαλάσσης Αἰθιοπίων καὶ βάλλει ῥομφαίαν καὶ ἐρήμωσιν ἕως Ἐθριμβον ἤτοι εἰς τὴν πατρίδα αὐτῶν, *op. cit.*, IV 40–41. Ethrimbos is of course the name of the city of Yathrib, in Arabia, later Medina. See for instance, *Theophanis Chronographia*, ed. de Boor, I, 365: τοῦ Ἐθρίβου; also index p. 600: Ἔθριβος, ἡ μεγάλη Ἀραβία.

[17] καὶ ἀνοικοδομήσουσιν τὰς πόλεις καὶ ἐλευθερωθήσονται οἱ ἱερεῖς ἐκ τῶν ἀναγκῶν αὐτῶν, *op. cit.*, 1897, IV, 43 (first version).

[18] Τότε ἀνοιχθήσονται αἱ πύλαι τοῦ βορρᾶ καὶ ἐξελεύσονται αἱ δυνάμεις τῶν ἐθνῶν, οἱ ἦσαν καθειργμένοι ἔνδοθεν, καὶ σαλευθήσεται πᾶσα ἡ γῆ ἀπὸ προσώπου αὐτῶν καὶ θροήσονται οἱ ἄνθρωποι καὶ ἐκφεύξονται καὶ κρύψουσιν ἑαυτοὺς ἐπὶ τὰ ὄρη καὶ τὰ σπήλαια καὶ ἐν τοῖς μνήμασι . . . τὰ γὰρ ἐρχόμενα ἔθνη ἀπὸ βορρᾶ ἐσθίουσι σάρκας ἀνθρώπων καὶ πίνουσιν αἷμα θηρίων ὡς ὕδωρ καὶ ἐσθίουσι τὰ ἀκάθαρτα, *op. cit.*, 1897, IV, 44 (first version).

[19] ἐξελεύσεται διὰ τῆς πύλης λεγομένης Χρυσίου (p. 62). Through the Golden Gate the emperors made their official entries into Constantinople.

victorious fight against the Arabs, he reached Yathrib-Medina, in Arabia, is doubtless an exaggeration; but it shows that Michael's war in the east was in reality unusually successful, and his brilliant victory gained over the Arabs at Poson in 863 has left in later popular tradition the legend that he reached the cradle of Muhammedanism in the depth of Arabia. The words of the *Revelation* that after the peace with the Arabs the Greeks will rebuild cities may reflect the historical fact of the restoration under Michael III of the walls of Nicaea and Ancyra. That the priests will be released from violence seems clearly a reference to the close of the iconoclastic period and the restoration of icon-veneration in 843. Finally the highly colored description of the abominable customs of the people who invaded the empire from the north, and who are without doubt the Russians, may be compared with the description of the Russian invaders, as we have it in Photius' sermons on the Ros, especially the second. With an exaggeration like that of Michael's advance to Yathrib-Medina in Arabia, the *Revelation* also has the Russians capture the city of Ioppe, that is to say, the city of Jaffa in Palestine. It is very well known that the most popular Archistrategus was named Michael. The end of the *Revelation* story narrating the coming of the Greek Emperor to Jerusalem and the birth of Antichrist is a pure legend, which was wide-spread in the Middle Ages.

If we turn now to the so-called interpolated Slavonic version of the *Revelation* of Methodius of Patara we find the name of the Emperor-Liberator: it was Michael. As early as about seventy-five years ago, in 1875, A. Veselovski, who was acquainted with the Greek text of the *Revelation* and its interpolated Slavonic versions, showed that the latter included some fragments from other apocryphal texts, a part of the *Vision of Daniel* and a part of the *Vision of Andrew the Simpleton.* Veselovski writes that, in comparison with older versions, the Russian interpolated versions of Methodius supply us with two new elements: they give the name of Michael as that of the Emperor-Liberator, and they mention that at the moment of danger Michael was not in Constantinople; he was absent, and an angel brought him from Rome. In his study Veselovski was inclined to identify Michael with the Emperor Michael Palaeologus, who in 1261 restored the Byzantine Empire; in the same study Veselovski compares Michael with Michaylik, who appears in the Ukrainian tale of *The Golden Gates.*[20] Five years later (in 1881), in his studies in South-Russian epics (*byliny*), Veselovski once more referred to the interpolated Russian version of the *Revelation of Methodius*, in which the

[20] A. N. Veselovski, 'Essays in the History of Christian Legend, II, Legend of a Returning Emperor,' *Journal of the Ministry of Public Instruction*, May, 1875, pp. 48–130; esp. pp. 60–63; 77; 78–79 (in Russian). On this study see Istrin, *op. cit.*, 1897, II, 175, 177–178, 180–182.

Archangel Michael brought the Tsar Michael from Rome to Saint Sophia in Constantinople, and the Tsar defeated the Ishmaelites. Finally Veselovski points out that the episode of the northern peoples Gog and Magog, who in their destructive advance reach Jerusalem, is inserted from the *Life* of Saint Andrew the Simpleton. In the same study Veselovski compares the Emperor Michael with a Russian epic hero (*Bogatyr*), Michael Danilovich.[21]   Michael III did not occur to Veselovski.   The statement that the Emperor in the moment of danger was out of Constantinople suggested to him the Emperor-Liberator Michael VIII Palaeologus, who came to save Constantinople from without.

In the interpolated Slavonic version occurs the name of Michael as the Emperor-Liberator.   We read: 'And then an endless multitude will be destroyed by the Tsar Michael, and others will be driven away like cattle; the pagan Ishmaelites will be humiliated from fear of God, and they will bow before the Tsar Michael saying "We are thy prisoners." . . . Michael's reign will last thirty-three years, as in the days of Noah . . . and the Lord will order Michael to hide himself in a sea island; Michael will go on board of a ship, and God will bring him by wind into a sea island and he will stay there till the fixed day; and God will open the western mountains, which Alexander of Macedon shut up. . . .   And after Michael's reign, for lawlessness of those men, God will open the western mountains, and Gog, Magog, and Aneg (Anak) will spring out of them . . . and men going from the north will start to eat human flesh and drink blood like water. . . .'[22]

Istrin is the first to identify the Michael of the Slavonic interpolated version of the *Revelation* and of some other Russian versions with Michael III.   He writes:

The most widely spread name of the Emperor-Victor, who in some texts appears as the last Tsar, is the name of Michael. . . .   The spread of Michael's name may have been due to some historical fact, and the history of Byzantium may have given foundation for it.   I am inclined to see the first stimulus to the popularity of the name of Michael in the Emperor Michael III, under whom the attack of Askold and Dir on Tsargrad occurred.   Such an event as the siege of Tsargrad by the Russians, which has left its trace in written literature, undoubtedly could not help being reflected in the popular imagination.   Photius' speech serves as a brilliant testimony of the importance of the event.   One may notice some common traits between the historical Tsar Michael and the legendary

---

[21] A. N. Veselovski, '*South-Russian Epics (Byliny)*,' *Supplement (Priložedie)* to vol. xxxix of the *Zapiski* of the Academy of Sciences, no. 5 (St Petersburg, 1881), 3–60; on the *Revelation of Methodius* pp. 9–10.   This study was reprinted with the same pagination in *Sbornik Otdelenija Russkago Jazyka i Slovesnosti of the Academy of Sciences* of St Petersburg, t. xxii, no. 2 (1881).   Both in Russian.

[22] Istrin, *op. cit.*, 1897, iv, 123–126.   The entire text of the interpolated version on pp. 115–131.

Michael. Not to mention the fact that under the Emperor Michael III the domination of the Arabs came to its close, we may observe some details common to the two. According to legend, during the attack of the enemies the Tsar-Victor is hiding himself somewhere, in various versions in various ways; during the attack of Askold and Dir the Emperor Michael was not in the city; he was on an expedition against the Arabs in Cappadocia; and in Greek texts the Tsar will come from the east. In the *Vision* of Andrew the Simpleton the Tsar who will deliver his empire to God in Jerusalem comes out of Arabia. It is not essential that reality did not correspond to legend; to the popular fancy Michael who had concluded a peace, although not a very honorable one, with his enemies, appeared a victor who had delivered the city from barbarians. All the more this fancy might have been strengthened and the people might have looked upon Michael as upon a messenger of God, because the deliverance of Tsargrad from the enemy took place at a solemn church ceremony: the Patriarch carried along the walls of the capital the sacred garment of the Mother of God.'[23]

I am myself not only inclined to share Istrin's speculations but I am absolutely sure that the *Revelation of Methodius of Patara* deals with Michael III and must serve as a new and decisive element in the rehabilitation of the name and brilliant military exploits of that undeservedly degraded emperor, whose vindication has been so energetically and justifiably proclaimed by Grégoire. Of course it is unfortunate that the Greek texts of the *Revelation* which are at present known to us fail to mention Michael's name. But it is not to be forgotten that we have no old Greek texts of the legend; if earlier versions of the legend had come down to us, they might have contained his name; the more so as, according to our best authorities on this question (A. Veselovski and Istrin) the legend of the Tsar Michael came to the Slavs by way of translation from Greek originals.[24]

Finally I wish to add one more detail, which in my opinion may serve as a decisive factor in this question. In the interpolated Slavonic version of the *Revelation*, as I have pointed out above, we read that the Lord commanded Michael to go to a sea island where he would stay till the fixed day (*do rečennago dni*). What is the origin of the story of Michael's going to a sea island? In 'the fixed or appointed day' of the *Revelation* I see the fatal day of Michael's murder. He was assassinated by Basil in the Palace of St Mamas September 24, 867. Now, after S. J. Pargoire's *Study on St Mamas*, we may say that the position of the suburb of St Mamas, where the palace, the church, and a private Imperial hippodrome were located, has been definitely demonstrated: the suburb of St Mamas was situated on the European shore of the Bosphorus, opposite to Scutari,

---

[23] Istrin, *op. cit.*, 1897, II, 182–184.   [24] See Istrin, *op. cit.*, 1897, II, 182, 184, 205.

at the modern Beshik-tash.[24a] But in Greek sources the location of St
Mamas is not exactly fixed, so that in historical literature it has been
located in various places, in Blachernae, on the Propontis, on the Euxine.[25]
Two Greek sources, Theophanes Continuatus and Genesius, place the
church of St Mamas on the Euxine and on the Propontis.[26] Probably in
connection with the indications of Theophanes Continuatus and Genesius
that the church of St Mamas was situated on the sea, on the Euxine or on
the Propontis, the idea of an island made its appearance. We have an
unexpected confirmation of this hypothesis in an Arab chronicle of
Eutyches of Alexandria. Eutyches, or in Arabic Sa'id-ibn-Bitriq, a
physician and historian, who was elected Patriarch of Alexandria in 933,
died in 940. In his brief chronicle, which begins with the creation of the
world, we read the following lines on Michael III and his favorite Basil:
'There was a general whose name was Basil. And (Michael) put him at
the head of all his generals and officials. And one day the Emperor Michael went for recreation to an island which was situated opposite to Constantinople, in the middle of the sea which is called Pontos. And the
General Basil assaulted him and killed him in the church which was in the
island.'[27] If we compare Eutyches' sea island where Michael went for
recreation and was assassinated with the sea island of the *Revelation* into
which our Lord brought him and in which he stayed till the fixed or fatal
day of his violent death, and if we take into account that the sea island in
Eutyches' chronicle was the place of the recreation and death of Michael
III, there is no doubt whatever that Michael of the *Revelation* means
Michael III.

As we know, a part of the apocryphal composition *Daniel's Vision* has
been incorporated in the interpolated Slavonic version of the *Revelation
of Methodius of Patara*. *Daniel's Vision* has come down to us in several
Greek versions and in Slavonic versions as well.[28] Greek versions, like

[24a] S. J. Pargoire, 'Le Saint-Mamas de Constantinople,' *Transactions (Izvestiya)* of the Russian
Archaeological Institute in Constantinople, vol. IX, nos. 1–2 (1904), 302. Pargoire repeats the same
conclusions in his paper read at a meeting of the Russian Archaeological Institute. J. Pargoire,
'St Mamas, le quartier russe de Constantinople,' *Echos d'Orient*, XI (1908), 203–210.

[25] See A. van Millingen, *Byzantine Constantinople* (London, 1899), p. 90: the Hippodrome of St
Mamas was in Blachernae. Millingen gives also other opinions. A. Vogt, *Basile I* (Paris, 1908),
p. 42: St Mamas, on the seashore, on the other side of Constantinople.

[26] *Theoph. Cont.*, p. 197: τὸν ἐν Εὐξείνῳ ἀνεγηρμένον ναὸν τοῦ ἁγίου Μάμαντος. *Genesius*, p. 102: ἐν
τοῖς κατὰ Προποντίδα παλατίοις περιφανέσιν, ἔνθα ναὸς τοῦ μεγαλομάρτυρος Μάμαντος.

[27] *Contextio gemmarum, sive Eutychii Patriarchae Alexandrini Annales*. Interprete Ed. Pocockio
(Oxford, 1658), II, 462. New edition by L. Cheikho, *Eutychii Patriarchae Alexandrini Annales*, II
(Beyrout-Paris, 1909), 67, lines 2–5 (*Corpus Scriptorum Christianorum Orientalium. Scriptores
arabici. Textus. Series tertia, tomi VI et VII*). Pocock's Latin translation is reprinted in Migne,
P. G., CXI, col. 1139. I have given a Russian version of this passage in my book, *Byzantium and the
Arabs during the Macedonian Dynasty* (St Petersburg, 1902), supplement, p. 20.

[28] Texts of *Daniel's Vision* in Istrin, *Chteniya* . . . 1898, I, 133–162.

those of the *Revelation*, fail to give the name of Michael.   One text calls
the Emperor-Liberator who will defeat the Ismaelites, John ('Ιωάννης),
probably John Comnenus, whom four angels will bring to St Sophia and
there crown emperor (p. 137. Mount Athos, Monastery Kutlumush, no.
217).   Three Greek texts mention invasions from the north: in one version we read that 'then will rise the peoples in the north, who never before
waged war' (p. 140. Bodl. Library, *Cod. Barrocianus, no. 145*); the same
manuscript relates that 'a fight will arise from the northern side, and the
people will roam about (περιπατήσει). and the coastland will suffer.'[29]
Then the third version says, 'And after him another emperor from the
north will rise, doing great foulness, much wrong, and great injustice.'[30]
It would be hazardous to conjecture that 'another emperor' (ἕτερος
βασιλεύς) hints at the Russian leader of the expedition on Constantinople,
Askold.   The last Greek version (Paris, Nat. Library, *Fonds grecs, no.
1295*), printed by Istrin (pp. 151–155), deals with the time of Manuel II
Palaeologus and has no relation whatever to this study.

Slavonic versions of *Daniel's Vision* are interesting for us because they
add the name of the Tsar Michael.   His legend has been discussed above.
It is not irrelevant to mention that a South Slavonic version puts *Solun'*
i.e., Salonika or Thessalonica, instead of Tsargrad, as the place where the
Emperor-Liberator, according to legends, was brought by the angels.
Evidently a South Slavonic compiler of this version, applying the prophecies to the Bulgarian Empire, replaced Tsargrad by a name better known
to him,   *Solun'* (Salonika), which had been several times in Bulgarian
hands.[31]   So the Tsar-Victor of Slavonic and Russian legends is the Tsar
Michael III, the last representative of the Amorian dynasty.[32]

Let us turn now to the *Life of Saint Andrew the Simpleton*, one of the
most precious documents for the cultural history of Byzantium, of which
a critical edition is badly needed.[33]   The saint lived in the tenth century,

---

[29] Here is the text (Cod. Barroc. 145): καὶ αὐτὴ (μάχη) ἐκ νοτίου μέρους ἀναφανθήσεται καὶ τὸ ἔθνος
περιπατήσει, καὶ πρὸ τούτου παράλια αὐτῆς οὐαί (Istrin, pp. 142–143).

[30] Bodl. Library, *Cod. Canonicianus, no. 19*, s. XV: καὶ ὀπίσω αὐτὸν ἀναστήσεται ἕτερος βασιλεὺς ἀπὸ
βορρᾶ καὶ ποιῶν ἀκαθαρσίας μεγάλας καὶ ἀδικίας πολλὰς καὶ ἀνομίας μεγάλας (Istrin, p. 147).

[31] Istrin, *op. cit.*, 1897, III, 262.   [32] *Ibid.*, p. 325.

[33] Detailed information on Saint Andrew the Simpleton or the Fool may be found in 'Commentarius
praevius Conr. Janninghi Vitae S. Andreae Sali,' in Migne, *P. G.*, CXI, coll. 621–628 (reprinted from
Acta Sanctorum, Maii die 28, t. VI).   For brief information on Saint Andrew see Archbishop Sergius,
The *Complete Liturgical Calendar (Menologion) of the Orient*, 2d ed. (Vladimir, 1901), II, 2, pp. 409–
410.   A. P. Rudakov, *Outlines in Byzantine Culture Based on Data from Greek Hagiography* (Moscow,
1917), p. 228.   Both in Russian.   On Saint Andrew the Simpleton there are two special studies, one
in Russian, the other in English.   Arch. Sergius' study was printed in the Russian magazine *Strannik*,
Sept.-Dec., 1898, and separately as well.   In English, Sara Murray, *A Study of the Life of Andreas
the Fool for the Sake of Christ*.   Munich Dissertation (Borna: Noske, 1910), pp. 135 and plate 1.
Unfortunately I have not been able to consult these.   But according to Paul Maas' brief review of

and his *Life* was compiled by his confessor, a presbyter of Saint Sophia, Nicephorus.   The former opinion that the saint lived in the fifth century under the Emperor Leo I (457–474) is to be discarded.   The name *Leo* which occurs in the *Life* is that of the Emperor Leo VI (886–912). As I have noted above, A. Veselovski has shown that a part of the *Life of Saint Andrew* has been incorporated in the interpolated Slavonic version of the *Revelation* of Methodius of Patara.   His prophecies are interesting for our study, especially one which, if I am not mistaken, has not been examined, and which unexpectedly gives decisive proof that it deals with the activities of Michael III and his successful fighting against Arabs and Russians.[34]

After saying that towards the end of the world the Lord would raise up an Emperor under whom prosperity would spread among all men, the author of the *Life* relates: 'And after that (the Emperor) will turn his face to the Orient and humiliate the sons of Agar; for the Lord will be irate because of their blasphemy, and because their offspring is bitter like that of Sodom and Gomorrah.   Therefore He will instigate and arouse the Emperor of the Romans against them, and he will annihilate them and will destroy their children by fire; and they, surrendered into his hands, will be given up to the most violent flame.   And Illyricum will be again restored to the Roman Empire, and Egypt will bring its tribute.   And he will put his hand upon the sea and will tame the fair peoples and will abase the enemies under his power; and his empire will last thirty-two years. . . .' [35]

In this passage of prophecy, we absolutely unexpectedly discover two historical facts: the restoration of Illyricum to the Empire, and the payment of tribute by Egypt to the Empire.   In my opinion these two historical facts belong to the period of Michael III.

The province of Illyricum was for long an apple of discord between Byzantium and the Papacy.   This question came to the fore again when Bulgaria was converted to Christianity and Pope Nicholas I, in his claims of the rights of the See of Rome over Illyricum, met such stiff resistance

---

Miss Murray's dissertation, it fails to give much new material, and the eschatological section of the *Life*, which particularly interests us in this study, has not been studied by the author, *Byz. Zeitschrift*, xxi (1912), 317–319.

[34] I use the edition of *Vita S. Andreae Sali* in Migne, *P. G.*, cxi, coll. 627–888. This is a reprint from *Acta Sanctorum, Maii* t. vi, coll. 1–101, supplement.   Some excerpts were published in A. Vasiliev, *Anecdota Graeco-Byzantina* (Moscow, 1893), pp. 50–58.   A complete Slavonic version in the *Collection of the Lives of Saints* by the Metropolitan Macarius, vol. iii, under Oct. 2.

[35] καὶ ἀποκατασταθήσεται πάλιν τὸ Ἰλλυρικὸν τῇ βασιλείᾳ Ῥωμαίων· κομίσει δὲ καὶ ἡ Αἴγυπτος τὰ πάκτα αὐτῆς.   Καὶ θήσει τὴν χεῖρα αὐτοῦ τὴν δεξιὰν ἐπὶ τὴν θάλασσαν, καὶ ἡμερώσει τὰ ξανθὰ γένη, καὶ ταπεινώσει τοὺς ἐχθροὺς ὑπὸ τὰς χεῖρας αὐτοῦ, καὶ τὸ σκῆπτρον αὐτοῦ ἔσται τριάκοντα δύο ἔτη . . . (col. 856).

from Michael III that he was forced to yield.[36] Saint Andrew's prophecy, then, is a repercussion of a historical fact connected with Michael's period.

Saint Andrew's prophecy that Egypt will bring tribute to the Empire is extremely interesting. In my opinion, this refers to the appearance of a Byzantine fleet in 853 before Damietta at the mouth of the Nile, when the city was plundered and burned and its inhabitants hastily fled. Probably six years later a Byzantine fleet reappeared before Damietta and Pelusium (al-Farama).[37] Egypt might well have paid money for deliverance, a sort of ransom. If it is true that these words of Saint Andrew's prophecy refer to the attack of Damietta and Pelusium — and I am certain that it is true — this statement has still greater value because it is the only Greek text which records this important event, all our information of the attack coming from Arabic sources which fail to mention any tribute paid to the Empire.

Since the words of Saint Andrew's prophecy have now been definitely attributed to Michael's time, the mention of 'fair peoples' (τὰ ξανθὰ γένη) whom he will 'tame' or vanquish may refer simply to the Russian attack of 860.[38]

I have devoted much space to the personality of Michael III; but it is high time now to show that our common stereotyped opinion of him and his activities should be reconsidered. It is not often that an emperor's activities leave so deep a trace in popular tradition as those of Michael III against the eastern Arabs, and — I may now say — against the Russians. Sharing Uspenski and Grégoire's speculations in general, I cannot go so far as Grégoire does in characterizing Michael as a genius. He was assassinated in 867 at the age of twenty-eight (he was born in 839), still quite a young man, who had not had time enough to develop and display whatever talents he may have had. He certainly possessed some highly undesirable qualities which have come down to us in the

---

[36] See a very clear presentation of the question in Fr. Dvorník, 'La lutte entre Byzance et Rome à propos de l'Illyricum au ixe siècle,' *Mélanges Charles Diehl*, ɪ (Paris, 1930), pp. 61–80; especially pp. 64–65. Also *idem, Les légendes de Constantin et de Méthode vues de Byzance* (Prague, 1933), pp. 265–267. The question of Illyricum had its continuation after the death of Michael III and Pope Nicholas I, and under Basil I in 870 Pope Hadrian II had a new rebuff. Dvorník, *op. cit.*, p. 269.

[37] See above, p. 56, where the sources of our information on these facts are given.

[38] It would not be irrelevant to mention here a curious translation of the Greek words τὰ ξανθὰ γένη or τὰ ξανθὰ μέρη in some Slavonic versions of apocryphal Greek texts. The Russian equivalent of the Greek adjective ξανθός is *rusy*, and later, probably in the seventeenth century, under the influence of political propaganda, the adjective *rusy* became *Russian*, and τὰ ξανθὰ γένη the *Russian peoples* (Russian *rody*). In some Slavonic versions instead of *rusye rody* (τὰ ξανθὰ γένη) we find *rusyje brady*, i.e., *blond beards*, as a result of confusion of the Greek word τὸ γένος = *race, people*, with τὸ γένειον = *beard*. See Istrin, *Chteniya*, . . . 1897, ɪɪɪ, p. 267, 325.

purposely distorted and exaggerated Macedonian tradition, which doubt-less was irreconcilably hostile to the memory of the last representative of the Amorian dynasty. But it must have had some foundation in fact, and it is clear that the imperial youth indulged himself to excess in his pleasures and dissipations, which after all is not unnatural for a young man invested with absolute power. But he had energy and initiative; and in addition — and this is probably more important — he managed to choose and keep near him very talented advisers and collaborators, like his uncle Bardas, his general Petronas, who was the hero of the de-cisive victory at Poson in 863, some other generals, and last but not least the powerful imposing figure of the Patriarch Photius. In popular tradition, in epic and in apocryphal writings, Michael's advisers and collaborators have vanished, and his own personality is the center around which are concentrated his military successes against the eastern Arabs and Russians.

THE PATRIARCH PHOTIUS

ALONG with the three personalities who played an important part in the event of 860, Michael III, his uncle Bardas, and his favorite and the future emperor Basil, stood a fourth who greatly influenced the Emperor and the masses of the people, and who took one of the most decisive parts in 860. This was the commanding figure of the Patriarch Photius.

In 860 Photius was about sixty years of age. Layman, erudite, writer, diplomat, strictly Orthodox, he was tonsured on December 20, 858, and five days later, on Christmas, was already raised to the highest dignity of the Church, that of Bishop, and became Patriarch of Constantinople.[1] In June 860, when the Russian attack took place, he was in the second year of his patriarchate and he displayed the first manifestation in the new office of his energetic effectiveness and acute skill in managing a dangerous situation. So in 860 Michael III was supported by two eminent officials, Bardas and Photius, and for the time being behind the scenes by the protostrator Basil.

[1] We are surprisingly ill informed on the chronology of Photius' life. According to Papadopoulos-Kerameus, Photius died in exile on February 6, 897, almost a centenarian, so that he was born about 800. Papadopoulos-Kerameus, Ὁ πατριάρχης Φώτιος ὡς πατὴρ ἅγιος τῆς Ὀρθοδόξου Καθολικῆς Ἐκκλησίας, *Byz. Zeitschrift*, VIII (1899), 650. Hergenröther, *Photius*, I (Regensburg, 1867), 315, thought that Photius' birthday should be set 'not after the year 827.' E. Amann writes that Photius was born in the first quarter of the ninth century, *Dictionnaire de theologie catholique*, XII, 2, col. 1537. According to Aristarkhes, Photius was born about 810. Τοῦ ἐν ἁγίοις πατρὸς ἡμῶν Φωτίου . . . Λόγοι καὶ Ὁμιλίαι, ed. by Σ. Ἀριστάρχης, I (Constantinople, 1900), p. γ(3).

THE PROPHET EZEKIEL AND THE RUSSIANS

FROM the first clash with the Russians, Byzantine writers have described them as an exceedingly cruel and ferocious people who devastated the Empire from the north. To represent their cruelty and ferocity in a more drastic form, several writers referred to Biblical texts from the Old Testament, and used their descriptions of some devastating campaigns from the north which had happened many centuries before our era. These descriptions to some extent lose in vividness and historical reality and become rather commonplace. But the essential fact remains clear: in the opinion of Byzantine writers and in the eyes of the people, the Russian invaders were cruel and ferocious.

In the first homily delivered by Photius during the Russian raid, the Patriarch, in order to represent more effectively the ferocity and savagery of the invaders, among other Biblical texts used freely the *Book of Jeremiah* and his *Lamentations* (θρῆνος), particularly those chapters and paragraphs where the Prophet describes a barbarian invasion 'from the north' and 'from the outermost part of the earth.'[1]

Another Biblical tradition has been used by Byzantine writers in connection with Russian incursions. This deals with the fabulous destructive peoples of Gog and Magog, whom, according to legendary sources, Alexander the Great enclosed somewhere in the Caucasian mountains. Scholars have tried many times to locate these two peoples. As the geographical horizon widened, Magog was placed north of the Caucasus. The Prophet Ezekiel gives his famous description of a devastating invasion from the north by Gog and Magog, saying: 'And the word of the Lord came unto me, saying, Son of man, set thy face toward Gog and the land of Magog, the prince of Rosh, Meshech, and Jubal. . . . And thou (Gog) shalt come from the place out of the uttermost parts of the north, thou and many peoples with thee, all of them riding upon horses, a great company and a mighty army . . . and every wall shall fall to the ground.'[2] Ezekiel's description of the invasion of Gog is probably an echo of the incursion of the Scythians, who descended by way of the pass of Derbend under the King of Assyria, Esar-Haddon (681–668 B.C.). Their inroads were so devastating that their victims believed that the end of the world was at hand. The term *Gog and Magog* has therefore become synonymous with barbarian, especially with the type of bar-

---

[1] Jeremiah, VI, 22. I use *The Old Testament in Greek according to the Septuagint*, ed. by H. B. Swete, III (Cambridge, 1912), 237.

[2] Ezekiel, XXXVIII, 1–2; 15; 20. In Greek: ἐπὶ Γὼγ καὶ τὴν γῆν τοῦ Μαγώγ, ἄρχοντα ῾Ρώς, Μέσοχ, καὶ Θοβέλ; see also XXXVIII, 3: ἐγὼ ἐπὶ ἄρχοντα ῾Ρώς, Μέσοχ, καὶ Θοβέλ; also XXXIX, 1: ἰδοὺ ἐγὼ ἐπὶ σὲ Γώγ, ἄρχοντα ῾Ρώς, Μέσοχ, καὶ Θοβέλ.

barian that burst through the northern frontier of civilization. When later the barbarian invasions breached the frontiers of the Roman Empire, Jews and Christians were prepared to recognize as Magog the Scythian hordes invading from the north.[3]

This was not the first time Ezekiel's prophecy was used in Byzantium to demonstrate the savagery and cruelty of invading barbarians. In the first half of the fifth century, under Theodosius II, the Hunnic troops of Roila, Attila's uncle, had invaded Thrace. The Empire was freed from danger by Roila's sudden death. In commemoration of this event the Patriarch of Constantinople, Proclus (434–437), preached a sermon in which he recalled Ezekiel's prophecy naming Gog, Ros, Misokh, and Thobel.[4]

Recently Professor G. Vernadsky, in accordance with his debatable theory of the southern origin of the ethnic term *Ros* or *Rus*, mentions Proclus' sermon and says: 'It is just possible that Proclus was induced to think of the biblical Rosh by the presence of the Ros or Rus (Rukhs-As) in Roila's army. In that case his sermon would contain the first mention of the Aso-Slavic Ros (Rus) in Byzantine literature.'[5]

In connection with the Russian attack of 860 and the subsequent wars between Byzantium and Russia, Ezekiel's prophecy reappears in Byzantine literature. 'It is quite possible that the biblical name of Rosh was first applied to the Russians in connection with their invasion in 860.'[6]

I have enlarged on Ezekiel's Book and recent interpretations of its reference to Gog and Magog because at the end of the tenth century the Byzantine historian Leo the Deacon, referring to Ezekiel's statements, identified the chief Ros (Rosh) with the name of the Russians, Ros ('Ρώς). Dealing with the wars of the Russian prince Svyatoslav against the

---

[3] A. R. Anderson, *Alexander's Gate, Gog and Magog, and the Inclosed Nations* (Cambridge, Massachusetts, 1932), pp. 7–9.

[4] Socratis *Hist. Eccl.* VII, 43 (Migne, *P. G.*, LXVII, col. 833). From him Nicephorus Callistus, *Eccl. Hist.*, XIV, 38 (Migne, *P. G.*, CXLVI, 1188). Theodoreti *Eccl. Hist.*, V, 36 (Migne, *P. G.*, LXXXII, coll. 1268–1269). Theodoretus recounts Roila's invasion, but fails to mention Proclus' sermon. Unfortunately this sermon has not survived. See Proclus' five sermons in Migne, *P. G.*, LXV, coll. 833–850. In coll. 887–888 there is a mention of Proclus' sermon on the Hunnic invasion, with references to Ezekiel, XXXVIII, 2, and Socrates, VII, 43. There are several sermons of Proclus in Syriac versions, which have not come down to us in their original Greek; but among them Proclus' sermon on the Hunnic invasion is not to be found. See J.-B. Chabot, *Littérature syriaque* (Paris, 1934), pp. 149–150. Also A. Baumstark, *Geschichte der syrischen Literatur* (Bonn, 1922), pp. 61–62. The best account of Proclus is in O. Bardenhewer, *Geschichte der altkirchlichen Literatur*, IV (Freiburg im Breisgau, 1924), pp. 202–208. Bardenhewer fails to mention the sermon of Proclus we are considering.

[5] G. Vernadsky, *Ancient Russia* (New Haven, 1943), p. 139. His notes, 50, 51, and 52, on p. 138, are subject to some corrections and change of order.

[6] Vl. Parkhomenko, *At the sources of Russian Statehood* (*U istokov russkoy gosudarstvennosti*) (Leningrad, 1924), pp. 55–56. Compare the preceding note.

Byzantines and Tauroscythians, he wrote, 'Many testify that the people (Russians) are desperate, warlike and strong, who fight all their neighbors; and the divine Ezekiel mentions them when speaking thus: "Behold, I bring against thee Gog and Magog, the Ros chief." '[7]   We need not concern ourselves because many versions of Ezekiel's text fail to contain the word *Ros* (*Rosh*) as a proper name, but instead emphasize more effectively the idea of *chief* or *prince*, like ἄρχων κεφαλῆς, *princeps capitis, der oberste Fürst, the chief prince, etc.*[8]   We are interested to observe, however, that in Byzantium at the end of the tenth century Leo the Deacon took the proper name Ros-'Ρώς from the Greek version of Ezekiel's book according to the Septuagint, and identified it with the Russians, who at his time were also known in Byzantium as Tauroscythians.   It may not be irrelevant to mention here that the tradition of the connection of the Russians, Ros, with the fabulous peoples of Gog and Magog, who were subjects to the prince of Rosh-Ros and of whom the Prophet Ezekiel speaks, appears later in Poland, whence it passes into Russia, where the *Gustinskaya Letopis* (*Chronicle*) and some other sources repeat it.[9]   Many years ago Kunik wrote that Leo the Deacon, whom he calls, probably by misprint, Johannes-Diaconus, was convinced that the Tauroscythians or Russians — 'Ρώς were identical with the Biblical Rôs, and thought that Ezekiel's prophecy concerning Γὼγ καὶ Μαγὼγ ἄρχων 'Ρώς had already been fulfilled.[10]

Thus references to biblical texts were made by some Byzantine writers in order to emphasize more drastically the cruelty, savagery, and destructive power of the Russian invaders.   These particular traits of the Russians of that time have been corroborated by Photius, as well as by some other sources which make no use of any book of the Old Testament.

---

[7] Leo Diaconus, IX, 6 (p. 150): ὅτι δὲ τὸ ἔθνος ἀπονενοημένον, καὶ μάχιμον, καὶ κραταιὸν, πᾶσι τοῖς ὁμόροις ἐπιτιθέμενον ἔθνεσι, μαρτυροῦσι πολλοί, καὶ ὁ θεῖος δὲ Ἰεζεκιὴλ μνήμην τούτου ποιούμενος ἐν οἷς ταῦτά φησιν " Ἰδοὺ, ἐγὼ ἐπάγω ἐπὶ σὲ τὸν Γὼγ καὶ Μαγὼγ, ἄρχοντα 'Ρώς."

[8] See A. Florovski, ' "Prince Rosh" with the Prophet Ezekiel' (ch. 38–39), Essays (*Sbornik*) in honor of V. N. Zlatarski (Sofia, 1925), pp. 506–507.   M. Syuzyumov, 'On the question of the origin of the word 'Ρώς, 'Ρωσία,' *Rossiya, Vestnik Drevnei Istorii*, II (1940), 121–123.   Both in Russian. They fail to mention Proclus' sermon.   Marquart, *Osteuropäische und ostasiatische Streifzüge* (Leipzig, 1903), p. 355, n. 3.

[9] See V. Mošin, 'Varyago-Russki vopros' (*The Varangian-Russian Question*), *Slavia*, x (Prague, 1931), 119; 524 (in Russian).

[10] Dorn, *Caspia. Mémoires de l'Académie des sciences de Saint-Pétersbourg*, VIIᵉ série, XXIII (1877), 404, n. 11 a (German edition).   A Russian writer, M. Syuzyumov, remarks that this interpretation of Ezekiel's words by Leo the Deacon is not his orgiinal conclusion; and here Syuzyumov refers to the oldest Greek commentary on the Apocalypse, written by Arethas, the archbishop of Caesarea, in the early part of the tenth century.   The text correctly given by Syuzyumov runs as follows: Εἶναι δὲ τὸν Γὼγ καὶ τὸν Μαγὼγ τινὲς μὲν Σκυθικὰ ἔθνη νομίζουσιν ὑπερβόρεια (Migne, *P. G.*, CVI, p. 416 B).   M. Syuzyumov, 'On the Sources of Leo the Deacon and Scylitzes,' *Vizantiskoe Obozrenie*, II (Yuryev, 1916), 166, n. 2 (in Russian).   But, as we see, Arethas fails to give the name of Ros — 'Ρώς — and mentions some Scythian peoples' only.

WHENCE DID THE RUSSIANS ATTACK
CONSTANTINOPLE IN 860?

A SEEMINGLY debatable question has been many times discussed and variously answered; whence did the Russians who
raided Constantinople in 860 come; from Kiev, after having sailed down
the Dnieper to its mouth, or from the Tauric Peninsula, the Crimea?
In the latter case we have to reckon, often reluctantly, with the 'mysterious' Russia called the Black Sea Rus (*Chernomorskaya Rus'*), which
the Russian annals usually mention in connection with the principality
of Tmutorokan.[1]   But this term when applied to the ninth century is
very vague; it rather obscures than throws light upon the subject.

It would be absolutely out of place to give here a complete picture of
the development of this question in literature; such a picture would give
us an endless list of names of authors and titles of studies.   Here I wish
to indicate only the most important and very often the most recent studies
which, in my opinion, may be useful for the reader of this book.

Many historians who deal with the first Russian attack on Constantinople fail to treat the question whence the invaders came.   Other historians favor the opinion that the invaders were the Russians of Kiev
who descended the Dnieper.[2]   But there is still an amazingly great number of historians who believe that the attack of 860 was made by the
Russians from the Tauric Peninsula.   And among the historians who try
to define these Russians, Golubinski, in the second corrected and augmented edition of his *History of the Russian Church* (1901), after having
defined the year 860 or the very beginning of 861 as the date of the
Russian attack, writes, 'If it is so, Askold and Dir not only could not attack Constantinople, but they had not yet come into Russia. . . .   It is
difficult to admit that the unknown Russians, who besieged Constantinople in the reign of Michael III and afterwards adopted Christianity,
were our Kievan Russians, under the leadership of Askold and Dir. . . .
Almost certainly we think that by these Russians are meant the Azovo-
Tauric or Azovo-Crimean Russians.'   Then, a little further on, Golu-

---

[1] Brutzkus has recently written that the Khazars employed Swedish warriors for the sea raid upon
Byzantium in 860.   Y. Brutzkus, 'The Khazars and the Kievan Rus,' in the Russian magazine of
New York City, *Novoselye*, no. 6 (1943), p. 79.

[2] Among many older historians see for example, V. Lamanski, *The Slavonic Life of St Cyril as a
Religious and Epic Work as well as an Historical Source* (Petrograd, 1915), pp. 47–48; 58–59 (in
Russian).   Among recent historians, F. Dvorník, *Les légendes de Constantin et de Méthode vues de
Byzance* (Prague, 1933), p. 179.   N. de Baumgarten, 'Aux origines de la Russie,' *Orientalia Christiana
Analecta*, no. 119 (Rome, 1939), 9.   A. Shakhmatov, *Outline of the Oldest Period of the History of the
Russian Language* (Petrograd, 1915), p. xxx (*Encyclopaedia of Slavic Philology* under v. Jagić, 11, 1).

binski says, 'The question of the Russians who attacked Constantinople under Michael III and afterwards adopted Christianity, remains unsolved; and that they were our Kievan Russians under the princes Askold and Dir is very doubtful, or better, totally incredible.'[3] Who were these Azovo-Tauric or Azovo-Crimean Russians? According to Golubinski, they were the Normans who had appeared and settled on the shores of the Black Sea in the Crimea, in the first half of the ninth century, before the establishment of the Normans in Kiev and Novgorod; in the Crimea the Normans became mixed with the remnants of the Crimean Goths. These Gotho-Normans attacked Constantinople in 860.[4]

In 1889, when the first edition of his study on the *Life of Stephen of Surozh* came out, Vasilievski thought that in the first half of the ninth century the Normans had not yet reached the shores of the Black Sea and believed that the Russians who were raiding the Black Sea down to the middle of that century were the Black Sea Russians, the Tauroscythians; and he regarded this people as a mixture of Goths and Taurians, i.e., the Alans, in other words he identified them with the Valangoths or Valagoths who are mentioned in some earlier sources.[5] Vasilievski's speculations are obscure, arbitrary, and, as far as the ninth century is concerned, devoid of historical ground. The time when in the third century A.D. the Goths took possession of the fleet of the Bosporan Kingdom and raided not only the shores of the Black Sea but also the coasts of the Propontis (the Sea of Marmora) and the islands and coasts of the Aegean and even Mediterranean, belonged to the remote past. In the ninth century the Goths in the Crimea, a minority group, were living under quite different conditions, and the two other powers, Byzantium and the Khazars, were playing predominant parts. So the hypothesis that the Crimean Goths played a leading role in the attack of 860 is to to be entirely eliminated.[6] As we have seen, Golubinski in his own speculations on the same subject is much more cautious than Vasilievski, admitting some mixture of Normans with Crimean Goths.

It seemed at the beginning of the twentieth century that the theory

---

[3] E. Golubinski, *History of the Russian Church*, I, 1 (Moscow, 1901), pp. 40, 41, 42, 45 (2d edition) The first edition came out in 1880, and in it the author expresses the same ideas.

[4] Concerning Golubinski's theory Miss Polonskaya writes, 'Golubinsky, who transferred the Varangians to the shores of the Sea of Azov, where, according to his own admission, nobody found them, but where they must have been'; N. Polonskaya, 'On the Question of Christianity in Russia before Vladimir,' *Journal of the Ministry of Public Instruction*, 1917, September, p. 76.

[5] Vasilievski, *Works*, III, pp. CCLXXX–CCLXXXII (in Russian).

[6] In connection with Vasilievski's theory, Miss Polonskaya remarks that of all his speculations only one is convincing: it was not the Kievan Ros who attacked Tsargrad. Polonskaya, *op. cit.*, p. 52. Polonskaya gives names of some scholars who held the same point of view before Vasilievski.

of the existence of the Black Sea or Tmutorokan Rus received a decisive blow.   In 1908 a Russian scholar, F. Westberg, in Riga, wrote of
the 'legendary Black Sea Rus,' of 'the legend which had been created by
historians in the second half of the nineteenth century'; he asserted that
'the hypothesis of the Black Sea Rus has done great harm to Russian
science,' and he expressed the hope of 'having done away with it for
ever,' and having proved its 'entirely chimerical character.'[7]   Another
Russian scholar, Th. Uspenski, after having examined Westberg's conclusions when they were still in manuscript form, declared that they
would henceforth be 'binding on anyone who worked on the events of the
ninth century.'[8]   So according to Westberg and Uspenski the so-called
Black Sea Rus (*Chernomorskaya Rus'*) is to be eliminated from the history
of ancient Russia.

But these conclusions are not convincing at all points.   The theory
that the Black Sea Rus carried out the attack of 860 has still a number
of adherents.   In 1913 Parkhomenko wrote: 'The incursions of Rus on
Surozh, Amastris, and Constantinople, more naturally and more appro-
priately from an historical and geographical standpoint, are to be attributed to maritime Russia, whose representatives only could have
reached such virtuosity in sea affairs, obtained such renown on the Black
Sea, and felt themselves the masters of the situation.   Such a role, especially early in the ninth century, was absolutely beyond the strength
of the Dnieper Russia, which was undoubtedly situated far from the
Black Sea and separated from it by such barriers as the steppes populated
by nomads and the Dnieper rapids; there is no use in even mentioning
more northern tribes.'   In another passage Parkhomenko remarks,
'We have no solid grounds at our disposal to attribute the attack of 860
to Askold and Dir, although, following the Russian annals, some scholars
accept this.'[9]   In 1917 Miss Polonskaya who, like Parkhomenko and
some older writers, regards the Black Sea Rus as Slavs, also is inclined
to believe that they attacked Tsargrad in 860.[10]   Most recently, in
many interesting studies, Mošin, following and enlarging upon Golubinski's speculations, also stresses the idea that the Russian attack of

[7] F. Westberg, 'On the Analysis of Oriental Sources on Eastern Europe,' *Journal of the Ministry
of Public Instruction*, 1908, March, p. 28.   *Idem*, 'The Report (Zapiska) of a Gothic Toparch,' *Viz.
Vremennik*, xv (1908), 227, 248, 250.   *Idem*, 'On the Life of Stephen of Surozh,' *ibid.*, xiv (1907),
234.   All in Russian.

[8] Th. Uspenski, in his review of Westberg's studies.   *Zapiski (Mémoires) of the Academy of Sciences
of St Petersburg*, 1904, no. 7, p. 257 (in Russian).

[9] V. Parkhomenko, *The Origin of Christianity in Russia* (Poltava, 1913), pp. 51–52, 63; also pp.
16–18, 68.   Parkhomenko regards the Black Sea Russians as Slavs.

[10] N. Polonskaya, 'On the Question of Christianity in Russia before Vladimir,' *Journal of the
Ministry of Public Instruction*, 1917, September, 50–51, 58, 77–78 (in Russian).

860 was made by the Black Sea or Tmutorokan Russians.[11]   Finally, in 1940–1941, Vernadsky attributes all the references to the Russians in Byzantium, beginning with 839, to the Tmutorokan Russians.   He writes: 'It is apparently from there (Tmutorokan) that the Russian envoys came, via Constantinople, to the court of the Emperor Lewis in 839 A.D.   It is likewise from there that the Russians set forth for their raids on Sugdaia, at the end of the eighth, or the beginning of the ninth century; on Amastris some time before 842; and on Constantinople in 860.'[12]   In 1940 Ostrogorski considers the starting point from which the Russians attacked Constantinople in 860 unsolved, whether Kiev or Tmutorokan.[13]

Very recently in 1943 G. Vernadsky, in his conscientious and stimulating volume on Ancient Russia, gives a new scheme of the Russian expedition in 860, very ingenious but too artificial to be accepted. He deviates from his former speculation that the expedition was undertaken exclusively by the Tmutorokan Russians, and tries to combine the activities of the Russian Khaganate of Tmutorokan with those of the Russian Khaganate of Kiev.   I give here Vernadsky's own words: 'It is not known what route the Russians chose to bring their fleet from the Cimmerian Bosporus (Kerch Strait) to the Thracian Bosporus (Bosporus Strait).   It seems certain that the Byzantines were caught unawares, having no intelligence of the advance of the Russians until Russian boats appeared at the Strait of Bosporus.   On the other hand it seems equally certain that the Byzantine navy must have kept watch over both the Crimean coast line and the shore of Asia Minor to prevent any Russian activities, especially after the Russian raid on Amastris in 840.   We may think therefore that the Russians appeared from a quarter in which the Byzantines never expected them.   They may have used the roundabout way through the Sea of Azov and northern Tauria to the mouth of the Dnieper; that is, crossing first the Sea of Azov to its northern shore, then going up the river Berda and down the river Konskaya, a tributary of the Dnieper.   Quite possibly it was in the lagoon formed by the Konskaya's approach to the Dnieper, below the present town of Zaporozhie, that the expeditionary force of the Russian Khaganate joined the unit of Askold and Dir coming from Kiev.   The joint flotilla of Russian boats must then have sailed down the Konskaya and

[11] V. Mošin, 'Essay on the First Conversion of Russia,' in the Serbian magazine *Bogoslovye*, v, 2 (Belgrad, 1930), 128–131 (in Serbian).   *Idem*, 'Varyago-Russian Problem,' *Slavia*, x (Prague, 1931), 131–132, 375, 516, 524.   *Idem*, 'The Origin of Russia.   The Normans in Eastern Europe,' *Byzantinoslavica*, iii (Prague, 1931), 295–296 (from the peninsula Taman).   *Idem*, 'Nicholas, Bishop of Tmutorokan,' *Seminarium Kondakovianum*, v (Prague, 1932), 48.   Last three studies in Russian.

[12] G. Vernadsky, 'Byzantium and Southern Russia,' *Byzantium*, xv (1940–1941), 73.

[13] G. Ostrogorsky, *Geschichte des Byzantinischen Staates* (Munich, 1940), p. 159, n. 3.

lower Dnieper to the Black Sea and crossed it directly south to the Bosporus.'[14]   In another place Vernadsky writes: 'with regard to the campaign we cannot think that Askold and Dir had a large enough army to undertake it by themselves. . . .   Only from the Russian Khaganate in the Tmutorokan area can assistance have been expected.   The campaign must have been, then, a joint undertaking of the Russian Khagan and of Askold and Dir.   Probably the Tmutorokan Khagan took the initiative in this matter.'[15]

I welcome Vernadsky's new approach to the question of the attack of 860 in admitting the participation of the Kievan Russians under Askold and Dir.   But I cannot accept his roundabout route for the southern Russians from Tmutorokan to the mouth of the Dnieper along the northern coast of the Sea of Azov and then by several small rivers. I repeat: this scheme is ingenious but unfounded.   It is perfectly true that the Byzantines were caught unawares, and I am certain that the enemy flotilla could not have passed by the southern coast of the Tauric Peninsula without being noticed by the Byzantine authorities at Cherson (Chersonesus), which belonged to the Empire.   But we have no positive evidence whatever for the roundabout route suggested by Vernadsky.

In my opinion the raid of 860 could not have been undertaken from the Tauric or from the Taman Peninsula.   It was not only a raid on a large scale; it was a real expedition.   According to our sources, the Russians had two hundred vessels.   A military undertaking of such large size must have been carefully prepared for a considerable span of time. If we take into consideration the situation in the Tauric Peninsula by the middle of the ninth century, we shall see at once that such a military enterprise as the attack of 860 could not have been organized in the Peninsula or in its vicinity.   Cherson and the neighboring region in the western part of the Peninsula belonged to the Byzantine Empire, who kept there a garrison under the command of a governor (*strategos*) who was at the head of the new Chersonesian *theme*, which had been established in the first half of the ninth century, under the Emperor Theophilus (829–842).[16]   Throughout the ninth century in the eastern part of the Peninsula the strong Khazar element predominated and friendly relations between the Empire and Khazaria continued to exist.   For that epoch we may call them two friendly governments.   Only at the opening of the tenth century did the period of Khazar predominance in the Crimea come to a close.   In the middle of the ninth century the

[14] G. Vernadsky, *Ancient Russia* (New Haven, 1943), pp. 343–344.

[15] Vernadsky, *op. cit.*, p. 342.

[16] See J. B. Bury, *A History of the Eastern Roman Empire* (London, 1912), pp. 416–417.   A. Vasiliev, *The Goths in the Crimea* (Cambridge, Massachusetts, 1936), pp. 108–109.

the so-called Crimean Goths with their center at Doros were so numerically small that they depended now upon Byzantium, now upon Khazaria, and they could not have taken any active part in the general policy of that epoch.   It is obvious that organization for such an undertaking as the expedition of 860 was quite impossible.   It is incredible that an expedition hostile to the Empire was equipped and launched under the eyes of the *strategos* of the Chersonesian *theme* and Khazar authorities friendly to the Empire.   There is no serious ground whatever for believing that the expedition of 860 might have been organized and carried out from the Tauric Peninsula.[17]

Then once more we have to keep in mind the very well known words from Photius' *Encyclical Letter*, which clearly reflect the process of gradual conquest of Slavonic tribes by the Scandinavian Russians around Kiev. Photius writes, 'The so-called Ros, after subjugating their neighboring tribes and becoming boundlessly proud and bold, rose against the Roman Empire.'[18]

And last but not least, the tradition which has been preserved in the Russian chronicles that the Russian leaders, Askold and Dir, undertook the expedition from Kiev, cannot be entirely discarded; this tradition reflects an historical fact, and is in no way a pure invention of the chronicler.   That this tradition does not appear in Byzantine chronicles proves nothing.   The names of the Russian leaders might naturally have easily escaped the attention of Byzantine writers.

The Russians, then, attacked Constantinople in 860, sailing from the estuary of the Dnieper, where they had come from Kiev.   They were mostly Swedes, in other words Normans, who undoubtedly had brought south with them some Slavs, several tribes of whom they had conquered in their onrush southwards.[19]

It is true that in their advance south certain groups of Normans reached the south of present-day Russia, including the Tauric Peninsula, before 860.   In this case their route was always along the Dnieper.   It is not to be forgotten that this river flows not straight south from Kiev, but

---

[17] The Russian Principality of Tmutorokan appeared much later at the end of the tenth and the beginning of the eleventh century, when general conditions in the Crimea and the Taman Peninsula had entirely changed.

[18] Τοῦτο δὲ τὸ καλούμενον τὸ 'Ρῶς, οἱ δὴ καὶ κατὰ τῆς 'Ρωμαϊκῆς ἀρχῆς τοὺς πέριξ αὐτῶν δουλωσάμενοι, κἀκεῖθεν ὑπέρογκα φρονιματισθέντες χεῖρας ἀντῆραν.   Migne, *P. G.*, CII, coll. 736–737, epistola 13 (from the old edition of *Photii Epistolae*, ed. Montakutius, London, 1651, p. 58, ep. 2).   Φωτίου 'Επιστολαί, ed. Valetta (London, 1864), p. 178, ep. 4.

[19] I merely mention here the speculations, of a Norwegian writer, E. Kvalen, who tries to prove that Norwegians, not Swedes, several times attempted to conquer Constantinople; he is endeavoring to eliminate the theory of any considerable Swedish activity in the Scandinavian enterprises east of Scandinavia.   E. Kválen, *The Early Norwegian Settlements on the Volga* (Vienna, 1937), p. 6; 22; 45, n. 1: 'Hroerekr (Rurik) in Holmgardr was a Norwegian chief.'

south-east, making a vast bend; and the eastern end of this bend goes a little south, to turn then southwest to reach its estuary.   So the south of present-day Russia, east of the Dnieper, was quite close and accessible to the Russian Normans who might have infiltrated into those regions, of course when general conditions in the steppes allowed such an advance. On the other hand it is not to be overlooked that the Normans before 860 might have reached the south of present-day Russia not only from the north-west but also from the north-east, through relations, mostly commercial, with the east and southeast, down the Volga and the Don.

But such an infiltration of Norman elements into the south of present-day Russia before 860 fails to change the general picture.   They were not sufficiently well organized to be able to equip and carry out a military expedition against the Empire.   Such an idea had never occurred to them.   Only a very well organized state could have thought out and executed such a daring attempt, and Kiev was at that time such a state.

NOTE ON THE NAME RUS IN THE SOUTH OF PRESENT-DAY RUSSIA

IT WOULD be beyond my capacities to discuss here the extremely important, interesting, and tantalizing question of the existence of the name of *Rus*, in one or another form, in the south of present-day day Russia from time immemorial. The question is complicated and has not yet been sufficiently investigated. The best presentation of it is now to be found in Vernadsky's recent book *Ancient Russia*, in which the author thinks it probable (p. 76) that the name *Rus* itself is derived from some Alanic clans known as the Rukhs-As (the Light As). Of course this is a stimulating hypothesis, which for the time being is not capable of proof. But the fact is that in South Russia and in the Caucasian regions, north and south of the central range, there are many geographical names, some ethnic terms, and some personal proper names as well, which contain the name of *Rus, Rush, Ros, Rosh*. For geographical names see, for instance, the old but still very valuable study of S. Gedeonov, *Varangians and Rus*, II (St Petersburg, 1876), 420–422; E. Golubinski, *History of the Russian Church*, 2d ed., I, 1 (Moscow, 1901), 42–43; and among recent writers, Brim, 'The Origin of the term Rus, Russia and the West,' *Rossiya i Zapad*, I (Petrograd, 1923), 9. On ethnic terms and personal names see, for example, N. Marr, 'An Inscription of Sardur II, son of Argishti,' *Zapiski of the Caucasian Museum*, series B-I (St Petersburg, 1919), 9–10, 14–15 (a tribe *Ras*). *Idem*, 'An Inscription of Rusa II from Maku,' *Zapiski of the Oriental Section of the Russian Archaeological Society*, XXV (1921), 26 (town *Rusa*); 28 (town of *Rusa-Rusy*); 49 (in the text of the inscription — town of *Rusa* or a small town of *Rusa*). I. Meshchaninov, 'Concerning the Inscription of Rusa, son of Argishti, at Maku,' *ibid.*, p. 258, n. 1 (in the dynasty of the kings of the Kingdom of Van there were three *Rusas*); 266 (not a town *Rusa*, but a town of the King *Rusa*); 267. All these publications are written in Russian. The last four studies are not mentioned in Vernadsky's book.

ASKOLD AND DIR

WITH the attack of 860 are closely connected two Russian leaders bearing Scandinavian names, Askold[1] and Dir. These names are not given in Byzantine sources, but have been preserved in old Russian tradition. But the name of Dir has probably survived in the Arab geographer of the tenth century, Masudi, who during his distant journeys in the East visited the countries around the Caspian Sea and compiled his great work *The Golden Meadows*. In chapter xxxiv of this work we have the following passage: 'The first among the kings of the Slavs is the King al-Dir, who possesses vast cities and many cultivated lands. Muhammedan merchants go to his capital with various kinds of merchandise.'[2] It is very tempting to see in Masudi's passage the name of Dir. But we must admit that there are some doubts as to the definite form of the name, because in the manuscripts of Masudi's work, this name has several variants — *Dir, Aldir, Din, Aldin*. But if we take into consideration that the prefix *Al* is merely the Arab definite article, we see that the variants differ only in the final letter *r* or *n*; and these two letters may be easily confused in Arab manuscripts.[3] Then some scholars try to discredit Masudi's evidence by pointing out that he lived in the tenth century and was therefore not contemporary with the Prince Dir, but that he regarded Dir as his contemporary.[4] But according to peculiarities of the Arab language, the phrase which we are interested in may be translated in either of two ways: 'The first among the Kings of the Slavs *is* the King al-Dir' or 'The first among the Kings of the Slavs *was* the King al-Dir.' Since Masudi speaks of al-Dir as the *first* king, I am inclined to believe that he refers him to a time before his own.[5] So in

---

[1] Brutzkus writes that the name of Askold is of Turkish origin and means in Turkish 'a maritime commander,' Y. Brutzkus, 'The Khazars and the Kievan Rus,' in the Russian magazine of New York City, *Novoselye*, no. 6 (1943), p. 79.

[2] Maçoudi (Masudi), *Les Prairies d'or*, ed. and transl. by Barbier de Meynard, iii (Paris), 64. In his translation Barbier de Meynard erroneously takes *Dir* for the name of a people, saying, 'Le premier d'entre les rois des Slaves est celui *des* Dir.'

[3] The French editor of *The Golden Meadows*, Barbier de Meynard, fails to give any variants to the name of *Dir*. See his *Variantes et notes*, iii, p. 446, where p. 64 is not mentioned. Variants are given in A. Harkavy, *Accounts of the Mohammedan Writers on the Slavs and Russians* (St Petersburg, 1870), p. 137; 167 (in Russian). See M. Hruševśky, *Geschichte des Ukrainischen (ruthenischen) Volkes*, i (Leipzig, 1906), 418, n. 2. Parkhomenko, *The Origin of Christianity in Russia* (Poltava, 1914), p. 71 n. 2 (in Russian).

[4] See for instance, V. Parkhomenko, *The Origin of Christianity in Russia* (Poltava, 1913), p. 71, n. 2. A. Presnyakov, *Lectures in Russian History* (Moscow, 1938), p. 45. Both in Russian.

[5] Because of the uncertainty of the spelling of this name and the chronological difficulty, Kunik thought it impossible to make use of Masudi's statement, *Caspia* (St Petersburg, 1877), p. xxxiii (German ed.); in the Russian edition (1875), p. xxiii.

spite of the lack of full certainty, Masudi's statement about the first King of the Slavs, whose name may be Dir, cannot be entirely ignored.[6]

According to the Russian Annals, Askold (Oskold) and Dir were two noblemen, two boyars, with Rurik, Prince of Novgorod; they were not related to him. They obtained permission to go to Tsargrad with their families and, sailing down the Dnieper, saw the small city of Kiev, where they remained. After gathering together many Varangians, they established their domination over the neighboring country. Thence they attacked Constantinople; and later on their return to Kiev, according to the Russian Annals, they were killed in 882 by Oleg who, after Rurik's death, had come to Kiev. There are many details which are not clear with regard to these two leaders, and it would be out of place to discuss the question here. I should mention that Shakhmatov, who calls them the first princes of Kiev, explained the story of their assassination by Oleg by the special predilection of the Russian chronicler in favor of Rurik's family: Rurik's descendants only were the sole legitimate rulers, and Askold and Dir were but usurpers.[7]

A few scholars have supposed that the names of Askold and Dir indicate not two persons but only one, one word being the first name and the other the surname. In 1850 Kunik apparently was doubtful when he wrote, "*Circa* 862 the Swede Askold (and Dir? Askold Dir?) as a Varangian will go to Constantinople.'[8] He was for a time inclined to accept Askold as a proper name, and Dir as the surname. A French historian, Rambaud, believing that Askold and Dir were only one person, regarded Dir as a proper name and Askold as a surname, saying, 'perhaps *Dir l'Oskylld, Dir l'Etranger;* Nestor would have simply doubled (*dédoublé*) this personage.'[9] Schlözer, acknowledging, as we have noted above, two Russian leaders, denies their participation in the invasion on

---

[6] I believe that Westberg's attempt to change the Arab form *al-Dir* into *Inguir* or *Ingur*, i.e., the Russian Prince of Kiev, Igor, who was contemporary with Masudi, is rather arbitrary. F. Westberg, 'On the Analysis of Oriental Sources on Eastern Europe,' *Journal of the Ministry of Public Instruction*, February, 1908, p. 396 (in Russian). *Idem,* 'Beiträge zur Klärung orientalischer Quellen über Osteuropa,' *Bulletin de l'Académie des sciences de Saint-Pétersbourg,* XI (1899), no. 5, p. 276.

[7] A. Shakhmatov, *The Earliest Fortunes of the Russian Nation* (Petrograd, 1919), pp. 58–59 (in Russian). A very clear presentation of the question in M. Hruševsky, *op. cit.,* I, 415–418.

[8] E. Kunik, 'Kritische Bemerkungen . . . , ' *Bulletin de la classe des sciences historiques, philologiques et politiques de l'Académie des Sciences de Saint-Pétersbourg,* VII (1850), 358; however, cf. p. 214, n. 43. This study of Kunik is often referred to as *Remarques critiques.* A French historian, Couret, is inclined to follow Kunik in this case. A. Couret, 'La Russie à Constantinople. Premières tentatives des Russes contre l'Empire Grec,' *Revue des questions historiques,* XIX (1876), 79, n. 5.

[9] A. Rambaud, *L'Empire Grec au dixième siècle* (Paris, 1870), p. 373, n. 5. The Greek scholar, Aristarkhes, accepts Rambaud's hypothesis. Τοῦ ἐν ἁγίοις πατρὸς ἡμῶν Φωτίου . . . Λόγοι καὶ Ὁμιλίαι, II (Constantinople, 1900), 29.

Constantinople.[10] Recently a Scandinavian historian, Ad. Stender-Petersen, wrote that the Russian chronicler on the campaign of 860 wished to connect the evidence of the Greek sources on the Russian campaign with the names of Hoskuld and Dyr, which were well known to him.[11] But the vast majority of scholars see in Askold and Dir two distinct persons. The Russian chronicles supply us with the best proof for this opinion in the story of their assassination by Oleg and their burial: two chiefs were buried in two different places. We read: 'And they killed Askold (Oskold) and Dir and carried (their bodies) to the hill which is (even) now called the Ugrian Settlement (*Ougorskoe*), where the Olma's Palace (*Olmin dvor*) stands. Over that tomb (Askold's) (he) built a church dedicated to St Nicholas, and Dir's tomb is behind St Irene's.'[12] Askold and Dir were not only two different literary characters, but real *historical* men. The Scandinavian names of all the first rulers of Russia, which the Russian chronicles contain, are absolutely authentic: Rurik, Askold and Dir, Oleg, Igor, and Olga. The fact that the last two names, Igor and Olga, are given not only in Russian chronicles but also are confirmed by Byzantine and Western sources, indirectly confirms the historicity of the first four names although they are not indicated in any other sources than Russian.[13]

Some later Russian sources give two stories about Askold and Dir's campaign on Constantinople, which are told under different years. In this connection I wish to discuss briefly the speculations of Th. Uspenski which are to be found in his interesting paper, *The First Pages of the Russian Annals and Byzantine Popular Tales* (Odessa, 1914). He asserts that Askold and Dir's expedition was probably the most definite and real fact, whose remembrance was still vividly preserved down to the time of the Russian chronicler. Uspenski asks: 'Why did the chronicler attribute the tradition of the campaign of Askold and Dir to the year 866? Why, ten years later, does Askold go again on Tsargrad? Of course,' Uspenski continues, 'because there were several tales of those campaigns,

---

[10] Schlözer, *Nestor, Russische Annalen*, ii, 258. See F. Kruse, *The first two Invasions of the Russians into Byzantium, Journal of the Ministry of Public Instruction*, 1840, December, p. 157 (in Russian).

[11] Ad. Stender-Petersen, 'Die Varägersaga als Quelle der altrussischen Chronik.' *Acta Jutlandica*, vi, 1 (Copenhagen, 1934), 249.

[12] According to the Laurentian and Hypatian versions of the Russian Chronicle. In English the Laurentian version translated by S. H. Cross, *The Russian Primary Chronicle* (Cambridge, 1930), p. 146 (in his translation the *Hunnish* hill is to be corrected to the *Magyar* or *Ugrian* hill); the Hypatian version in G. Vernadsky, 'Lebedia. Studies on the Magyar Background of Kievan Russia,' *Byzantion*, xiv (1939), 197.

[13] I purposely omit the Jewish mediaeval text edited by Schechter, where the name of 'Helgu (Oleg) the King of Russia' is given. This document presents many chronological and topographical difficulties which have not been satisfactorily explained.

and with various details. Under 866 the Byzantine Annals recorded the campaign of Rus on Constantinople; this was, for the Russian chronicler, the first basis to which he might link the tale of Askold and Dir. In fact, there are no grounds whatever for thinking that in 866 Askold and Dir were under Constantinople, for the Greek chronicle fails to name the leaders of the Russian fleet. But what is especially important to us is the information under the year 876. "The tribes, who are called Russians and who are also Cumans, lived in Euxinopontus; and they began to devastate the Roman land, and wished to go to Constantinople; but Divine Providence prevented them (from doing so); and the Divine wrath struck them; and then their princes, Askold and Dir, returned empty-handed."' Then Uspenski concludes, 'One may hardly doubt that we have here a tradition about some other Russian military enterprise. The difference between the first and second fact is evident: the first fact was written down on the basis of a Byzantine chronicle . . . the second fact on the basis of a local tradition.'[14] For these statements Uspenski gives no references.

I wish to enlarge on Uspenski's conclusions, because in my opinion, they require some correction. The Russian attack on Constantinople, as we know, already appears in the oldest versions of the Russian Annals in the Laurentian and Hypatian versions. The campaign is mentioned there only under the year 6360 (852): Askold and Dir are not named, and the source of the chronicle is indicated, 'as is written in the Greek Chronicle.' Then under the year 6374 (866), the Chronicles give the story itself, which is told according to the Continuator of George Hamartolus, with the addition of the names of Askold and Dir, which are lacking in the Greek source. This version has passed into the later Russian Annals. Now comes other information, which appears under the year 876, and which Uspenski attributes to a local Russian tradition. Uspenski fails to indicate where this second piece of information is to be found.

It is known that this story, which mentions the Russians living Euxinopontus, has passed into the later *Nikonovski* or *Patriarchal Chronicle* and into the *Stephennaya Kniga* from the Slavonic *Paralipomena* of Zonaras, which has been discussed above.[15] I do not understand why

---

[14] Th. Uspenski, *The First Pages of the Russian Annals and Byzantine Popular Tales* (Odessa, 1914), pp. 8–9 (in Russian). I use a reprint from vol. xxxii of *Zapiski of the Odessa Society of History and Antiquities*, pp. 199–228.

[15] Bodyanski, 'Paralipomena of Zonaras,' in *Chteniya* of the Moscow Society of Russian History and Antiquities (Moscow, 1847), no. 1, pp. 99–103. See V. Ikonnikov, *Essay on the Cultural Influence of Byzantium in Russian History* (Kiev, 1869), p. 529 (in Russian). *Nikonovskaya letopis*, in the *Complete Collection* (*Polnoe Sobraniye*) of Russian Chronicles, ix (St Petersburg, 1862), 13. *Stephennaya Kniga, P. S. R. L.*, xxi, 1 (St Petersburg, 1908), 35. I may add that the same story has been reproduced in the *Russian Chronograph* of the version of the year 1512, and in the *Russian*

Uspenski attributes this story to a local Russian tradition. The story, as I have noted above, passed into later Russian chronicles from the *Paralipomena* of Zonaras. But if we turn to the original Greek text of Zonaras, we discover in the latter the complete story which is given by Uspenski and which he attributes to a local Russian tradition.[16] This story, if we read Zonaras' text attentively, is to be referred to the attack of 860 because he mentions only one attack, and because immediately after this story Zonaras mentions a devastation of the Cyclades and coastal regions by the Cretan Arabs, which happened, as we have told above, in 861. Uspenski is inclined to see in their story another episode, another attempt to raid Constantinople, which was not indicated in Byzantine sources. But this is an absolutely arbitrary hypothesis, because there is no contradiction whatever between Zonaras' story and that of other Byzantine sources. Zonaras correctly says that the Russians began to devastate the Byzantine territory; but in their attempt to take Constantinople they failed. All this is in absolute accordance with our standard information on the campaign of 860. I have dwelt on Uspenski's speculations on this subject, because if I am not mistaken they have never been discussed.

As a convinced adherent of the historicity of Askold and Dir, I am inclined to accept the version of the Russian Chronicles concerning their leadership in the campaign of 860, although their names are not given in Byzantine sources. The raid of two hundred ships was an expedition on a rather large scale, and it must have been organized and directed by a leader, or, in this case, by two leaders pursuing the same end. We know that the Norman raids in Western Europe were always directed by energetic and courageous vikings, the names of many of whom have survived. The eastern raid on the Empire in 860 was organized and led in the same manner. Bjorn Jernside, Hasting, and other Norman leaders in the ninth century upheld the same Viking tradition in the west as Askold and Dir in the east.[17]

Chronograph of the western-Russian version (compiled probably at the beginning of the second half of the sixteenth century). *Complete Collection of Russian Chronicles*, XXII, 1 (St Petersburg, 1911), 352; XXII, 2 (Petrograd, 1914), 153.

[16] *Zonaras*, XVI, 5 (Bonn, III, 404): Τὸ δ'ἔθνος τῶν ῾Ρῶς Σκυθικὸν, ὃν τῶν περὶ τὸν Ταῦρον ἐθνῶν στόλῳ τὸ τοῦ Εὐξείνου πόντου κατέτρεχε καὶ αὐτῇ Βυζαντίδι ἐπιέναι διεμελέτα. ἀλλ' οὐκ εἰς ἔργον ἤχθη σφίσι τὸ βούλευμα, κωλυσάσης τοῦτο τῆς προνοίας τῆς ἄνωθεν, ἢ καὶ ἄκοντας αὐτοὺς ἀπράκτους, μᾶλλοε δὲ καὶ θείου πειραθέντες μηνίματος, ἀπελθεῖν ᾠκονόμησεν. More briefly the same story is told in Cedrenus, II, 173 (the *Euxinopontos* is not mentioned.)

[17] In a recent history of Russia, published in Moscow in 1939, we read, 'With the Prince Dir is connected our information on the first great attack of Kievan Russia on Tsargrad.' But before this statement both names, Askold and Dir, are mentioned. *History of USSR*, I (Moscow, 1939), 92 (in Russian). The author does not explain why he uses Dir only as the leader of the raid of 860.

As I have noted above, the Byzantine writers who dealt with the Russian attack of 860 were merely not acquainted with the names of the Russian leaders, as was quite natural. So the silence of the Byzantine sources on the names of Askold and Dir can in no way serve as proof that the names are fictitious, and the leaders themselves never existed.

Shakhmatov believes that Askold and Dir were the leaders of the campaign, and that they had conducted it from Kiev. Shakhmatov, 'Outline of the Oldest Period of the History of the Russian Language,' *Encyclopedia of Slavonic Philology*, II, 1 (Petrograd, 1915), p. xxx.

THE MONTH OF THE EXPEDITION

WE know that the Russian ships appeared before Constantinople on June 18, 860. This was the typical month for Russian expeditions, whether peaceful, connected with trade or commerce, or warlike. The famous passage which the Emperor Constantine Porphyrogenitus in the tenth century inserted in his book *On the Administration of the Empire*, also says that usually in the month of June the well-equipped flotilla of Russian traders left Kiev to start down the Dnieper, in order to reach Constantinople after difficulties and dangers. Difficulties and dangers were twofold: the Dnieper rapids and the savage Patzinaks (Pechenegs) who in the tenth century infested the steppes along the river.[1] In 860 the Russian raiders under the leadership of Askold and Dir must have overcome, like their descendants in the tenth century, the natural obstacle of the Dnieper rapids. But the danger of which Constantine Porphyrogenitus, writes, the Pechenegs, did not yet exist in that region in the middle of the ninth century, for this terrible nomadic people succeeded in dominating the whole expanse of the southern steppes from the Don to the Dneister and probably beyond this river, at the end of this century only.[2] Apparently the Magyars who from the beginning of the ninth century roved and raided in the south Russian steppes as far west as the lower Danube, were not strong enough to form serious obstacles to the Russians in their steady drive southwards,[3] although Magyar predatory instincts in the middle of the ninth century have been noticed in some sources. It is known that one of the two 'Apostles to the Slavs,' Constantine the Philosopher, who later took the name of Cyril, on his mission to the Khazars, probably in 861, was attacked by the Magyars somewhere in the Crimea. Referring to the passage from Constantine Porphyrogenitus quoted above, Bury wrote that the journey down the Dnieper could not safely be made except by a formidable company; a small body would have fallen a prey to predatory nomads like the Hungarians and the Patzinaks.[4]

Apparently a flotilla of two hundred vessels, like that which attacked Constantinople in 860, was strong enough to overcome the dangers which lay in its way south.

[1] *Constantini Porphyrogeniti De administrando imperio*, ch. IX (Bonn edition, pp. 74–79).

[2] See D. A. Rasovsky, 'Pechenegs, Torki and Berendei in Russia and Ugria,' *Seminarium Kondakovianum*, VI (1933), 3 (in Russian).

[3] On Magyar migrations see K. Grot, *Moravia and Magyars* (St Petersburg, 1881), pp. 180–206 (in Russian). In connection with Grégoire's new hypothesis on the length of the stay of the Magyars in South Russia see G. Vernadsky, 'Lebedia. Studies on the Magyar Background of Kievan Russia,' *Byzantion*, XIV (1939), especially pp. 200–201. See also above, p. 69.

[4] J. B. Bury, *A History of the Eastern Roman Empire* (London, 1912), pp. 413–414.

THE CAUSE OF THE EXPEDITION

OUR sources fail to mention the cause of the attack of 860. But scholars have naturally been interested in this question; and it is not to be forgotten that, owing to a blunder made by the first editor and translator of Photius' homilies on the Russian incursion, an erroneous idea of the cause has survived down to our own day. Even before the publication of Photius' homilies, a German scholar, Wilken, in 1829, as we have noted above, wrote that the cause of the incursion was probably not only rapacity, but the wish of the Russians to take revenge for an offense which had been passed over in silence by Byzantine historians, an offense of the kind which at that time the Greeks often indulged themselves against the peoples whom they considered crude barbarians.[1]

As we know, the first edition of Photius' two homilies on the Russian incursion by the Archimandrite Porphyrius Uspenski came out in 1864. One passage in the first homily reads in this edition as follows: πολλῶν καὶ μεγάλων φιλανθρώπως ἐλευθερωθέντων ὀλίγους ἁλοεῖς ἀφιλανθρώπως ἐδουλώσαμεν. Porphyrius' translation of this rather awkward phrase runs as follows: 'Many and the great among us were liberated from captivity by charity; and we have mercilessly made a few threshers our slaves.' The sense of this statement is not very clear either in Russian or in English. 'A few threshers' (in Greek ἁλοεῖς; in Russian *molotil-shchiki*) is not easily understood. Then P. Uspenski translated one passage from the second homily as follows: 'Indeed, these barbarians (i.e., Russians) became justly enraged on account of the murder of their compatriots, and, with hope of success, demanded and awaited punishment equal to the crime. And we because of fear and defeat have weakened.' But in the Greek text we discover something quite opposite to Uspenski's translation; we read, 'The blood guiltiness (μιαιφονία) of the barbarians (i.e., Russians) towards (our) compatriots (i.e., the Greeks) must have provoked the latter's just wrath and brought about with reasonable hopes (of satisfaction) a demand for proper revenge; instead of that they (i.e., the Greeks) because of fear and fright, have weakened.' In other words, it was not the Greeks who murdered the Russians, who were therefore enraged and anxious to avenge the crime; but, on the contrary, Russians had murdered Greeks, who instead of feeling resentment and craving for revenge, lost their courage and grew craven. In 1867 as we have noted above, there came out a new and critical edition of

---

[1] F. Wilken, 'Ueber die Verhältnisse der Russen zum Byzantinischen, Reiche in dem Zeitraume vom neunten bis zum zwölften Jahrhundert,' *Abhandlungen der Akademie der Wissenschaften zu Berlin.* 1829, Historisch-Philologische Klasse, p. 89.

Photius' homilies on the Russian incursion by A. Nauck, *Lexicon Vindobonense* (St Petersburg, 1867). To our surprise and great satisfaction, instead of the words in P. Uspenski's edition which have been quoted above, ὀλίγους ἀλοεῖς ἀφιλανθρώπως ἐδουλώσαμεν, the manuscripts give ὀλίγων ἄλλους καὶ ἀφιλανθρώπως ἐδουλώσαμεν.[2] In other words, for the mysterious ἀλοεῖς = threshers we have simply ἄλλους = others. All this was thoroughly explained by Vasilievski as early as 1878.[3]

Though after 1878 the 'threshers' disappeared from historical literature, P. Uspenski's other blunder about the hypothetical Russians murdered in Constantinople not long before 860 has surprisingly survived down to our own day and can be discovered even in the works of very eminent historians.

Before 1878 Bestuzhev-Ryumin wrote that Photius' second homily represents the assassination of several Russians in Constantinople as the cause of the attack.[4] The same cause we find given by D. Ilovaiski and Golubinski.[5] Klyuchevski writes, 'The attack was provoked, according to Photius, by the fact that the Greek people had broken the treaty, and it was undertaken by the Rus in order to avenge the offence which had been inflicted upon their compatriots, Russian merchants, seemingly for nonpayment of a debt; consequently (the attack) had in view the restoration by force of trade relations which had been violently broken off by the Greeks.'[6] Even in 1915, Lyubavski held to the same opinion saying, 'At times, the Byzantines offended the Russian merchants, who came to them to Constantinople. The first Varangian princes were the avengers of these offenses. Askold and Dir attacked Constantinople in 860, according to Patriarch Photius, because the Byzantines had murdered some

---

[2] A. Nauck, *Lexicon Vindobonense, Appendix*, p. 20. See ed. C. Müller, *Fragmenta Historicorum Graecorum*, v, 1 (Paris, 1870), p. 163, §5. Ed. Ἀριστάρχης, II, pp. 7–8, §1.

[3] Vasilievski, 'Russo-Byzantine Fragments, VIII. The Life of George of Amastris,' *Journal of the Ministry of Public Instruction*, March, 1878, p. 175, n. 2 (on pp. 175–177). In the following editions of the *Life of George of Amastris*, Vasilievski omitted his discussion of P. Uspenski's errors. See Vasilievski, *Works*, III, p. CXXVI, n. 2. See Ch. Loparev, *Some Old Evidence for the Placing of the Garment of the Mother of God in Blachernae*, *Viz. Vremennik*, II (1895), p. 582 (in Russian).

[4] K. Bestuzhev-Ryumin, *A Russian History*, I (St Petersburg, 1872), p. 99, n. 7 (in Russian). See above.

[5] D. Ilovaiski, *Studies on the Origin of Russia*, sec. ed. (Moscow, 1882), pp. 278–279. Cf. *idem, A History of Russia*, sec. ed. (Moscow, 1900), p. 18 (the cause of the attack of 860 is the breaking of trade treaties with Russia). Golubinski, *History of the Russian Church*, I, 1 (Moscow, 1880), 20; sec. ed. (Moscow, 1901), 40.

[6] V. Klyuchevski, *The Course of Russian History*, I (Moscow, 1904), p. 170. In the English translation of the book by C. J. Hogarth, we read: 'As regards Askold's expedition, Photius tells us that Rus was first angered by the murder of some of her merchants in Constantinople, and finally moved to action by the refusal of the Byzantine government to make reparation for the insult or to renew the trading relations thus broken off,' V. Klyuchevski, *A History of Russia*, transl. by C. J. Hogarth, I (London-New York, 1911), p. 81.

of their compatriots and refused the Rus satisfaction for that offense.'[7]
Evidently basing his opinion on Klyuchevski's book, the late American
historian, J. W. Thompson, wrote, 'Although the details of the attack
are of no interest to us, we should, however, take note of the fact that,
according to Photius, this expedition was undertaken for the purpose of
revenging an insult done to some Rus merchants.   This insult probably
consisted of nonpayment of some debt due to them.'[8]

These examples clearly show how the blunder which was made many
years ago and definitely explained in 1878, has survived down to our own
time.   Of course Photius fails to mention any story of the murder of
Russian merchants in Constantinople before 860.   No particular cause
for the attack of 860 is known.   We must explain it, for the time being,
by the same causes which stimulated the Normans to make their raids
over Western Europe, rapacity, and desire for devastating, and for ac-
quiring booty and wealth.   Of course Constantinople may have allured
them more than Paris, Seville, and other West European cities.   Only
one West European city could match Constantinople, this New Rome; it
was the Old Rome in Italy.   And we know that the Normans made an
unsuccessful attempt to attack the papal residence.   Rumor of the
fabulous wealth of Constantinople was widespread, and this was the
chief reason for the Russian attack of 860.

[7] M. K. Lyubavski, *Lectures on Ancient Russian History to the end of the sixteenth century* (Moscow,
1915), p. 82 (in Russian).

[8] J. W. Thompson, *An Economic and Social History of the Middle Ages* (New York-London, 1928),
pp. 342–343.

NOTE ON THE NAME ROS BEFORE 860

WERE the Russians known in Byzantium before 860? We know that the name of the people *Ros* was mentioned under 839 in a Western chronicle, that is, not in a Greek but in a Latin text. Since we have eliminated the texts of the *Life of Stephen of Surozh* and the *Life of George of Amastris* for the period previous to the year 860, the name *Ros*, in a Greek text, appears for the first time in the homilies of Photius. In his second homily Photius, among other qualifications attributed to the Ros, calls them ἔθνος ἄγνωστον, i.e., unknown (ed. Müller, p. 168, §10). Vasilievski objects to the translation 'unknown,' preferring 'unnoted, obscure.' According to him, 'Had Photius said that Rus was unknown before 865 (now 860), he would have contradicted himself.'[1] In my opinion the Russians, of course, had been known in Byzantium before 860, but not under the name of *Ros* — 'Ρώς. They were known under the name of Tauroscythians, which, as we know, in the ninth and tenth centuries, indicated the Russians. For instance, in 856 they took a decisive part in the murder of Theoctistus, Logothete of Course and all-powerful minister under Theodora, mother of Michael III.[2] So if we take the adjective ἄγνωστος in its original meaning 'unknown,' we may explain it by the fact that in the Byzantine usage the northern invaders appeared for the first time in 860 under their own name Ros, but had been previously known as Tauroscythians or even simply Scythians. I think that Kunik was right in saying that 'the originally undeclinable word 'Ρώς, like the 'Ρώς in the Septuagint, received its full confirmation (*Weihe*) through Photius' two homilies.'[3] Perhaps some new Greek texts, undoubtedly compiled before 860, will be discovered. In this case we may change our opinion; but for the time being we must state that the name 'Ρώς — Ros appeared for the first time in Byzantine Greek sources in Photius' homilies, and the discovery of this name in *Annales Bertiniani* under 839 presents no contradiction whatever to this statement.

---

[1] Vasilievski, *Works*, III, p. CXXVI–CXXVII. In the very accurate Russian translation of Photius' two homilies by E. Lovyagin, the adjective ἄγνωστος is rendered by 'unknown.' E. Lovyagin 'The Two Homilies of the Holiest Patriarch of Constantinople Photius on the Occasion of the Attack of Ros on Constantinople,' *Christyanskoe Čtenie*, September-October, 1882, p. 432, §2.

[2] Genesius, lib. IV, Bonn., p. 89: τοὺς ἐκ Ταυρικῆς καθ' ἑταρείαν Σκίθας ὁ βασιλεὺς ῥαγδαίῳ προστάγματι διαφώννυσιν ἐπελθεῖν κατ' αὐτοῦ (i.e., Theoctistus) καὶ συντόμως διαχειρίσασθαι. See Bury, *A History of the Eastern Roman Empire* (London, 1912), p. 159. Bury fails to mention that the guards were Tauroscythians.

[3] Dorn-Kunik, *Caspia* (1877), p. 395, n. 6 (German ed.).

THE STORY OF THE ATTACK

THE year 860 began not very promisingly for the Empire in Asia Minor, where the Arab danger never ceased. In the south-eastern corner the garrison troops of the border were stationed at the fortress of Lulon (Lulu), erected on an impregnable height, the key to the Cilician pass. It belonged at that time to the Empire, but in March 860, quite unexpectedly, it surrendered to an Arab captain. Along with the fortress, the Byzantine patrician who had been sent from Constantinople to take charge of the situation was also handed over to the Arabs. This special imperial envoy was carried into captivity and threatened with death. The Emperor was seriously concerned for his fate and very anxious to recover him. At the very end of April or, more probably, at the outset of May, 860, an exchange of captives was effected on the banks of the River Lamos, about a day's march from Tarsus, and the patrician was released. It would seem that with the exchange of captives hostilities between the Empire and Caliphate for a time at least should have ceased. But for reasons so far unknown, the Emperor left Constantinople for Asia Minor as early as the beginning of June to invade the Caliph's dominions.[1]

On his departure for the eastern campaign, Michael committed the charge and defense of the capital to Ooryphas (Oryphas), the Prefect of the city. When the Emperor was at Mauropotamos, amazing tidings arrived from the capital. Ooryphas sent him a message that a Russian host had sailed in two hundred boats across the Euxine towards Constantinople, entered the Bosphorus, wrought wreck and ruin in the suburbs, and slaughtered many inhabitants. Michael with all speed returned to the capital and was barely able to get across the Bosphorus. Meanwhile the Russians not only plundered the monasteries and suburbs on the banks of the Bosphorus; they entered the Sea of Marmora and overran the Islands of the Princes. On one of these islands, Terebinthos, at that time the ex-Patriarch Ignatius was living in exile. His biographer, Nicetas Paphlagon, gives the following description of the Russian attack: 'The bloody race of the Scythians, the so-called *Ros* (οἱ λεγόμενοι 'Ρῶς), having come through the Euxine to the Stenon (Bosphorus) and plundered all the places and all the monasteries, overran likewise the islands around Byzantium, carrying off all the sacred vessels and property, and slaughtering all the captives. In addition, in their barbarous drive and spirit, they overran the monasteries of the Patriarch, took away all

---

[1] On these events see A. Vasiliev, *Byzance et les Arabes*, ɪ (Brussels, 1935), 239–241; Russian ed. (St Petersburg, 1900), pp. 186–189. J. B. Bury, *A History of the Eastern Roman Empire* (London, 1912), pp. 279–281.

the property, seized twenty-two of his devoted servants, and cut all of them in pieces with axes on the stern of a ship.'[2] Michael managed to reach the capital, clashed with the invaders, and routed them. The Russians, in speedy flight, left the shores of the Empire and returned northwards. Such is the historical skeleton of the Russian attack.[3]

The Russians undertook their raid in two hundred boats. This round number is given in our Greek and Slavonic evidence and can be accepted as a real historical indication of the size of the expedition; it consisted of about two hundred ships.[4] We know now that the number of Norman ships, three hundred and sixty, given by Johannes Diaconus and his Venetian followers, does not refer to the Russian expedition of 860. As has been noted above, these 360 ships raided the coasts of the Sea of Marmora and the suburbs of Constantinople from the south in 861, and have nothing to do with the northern Russian activities in the Black Sea and Bosphorus.[5]

[2] Nicetae Paphlagonis *Vita S. Ignatii archiepiscopi Constantinopolitani*, Migne, *P. G.*, cv, coll. 516–517; also col. 532. Mansi, *Conciliorum Collectio Amplissima*, xvi, col. 236.

[3] *Anecdota Bruxellensia*. i. *Chroniques Byzantines du Manuscrit* 11376 par Franz Cumont (Gand, 1894), p. 33 (Recueil de Travaux publiés par la Faculté de Philosophie et Lettres, 9-me fascicule). The Byzantine chronicles representing various versions of the unpublished original text of Symeon Logothete: *Georgii Hamartoli Continuator*, ed. Muralt, 736–737; ed. V. Istrin, *The Chronicle of George Hamartolus in an Old Slavonic Version*, ii (Petrograd, 1922), pp. 10–11, §12; *Symeon Magister*, ed. Bonn., p. 674, ch. 37; *Leo Grammaticus*, pp. 240–241; *Theodosii Meliteni Chronographia*, ed. J. L. F. Tafel (Munich, 1859), p. 168. Then Cedrenus, ii, 173. Zonaras, xvi, 5 (Bonn., iii, 404). The earlier Russian Annals mostly depend on George Hamartolus' Continuator. *The Laurentian Version*, sec. ed., (Leningrad, 1926), pp. 17 and 21–22 (Complete Collection of Russian Annals, i). *The Hypatian Version*, sec. ed. (St Petersburg, 1908), pp. 12 and 15 (Comp. Coll., ii). *The First Pskov Chronicle*, C. Coll., iv (St Petersburg, 1848), 174. *Voskresenki Chronicle*, C. Coll., vii (St Petersburg, 1856), pp. 7–9, 269. *Patriarshi* or *Nikonovski Chronicle*, C. Coll., ix (St Petersburg, 1862), pp. 7–9. *Russian Chronograph*. i. Chronograph of the version of the year 1512 (St Petersburg, 1911), pp. 348 and 352; ii. Chronograph of the West Russian version (Petrograd, 1914), p. 150, 153, 154 (C. Coll. vol. xxii). *The Chronicle of Avraamka*, C. Coll., xvi (1889), col. 35. *Simeonovski Chronicle*, C. Coll., xviii (1913), p. 8 (fragments of the beginning of the *Troitski Chronicle;* the latter entire chronicle burned in Moscow in 1812). *Lvovski Chronicle*, C. Coll., xx (1910), p. 44. *Yermolinski Chronicle*, C. Coll., xxiii (1910), p. 3. *Tipografski Chronicle*, C. Coll., xxiv (1921), p. 7. The old Slavonic version of Symeon Logothete: *Simeona Metafrasta i Logotheta Spisanie mira ot bytiya* . . . ed. A. Kunik, V. Vasilievski, V. Sreznevski (St Petersburg, 1905), p. 106. M. Weingart, *Byzantské Kroniky v Literatuře Cirkoněslovanské*, ii, 1 (Bratislava, 1923), 135–136. An Old Slavonic Version of George Hamartolus' Continuator: M. Istrin, *An Old Slavonic Version of George Hamartolus and His Continuation*, i (Petrograd, 1920), 511. *Paralipomena Zonarae*, ed. Bodyanski, *Chteniya of the Moscow Society of Russian History and Antiquities*, 1847, no. 1, pp. 99–103 (in Old Slavonic).

[4] As early as 1844 a Russian historian, A. Chertkov, wrote that the information of two hundred Russian ships is testified to by Russian and Byzantine sources, and we may call it authentic and positive with regard to the number of ships. A. Chertkov, 'On the number of the Russian Troops who Conquered Bulgaria, and fought against the Greeks in Thrace and Macedonia in the years 967–971,' *Zapiski* of the Odessa Society of History and Antiquities, i (Odessa, 1844), 170, n. 1; also 173 (in Russian).

[5] Cf. Kunik, who wrote that in 865 Askold appeared under the walls of Constantinople with a piratic fleet, of over 300 ships. *Accounts of al-Bekri and other authors on Russia and the Slavs*, ii (St Peters-

If we compare the number of ships which participated in the Russian raid of 860 with some Viking expeditions in Western Europe, we may call the Russian raid an enterprise of medium size. Let us give some examples: in 845 King Horik sent a Viking fleet of 600 ships to the river of Elba; in the same year a fleet of 120 ships, under command of Regner, entered the Seine. In 844 a fleet of 54 ships and a number of smaller boats plundered the western coasts of the Iberian Peninsula. In the siege of Paris in 885 took part, in addition to numberless small boats, 700 large ships, containing between 30,000 and 40,000 raiders. The latter figure is the highest known in Western sources.[6] The Norman flotilla which operated in the Eastern Mediterranean and raided the coasts of the Sea of Marmora in 861 consisted, according to Joannes Diaconus, of 360 ships.

Some scholars have held the opinion, in connection with the raid of 860, that the Russians attacked Byzantine territory in their small vessels, the so-called *monoxyla* (dugouts), made of a single piece of timber, formed by simply hollowing out the trunk of a tree. The *monoxyla* are mentioned in various sources for the siege of Constantinople by the Avars, Slavs, and Scythians in 626; some later evidence on the subject has identified these Scythians with the Russians. The famous account of the route of the Russian traders down the Dnieper to Byzantium, which was compiled in the tenth century by the Emperor Constantine Porphyrogenitus, also mentions the Russian dug-outs, *monoxyla*, which rowed down from the northern cities of Novgorod, Smolensk, Lyubech, Chernigov, and Vyshegrad as far as Kiev. Here the *monoxyla* were to be replaced by new boats, evidently by larger vessels, which started farther south, in order to reach, after many perils and mischances, the imperial capital.[7]

The Greek sources on the attack of 860 never use the term *monoxyla*. Russian vessels are called, πλοῖα, σκάφη, νῆες, or, as in Cedrenus and Zonaras, simply ὁ στόλος. The Patriarch Photius calls them 'the barbarian ships' (αἱ βαρβαρικαὶ νῆες).[8] Even the word τὸ σκάφος, originally meaning *anything hollowed, the hull of a ship*, means also *ship* in general. It is not surprising that in 860 the Russians for their maritime expedition made

---

burg, 1903), 108. Here of course Kunik is wrong both as to the year 865 and as to the figure, 'over 300,' taken by him from Joannes Diaconus, where the figure 360 is given. This study was published after Kunik's death (he died in 1899).

[6] See J. Steenstrup, *Normannerne*, II (Copenhagen, 1878), 153, 154, 217, 290. See also the list of Norman raids in the ninth century and the number of ships which took part in them, in Steenstrup, *op. cit.*, I (1876), 214–217.

[7] Bury calls *monoxyla* by an uncommon English word, 'one-plankers.' Bury, *A History of the Eastern Roman Empire*, p. 413, n. 3.   [8] Ed. Müller, p. 169, §18. Aristarkhes, II, 39, §2.

no use of *monoxyla*, which were too small for such a purpose.[9] The Vikings in the ninth century already had much more experience in maritime enterprises after their numerous activities in Western Europe than the Avars, Slavs, and Scythians had had in 626. They would have never seriously considered the *monoxyla* as vessels destined to cross the Black Sea, reach the shores of the Byzantine Empire, and carry out a real expedition against Constantinople and other places. In the tenth century, Constantine Porphyrogenitus himself, as we know, writes that at Kiev the *monoxyla* were replaced by larger boats to continue the journey south.[10] The Arab geographer of the tenth century, Masudi, speaks of the Russians who carried on trade with Andalus (Spain), Rome, Constantinople, and the Khazars; and at the beginning of the tenth century (in 912–913, the year 300 of the Hegira), they used for their commercial purposes 500 vessels, and each vessel was manned with a hundred men.[11] If we apply the figure of a hundred men for a boat, given by Masudi, for the Russian boats which participated in the attack of 860 — which is quite permissible — we shall arrive at the number of approximately 20,000 raiders (200 vessels, each with a crew of one hundred). According to Russian sources, on an average a Russian ship of the tenth to the twelfth centuries carried 40 to 60 men, and sometimes more, up to 100, especially for sea navigation.[12]

Archaeological discoveries permit us to supplement our idea of Viking ships from descriptions in literary sources, so that, in spite of the deficiencies of the ships unearthed, we can see how they looked in reality, many centuries ago, in the period of the Viking raids. I give here at random a few examples. In 1880 a ship was found in Norway in a burial mound. The ship is supposed to date from about 900. In 1904 another ship, packed with goods, was unearthed in southern Norway. The find dates from about 800 A.D.[13] In the grounds back of the central building

---

[9] Bury still believes that the Russians used *monoxyla*. He writes: 'It is clear that the Russians must have been informed of the absence of the fleet, for otherwise they would never have ventured in their small boats into the jaws of certain death,' Bury, *A History of the Eastern Roman Empire*, p. 421.

[10] Toynbee calls the vessels of 860 *war-canoes*. A. J. Toynbee, *A Study of History*, v (London, 1939), 289, 290. In my opinion, the word *canoe* or *war-canoe* is rather misleading in this case.

[11] Maçoudi (Masudi), *Les Prairies d'or*, ed. and translated by Barbier de Meynard et Pavet de Courteille, II, 18. A German translation in J. Marquart, *Osteuropäische und ostasiatische Streifzüge* (Leipzig, 1903), p. 330. In addition to the manuscripts of the Parisian edition, Marquart employs for this story the fine manuscript of Leiden Hs. 537 a.

[12] M. Pokrovski, *History of Russia*, translated and edited by J. D. Clarkson and M. R. M. Griffiths (New York, 1931), p. 35. G. Vernadsky, *Links (Zvenya) of Russian Culture: Ancient Rus*, I (1938), p. 66 (in Russian).

[13] See K. Gjerset, *History of the Norwegian People*. Two volumes in one (New York, 1932), pp. 34–35.

of the University of Oslo is a wooden shed containing a 'Viking ship' of the ninth century, found in 1889 at Gogstad, near Sandefjord. Its total length from stem to stern is 77 feet, its breadth 16 feet. A second shed contains fragments of a similar boat found in Smaalene in 1867. In 1938 in England near Woodbridge, Suffolk, was unearthed a great open rowing-boat some 80 feet long. In the early stages of the work it was expected that the ship would prove to be of the Viking Age, but later it became quite clear from its construction, apart from the articles buried in it, that the ship belonged to the pagan Anglo-Saxon period. It is probably the finest monument of the pagan Anglo-Saxons that has come down to us, and the first known English war-vessel.[14] Although it is not a Viking ship, it possesses interest for us as a specimen which in the earlier Middle Ages was used for maritime undertakings similar to those of the Vikings.

The attack of 860 was swift and absolutely unexpected 'as a swarm of wasps.'[15] In this respect it differed in no way from Norman raids in Western Europe. The moment of the attack was very much in favor of the Russians, because the Emperor and his army were fighting the Arabs in Asia Minor, and the fleet was absent fighting the Arabs and Normans in the Aegean and Mediterranean. This exceptional double advantage, on land and sea, suggests that the Russians may have been informed of the situation, especially of the absence of the fleet.[16] The land defense of the capital was also weakened, because the Imperial army which was fighting against the Arabs consisted not only of the troops stationed in Asia Minor but also of those regiments (*tagmata*) which were usually stationed in the neighborhood of the capital.[17] Undoubtedly the Constantinopolitan garrison, as we have pointed out above, was at hand and could defend the city itself. But as far as we are aware of the course of the attack, the coasts of the Black Sea, the Bosphorus, and the Sea of Marmora, including its islands, were almost defenseless and exposed helplessly to Russian attacks.

The record of the *Nikonovski Chronicle* which positively states that the Kievan princes, Askold and Dir, were aware of the Arab campaign from the east is extremely interesting; and only after having obtained

---

[14] C. W. Phillips, 'The Excavation of the Sutton Hoo Ship-burial,' *The Antiquaries Journal*, xx (April, 1940), no. 2, pp. 177–178, 192.

[15] A. Toynbee, *A Study of History*, v (London, 1939), 289. 'In this element of suddeness and surprise,' Toynbee writes, 'the Russian attack is reminiscent of the Gothic naval attack on the Black Sea coasts *post* A.D. 250 and of the Cossack naval attack on the Black Sea coasts of the Ottoman Empire *post* A.D.1637.'

[16] Bury is more positive, saying, 'The Russians *must* have been informed of the absence of the fleet' (*op. cit.*, p. 421). See above.

[17] The observation on *tagmata* in Bury, *A History of the Eastern Roman Empire*, p. 419. See above.

this information did they decide to undertake their expedition against Constantinople.[18]   The question arises how the Russians could have been informed of the situation in Byzantium in 860.   A number of Russians or Tauroscythians were at that time, as we know, in Constantinople, serving in the imperial guard; and some Russians or Normans were also in the Tauric Peninsula, near the Byzantine possessions at Kherson. They might have known something about the situation in the capital and informed their compatriots at Kiev.   But owing to primitive means of communication, it would not have been easy to get the message to Kiev in time.   However this may have been, the record of the *Nikonovski Chronicle*, whose source has not yet been identified, is not to be discarded, for it agrees well with the general situation in Byzantium.[19]

The Emperor's absence at the moment of the Russian incursion is testified to by a group of Greek sources connected with the unpublished Chronicle of Symeon Logothete, by Russian chronicles, which depend on Greek sources, and by the contemporary eye-witness of the event, the Patriarch Photius.   In his first Sermon, which he preached just after the appearance of the Russian flotilla and the first stages of their destructive operations, Photius exclaims: 'Where is the Christ-loving Emperor now?   Where are the armies?   Where are arms, machines, military counsels, equipment?   Are not all these withdrawn to meet an attack of other barbarians?   And the Emperor endures far distant labors beyond the frontiers (of the Empire); along with him the army went to share in his hardships; manifest ruin and slaughter confront us.'[20]

On the question when the Emperor returned to the capital, there is considerable divergence.   A group of Greek chronicles depending on the unpublished Greek text of Symeon Logothete describes how the Emperor immediately on receiving Ooryphas' message returned home and could hardly get across the Bosphorus, where Russian ships were operating. He went to the church of Blachernae and, along with the Patriarch Photius, took from there the precious garment (ὠμοφόριον, μαφόριον) of the Virgin Mother, which in solemn procession they bore round the walls of the city; then they dipped it in the waters of the sea.   There was a dead calm.   But immediately after the relic had been dipped a strong wind and storm arose, and the ships of the 'godless' Russians were wrecked, and the invaders with great speed and in complete defeat fled

---

[18] *P.S.R.L.*, IX, 8.

[19] Aristarkhes' conjecture that Ooryphas might have been warned concerning the impending Russian attack by the Patzinaks (Pechenegs), who were hostile to the Russians, is devoid of foundation. Aristarkhes, Φωτίου Λόγοι καὶ Ὁμιλίαι, II, 2.

[20] *Photii Homilia* I, ed. C. Müller, p. 165, §§22–23; ed. Aristarkhes, p. 51.   A Russian translation by E. Lovyagin, in *Khristyanskoe Chtenie*, Sept.-Oct., 1882, p. 425.

home. In other words, the data on the Emperor's arrival in the capital given in the so-called chronicles of George Hamartolus' Continuator, Leo Grammaticus, Theodosius Melitenus, Symeon Magister, Georgius Monachus, and the Slavonic version of Symeon Logothete, are only different versions of the full unpublished text of Symeon Logothete, i.e., is information supplied only by one source, Symeon Logothete, who lived himself in the second half of the tenth century.[21] Neither the *Anonymus Bruxellensis*, which gives the exact date of the invasion, nor Nicetas Paphlagon, nor Cedrenus (Scylitzes) nor Zonaras mention the Emperor at all. But the most surprising fact in the literary history of the invasion of 860 is that the eye-witness Photius, in his second sermon which was delivered after the enemy had departed, fails to mention the Emperor's presence. It is quite impossible to see any reference to the Emperor in the following passage of his second sermon: 'Along with me the *entire city* bore Her (i.e., the Virgin Mother's) garment for repulse of the besiegers and for protection of the besieged ones, and we addressed prayers and made a litany.'[22] It would have paid far too little deference to the Emperor to have included him under the words *the entire city*. We shall discuss this question below in connection with religious processions during the Russian invasion.

Evidently Michael's uncle, the all-powerful Bardas, was with the Emperor during the latter's campaign in Asia Minor. His absence from the capital may be inferred from the fact that only Ooryphas, the prefect of the city, is mentioned as being left in charge of Constantinople.[23]

Most probably Michael's new favorite, Basil, was also in Asia Minor.[24] We remember that in 859 he was in charge of the reconstruction of the walls of Ancyra, and in 860 he may have accompanied the Emperor.

As we know, the defense of the capital was entrusted to the prefect of the city, Ooryphas (Oryphas). This name was very well known under the Amorian dynasty, when several persons of this name held different offices.[25] The prefect of the city in 860 was Nicetas Ooryphas who, according to Nicetas Paphlagon, oppressed the ex-Patriarch Ignatius in the

---

[21] References to all these chronicles have been given above. On the complicated question of Symeon Logothete see the excellent study by G. Ostrogorsky, 'A Slavonic Version of the Chronicle of Symeon the Logothete,' *Seminarium Kondakovianum*, v (Prague, 1932), pp. 17–36 (in Russian).

[22] καὶ τὴν περιβολὴν εἰς ἀναστολὴν μὲν τῶς πολιορκούντων φυλακὴν δὲ τῶν πολιορκουμένων σὺν ἐμοὶ πᾶσα ἡ πόλις ἐπιφερόμενοι τὰς ἱκεσίας ἐκουσιαζόμεθα, τὴν λιτανείαν ἐποιούμεθα. Ed. Müller, p. 169, §22; Aristarkhes, ii, pp. 41–42, §4.

[23] See Bury, *op. cit.*, p. 419, n. 5. F. Dvorník, *Les légendes de Constantin et de Méthode vues de Byzance* (Prague, 1933), p. 148: 'In June 860, as the Emperor and Bardas conducted a military expedition against the Arabs in Asia Minor. . . . '

[24] The Russian *Nikonovski Chronicle* plainly writes that the Emperor Michael and Basil marched against the Agarenes (Arabs). *P.S.R.L.*, ix, 9.   [25] See Bury, *op. cit.*, p. 143, n. 7.

island of Terebinthos, where the latter lived in exile. Later Ooryphas became commander (*drungarios*) of the Imperial fleet and was the chief admiral of the age. From his general career it may be inferred that he displayed energy and vigor in defending the capital in 860.

Another question connected with the attack of 860 is the location of Mauropotamos, where the Emperor and his army stood when he received Ooryphas' message concerning the Russian raid. The river named Mauropotamos — Μέλας ποταμός — in Turkish Qarasu — the Black River, occurs often in Asia Minor.[26] It is not irrelevant to mention here that a river of the same name is also to be found in the Balkan Peninsula, close to Constantinople; and in 1829 a German historian, F. Wilken, as I have noted above, wrote of this Russian raid that Μαῦρος ποταμος is certainly no other than the River Melas, which, after its union with the River Athyras, discharges itself into the Propontis, six hours' distance southwest of Constantinople.[27] This statement, of course, is a mere curiosity.

The name of the place is indicated by various Greek versions of the yet unpublished Greek text of Symeon Logothete and by their Slavonic versions. What was the real name of the place, ὁ Μαυροπόταμος or τὸ Μαυρο-πόταμον? Bury thinks that the weight of manuscript authority is in favor of the latter form; in this case the name would mean a place (of course on a river), not the river itself.[28] It is true that in the printed texts we find both forms in the accusative, τὸν Μαμροπόταμον (Theod. Melit, 168; Georg. Mon., p. 826) and τὸ Μαυροπόταμον (Georg. Hamart., ed. Istrin, p. 10;[29] Sym. Mag., p. 674). But in the text of Leo Grammaticus we have τὸν μαῦρον ποταμόν, i.e. the river. The Slavonic version of Simeon Logothete gives 'on Mauropotamon, which is the Black River.'[30] In my opinion, we must interpret this name as that of a river, not of a place.

There is a discrepancy as to the location of this river. In 1900 I rejected Μέλας ποταμός, a tributary of the Sangarios, which connects the

---

[26] See E. Honigmann, *Die Ostgrenze des Byzantinischen Reiches* (Brussels, 1935), p. 71. See also several references to Mauropotamos in de Boor, 'Der Angriff der Rhos auf Byzanz,' *Byz. Zeitschrift*, IV (1895), 450, n. 1.

[27] F. Wilken, 'Ueber die Verhältnisse der Russen zum Byzantinischen Reiche in dem Zeitraume vom neunten bis zum zwölften Jahrhundert,' *Abhandlungen der Akademie der Wissenschaften zu Berlin* (1829). *Historisch-Philologische Klasse*, p. 83. The Melas (now Kara-su) and Athyras flow from the hill of Kushkaya near the Anastasian Wall.

[28] Bury, *op. cit.*, p. 274, n. 4.   [29] In Istrin's edition τὸ[ν] Μαυροπόταμον.

[30] *Simeona Metafrasta i Logotheta Spisanie mira* . . . ed. Kunik, Vasilievski, Sreznevski (St Petersburg, 1905), p. 106. M. Weingart, *Byzantské kroniky v literatuře církevněslovanské*, II, 1 (Bratislava, 1923), 135. In the Slavonic version of George Hamartolus' Continuator we read, 'When (the Emperor) reached the so-called Black River,' ed. Istrin, I (Petrograd, 1920), 511.

latter river with Lake Sobandja, west of Ismid (Nicomedia), as too close
to Constantinople,[31] and preferred another river, the Kara-Su, i.e.,
Μέλας ποταμός, a tributary of the Halys, the greatest river of Asia Minor,
north of Mount Argaios, in Cappadocia.[32]   In his note added to my
original Russian text, Grégoire rejected my supposition and identified the
Mauropotamos with the tributary of the Sangarios.[33]   Lamanski simply
says, 'The river Μέλας ποταμός, in Turkish Kara-Su, a tributary of Sangarios, west of Nicomedia, as Ramsay accepts, or the River Kara-Su,
Μέλας ποταμός, in Cappadocia . . . , as Vasiliev believes.'[34]   Bury remarks that this place has not been positively identified.[35]   A rather
strange contradiction appears in Th. Uspenski who, having recounted
the defeat of Theoctistus by the Arabs in 843–844 'on the borders of the
Empire near the mountain Tauros,' notes, 'This battle took place at the
Black River, where the Emperor was also in 860.'[36]   As far as I am concerned, I hesitate to abandon my opinion that Mauropotamos is in Cappadocia and to accept Grégoire's point of view.   I can now adduce another
proof refuting Grégoire's suggestion, a point which I overlooked in 1900.
In his first sermon Photius, after mentioning the Emperor's absence from
the capital, exclaimed, 'And the Emperor endures far distant labors
beyond the frontiers (of the Empire).'[37]   Photius would never have used
these words had the Emperor been at that time in the neighboring basin
of the Sangarius.

It should be added that in some printed texts of Symeon Logothete's
group we have the following reading: τὴν τῶν ἀθέων ῾Ρῶς ἐμήνυσεν ἄφιξιν,
γεγενημένους ἤδη κατὰ τὸν Μαυροπόταμον.[38]   From this gramatically
rather corrupt Greek text one might infer that the Emperor was informed
of the appearance of the Russians, when the latter — not the Emperor —
were at Mauropotamon.   Of course this reading and intepretation depend on the defectiveness of the printed text and cannot be seriously
considered.[39]

---

[31] See W. M. Ramsay, *The Historical Geography of Asia Minor* (London, 1890), p. 210 and 460.
Ramsay says that the Melas is now the river Tchark Su, which has now no connection with the San-
garius. See also W. Tomaschek, 'Zur historischen Topographie von Kleinasien im Mittelalter,'
Sitzungsberichte der Akademie der Wissenschaften in Wien, cxxiv (1891), pp. 7–8.

[32] Vasiliev, *Byzantium and the Arabs*, i (St Petersburg, 1900), p. 155, n. 2 (in Russian). My note
is reproduced in full in the French edition of my book (p. 196, n. 2).

[33] Vasiliev, *Byzance et les Arabes*, i, 196, n. 2.

[34] Lamanski, *The Slavonic Life of St Cyril* . . . (Petrograd, 1915), p. 59 (in Russian).

[35] Bury, *op. cit.*, p. 419, n. 2.

[36] Th. Uspenski, *History of the Byzantine Empire*, ii, 1 (Leningrad, 1927), 320 and n. 1 (in Russian).

[37] καὶ βασιλεὺς, μὲν ὑπερορίους πόνους καὶ μακροὺς ἀνατλᾷ. Müller, i, p. 165, J23.

[38] *Theodos. Melit.*, ed. Tafel, p. 168.   *Leo Gramm.*, p. 240.   *Georg. Mon.*, p. 826.

[39] See A. Kunik and V. Rosen, *Accounts of al-Bekri and other authors on Russia and the Slavs*, i
(St Petersburg, 1878), 190: 'the governor of Tsargrad, Oryphas, informed Michael of the appearance

The Greek sources which depend on the unpublished Symeon Logothete and the Slavonic version of the latter relate that in their raid on Constantinople, the Russians entered the Hieron (τὸ Ἰερόν) and began their devastations there.[40]   Nicetas Paphlagon, in his *Life of Ignatius*, completing the picture, says that the Russians coming from the Euxine passed through Stenon (τῷ Στενῷ), penetrated into the Sea of Marmora, and devastated the Islands of the Princes.[41]   The Hieron was originally a promontory on the Bosphorus near the Euxine, in the narrow section of the Straits, on the top of which are still to be seen the ruins of the so-called Genoese Castle, and at its foot the Turkish fort and village of Anadoli-Kavak.   The name τὸ Ἰερόν itself goes back to an ancient temple which attracted many pilgrims in pre-Christian times.[42]   In the texts connected with the raid of 860, as in other Byzantine sources as well, Hieron means the straits of Bosphorus, and is identical with the name of Stenon given by Nicetas Paphlagon.   Thus the Russians passed through the Bosphorus, which, in Greek sources, is called Hieron or Stenon. Later Byzantine historical evidence, like Cedrenus (Scylitzes) and Zonaras, fails to mention the Straits.

The old Russian Chronicles which deal with the Russian raid of 860 and the Slavonic version of George Hamartolus' Continuator give for Hieron or Stenon the name *sud*, which has been discussed and interpreted in various ways by many scholars for many years.   Now, I think, we may return to the old interpretation of the term as the Germanic word *Sund*, *a strait*, which was taken into the Russian language from the Norse; and we must dismiss any connection of the word *sud* with a sort of Greco-Byzantine fortification σοῦδα-*suda*, which has been sometimes pointed out.[43]

---

of the Russian pirates at the Black River (Mauropotamon, on the eastern shore of the Bosphorus?)' This passage and interrogation mark belong to Kunik.

[40] *Georg. Hamartoli Continuator*, ed. Istrin, p. 11; ed. Muralt, p. 736. *Sym. Mag.*, p. 674. *Leo Gramm.*, p. 241. *Theodos. Melit.*, ed. Tafel, p. 168. *Georg. Mon.*, p. 826. Symeon the Logothete's Slavonic version, ed. Sreznevski, p. 106; Weingart, *Byzantské kroniky*, II, 1, p. 135 (inside Iera).

[41] *Nicetae Paphlagonis Vita Ignatii*, Migne, *P. G.*, CV, vol. 516; Mansi, *Conciliorum Collectio*, XVI, col. 236.

[42] See P. Dethier, *Le Bosphore et Constantinople* (Vienne, 1873), pp. 70–71. In later times the crusaders called the place al-Giro = τὸ Ἰερόν. Tomaschek, 'Zur historischen Topographie von Kleinasien im Mittelalter,' *Sitzungsberichte der Ak. der Wissenschaften in Wien*, CXXIV (1891), p. 3. E. A. Grosvenor, *Constantinople*, I (Boston, 1895), p. 207.

[43] We have recently had a number of attempts to interpret the term σοῦδα, especially by Fr. Dölger and H. Grégoire. See, for instance, F. Dölger, 'Zur Σοῦδα - Frage,' *Byz. Zeitschrift*, XXXVIII (1938), 36, where in note 2 he lists Grégoire's four articles on the subject. In 1937 Grégoire entirely renounced the idea of the connection of the old Russian *sud* with σοῦδα and concluded that *Sud* is a Scandinavian word and the Germanic *Sund*. Grégoire, 'Etymologies byzantino-latines,' *Byzantion*, XII (1937), 294, n. 1. There is a special Russian study by V. Istrin, 'Sud', in the Annalistic Accounts on the Attacks of the Russian Princes on Constantinople,' *Journal of the Ministry of Public Instruc-*

A valuable addition to our knowledge of the Russian invasion is supplied by Nicetas Paphlagon, who, as we have noted above, describes how the 'bloodiest people of the Scythians, the so-called Ros' entered the northern section of the Sea of Marmora and devastated the Islands of the Princes.

This group consists of nine islands of unequal size. Four of them are relatively large: Proti, Antigoni, Halki, and the largest, Prinkipo. Then there are five other small islets, the tiniest of the group: Pita, between Antigoni and Halki; Terebinthos (Τερέβινθος, now ᾿Αντερόβινθος or ᾿Αντερόβιθος), about two miles east of Prinkipo;[44] Niandros (Ύάτρος or ῎Ιατρος), south of Prinkipo; Plati (Πλάτη, less often Πλατεῖα), west of Antigoni and south-west of Proti; and Oxia (᾿Οξία), the westernmost islet of the group.[45]

In his biography of Ignatius, Nicetas was interested only in those islets where his hero had established his monasteries. They were three: Plati, Hyatros, and Terebinthos.[46] Nicetas does not mention the larger islands. His first statement deals with Terebinthos. In February 860, Ignatius had been permitted by the Byzantine authorities to return to Terebinthos from Mytilene, where he had remained six months under strict supervision. Before the foundation by Ignatius of the monastery of Satyros on the opposite coast of Asia Minor in 873, Terebinthos seems to have been Ignatius' favorite dwelling place.[47] According to him, the Russians raided Terebinthos, despoiled his monastery, seized twenty-two of his household, and dismembered them with axes on the stern of a ship. Here not without malice, Nicetas remarks that, when the Byzantine high authorities, who had no sympathy whatever with Ignatius' tribulations, learned about this disaster, they rather regretted that Ignatius himself had failed to fall into barbarous hands and that he had not been slain with the other captives.[48]   The second episode of the Russian incursion on the

---

tion (December, 1916), pp. 191–198. Istrin still admits a connection between *sud* and σοῦδα. See also Istrin, *The Chronicle of George Hamartolus in an Old Slavo-Russian Version*, ii (Petrograd, 1922), p. 210. Cf. Kunik's statement: *sud*, the Norman *Sund*, =τὸ Στενόν=the Narrow Sea=the Golden Horn=Saevidharsund. Dorn, *Caspia* (St Petersburg, 1875), p. 377 (Russian ed.). Also Tomaschek, *op. cit.*, p. 3: 'the East Slavs inherited the form *sud* from their Norman dukes (Herzogen) from the word *Sund*=τὸ Στενόν.'

[44] Schlumberger writes that this island is now sometimes called 'the Island of Rabbits.' G. Schlumberger, *Les Iles des Princes*, (Paris, 1884), p. 254. A new reprint of this book appeared in 1925.

[45] See J. Pargoire, 'Les monastères de saint Ignace et les cinq plus petits îlots de l'Archipel des Princes,' *Izvestiya* of the Russian Archaeological Institute in Constantinople, vii (1902), pp. 56–91. R. Janin, 'Les Iles des Princes, Étude historique et topographique,' *Echos d'Orient*, xxiii (1924), pp. 178–194; 315–338; 415–436.

[46] Nic. Paphl. *Vita Ignatii*. Migne, *P.G.*, cv, col. 496: Πλάτη μὲν οὖν καὶ Ύάτρος τότε καὶ Τερέβινθος, αἱ Πριγκίπειοι νῆσοι προσαγορεύονται. Mansi, *Conciliorum Collectio*, xvi, col. 217. See Pargoire, *op. cit.*, p. 57.   [47] Pargoire, *op. cit.*, p. 64. Janin, *op. cit.*, p. 429.

[48] *Vita Ignatii*, col. 516. Mansi, xvi, col. 236. Referring to this Russian raid on Terebinthos, Presnyakov makes a strange blunder, locating this island 'near Sinope.' A. Presnyakov, *Lectures in Russian History*, i (Moscow, 1938), p. 46 (in Russian).

Islands of the Princes told by Ignatius is his relation of the Russian raid on the island of Plati (Πλάτη, Πλατεῖα). Here were located the Church of the Forty Martyrs of Sebasteia and the Chapel (εὐκτήριον) of the Holy Virgin. Among other things which were wrecked on this islet, the Russians cast down to the ground the communion table in the Chapel. Several years later the deposed Patriarch Ignatius repaired the table and restored it to its former place.[49] Nicetas fails to mention any particular fact as to the third islet, Hyatros, where the third monastery of Ignatius was established.

Although Nicetas says nothing about other islands of the group, especially about the large islands like Proti, Antigoni, Halki, and Prinkipo, we may be almost certain that they were also raided by the Russians. Pillaging was very easy, because the islands were not fortified, and at the same time they contained monasteries, churches, and settlements. Nicetas fails to mention these raids, because in these islands the monasteries and churches had not been established by the ex-Patriarch Ignatius, Nicetas' hero. But the islands of the group are located so near each other that none could have escaped the Russian invader.[50]

At one time, on account of chronological uncertainty, the Terebinthos episode was considered to be one of the Russian raids prior to the main invasion which, as we know, was attributed by the vast majority of scholars to the year 865–866. In 1867, referring to the raid on Terebinthos, Hergenröther, as I have pointed out above, wrote that this Russian expedition of course is not identical with the direct Russian attack on Constantinople to be described below.[51]

A characteristic feature of the raid of 860, as it is reflected in our sources is the extreme ferocity, rapacity, savagery, and destructive activities of the Russians. All these piratical qualities may be observed in the raids of their Norman compatriots also all over Western Europe, and in the Russian campaigns at the beginning of the tenth century on Tabaristan and other places along the Caspian coast. Masudi writes of these campaigns that the Russians shed blood, carried off women and children, plundered property, and spread everywhere destruction and fire.[52] The recently published and translated Persian geographer of the tenth century calls the Russians evil-tempered, intractable, arrogant-looking, quarrelsome, and warlike.[53] But it is not to be forgotten that these destructive

---

[49] *Vita Ignatii*, col. 532: Τούτου τὴν τράπεζαν πρώην οἱ Ῥῶς τὴν νῆσον πορθοῦντες κατέβαλον εἰς γῆν, ὁ Ἰγνάτιος δὲ ταύτην αὖθις ἀνεθρόνισε.

[50] See a minuscule map of the Islands of the Princes in Janin, *op. cit.*, p. 316.

[51] J. Hergenröther, *Photius*, I (Regensburg, 1867), 421.

[52] Masudi (Maçoudi), *Les Prairies d'or*, ed. Barbier de Meynard, II, p. 21. Marquart, *Osteuropäische und ostasiatische Streifzüge*, pp. 331–332.

[53] Hudud al-'Alam, *The Regions of the World. A Persian Geography* 372 A.H.–982 A.D. Translated and explained by V. Minorski (Oxford, 1937), p. 159, §44 (Gibb Memorial, New series, XI).

qualities of the Russians revealed themselves during the raids only; as we
know, Russian merchants, in the ninth and tenth centuries, peacefully
carried on their business transactions, and were known in Spain (Andalus),
Rome, Constantinople, Bagdad, and among the Khazars as peaceable
traders.

The sources connected with the unpublished Greek text of Symeon
Logothete say briefly that the Russians 'made much slaughter,'[54] or 'made
much slaughter on Christians,'[55] or 'made much destruction to Christians
and shed innocent blood.'[56]   A very dramatic picture of the savage Russian raid on the Islands of the Princes, especially on the island of Terebinthos, has already been described.

The Patriarch Photius devoted much attention to the Russian atrocities
in his two sermons.   Photius' aim was not to give his congregation an
exact picture of the event, but to impress his hearers, to make them feel
how great were their sins and transgressions, and to bring them to repent-
ance, atonement, and moral regeneration.   So we should not be surprised that in several respects Photius' presentation is highly colored and
not without exaggeration.   But the passages in his sermons devoted to
Russian atrocities do not contradict our general knowledge of their excesses and may be accepted as reliable.   Here I wish to give the passages
from his two sermons which refer to this aspect of the raid.   Of course
the passages where Photius pictures Russian cruelty by Biblical quotations are not of much historical value; as, for instance, in his first sermon
he quotes the book of Jeremiah (VI, 22–24), exclaiming, 'Behold, a people
cometh from the north country . . . they shall lay hold on bow and spear;
they are cruel, and have no mercy; their voice roareth like the sea,' *etc.*[57]
But in several other passages Photius clearly reflects the real situation.
As we know, the first sermon was preached at the very beginning of the
invasion.   'I see,' Photius exclaims, 'that a cloud of barbarians floods
with blood our city which is withered because of our sins. . . .   Alas for
me, that I see how the savage and cruel people surround the city and
plunder the city suburbs, destroy everything, ruin everything, fields,
houses, cattle, herds (beasts of burden), women, children, old men, youth;
they strike all with the sword, feeling pity for no one, sparing no one.
Destruction for all of us!   Like locust on corn-field, like mildew on vine-

---

[54] πολὺν εἰργάσαντο φόνον. Sym. Mag., p. 674.

[55] πολὺν φόνον κατὰ χριστιανῶν κατεργάσαντο. *Georg. Ham. Cont.*, ed. Istrin, p. 11 (ed. Muralt,
p. 736).

[56] πολὺν εἰργάσαντο φθόρον χριστιανῶν καὶ ἀθῷον αἷμα ἐξέχεον. *Theodos. Melit.*, 168. *Leo Gramm.*,
p. 241. *Georg. Mon.*, pp. 826–827.   The same words are in the Slavonic version of Symeon the
Logothete, ed. Sreznevski, p. 106; Weingart, *op. cit.*, II, 1, p. 135.

[57] I refer to C. Müller's (*Fragm. hist. graecorum*, V, 1) and Aristarkhes' (Constantinople, 1900)
editions.

yard, or rather like a hurricane or typhoon or flood or I cannot say what, they have attacked our country and eliminated the whole generations of inhabitants. . . . It is much better to die once than constantly to expect to die and be unceasingly pained and afflicted in mind about the sufferings of our neighbors. . . . This savage and barbarous people having spread out from the very suburbs of the city, like wild boars, have overrun its surroundings.'[58]

In the second sermon, which was delivered after the Russian departure, there are several passages referring to Russian ferocity, some of which are repetitions of what was said in the first sermon.

'Indeed (this disaster),' Photius says, 'does not resemble other inroads of barbarians; but the unexpectedness of the incursion and its extraordinary speed, the mercilessness of the barbarous race and the harshness of their temper and the savagery of their habits, prove that this blow has been sent from heaven like a thunderbolt. . . . They despoiled the surroundings and plundered the suburbs, cruelly massacred captives and safely established themselves around all this (city), showing in their greed for our wealth such conceit and arrogance that the inhabitants did not even dare to look on them with level and undaunted eyes. . . . (This people) poured upon our frontiers all at once, in the twinkling of an eye, like a billow of the sea, and destroyed the inhabitants on the earth, as the wild boar (destroys) grass or reed or crop.[59] One might have seen how infants were torn away from the (mother's) breast and (deprived) of milk and life itself; and the extemporaneous grave for them was — alas — the rocks against which they were dashed; and the mothers pitiably cried aloud and were slaughtered along with the babes who were mangled and mutilated before death. . . . Their cruelty did not confine itself to humans; but their savagery destroyed all speechless animals — oxen, horses, birds, and other (animals) whom they met. By an ox lay a man, and both child and horse had a common grave, and women and birds were mixed in each other's blood. Everything was filled with dead bodies; the water in the rivers turned to blood . . . dead bodies made the arable land rotten, crowded the roads; because of them the groves became wild and waste like bushes and wilderness; caverns were full of them; mountains and hills, gullies and ravines differed in no way from the cemeteries of the city.'[60]

Of course these excerpts of Photius' two homilies contain rhetoric and oratory as well as some commonplaces. I repeat that Photius' homilies are not a chronicle; they are a special form of elaborate writing intended to impress as far as possible the imagination and spirit of the congregation. But they have an historical basis, a reality which was still before the eyes

---

[58] C. Müller, p. 165, §§ 18–23. Aristarkhes, II, 15–18, §§ 2–3. In connection with the last phrase cf. *Psalms*, LXXIX (LXXX), 14 (according to the Septuagint): καὶ ὄνος ἄγριος κατενεμήσατο αὐτήν. Photius: μονιοῦ δίκην ἀγρίου τὰ πέριξ αὐτῆς κατενεμήσατο.

[59] As in the first sermon, this is reminiscent of *Psalms*, LXXIX (LXXX), 14 (see above).

[60] Ed. Müller, pp. 167–168, §3, 6, 10–13. Aristarkhes, II, pp .31–37.

of the hearers.   From Photius' homilies we realize that the Russian devastation and destruction greatly affected all aspects of the daily life of the people, and his description differs in no way from what we know about the Norman incursions and raids all over Western Europe.   One very important conclusion must be drawn from Photius' sermons, and from other sources too, that all this destruction was carried out in the suburbs and vicinity of the city and the neighboring regions only; the capital itself remained unharmed and unmolested.

Kunik once wrote, 'It is unknown to us whether the Russians in 865 quenched their bloody ferocity chiefly on the representatives of the clergy.'   Such a question is quite superfluous, because, from various descriptions dealing with West and East, we are well informed that all classes of people, including of course the clergy, suffered equally from Norman violence.[61]

[61] Kunik and Rosen, *Accounts of al-Bekri* . . . , I, 177 (in Russian).

DURATION OF THE RUSSIAN INVASION

THANKS to the Brussels *Anonymous Chronicle*, we know exactly that the Russians came in two hundred boats on the eighteenth of June, 860. But we have no definite information as to when they withdrew.

If I am not mistaken, the question of the duration of the Russian campaign of 860 arose in 1842 when Bishop Porphyrius Uspenski published the following note from a Greek *synaxarion* (Ms. of the year 1249), referring to 5 June: '(On this day) is commemorated the disaster inflicted upon us by invasion of the pagans, when, beyond any hope, we were yet liberated through the prayers of the Immaculate Lady the Virgin Mary.'[1]

In 1903–1904 Lamanski wrote, 'There is reason to believe that the siege of Constantinople by the Rus of Askold was prolonged even more than a year. Such was the opinion of Bishop Porphyrius.' In another place the same author remarks that if Porphyrius' note refers to the liberation of Tsargrad from Askold's Rus, the withdrawal may be referred to the beginning of June, 861. In a third reference Lamanski says, 'If we believe Nicetas (Paphlagon) that Ooryphas was searching for Ignatius in the Islands of the Princes and along the coastland in May or at the beginning of June, 861, we may conclude that at that time the Rus had already withdrawn, and consequently the note of the *synaxarion* which was indicated by Archbishop Porphyrius on June 5 does not refer to Russia.'[2] Lamanski was, then, uncertain as to the duration of the Russian raid. In 1903 Papadopoulos-Kerameus, in the study mentioned by Lamanski, takes the positive view that the commemorative note which refers to Ros must be that of June 5, so that the invasion and siege by the Rus lasted probably almost a whole year, i.e., from June 18, 860 to June 5, 861. He admits that there is no direct evidence on the subject: but (1) the so-called Chronicle of Symeon Magister refers the time of the invasion to the ninth year of Michael, and that of the siege of Constantinople to the tenth year

---

[1] A. Vostokov, *Description of the Russian and Slavonic manuscripts of the Rumyantsev Museum* (St Petersburg, 1842), p. 450, *prologue*, no. cccxix. Here Vostokov remarks that this commemorative note is also inserted in the *Menologium* of the Gospel of Lutsk, and adds, 'But to what invasion does this refer? In the *Menologium* of the Gospel of Lutsk we read a note on 'the commemoration of a terrible disaster inflicted upon us by invasion of the pagans' (Vostokov, *op. cit.*, p. 177, no. cxii, under 5 June). Here Vostokov says, 'In no other menologium do we find this commemorative note. Here of course the reference is to the Mongol invasion, which seems to have been commemorated by the Church only in South Russia.' See also Lamanski, *The Slavonic Life of St Cyril*, p. 97, n. 1; 112. Both publications in Russian. In Russian liturgical literature, the *prologue* (Greek word Πρόλογος) is a book containing condensed stories of the saints and religious feast days. The Greeks call this book *synaxarion* (συναξάριον), in the Latin form *synaxarium*.

[2] Lamanski, *op. cit.*, 97, n. 1; 112; 117. Lamanski mentioned that Papadopoulos-Kerameus had prepared for print speculations and proofs of his own concerning the duration of this siege (a year more or less), p. 97, n. 1.

(p. 674).   Therefore, Papadopoulos-Kerameus proceeds, the apprehensions of the Byzantines started, not on the day of the siege of the city itself, in the strict sense of the word, but from the appearance of the Rus in Thrace, Paphlagonia, and Mysia, and their spread along the shores of the Bosphorus and in the Sea of Marmora, so that the people had been forced earlier to close the city gates.   (2) That the siege of Byzantium really dragged on a considerable time we have testimony in the sermon of George, under Photius the *chartophylax* of Saint Sophia, who later was metropolitan of Nicomedia.   George's sermon was delivered at the festival of the Presentation in the Temple of the Mother of God, i.e., in November, 860.   In it we discover a direct hint at a barbarian invasion and siege, which can refer only to the Rus (Migne, c, col. 1456).   Here Papadopoulos-Kerameus gives the Greek text and a Russian translation of the appropriate passage.   (3) We find the third proof of the duration of the siege in Photius' second homily, when, as if speaking of events some time in the past, he says, 'Do you remember that shuddering, those tears and sobs, with which then we were all seized in the utmost despair?,' and once more, 'You all know, of course, that at that time everyone, urged by his conscience, if he had done wrong, gave promise to God never again to do evil.'[3]

In 1914 F. Uspenski admitted that the Russians, after failing under Tsargrad, withdrew at the beginning of the autumn of 861.[4]   In 1917 Miss N. Polonskaya, in her conscientious study on Christianity in Russia before Vladimir, gives the following rather inexact statement: 'Now on the basis of Cumont's Brussels *Byzantine Chronicle*, one may regard as firmly established the fact that the siege of Tsargrad by the Russians lasted from June 18, 860 to July 5, 861.   Other sources also confirm this: the *Life* of St Clement and the testimony of Joannes the Deacon of Venice.   Thus,' Miss Polonskaya concludes, 'one debatable question is to be regarded as settled.'[5]   Of course her opening lines must be corrected because the *Brussels Chronicle* mentions only the date of the beginning of the invasion and fails to indicate any date for the withdrawal of the Russians.   Evidently she took the date of the Russian retreat from Papadopoulos-Kerameus' study cited above (her reference to p. 39 of his work is inaccurate).   It should also be pointed out that Papadoupoulos-Kerameus gives as the date of the Russian retreat June 5, not July 5, as is

[3] Papadopoulos-Kerameus, 'The Akathistos of the Mother of God, Rus, and the Patriarch Photius,' *Viz. Vremennik*, x (1903), pp. 391–393 (in Russian).

[4] Uspenski, 'The First Pages of the Russian Annals,' p. 19. *Zapiski* of the Odessa Society of History and Antiquities, xxxii (1914).   I refer to the pagination of an offprint.

[5] N. Polonskaya, 'On the Question of Christianity in Russia before Vladimir,' *Journal of the Ministry of Public Instruction*, 1917, September, p. 44 (in Russian).

stated in Polonskaya's study.   I do not know in what respect the *Life* of St Clement may help her as to the Russian campaign; she merely mentions this *Life* without any reference and without any specific indication of its relation to her study.   As we have shown above, the reference to Ioannes the Deacon of Venice is to be discarded.

Quite a different point of view is represented by the Greek editor of Photius' sermons, S. Aristarkhes.   Accepting the year 861 as that of the Russian invasion, he thinks that the invasion began in the spring of 861, or, as he says in another place, at the outset of June, 861, and ended in July of the same year.   According to him, the first sermon was preached by Photius on Sunday, June 5, and the second on Saturday, July 2.[6] Aristarkhes' dating of the Russian incursion, especially if we remember that his speculations were written after the publication of the *Brussels Chronicle*, is arbitrary and cannot be seriously considered.

Let us examine our sources on the Russian invasion from the point of view of its duration.

A very important source for this question is the *Chronicle* of the so-called Symeon Magister or Pseudo-Symeon.   Many years ago, in 1876 to be exact, a German scholar, F. Hirsch, proved that the chronological data in which this *Chronicle* abounds cannot be accepted;[7] and much later, in 1912, Bury, referring to Hirsch's study, wrote, 'It is important to observe that the chronological data by which this chronicle is distinguished are worthless.'[8]   Among these worthless chronological data of Pseudo-Symeon we must include his attribution of events to appropriate 'exact' years of Michael's reign.   In this respect Pseudo-Symeon is absolutely unreliable.   But, from a general point of view, his chronicle as we have it now in printed form is a very important source for the history of the ninth and tenth centuries.   He lists the Russian invasion under two successive years of Michael's reign, the ninth and tenth, which is of course absolutely wrong.   But if these years are wrong, the idea may be right that the Russian incursion lasted over a year and according to the Byzantine calendar started in one year and continued into the next.   The *Brussels Chronicle* supplies us with an amazingly exact date of the appearance of Russian ships before the capital: on the eighteenth of June, the eighth indiction, the year 6368, in the fifth year of Michael's reign. These three definitions, in complete accord with each other, give the year

---

[6] 'Αριστάρχης, Φωτίου Λόγοι καὶ 'Ομιλίαι (Constantinople, 1900), i, p. κζ΄; ii, 2–3; the dates of Photius' sermons, p. 4.   The dates of June 5 and July 2, 861, do not fall on Sunday and Saturday.   See E. Gerland, 'Photios und der Angriff der Russen auf Byzanz,' *Neue Jahrbücher für das klassische Altertum, Geschichte und deutsche Literatur*, xi (Leipzig, 1903), 718, n. 2.

[7] F. Hirsch, *Byzantinische Studien* (Leipzig, 1876), p. 342 sq.   See above.

[8] Bury, *op. cit.*, p. 459.

860. The fifth year of Michael's reign is to be accepted as the year of his sole reign after Theodora's fall in 856. The year 6368 of the Creation ended on the thirty-first of August, and a new year, 6369, began on the first of September. So, had the Russian invasion lasted only just over two months and a half, it would have belonged to the two consecutive years, 6368 and 6369 from the point of view of the Byzantine calendar. Let us see what Pseudo-Symeon tells under the first year of the invasion, i.e., from June 18, 6368 to September 1, 6369. In this year Michael marched against the Arabs, leaving the prefect Ooryphas in charge of the capital. The latter informed the Emperor, who had already reached Mauropotamos, of the appearance of the Ros in two hundred boats. The Emperor, having had no time to achieve anything in Asia Minor, immediately returned (ed. Bonn., 674, ch. 37). Then under the following year, i.e., after the first of September, 6369, Pseudo-Symeon narrates how the Russians entered the Bosphorus (τὸ Ἱερόν), surrounded the city, and slaughtered a great number of people. The Emperor was hardly able to cross the Bosphorus. And then follows the well-known story of how the Emperor and Photius dipped the precious relic in the sea, and how the violent storm which suddenly arose dispersed the Russian ships (ed. Bonn., 674, ch. 38). In these two chapters of Pseudo-Symeon's chronicle we have a very valuable indication that the Russian incursion might have lasted not merely several days or a week, but at least several months.

Some scholars are inclined to believe that the Russian raid was of very short duration. In 1895 Loparev wrote that the siege lasted only one week, from June 18 to June 25.[9] Although Loparev's speculations, as we have seen above, were rightly refuted by Vasilievski, Shakhmatov, in 1919, following Loparev, stated that the Russians withdrew from the capital on June 25, 860.[10] In 1930 V. Mošin, referring to Archbishop Porphyrius' note on June 5, wrote that it was absolutely impossible to admit that the siege might have lasted a year; it is difficult to believe that the pirates could have spent a whole year under Constantinople; in that time the Emperor might have gathered an army and liberated the city.' Cyril,'[11] Mošin proceeds, 'left Constantinople for Kherson in the Crimea and found there the relics of St Clement in January 861. He could not have left Constantinople when the city was surrounded by the Russians. Nicetas Paphlagon brings confirmation by saying that the Russian assault took place before the Council of Tsargrad in May, 861, and before the earthquake in August, 860, so that the Russians could not have stayed under

---

[9] Ch. Loparev, 'An Old Source on the Placing of the Garment of the Mother of God in Blachernae,' *Viz. Vremennik*, II (1895), 626 (in Russian).

[10] A. Shakhmatov, *The Earliest Fortunes of the Russian Nation* (Petrograd, 1919), p. 60 (in Russian).   [11] Here Mošin has in view Cyril (Constantine), the apostle to the Slavs.

Constantinople more than two months.'[12]   Bury also believed in a short Russian campaign.   From his point of view, the Russian defeat was inflicted at the moment of the Emperor's arrival.   Bury writes, 'He must have intercepted the barbarians and their spoils in the Bosphorus, where there was a battle and a rout.'[13]

Before 900 there were four famous sieges of Constantinople which have left a deep impression on popular imagination, have survived in the ritual of the Byzantine Church, and, through the latter, in that of the Greek-Orthodox Church in general down to our own day.   The four sieges were: the siege by the Persians and Avars in 626 under Heraclius; the siege by the Arabs in 674–678 under Constantine IV; the siege by the Arabs in 717–718 under Leo III the Isaurian; and the siege by the Russians in 860 under Michael III.   I do not include here the siege of Constantinople in 821–823 by the rebel Thomas the Slavonian under Michael II the Stammerer, because Thomas' insurrection, although supported by the Arabs, was considered to belong to the internal life of the Empire, and has left no particular trace in later ecclesiastical tradition.   The sieges of 626 and 717–718 can be identified with absolute certainty in liturgical tradition.

The siege of 626 was commemorated in the Byzantine ecclesiastical ritual under August 7.   This was the day of the liberation of Constantinople from the Persians and Avars under Heraclius.   The *synaxarion* of the Constantinopolitan Church has preserved a detailed story of the siege with the names of the Emperor Heraclius, the Persian King Chosroes, the Khagan of the Avars, and the Scythians.   In conclusion we read, 'Therefore we all celebrate the memory of this event yearly in the holy building of the Holy Virgin, which is in Blachernae.'[14]   A manuscript of the Library of the Monastery of Saint Catherine on Mount Sinai also preserves the statement that on August 7 is commemorated 'the invasion of the Avars in the time of the Emperor Heraclius and the Patriarch Sergius.'[15]   In Slavonic tradition the liberation of Tsargrad from the Persians and Avars is also commemorated under August 7.[16]   The liberation of Constantino-

---

[12] V. Mošin, 'A Study on the First Conversion of Russia,' *Bogoslovie*, v, 2 (Belgrad, 1930), pp. 66–67 (in Serbian).   We shall show below that the earthquake referred to occurred in 862, not 860.

[13] Bury, *op. cit.*, p. 421.

[14] *Prophylaeum ad Acta Sanctorum Novembris.   Synaxarium ecclesiae Constantinopolitanae e codice sirmondiano nunc berolinensi adjectis synaxariis selectis* ed. Hippoliti Delehaye (Brussels, 1902), coll. 872–876.   See also A. Dmitrievski, 'Description of the Liturgical Manuscripts preserved in the Libraries of the Orthodox East,' ɪ, *Typica* (Kiev, 1895), 101 and n. 3 (under August 7).   In these two brief notes no proper names are given.   [15] Dmitrievski, *op. cit.*, ɪ, 101, n. 4.

[16] Archbishop Sergius, *The Complete Liturgical Calendar (Menologion) of the Orient*, sec. ed., ɪɪ, 1 (Vladimir, 1901), p. 239.   See also A. Vostokov, *Description of the Russian and Slavonic Manuscripts of the Rumyantsev Museum* (St Petersburg, 1842), p. 451 (Prologue no. cccxix).

ple from the Agarenes under Leo III the Isaurian in 717–718 is commemorated by the Byzantine and Greek-Orthodox Church on August 16.[17]   In the *Menologium* of Archbishop Sergius under August 16 we read the following passage in Old Slavonic: 'The charity of God, when He repelled with shame the impious Agarenes under Leo the Isaurian in 717, is commemorated.'[18]

Now we turn to the siege of Constantinople by the Arabs, especially by an Arabian fleet, which for five successive years, from April to September, came to blockade the capital, and finally in 678 started home to Syria to be destroyed by a severe winter storm off the southern coast of Asia Minor.   Of course an event of such magnitude must have left a deep impression on the Empire.   The West was also greatly impressed.   The Khagan of the Avars and other Western rulers 'sent ambassadors with gifts to the Emperor and begged him to establish peaceful and loving relations with them . . . and there came a time of great peace in the East and in the West.'[19]   The siege of Constantinople by the Arabs under Constantine IV apparently is commemorated by the Byzantine Church under 25 June.   Under this day, in a Greek manuscript, probably of the tenth century, which has been preserved in the library of the Monastery of St John the Theologian in the island of Patmos, we have a brief note: 'The attack (ἔλευσις) of Saracens and *Roun*, and the religious procession in Blachernae.'[20]   Referring to this note, two manuscripts of the Patriarchal Library of Jerusalem, no 53 and no. 285, give the following statement: 'We perform this commemorative rite because God liberated us from the Saracens, who surrounded us by land and by sea.'[21]

In one of the Old Slavonic *Prologues* or *Synaxaria* which is preserved at the Rumyantsev Museum in Moscow, we have the same event commemorated under June 25.   We read, 'The withdrawal of impious Saracens by land and by sea from our imperial city is commemorated.'[22]   We see that in this version there is no mention of the *Roun;* it deals exclusively with the Saracens.

---

[17] *Propylaeum*, coll. 901 (3)–904: ἐν ἀρχῇ γὰρ τῆς βασιλείας Λέοντος τοῦ Ἰσαύρου (col. 901).   Dmitrievski, *op. cit.*, i, 106 (a Jerusalem manuscript).   [18] Sergius, *op. cit.*, ii, 1, p. 248.

[19] *Theophanis Chronographia*, ed. de Boor, p. 356.   On the general importance of the event see the recent work of G. Ostrogorski, *Geschichte des byzantinischen Staates* (Munich, 1940), pp. 80–81.

[20] καὶ τῶν Σαρακινῶν καὶ τῶν ῾Ροῦν ἡ ἔλευσις, καὶ λιτὴ ἐν Βλαχέρναις.   A. Dmitrievski, *Description of the Liturgical Manuscripts preserved in the Libraries of the Orthodox East*, i, *Typica* (Kiev, 1895), p. 83. The same text in *Propylaeum*, coll. 769–770, *Synaxaria selecta*.

[21] Dmitrievski, *op. cit.*, i, 83, n. 1.

[22] A. Vostokov, *Description of Russian and Slavonic manuscripts of the Rumyantsev Museum* (St Petersburg, 1842), p. 450, *Prologue* no. cccxix. Vostokov concludes from the words of the *Prologue*, 'our imperial city,' that its compiler or copyist lived in Constantinople. For a few words on this *Prologue* see Arch. Sergius, *The Complete Menologion of the Orient*, sec. ed. i (Vladimir, 1901), 304 (in Russian).

In connection with this commemoration of the siege of 674–678, if our text really deals, as we believe, with this event, we may conclude that the Arabs who, every year, as we have noted above, laid siege to Constantinople from April to September, departed during the last year of the siege some day in the summer, in June, for the Church commemorated the liberation on June 25. It is to be noted that the Greek text deals not only with an attack by Saracens but also with one by *Roun*, a name which, for the time being at least, has no meaning for us whatever. Our first reaction is that in this name we may have a distorted form of *Rus* or *Ros* ('Ρώς, 'Ρῶς) i.e., Russians. If this were true, it would be evidence for a combined Arab-Russian attack, of which we know absolutely nothing. In 1892 A. Krasnoseltsev was inclined to believe this a distorted form Ρως or Ρους; but he referred this commemoration of June 25 not to the days of Constantine IV but to the Russian attack of 860, and tried to explain the presence of Saracens by Photius' testimony that at the beginning of the siege the Emperor Michael was not at home, and that he was fighting the Saracens, from whom he succeeded in escaping.[23] Krasnoseltsev's opinion was shared in 1895 by Chr. Loparev, who wrote that, 'as an easily understood matter of convenience, the Church commemorated on the same day the liberation from the Saracen invasion of the Empire and the liberation from the Russian invasion upon Constantinople, 'although that liberation cost the moral dignity of Tsargrad dear; Michael fled from the Saracens and made a peace shameful for Byzantium with the Russians.'[24] In 1901 Archbishop Sergius also refers the mention of the attack of the Saracens and *Roun* to the invasion of Askold and Dir in 860.[25] But the enigmatic name *Roun* occurs only once, in a very defective manuscript, full of errors, so it is impossible to draw any definite conclusion from such doubtful ground. When a better manuscript is discovered the form *Roun* itself may disappear.[26] Since the name *Roun* is thus eliminated from our discussion, June 25 at present commemorates only a Saracen attack and a religious procession to be performed every year on that day to celebrate the liberation of the capital. Since the sieges of 626 and

[23] N. Krasnoseltsev, 'The Rule (*Typikon*) of the Church of St Sophia in Constantinople,' *Annals* (*Letopis*) of the Historico-Philological Society at the University of Novorossisk, II, Byzantine Section (Odessa, 1892), 216–217 (in Russian).

[24] Chr. Loparev, 'An Old Source for the Placing of the Vestment of the Holy Virgin in Blachernae, in a new interpretation in connection with the Russian Invasion upon Byzantium in 860,' *Viz. Vremennik*, II (1895), 627 (in Russian).

[25] Serg. Sergius, *The Complete Liturgical Calendar (Menologion)* sec. ed., II, 1 (Vladimir, 1901), 191.

[26] See Vasilievski, 'Avars not Russians, Theodore not George,' *Viz. Vremennik*, III (1896), p. 95. The same doubts in Papadopoulos-Kerameus, 'The Acathistus of the Mother of God, Rus, and Patriarch Photius,' *ibid.*, X (1903), 391 (both in Russian).

717–718 are definitely commemorated on August 7 and August 16, June 25 must commemorate the Arab siege of Constantinople in 674–678. No other siege of the capital by the Arabs is known.[27]

In addition to these three dates in Greek *synaxaria* we have a fourth, under 5 June. The text of the Constantinopolitan *synaxarion* referring to this day is quite valuable. I give the text in an English version: '(On this day) is commemorated the terrific disaster which was inflicted upon us in the form of an incursion of the barbarians; when all were ready to be deservedly captured by them and subjected to slaughter, the merciful and benevolent God, by the bowels of His mercy, contrary to all hope, delivered us, through the intercession in our behalf of our Immaculate and All-holy Lady with Him Who through Her protects humanity.'[28] Like other religious services on special occasions, this commemorative service was held at the Campus, on the plain of the Hebdomon (the modern village of Makri Keui) on the shore of the Sea of Marmora at a distance of three miles to the west of the Golden Gate or seven miles from the center of the city.[29] Then in an Old Slavonic version of a Greek *synaxarion*, preserved at the Rumiantsev Museum in Moscow, the following note occurs under June 5: '(On this day) is commemorated the liberation from an invasion of the pagans through the prayers of the Immaculate Lady the Virgin Mary.'[30]

If we read attentively the text of the Constantinopolitan *synaxarion* quoted above, we see, even taking into consideration that the aggressors are not called by name, that the terrific incursion of the barbarians, the capture and slaughter of the people, and ultimately the miraculous intercession of the Holy Virgin, which, when the people were in despair, saved

---

[27] L. Bréhier has recently accepted the date of 25 June as that of the withdrawal of the Arabs from the capital, and pointed out that this date is commemorated every year by the Churches. *Histoire de l'Eglise depuis les origines jusqu'à nos jours*, publiée sous la direction de A. Fliche et V. Martin. 5. *Grégoire le Grand, les états barbares et la conquête arabe* (Paris, 1938), p. 184 and n. 2.

[28] *Propylaeum*, coll. 729–731: Ἡ ἀνάμνησις τῆς μετὰ φιλανθρωπίας ἐπενεχθείσης ἡμῖν φοβερᾶς ἀνάγκης ἐν τῇ τῶν βαρβάρων ἐπιδρομῇ, ὅτε μέλλοντας πάντας ὑπ' αὐτῶν δικαίως αἰχμαλωτίζεσθαι καὶ φόνῳ μαχαίρας παραδίδοσθαι ὁ οἰκτίρμων καὶ φιλάνθρωπος Θεὸς διὰ σπλάγχνα ἐλέους αὐτοῦ παρ' ἐλπίδα πᾶσαν ἐλυτρώσατο ἡμᾶς, πρεσβευούσης αὐτὸν ὑπὲρ ἡμῶν τῆς ἀχράντου καὶ παναγίας δεσποίνης ἡμῶν τὸν τὸ ἀνθρώπινον γένος δι'αὐτῆς φυλαττόμενον.

[29] See Dmitrievski, *op. cit.*, ι, pp. 78–79: καὶ ἡ ἔλευσις τῶν βαρβάρων, καὶ λιτὴ ἐν τῷ κάμπῳ; then follows an interesting description of the particular religious service on that day. Dmitrievski gives also excerpts from three other manuscripts which contain references to the commemoration of the same event, and mention ἡ λιτὴ ἐν τῷ κάμπῳ. The two best studies on the Hebdomon are: Al. van Millingen, *Byzantine Constantinople* (London, 1899), pp. 316–341. D. Beliaev, 'Byzantina,' ιιι (St Petersburg, 1907), pp. 57–92. *Zapiski* of the Classical Section of the Russian Archaeological Society, vol. ιv (in Russian).

[30] A. Vostokov, *Description of the Russian and Slavonic manuscripts of the Rumyantsev Museum* (St Petersburg, 1842), p. 450, no. cccxix. This text has also been reproduced by V. Lamanski, *The Slavonic Life of St Cyril* (Petrograd, 1915), 112.

the city — all these points in every detail coincide with the story told by our evidence on the invasion of 860. The Archimandrite Porphyrius Uspenski, the first editor and translator of Photius' Homilies on the Russian invasion, who for the first time called attention to the note quoted above on the pagan invasion mentioned under June 5, as well as Philaret, bishop of Chernigov, and Archbishop Sergius, was inclined to believe that the note refers to the Russian invasion under Askold and Dir. In 1892 Krasnoseltzev wrote that this is not very conceiving.[31] In 1903 Papadopoulos-Kerameus flatly stated that the note could refer only to the Russian invasion.[32] Referring to the *synaxarium* published by Nikodemus in Athens, 1868, whose text is identical with *Propylaeum* (coll. 729–731), Aristarches in 1900 also accepts 5 June as the date of the celebration of the Russian withdrawal.[33]

After considering the four events which have been observed and celebrated by the Greek-Orthodox Church tradition, we may certainly conclude that the celebration on 5 June of the final withdrawal of the pagans from under the walls of Constantinople refers to the Russian withdrawal from Byzantine territory. Since we know now that the Russians made their appearance before Constantinople on June 18, 860, the commemoration of their withdrawal on 5 June, as has been noted above, clearly shows that the Russian invasion lasted about a year, from June, 860 to June, 861; but as we shall see later, towards the close of March, 861, the danger was evidently already much less.

Unfortunately Constantinople in 860–861 had no special historian or chronicler to give us a detailed and exact story of life in the capital during those tragic months. The two eye-witnesses, Photius and Nicetas Paphlagon, were not historians. We are much more fortunate in the siege of 626, of which we have the valuable description written by Theodore Syncellus, who was both a professional writer and an eye-witness of this important event.[34] A quarter of a century after the Russian invasion, there took place in Western Europe the famous great siege of Paris in 885–886 by the Normans. Of course Paris of the ninth century was not a

[31] Krasnoseltsev, 'The Rule (*Typikon*) of the Church of St Sophia in Constantinople,' *Annals (Letopis)* of the Historico-Philological Society at the University of Novorossiya. II. *Byzantine Section* (Odessa, 1892), pp. 215–216. On Krasnoseltzev's doubts see above. Cf. Arch. Sergius, *op. cit.*, II, 1, p. 169; II, 2, pp. 210–211.

[32] Papadopoulos-Kerameus, 'The Akathistos of the Mother of God, Rus, and Patriarch Photius,' *Viz. Vremennik*, X (1903), p. 391 (in Russian).

[33] 'Αριστάρχης, Φωτίου Λόγοι καὶ 'Ομιλίαι, II (Constantinople, 1900), p. 4.

[34] Published by A. Mai, *Nova Patrum Bibliotheca*, VI, 2 (Roma, 1853), pp. 423–437. A much better edition by L. Sternbach, *Analecta Avarica* (Gracow, 1900), pp. 297–320. On the author, Vasilievski, 'Avars not Russians, Theodore not George,' *Viz. Vremennik*, III (1896), p. 92. Sternbach, *op. cit.*, p. 333.

Constantinople. At that time Paris was still an island city (now *la Cité*) washed by the Seine. This siege also is recorded for us by a writer, an eye-witness, the monk Abbo. No matter how wretched is the verse of his long poem, he is our only authority for the details of the great siege of Paris, and in his eyes Paris was the 'Queen of Cities who surpasses all other cities.[35] But in 860–861 Constantinople had not even an Abbo.

Since we know that the Russian invasion was protracted into the year 861, we may say almost with certainty that Russian ships from the north and Norman vessels from the south, as has been noted above, were raiding simultaneously, or within a few months of each other at least, in the Sea of Marmora and in the suburbs of Constantinople. But these simultaneous or almost simultaneous operations of the two Norman-Viking undertakings do not necessarily mean that both sides were acting in complete accordance with each other, fulfilling a general plan, fixed and dictated in advance by one or the other leader. We shall discuss this possibility below.

In addition to the two eye-witnesses of the Russian invasion, Photius and Nicetas Paphlagon, there was a third eye-witness of the invasion of 860, of whom we hear very little. This was George of Nicomedia. He was Photius' close friend and occupied a very high and important position in Constantinople as the *chartophylax* of Saint Sophia, i.e., he was the Patriarch's chancellor and his official secretary, dealt with difficulties of ecclesiastical jurisdiction, assisted Photius with his correspondence, and their relations were always very close.[36] Apparently Photius ordained him metropolitan of Nicomedia in Bithynia in 860, the very year of the Russian invasion. If I am not mistaken, only ten of George's sermons in their vernacular Greek have at present been published; nine of them deal with the festivals connected with the life of the Holy Virgin and according to Ehrhard they are entirely devoid of historical interest.[37]

---

[35] Abbonis *Bella Parisiacae Urbis*, I, vv. 10–12: 'Nam medio Sequanae recubans, culti quoque regni Francigenarum, temet statuis per celsa canendo. Sum polis, ut regina micans omnes super urbes,' *M. G. H., Poetae Latini Aevi Carolini*, IV, 1, ed. P. de Winterfield (Berlin, 1899), p. 79. The Norman attacks on Paris and the siege of the city lasted from the end of November 885 to September 886.

[36] On the *chartophylax*, the most important of the six chief officials under the Patriarch, each of whom controlled some special department, see N. Skabalanovich, *Byzantine State and Church in the Eleventh Century* (St Petersburg, 1884), p. 364 (in Russian). J. M. Hussey, *Church and Learning in the Byzantine Empire, 867–1185* (London, 1937), pp. 122–123. Hussey follows Skabalanovich's work.

[37] Krumbacher (Ehrhard), *Geschichte der byz. Litteratur* (München, 1897), p. 166. A few insignificant words in Montelatici, *Storia della letteratura bizantina* (Milan, 1916), p. 178. A. Vogt, 'Deux discours inédits de Nicetas de Paphlagonie' (Rome, 1931) p. 10 (*Orientalia Christ.*, XXIII, I; no. 71, July 1931). Under November 21 George's canon and canticles are mentioned in Sergius, *op. cit.*, II, 1, p. 360 (in Russian). George's ten sermons and three very short chants in prose (the so-called *idiomela*) are to be found printed in Migne, *P. G.*, c, coll. 1335–1530. Some former data on George's life and works, *ibid.*, coll. 1327–1334.

As has been pointed out above, Papadopoulos-Kerameus stressed the fact that in his sermon, which was preached at the festival of the Presentation in the Temple of the Mother of God, i.e., on November 21, 860, George clearly hints at the Russian invasion. Here Papadopoulos-Kerameus refers to George's seventh sermon, which bears a rather unusual and obscure title: 'Sermon seven. On the same festival[38] and on that which happened thereafter.[39] After finishing the sermon itself, which has no connection with contemporary events, George closes with a sort of appeal to the Holy Virgin. Not much may be drawn from it for our knowledge of the Russian invasion. I give here some excerpts from the concluding part of this sermon:

Stop, by Thy intercession, wars against Thy people; come to aid, with Thy strong power, the flock who rely upon Thee. We hold before ourselves no stronger trophy than Thy aid. . . . Thou movest the boundless clemency of Thy Son towards our misery; Thou revealest wakeful intercession in our behalf. . . . Demand is reasonable; expectation is fine; hope is not deceitful. . . . We hold Thee as mediatress. Thou seest that all Christians entertain hope in Thee. Thus do through Thy power that hope may be fulfilled. There is no other resort from the dangers which oppress us, but Thy impregnable aid. Our rulers have cherished their hopes in Thee. They hold Thee instead of all weapons; they employ Thee as shield and breastplate; they bear Thee around as a crown of glory; they have considered Thee the stronghold of their own empire; they have entrusted to Thee the scepter of the realm. Thus arise in Thy strong power before the people and disperse the enemies of Thy Son, in order that we, being liberated from their impious madness (ἀθέου μανίας), may enjoy general delight and exultation.

This sermon was preached, doubtless, when George was already metropolitan of Nicomedia. Since he was a contemporary of the invasion of 860, his allusions to the impious (ἄθεοι) enemies who menace the country refer to the Russians. Words like 'the dangers which oppress us' or 'arise . . . and disperse the enemies' show that the Russians had not yet withdrawn. The sermon was delivered when they were still raiding and devastating. The sermon celebrated the religious festival of the Presentation in the Temple of the Holy Virgin which was commemorated in Byzantium and is still commemorated in the Greek-Orthodox world in general on November 21. So we may conclude, as Papadopoulos-Kerameus believes, that in November 860 the Russians were still continuing their raiding operations. The words 'they bear Thee around as a crown of glory' allude to the solemn procession with the precious garment of the

---

[38] I.e., that dealt with in the sixth sermon, *On the Presentation in the Temple of the most holy Mother of God*, Migne, c, col. 1420.

[39] Εἰς τὴν αὐτὴν ἑορτὴν καὶ εἰς τὰ ἑξῆς τῆς ἱστορίας. Migne, *op. cit.*, c, col. 1440. The whole sermon coll. 1440–1456.

Holy Virgin.   It is of course regrettable that George did not follow Photius' example and call the Russians specifically by name.

The two passages from Photius' second homily which Papadopoulos-Kerameus cited and which have been given above in this study may be interpreted as indicating a much longer attack than one of several days or two weeks only.   Re-reading the homily, one gets the impression that, even allowing for all sorts of rhetorical embellishments and oratorical exaggerations, the facts described in the homily could not all have happened in a few weeks; the more so since Photius fails to mention the Russian raiding operations in the islands and shores of the Sea of Marmora, which have been authentically described by Nicetas Paphlagon.   It seems to me that Photius' second homily has not reached us in the form in which it was delivered.   The homily consists of two parts.   The first describes the Russian invasion and retreat; the second half, beginning with §26 and down to the end (ed. Müller, pp. 170–173) contains nothing but pious ejaculations and quotations from the Bible, which have no connection with the event.   As I have pointed out above, had Photius' homilies been preached in the form which we have now, they would have been unintelligible and somewhat boring to a congregation.

In 1900, believing with the majority of scholars that the Russian raid was of short duration, I wrote in the Russian version of my book *Byzantium and the Arabs during the Amorian Dynasty* that after the repulse of the Russians Michael III went to Asia Minor again in the summer of the same year, 860, fought the Arabs, and was pitifully defeated, so that he barely escaped captivity by flight.   His general Manuel deserves the credit for the Emperor's escape.[40]   Of course, had Michael's campaign against the Arabs in Asia Minor been undertaken in the summer of 860 after the Russian retreat, the theory of the long Russian expedition would be untenable; for it would be impossible to imagine that the Emperor would leave the capital for a new expedition when the Russians were still raging around the city, along the Bosphorus, and in the Sea of Marmora. But H. Grégoire, in a convincing and illuminating study, has definitely proved that this Asia Minor campaign never book place, and that the allusions supposed to refer to it in Byzantine sources are merely repetitions of the story of the rescue of the Emperor Theophilus in 838 by the general Manuel.   No Arabic evidence mentions Michael's defeat.[41]   Since a sec-

---

[40] Vasiliev, *Byzantium and the Arabs* (St Petersburg, 1900), p. 194 and n. 5.   Bury (*op. cit.*, p. 282) follows Vasiliev.

[41] See H. Grégoire, 'Etudes sur le neuvième siècle,' *Byzantion*, VIII (1933), pp. 520–524 ('Un singulier revenant: Manuel le Magistre dans ses rôles posthumes').   *Idem*, 'Manuel et Théophobe ou la concurrence de deux monastères,' *ibid.*, IX (1934), pp. 184–185, 202–203.   *Idem*, in his note to the French edition of A. Vasiliev, *Byzance et les Arabs*, I (Brussels, 1935), 245, n. 2.   Grégoire writes that

ond campaign of Michael against the Arabs in the summer of 860 is thus to be eliminated, one of the objections to the length of the Russian invasion disappears.

Probably taking advantage of the absence of the Emperor, who was very busy in the capital, the Arabs in Asia Minor started several successful inroads.[42]

Another proof of the length of the Russian invasion is the location of Mauropotamos in Cappadocia, far from the capital, where the Emperor received Ooryphas' message. It must have taken a long time for Michael III, after having left the bulk of his army, to reach the Bosphorus, and he reached it when the Russians were already holding the straits and the approaches to the capital, so that the Emperor was barely able to cross the straits to enter the city. In other words the Russian invasion was in full swing.

I wish to adduce here an observation from a source which has never been used in connection with the question of the duration of the Russian invasion, namely the *Libellus Ignatii*, written by Ignatius' biographer, Nicetas Paphlagon. At the end of March and in April, 861, the so-called First and Second Council, attended by Papal legates, assembled in Constantinople in the Church of the Apostles.[43] The delegates went from Italy by sea, when, after passing the Hellespont, they entered the Sea of Marmora. They were shifted from their direct sea route to Constantinople, northwest to the port of Rhaedestos, on the western shore of the Sea of Marmora, where they landed. On their arrival there they received from Photius costly presents: dresses, chasubles, and pectoral crosses.[44] It is quite possible that the papal legates landed at Rhaedestos to continue their journey to the capital by land for the reason that the sea

---

Miss Michaux will study this question in detail. In my Russian edition of *Byzantium and the Arabs* (I, p. 192, n. 5), I noted that Genesius tells the story of the rescue of Michael III, which is almost identical with the story under Theophilus.

[42] Vasiliev, *Byzance et les Arabes*, I, pp. 245–246.

[43] Up to 1936, the date of this assembly which was universally accepted was May, 861. But in 1836, V. Grumel, from the notes of the cardinal Deusdedit, who attended the Council, learned that the sessions of the Council were interrupted by the celebration of Easter and resumed with the third session after the feast. In 861 Easter fell on Sunday, April 6; so that the two first sessions of the Council took place most probably at the very end of March, because the week just before April 6 was the Passion week, when the Church was busy with many religious services. V. Grumel, *Les regestes des actes du Patriarcat de Constantinople*. Fasc. II (*Socii Assumptionistae Chalcedonenses*, 1936; printed in Turkey), p. 77, no. 466. Grumel refers to Wolf von Glanwell, *Die Kanonensammlung des Kardinals Deusdedit*, I (Paderborn, 1905), CCCCXXVIII–CCCCXXXI; pp. 603–610. I have not seen this book.

[44] *Libellus Ignatii*, Mansi, *Conciliorum Collectio Amplissima*, XVI, col. 297: καὶ τὰ δῶρα αὐτοῦ (i.e., of Photius) μακρόθεν ἐδέξασθε, κατὰ γὰρ τὴν 'Ραιδεστὸν ὑμῖν αὐτὰ ἀπηντήκασιν, ἱμάτιά τε καὶ φελώνια, καὶ ἐγκόλπια.

route to Constantinople was not safe on account of the Russian raids in the Islands of the Princes and the siege of the capital. The legates landed at Rhaedestos because between this city and Constantinople there was a very well known strategic and commercial road along the coast, through Heraclea, on the Propontis, and Selymbria.[45] We know that on the arrival of the papal legates at Constantinople they were kept in isolation for three months so that they were not allowed to converse with the Ignatian party, but only to hear the Photian arguments. If the synod assembled at the very end of March, then the legates must have spent in isolation January, February, and March, 861. In other words, they had arrived at Constantinople from Rhaedestos by Christmas of 860. From these chronological calculations we may infer that in December 860, the Russian danger was not yet over, and the sea route to the capital in the northern section of the Sea of Marmora was not yet safe. We may be surprised that a council so remarkable for its large number of bishops and papal legates, with the Emperor himself present, should have assembled in Constantinople when the Russians were still raging under its walls. But the city was not entirely blocked; the land route was open and the Russians were not able to cut it off. Unfortunately we have very little information about this Council which confirmed the deposition of Ignatius, because its records were burnt in 869, when another Council deposed Photius and reinstated Ignatius.

In my opinion, the hymn *Acathistus* (*Akathistos*, ὁ ἀκάθιστος ὕμνος) which has been discussed above, is of great value in this connection. As I have already noted, I am inclined to believe, along with some other scholars, that its composition is due to the Russian invasion of 860. The yearly performance of the *Acathistus* in the Byzantine Church, as we know, was fixed for the Saturday of the fifth week in Lent. In 861, when Easter fell on Sunday, April 6, the Saturday of the fifth week in Lent was March 22. Very often in such church commemorations an historical fact is involved in assigning the commemoration to one day or another. Now we know that the Russian invasion was not a mere raid, but an expedition which not only had in view of course devastation and pillaging, but also perhaps a foolish idea of capturing Constantinople, which doubtless was besieged from the sea; now we are certain that the expedition lasted not a few weeks but several months and ended some time in 861. Evidently the hymn *Acathistus* was composed and first performed in commemoration of the solemn procession which has been described with many details in

---

[45] See W. Tomaschek, 'Zur Kunde der Hämus-Halbinsel,' *Sitzungberichte der philos.-histor. Classe der Akademie der Wissenschaften zu Wien*, cxiii (1886), 330–332. Rhaedestos was the ancient fort Βισάνθη.

our sources, and which, according to a later local religious tradition, led to the final defeat of the Russians. Since the yearly performance of the *Acathistus* was fixed for March 22, we may consider this date as the day when the solemn procession with the sacred vestment of the Holy Virgin took place. In other words, at the close of March, 861, the Russians were already withdrawing from under the walls of Constantinople. Their invasion left so deep an impression on the minds of the people that the *Acathistus* has remained permanently fixed in the ritual of the Greek-Orthodox Church. Since the performance of the *Acathistus*, this song of triumph, is set on March 22, the day which, according to later tradition, led to the final victory over the aggressor, we may conclude that towards the end of March the Russian danger although not entirely over was definitely on the wane. This circumstance may to some extent explain why in March and April 861 the so-called First and Second Council in the presence of the papal legates, could have been held in Constantinople with little fear of the Russian raiders.

From my discussion of the question of the duration of the Russian campaign against Constantinople, we may come to the following conclusion: the campaign, which started from the Byzantine point of view on June 18, 860, when two hundred Russian boats made their appearance at the shores of the Empire, lasted not a few days or a few weeks, but some months, and was still in progress in the opening months of the following year, 861. It is impossible to say definitely when the campaign came to its close. It is quite plausible to surmise that the Russian failure under Constantinople was already an accomplished fact in March 861, when the triumphal hymn, the *Acathistus*, was first performed on March 22 during the religious service and solemn procession celebrating the enemy's withdrawal from Constantinople. It is also possible to believe that certain groups of Russian invaders, after their withdrawal from under the walls of Constantinople and from the Sea of Marmora, for a while continued their pillaging in the upper part of the Bosphorus and some adjoining regions. But these pirate raids failed to menace the capital, which probably considered itself safe and free. In this case, the date June 5, which we discover in liturgical tradition and in the *synaxaria*, may mean the final liberation of the Empire from Russian danger, when the last Russian boats left the Byzantine shores. The date of June 5 in our sources cannot be accepted as a definite and exact date of the final event; it is only the date which was later fixed by the Church, and is to be regarded as an approximate chronological indication of the close of the Russian campaign. The final withdrawal of the Russian flotilla from the Byzantine shores may have taken place some time in April or May. But one thing is now certain: the idea of a short raid of a few days or a few weeks must be entirely discarded.   The Russian campaign of 860 lasted ten months at least.[46]

[46] Kunik knew the date June 5, but he was inclined to consider this day as the date of the beginning of the expedition.   E. Kunik, 'Bemerkungen über den Tag der Befreiung Constantinopels i. J. 865,' *Bulletin de l'Académie Impériale des Sciences de St Pétersbourg*, XXVII (1881), coll. 356–362; especially col. 360.

RELIGIOUS PROCESSIONS

WITHOUT doubt some of the most impressive moments during the invasion of 860–861 were those of the solemn processions headed by Photius, when the precious garment of the Virgin Mary, which was preserved in the Church of the Virgin at Blachernae, was borne round the walls of the city. It was not the first time that this venerated relic was used during a critical experience for the capital. The best known occasion was during the siege of the city by Avars, Scythians, and Persians in 626 when, according to a legendary tradition, the relic had saved the capital. Doubtless such religious performances deeply impressed the superstitious populace and furnished them real consolation and comfort. But I am not sure that these religious manifestations deeply impressed the barbarians who at that time were laying siege to the city and might have seen a procession moving round the walls. I am thinking here of Lamanski's speculations concerning the ceremony which took place during the siege of 860. According to him, the superstitious barbarians, who had been physically and morally weakened by all sorts of excesses, pillages, and massacres, at seeing these strange processions round the walls and hearing the chants which reached their ears, concluded that all their failures to take the city by storm, the quarrels among themselves, and the increasing mortality among them (caused by the unburied and putrifying corpses), came from the charm and magic conjurations of processions and prayers which were directed against them. The exhausted Vikings, he continues, lost their faith in themselves and in the power of their gods, and had already several times thought of returning to their own country. They were struck by the coincidence between the procession on the walls of the city and the strong wind which suddenly arose, and this was enough to make the besiegers retreat and rush in a disorderly rout to their boats.[1] Of course these psychological observations of Lamanski on the Russian morale and the influence of the religious ceremonies upon them have no confirmation whatever from our evidence. It is also impossible to accept Gerland's imaginary view that the battle was fought during the procession, perhaps in sight of the praying people, while the Emperor himself led on the troops.[2]

Since we know now that the Russian aggression lasted not several days or a few weeks but some months, the question of religious ceremonies connected with it is to be reconsidered. We have two pieces of evidence

---

[1] Lamanski, *The Slavonic Life of St Cyril* (Petrograd, 1915), pp. 130–131.

[2] E. Gerland, 'Photius und der Angriff der Russen auf Byzanz,' *Neue Jahrbücher für das klassische Altertum, Geschichte und deutsche Literatur*, XI (1903), 719, n. 4. See also Bury, *op. cit.*, p. 421, n. 1.

concerning such religious processions: the first, that of a contemporary and eye-witness, Patriarch Photius, and the second, a later tradition of the second half of the tenth century, which belongs to the Greek chronicles of Symeon Logothete's group. Theophanes' Continuator, Cedrenus (Scylitzes), and Zonaras fail to mention any procession.

In his second homily, which was preached not, as Bury writes, when the enemy *were departing* (p. 420) but after they *had departed*, Photius gives a full picture of the Russian retreat. He said:

When we were beseeching God with litanies and chants, when in contrition of our hearts we were repenting . . . then we were relieved from disaster . . . then we saw the disappearance of the threat, and the wrath of God seemed to recede from us; for then we saw our enemies withdrawing, and the city, which had been menaced with pillaging, free of devastation. Since we were deprived of any help and were in great want of power of men, we rested our expectations upon the Mother of our Lord and God, and were comforted; we implored Her to appeal to Her Son for the atonement of our transgressions; we called upon Her intercession for our rescue, upon Her protection to watch upon the impregnable wall; we implored Her to break down the audacious rashness of the barbarians, to pull down their insolence, to defend the people in despair, to fight for Her own flock. The entire city bore with me Her garment for the repulse of the besiegers and the protection of the besieged; we offered prayers and made a litany. Thus through the marvelous benevolence of the free petition of the Mother, God has inclined towards us, wrath has been averted, and the Lord has shown mercy upon His flock. This venerable garment is, indeed, the dress of the Mother of God. It went round the walls, and the enemy inexplicably (ἀρρήτῳ λόγῳ) turned their backs (and fled). It protected the city, and the stronghold of the enemies collapsed as if by a sign. It (the garment) covered the city, and the enemy were deprived of their hope upon which they depended. As soon as the Virgin's garment had been borne round the wall, the barbarians raised the siege and withdrew (ἀνεσκευάσαντο), and we were released from impending captivity and received unexpected salvation. Unexpectedly befell the aggression of the enemies; beyond all hopes has proved their withdrawal.[3]

From this description of the Russian retreat we clearly see that the sermon itself was delivered some time after the event; Photius reports it as an accomplished fact. There is no hint of any miracle in Photius' presentation unless we point out one detail; he said that the retreat occurred 'in an inexplicable way' (ἀρρήτῳ λόγῳ), that is, because of the relic. The Emperor is not mentioned as being present in this procession, so that we may infer that, although he was in the capital, he took no part in this particular ceremony.

Our further evidence on a religious ceremony comes from various ver-

---

[3] Ed. Müller, pp. 169–170, §§21–23, 25. Aristarkhes, II, pp. 40–43, §4.

sions of Symeon Logothete. It is clear that these texts deal with another procession. They narrate that this procession was held immediately on the Emperor's return from Asia Minor to the capital. It was led not only by Photius but also by the Emperor himself. According to this tradition, the relic was not only borne in procession round the walls but was dipped in the sea, which at that time was dead calm; suddenly a violent storm arose and dispersed the ships of the 'godless' Russians, so that only a few of them escaped danger and in complete defeat returned to their own country.[4] This second relation gives a later tradition which was formed in the second half of the tenth century; this tradition introduced the element of a miracle and made the ceremony the final act of the Russian catastrophe.

Since the Russian invasion lasted several months, during that time not only one but several religious processions were performed to comfort the populace. In the first solemn procession which was performed on the return of Michael III to the capital, both the Emperor and the Patriarch took part. The effect of their cooperation on such an exceptional occasion must have been tremendous. But in the procession which was organized at the end of the Russian campaign, which Photius describes in his second homily, the Emperor took no part. The Emperor's presence at such ceremonies was not obligatory. During the months of the Russian siege several such processions might have been held.

The miraculous storm of wind needs no miracle for explanation. A sudden storm is a phenomenon which occurs often and suddenly in the Black Sea. We may very reasonably assume that such a storm arose and dispersed the Russian ships. The weather in the Black Sea in January, February, and March is often very stormy, and we have tried to show above that the Russians withdrew from under the capital before March 22. In this connection A. van Millingen writes, 'Other natural allies to withstand a naval attack were moreover found in the violent storms to which the waters around the city are liable . . . in 865 a storm destroyed the first Russian flotilla that entered the Bosphorus.'[5]

We know now that, in the ceremony which Photius described in the second homily, the Emperor took no part, so that when Photius said that the entire city had borne the precious relic round the walls with him, he meant that the whole population of the capital participated in this manifestation of religious enthusiasm. As we have already pointed out, he did not of course include the Emperor in words of such general character

---

[4] *Georgii Hamartoli Continuator*, ed. Istrin, p. 11; ed. Muralt, pp. 736–737. *Sym. Mag.*, p. 674, ch. 37. *Theodos. Melit.*, p. 168. *Leo Gramm.*, p. 241. *Georg. Mon.*, p. 827. Slavonic version of *Symeon Logothete*, ed. Sreznevski, p. 106. Weingart, *Byzantské Kroniky*, II, 1, p. 136.

[5] A. van Millingen, *Byzantine Constantinople* (London, 1899), p. 179.

as 'the entire city'; he would have made a specific reference to the personal presence of the Emperor.   But many scholars have been influenced by later sources which erroneously mentioned the imperial presence in the procession.   Some scholars believed that when Photius preached his second sermon the Emperor was not yet at Constantinople for, if he had been, Photius would have mentioned him; the later chroniclers, then, are responsible for this factual inaccuracy.[6]

It is interesting to point out that, at the end of the eleventh century, the Patriarch of Antioch John (Joannes) IV (1092–1098),[7] in his letter to the Emperor Alexis Comnenus (1081–1118), wrote: 'Do you not hear that in the reign of Michael, Theophilus' son, the Tauroscythians, having attacked with a heavy fleet and taken (the country) all around, held the whole (city) as if in nets?   After the Emperor, with the Archbishop and the whole population of the city, had come to the Church of Blachernae and all together made prayers to God, the very holy garment of the Mother of God was dipped in the sea.'   Then follows the well known story of the storm, the ruin of the barbarian ships, and their miserable return home to inform their countrymen of their disaster.[8]   Doubtless the text

---

[6] I cite some historians who share this point of view.   D. Ilovaiski, *A History of Russia*, sec. ed., I (Moscow, 1900), p. 12 (in Russian).   C. de Boor, 'Der Angriff der Rhos auf Byzanz,' *Byz. Zeitschrift*, IV (1895), p. 460. V. Lamanski, *The Slavonic Life of St Cyril* (Petrograd, 1915), p. 124, 127, 129, 130 (in Russian).   J. Bury, *op. cit.*, p. 420, n. 3 and 5.   Aristarkhes writes that the Russian danger came to its close with the Emperor's arrival (in July 861).   Φωτίου Λόγοι καὶ 'Ομιλίαι, II, 3, 28.   Gerland remarks, 'If one admits that the Emperor led the troops, and simultaneously the Patriarch escorted the procession, the words σὺν ἐμοὶ πᾶσα ἡ πόλις do not seem at all surprising.'   E. Gerland, 'Photius und der Angriff der Russen auf Byzanz,' *Neue Jahrbücher für das klassische Altertum, Geschichte und deutsche Literatur*, XI (Leipzig, 1903), p. 719, n. 4.

[7] The years of John IV's patriarchate I have taken from Arch. Sergius, *The Complete Liturgical Calendar (Menologion) of the Orient*, 2d ed., II, 1 (Vladimir, 1901), p. 687.   He himself took the years from Arch. Porphyrius' studies published in the *Trudy* of the Kievan Spiritual Academy, years 1874–1875.   Both in Russian.   In Western Europe in the eighteenth century, Casimir Oudin wrote that John IV of Antioch lived at the end of the eleventh century and was a contemporary of Pope Urban II (1088–1099).   C. Oudini *Commentarius de scriptoribus Ecclesiae antiquis* (Frankfort a/M., Leipzig, 1722), II, p. 842.   J. B. Cotelerius, *Monumenta Ecclesiae Graecae*, I (Paris, 1677), p. 159, ascribed John IV's life to the middle of the twelfth century.   See *Notitia de Joanne Antiocheno*, reprinted from Cotelerius' *Monumenta*, in Migne, *P. Gr.*, CXXXII, coll. 1115–1118.   John IV's letter to Alexis Comnenus, which we quote in the text, solves the question: he lived at the end of the eleventh or at the outset of the twelfth century.

[8] This text is published in the Greek periodical Ἐκκλησιαστικὴ Ἀλήθεια, XX (1900), 358. Since I am unable for the time being to procure this periodical, I have taken the text and reference from Papadopoulos-Kerameus' study, 'The Akathistos of the Mother of God, Russia, and Patriarch Photius,' *Viz. Vremennik*, x (1903), p. 381.   This is the beginning of the Greek text: οὐκ ἀκούεις ὅτι ἐν ταῖς τοῦ βασιλέως Μιχαὴλ ἡμέραις, τοῦ Θεοφίλου παιδός, Ταυροσκίθαι βαρεῖ στόλῳ προσενεχθέντες καὶ κύκλῳ διαλαβόντες ὥσπερ ἐντὸς δικτύων ἄπασαν εἶχον; τοῦ βασιλέως σὺν ἀρχιερεῖ καὶ παντὶ τῷ τῆς πόλεως πλήθει τὸ ἐν βλαχέρναις καταλαβόντων τέμενος καὶ κοινῇ τὸ θεῖον ἐξιλασαμένων, εἶτα βάπτεται μὲν κατὰ τῆς θαλάσσης ἄκρως τὸ ἅγιον τῆς Θεομήτορος ῥάκος . . . Papadopoulos-Kerameus ascribes John IV's letter to the twelfth century (p. 381).

of John IV's letter to Alexis Comnenus depended on the tradition of the Greek chronicles.

It would not be amiss to mention that the foundation of the Church of Blachernae in a later legendary tradition may be connected with some Russian tales. The Vatican *Manuscript 153* of George Hamartolus' Continuator states that the name of that church goes back to the name of a certain Scythian chief, Blachernos by name (Βλαχέρνου καλουμένου), who was killed on the spot of the future sanctuary.[9] This story passed later into Slavonic and Russian chronographs, and in one of these, *On the Origin of the Russian Land and Foundation of Novgorod*, we read that two Russian princes, Khalokh and Lakhern, came with numberless troops to the walls of Constantinople, and the brave Lakhern was killed on the spot where afterwards was built the Lakhern (=Blachernae) Church of the Holy Virgin.[10] So in a later Russian tradition the Scythian chief of the Greek evidence, Blachernos, has become the Russian prince Lakhern.

[9] Ed. Istrin, p. 11; ed. Muralt, p. 737. See also Genesius, p. 85. On some other etymologies of Blachernae see J. Papadopoulos, *Les palais et les églises des Blachernes* (Thessalonica, 1928), pp. 15–16.

[10] See V. Vasilievski, 'The Pilgrimage of the Apostle Andrew to the Land of the Myrmidons,' *Works*, ii, 1 (St Petersburg, 1909), pp. 292–293 (in Russian). Vasilievski gives references to appropriate sources.

THE EARTHQUAKE OF 862

A MINOR detail which is sometimes connected with the invasion of 860 is to be mentioned. This relates to an earthquake which occurred about this year. Uspenski wrote that in August, 861, an earthquake shook Constantinople; the populace saw in it punishment for the unjust condemnation of Ignatius; and in a note referring to this statement Uspenski remarks, 'In his homilies on the invasion of Russia Photius mentions this earthquake.'[1] Lamanski says 'Photius fails to mention the earthquake.'[2] This earthquake is described in the *Life* of Ignatius by Nicetas Paphlagon, who writes, 'The month of August began, and the capital was terrified by violent earthquakes. . . . The earthquake lasted for forty days,'[3] in other words, as is usually admitted, the earthquake lasted from the first of August to September 7. The year of the earthquake must be defined in connection with the life and tribulations of the ex-Patriarch Ignatius. In my opinion, the most plausible year is 862, as we find it in Bury's work. 'In August and September (862) Constantinople was shaken by a terrible earthquake for forty days, and the calamity was ascribed by superstition to the unjust treatment of Ignatius.'[4] Lamanski speculates that if the earthquake which is mentioned by Nicetas happened in 860 and not in 861, it might have been one of the chief causes of the retreat and catastrophe of the Russians.[5] Finally Aristarkhes and Mošin merely ascribe the earthquake to the year 860.[6]

Since we now know, according to Bury's careful study, that this forty days' earthquake took place in 862, this terrible phenomenon has nothing to do with the Russian campaign. Even if it shook the territory of the capital and its vicinity, not in 862, but in 861, the result would be the same: it had no connection whatever with the Russian incursion, because in August and September of 861 the Russians had already left Constantinople. Aristarkhes and Mošin have no ground for ascribing the earthquake to the year 860.

Now the question arises why Uspenski, as we have noted above, stated that this earthquake is mentioned in Photius' homilies. This may be explained in several ways: Uspenski may have by oversight named Pho-

---

[1] F. Uspenski, *History of the Byzantine Empire*, II, 1 (Leningrad, 1927), 441 and n. 1 (in Russian).

[2] V. Lamanski, *The Slavonic Life of St Cyril* (Petrograd, 1915), p. 112 (in Russian).

[3] Migne, *P. G.*, cv, col. 525. See also George Hamartolus' Continuator: σεισμοῦ γὰρ γεγονότος φρικωδεστάτου (ed. Istrin, p. 12, Muralt, p. 739).

[4] Bury, *op. cit.*, p. 198, n. 4; also p. 445, n. 1.

[5] Lamanski, *op. cit.*, pp. 111–112.

[6] Aristarkhes, Φωτίου Λόγοι καὶ Ὁμιλίαι, I, p. κγ. V. Mošin, 'Study on the First Conversion of Russia,' *Boqosloviye*, v, 2 (Belgrad, 1930), p. 67 (in Serbian).

tius for Nicetas Paphlagon; or Uspenski may have remembered that Photius in his second sermon used the word σεισμός when he was describing the horrors of the Russian incursion.   But Photius used this word here not in the sense of *earthquake*, but in its original meaning, *shock, palpitation, shaking*.   He exclaimed, 'When shock and gloom (darkness) have seized our minds.'[7]   Or finally, Uspenski may have had in view a passage from Pseudo-Symeon's chronicle, where the latter, probably referring to the earthquake of 862, mentions that Photius preached a sermon to show that earthquakes are not a consequence of our sins but are due to natural causes.[8]   However this may be, this earthquake has no connection with the Russian campaign.

[7] ὅτε σεισμὸς καὶ γνόφος κατεῖχε τοὺς λογισμούς.   Ed. Müller, p. 169, § 18; Aristarkhes, ii, 39, § 3.

[8] Symeon Magister, ed. Bonn., p. 673: αὐτὸς ὁ Φώτιος ἀναβὰς ἐπὶ τοῦ ἄμβωνος δημηγορῆσαι εἶπεν ὅτι οἱ σεισμοὶ οὐκ ἐκ πλήθους ἁμαρτιῶν ἀλλ' ἐκ πλησμονῆς ὕδατος γίνονται.   See Bury, *op. cit.*, p. 445, n. 1.

THE RUSSIAN RETREAT

THE Russian enterprise of 860–861 ended without doubt in failure. The Russians abandoned the Byzantine territory in great haste and disorder. In his second sermon Photius preached: 'Unexpectedly the invasion of the enemy befell, their withdrawal has proved beyond all hopes; the trouble was portentous, but the close (of it) was beyond expectation; unspeakable was the fear of them; they were despicable in flight; with wrath they had overrun us; we have found that the benevolence of God (toward us) combatting them has kept back their onslaught.'[1] From these rhetorical words we may conclude that the Russians finally fled, but the Patriarch fails to emphasize the immediate cause of their flight. The group of Symeon Logothete's chronicles attribute the Russian defeat and destruction to a miraculous storm. The Brussels Chronicle says that the Russians were defeated and destroyed through the intercession of the Mother of God. Theophanes' Continuator, Cedrenus (Scylitzes), and Zonaras vaguely write that the Russians returned home through the agency of celestial power.[2] Russian chroniclers say that Askold and Dir returned to Kiev with a small force (*druzhina*), and the *Nikonovski Chronicle* adds, 'And there was in Kiev great weeping.'[3] No source supplies us with any plausible reason for the Russian defeat. But, by whatever means, the Russian invasion of 860–861 ended in complete failure. Rambaud calls it a disaster; Uspenski, 'a defeat of Askold and Dir under Constantinople'; Grégoire, an attack 'which was gloriously repulsed' by Michael III; Toynbee, 'the repulse of the surprise attack of Askold's war-canoes'; Dvorník, 'unlucky adventure.'[4]

Since all historians have referred the story of Joannes Diaconus and his Venetian followers to the Russian aggression of 860–861, we read in many studies that probably, in spite of the assertions of Photius and the Byzantine chronicles, the Russian aggression ended not in total defeat but in an honorable peace at least if not in a real victory. Even Photius' rather vague statements about the Russian flight permit some scholars to believe

[1] Ἀπροσδόκητος ἐπέστη ἡ ἔφοδος τῶν ἐχθρῶν, ἀνέλπιστος ἐδείχθη ἡ ἀναχώρησις αὐτῶν. ἐξαίσιος ἡ ἀγανάκτησις, ἀλλ' ὑπὲρ λόγον τὸ τέλος. ἄφατος ἦν αὐτῶν ὁ φόβος, εὐκαταφρόνητοι γεγόνασι τῇ φυγῇ. ὀργὴν εἶχον εἰς τὴν καθ'ἡμῶν ἐπιδρομήν, συνελαύνουσαν αὐτοὺς φιλανθρωπίαν εὕρομεν θεοῦ τούτων ἀναστέλλουσαν τὴν ὁρμήν. Ed. Müller, ii, p. 170, § 25; Aristarkhes, ii 43 § 4.

[2] *Cont. Theoph.* p. 196, c. 33: θείας ἐμφορηθέντες ὀργῆς. Cedr. ii, 173: τῆς θείας πειραθέντες ὁρμῆς. Zonaras, xvi, 5 (Bonn, iii, 404): θείου πειραθέντες μηνίματος. [3] *P.S.R.L.*, ix, 9.

[4] A. Rambaud, *L'Empire grec au dixième siècle* (Paris, 1870), pp. 382–383. Th. Uspenski, *The History of the Byzantine Empire*, ii, 1 (Leningrad, 1927), p. 398. H. Grégoire, 'Etudes sur le neuvième siècle,' *Byzantion*, viii (1933), p. 532. A. Toynbee, *A Study of History*, v (London, 1939), p. 290. F. Dvorník, *Les légendes de Constantin et de Méthode vues de Byzance* (Prague, 1933), p. 148.

that the Russians quit the Byzantine territory unharmed.[5] But of course the central source for these scholars was the Venetian Chronicle of Joannes the Deacon, who wrote that the Normans had returned in triumph. In 1930 Laehr wrote that, without any doubt, the destruction of the Russian fleet belongs to the realm of legend, and then, referring to Joannes the Deacon, concludes that the Russians returned to their own country in triumph.[6] In 1919, Shakhmatov, accepting Loparev's erroneous conclusions, affirmed that the Russian campaign had ended in an entirely different way from that related in Symeon Logothete's or Hamartolus' Continuator's Chronicle; it had ended in a peace honorable for the Russians, which was concluded under the walls of Tsargrad; after this, on the twenty-fifth of June, they withdrew from under the city.[7] Some historians have referred to a letter of Pope Nicholas I to Michael III, where the Pope mentions that the pagans devastated the suburbs of Constantinople, slew many people, and still remained unpunished. And, sharing the view that this statement refers to the Russian aggression, these scholars add the papal letter to their documents to prove that the Russians were not defeated.[8] But all these speculations have been based on the erroneous postulate that all the Italian sources under consideration refer to the Russian aggression. We know now that all this Western evidence describes the Norman aggression from the south, which has no connection with the Russian aggression from the north.

We must admit that we do not know the exact circumstances under which the Russian campaign ended in failure. The Byzantine fleet, which was absent at the time of the invasion, may finally have returned from the Aegean and Mediterranean to inflict a decisive blow on the Russian flotilla. But none of our evidence, including Photius' second sermon, even mentions the interference of the fleet. Bury's supposition that possibly on receiving the news of the Russian invasion the Emperor ordered ships to sail from Amastris to the Bosphorus is totally without foundation.[9] We have no notion whether the land forces of the Emperor operated against the Russians. At any rate Bury's statement that 'it is evident that the Russians became aware that the Emperor and his army were at hand and that their only safety lay in flight,' is too positive.[10]

[5] See, for instance, 'Kunik in *Accounts of al-Bekri* . . . ', I (St Petersburg, 1878), p. 175, n. 7 (in Russian). C. de Boor, Der Angriff der Rhos auf Byzanz, *Byz. Zeitschrift*, IV (1895), p. 460; but cf., pp. 462–463. Bury, *op. cit.*, p. 420, n. 4.

[6] G. Laehr, *Die Anfänge des Russischen Reiches* (Berlin, 1930), p. 94.

[7] A. Shakhmatov, *The Earliest Fortunes of the Russian Nation* (Petrograd, 1919), p. 60 (in Russian).

[8] See, for instance, Kunik, *Accounts of al-Bekri*, I (1878), pp. 173–174 (in Russian).

[9] Bury, *op. cit.*, p. 421, n. 2.

[10] Bury, *op. cit.*, p. 421. In note one to this page Bury adds, 'This is obviously the true explanation of the sudden retreat, which began spontaneously, before the battle.' Some other scholars also see

As we have shown above, the earthquake as a factor in the Russian defeat is to be eliminated on the grounds of simple chronology.

To sum up, the general cause of the Russian failure — for such it undoubtedly was — may be found in the exhaustion of the Russians, who had already spent several months in devastation and pillaging, whereas during that time resistance on the part of the Byzantines was being organized. In addition some reinforcements may have arrived from the east. Also, the Russian aim of capturing Constantinople was of course beyond their strength or ability.[11] It is no exaggeration to assume that such a daring and frankly foolish plan did exist in the overexcited minds of the Russian Vikings. In several places Photius plainly speaks of it. I give here some examples: 'Mourn along with me this Jerusalem, which has not yet been brought to captivity but has already lost the hope of salvation. . . . They lifted up and struck vehemently their hands together in hope to capture the imperial city like a nest of young birds . . . they settled fearlessly all around this city . . . the whole city was on the point, as one says, of becoming captive of the spear (δοριάλωτος, *i.e.* taken in war) . . . our ears have been open to nothing but the rumor that the barbarians had rushed within the walls, and the city had been subdued by the enemy,' *etc.*[12] The Byzantine chronicles of Symeon Logothete's group also plainly state that the Russians surrounded the city. In spite of the final failure, during several months of their operations, the Russians must have seized plenty of spoils of various sorts. But it is quite possible that at the conclusion of their piratic operations high winds aided in the work of their destruction, so that it is rather unlikely that the invaders could bring all their plundered spoil safely back across the sea. The Russian sources frankly affirm that Askold and Dir returned to Kiev in a pitiful condition.

---

the approach of the Byzantine land forces as the cause of the Russian retreat. F. Dvorník, *Les légendes de Constantin et de Méthode vues de Byzance* (Prague, 1933), p. 148.

[11] Cf. A. Toynbee, *A Study of History*, ii (London, 1934), p. 349: In 860 the Vikings only just failed to take the Imperial City by surprise.

[12] Ed. Müller, I, 165, §24; ii, 168, §5; 169, §15; §18; 170, §23. Aristarkhes, ii, 18, §3; 33–34, §1; 37–39, §3; 41–42, §4.

TREATIES BETWEEN BYZANTIUM AND RUSSIA AFTER 860–861

IT is a very interesting question whether the Russian invasion of 860–861 ended in a definite agreement with the Byzantine government or not. Our evidence fails to give any positive answer to this question. In the middle of the nineteenth century a Russian scholar, Macarius, archbishop of Kharkov, wrote, 'The aggression of the Russians upon Byzantium took place in the time of the princes in Kiev, Askold and Dir, and ended, according to the testimony of Constantine Porphyrogenitus (*Vita Basilii*), in the conclusion of an alliance between the Russians and Greeks.'[1] In 1938 Ravndal said that, after Askold's invasion, 'a formal treaty had been concluded between Byzantium and Kiev, perhaps confirming previous conventions, but of it we have not the text.'[2]

What ground have we for such statements? Theophanes' Continuator writes that shortly after the Russian withdrawal a Russian embassy came again to Constantinople beseeching to be converted to Christianity, and that this conversion indeed took place.[3] From this text we may conclude that shortly after 860–861 a Russian embassy came *again* to Constantinople; in other words, before the latter embassy another embassy had already been in the capital. If the embassy which is mentioned in Theophanes' Continuator took place shortly after the Russian withdrawal, the previous embassy might have occurred immediately after the withdrawal or even just before the withdrawal. So we conclude that negotiations initiated by the defeated Russians took place at once after the campaign of 860–861 and ended in a friendly agreement; otherwise the subsequent peaceful embassy which is clearly described in the Byzantine Chronicle would not be understandable. It is not to be forgotten that in his circular letter to the Oriental Patriarchs, which is now ascribed to the spring or summer of 867, Photius remembers the invasion upon the Empire by the race which in cruelty and bloodthirstiness left all other peoples far behind, the so-called Ros, and adds that now indeed, even they have changed their Hellenic and godless religion for the pure and unadulterated faith of the Christians, and have placed themselves under the protection of the Empire, becoming good

---

[1] Archbishop Macarius, *History of Christianity in Russia before the Isoapostolic Prince Vladimir* sec. ed. (St Petersburg, 1868), p. 220 (in Russian).

[2] G. Bie Ravndal, *Stories of the East-Vikings* (Minneapolis, Minnesota, 1938), p. 190.

[3] Cont. Theoph., p. 196, c. 33: καὶ μετ'οὐ πολὺ πάλιν τὴν βασιλεύουσαν πρεσβεία αὐτῶν κατελάμβανεν, τοῦ θείου βαπτίσματος ἐν μετοχῇ γενέσθαι αὐτοὺς λιτανεύουσα, ὃ καὶ γέγονεν. From Cont. Theoph., Cedrenus, ii, 173, and Zonaras, xvi, 5; Bonn, iii, 404.

friends instead of continuing their recent robbery and daring adventures.[4]

Photius' letter allows us to fix more exactly the time of the appeal of the Russians to Byzantium. He mentions Russian affairs just after stating that the Bulgarians adopted Christianity. The year of the Bulgarian conversion has been now definitely fixed: the baptism of the Bulgarian King Boris took place in 864, but his envoys had already been baptized in Constantinople at the end of the year 863.[5] So, according to Photius' letter, the Russian appeal and the new conditions which were established between Byzantium and Russia occurred between 864 and the spring or summer of 867, when Photius' encyclical letter was written and dispatched. According to these chronological calculations, Photius in his letter probably meant the second Russian embassy which is mentioned in the *Chronicle* of Theophanes' Continuator. Doubtless a certain friendly treaty, or possibly two, were made between Byzantium and Russia, after the invasion of 860–861, still during the reign of Michael III and the incumbency of the Patriarch Photius.

How long this first peace lasted it is not very easy to determine because, in the biography of his grandfather the Emperor Basil, Michael's successor, Constantine Porphyrogenitus, wrote that Basil, by many precious gifts, made an agreement with the 'most unconquerable and most impious people of the Russians' and concluded with them a treaty of peace.[6] This happened after Photius' deposition under the reinstated Patriarch Ignatius, in other words, after 867. According to the same text Basil, after peace had been made, persuaded the Russians to adopt Christianity, and the Patriarch Ignatius sent an archbishop to them.[7] Putting aside the very complicated question of the first conversion of the Russians to Christianity, the text of Basil's biography implies that some new troubles broke out between Byzantium and Russians after the campaign of 860–

---

[4] Καὶ τὸ παρὰ πολλοῖς πολλάκις θρυλλούμενον καὶ εἰς ὠμότητα καὶ μιαιφονίαν πάντας δευτέρους ταττόμενον, τοῦτο δὴ τὸ καλούμενον τὸ 'Ρῶς . . . ἀλλ' ὅμως νῦν καὶ οὗτοι τὴν τῶν χριστιανῶν καθαρὰν καὶ ἀκίβδηλον θρησκείαν τῆς Ἑλληνικῆς καὶ ἀθέου δόξης, ἐν ᾗ κατείχοντο πρότερον, ἀντηλλάξαντο ἐν ὑπηκόων ἑαυτοὺς καὶ προξένων τάξει, ἀντὶ τῆς πρὸ μικροῦ καθ'ἡμῶν λεηλασίας καὶ τοῦ μεγάλου τολμήματος ἀγαπητῶς ἐγκαταστήσαντες. Photii *Epistolae*, ed. Montakutius (London, 1651), p. 58, ep. 2. Migne, *P. G.*, CII, coll. 736–737, ep. 13 (printed τορῶς for τὸ 'Ρῶς). Φωτίου Ἐπιστολαί, ed. Valetta (London, 1864), p. 178, ep. 4. On dating, V. Grumel, *Les regestes des acts du Patriarcat de Constantinople.* Fasc. II (Socii Assumptionistae Chalcedonenses, 1936, printed in Turkey), pp. 88–89. Among recent Russian writings on this circular or encyclical letter see T. M. Rosseikin, *The First Rule of Photius, the Patriarch of Constantinople* (Sergiev Posad, 1915), pp. 392–405.

[5] A. Vaillant et M. Lascaris, 'La date de la conversion des Bulgares,' *Revue des études slaves,* XIII (1933), p. 13. Ch. Gerard, *Les Bulgares de la Volga et les Slaves du Danube* (Paris, 1939), p. 183.

[6] *Cont. Theoph.*, p. 342, c. 97: 'Αλλὰ καὶ τὸ τῶν 'Ρῶς ἔθνος δυσμαχώτατόν τε καὶ ἀθεώτατον ὂν χρυσοῦ τε καὶ ἀργύρου καὶ σηρικῶν περιβλημάτων ἱκαναῖς ἐπιδόσεσιν εἰς συμβάσεις ἐφελκυσάμενος, καὶ σπονδὰς πρὸς αὐτοὺς σπεισάμενος εἰρηνικάς.

[7] This information about the Russians' adoption of Christianity and an archbishop who was sent to them is also to be found in Michaelis Glycae *Annales*, part IV, Bonn., p. 553.

861. Referring to the text just quoted, Dvorník positively asserts that certainly the expedition of 860 was not the last of its sort.[8]   On the other hand Constantine Porphyrogenitus, in his laudatory biography of his grandfather, might have ascribed to him the honor of the conclusion of the first treaty of peace with the Russians, which in reality might have been made by Michael III.   The hostile attitude towards Michael III of the Macedonian dynasty, especially its first representative Basil, Michael's murderer, is very well known and has already been emphasized in this study.

At any rate, if another conflict took place between Byzantium and Russians under Basil I, it was the last one before the expedition of the Russian prince Oleg against Constantinople, a very important event which, according to the Russian chronicles, occurred in 907.   Otherwise some passages in the treaty which was concluded in September 911 between the belligerents would not be understandable.   One of the aims of the treaty was 'to maintain and proclaim the amity which for many years has joined Christians (i.e., Greeks) and Rus.'[9]   This statement very well explains the peaceable relations between the two countries which began in 861 or shortly after.   Over forty years of peace between Byzantium and Russians were broken by Oleg in 907.

Another very interesting point in Russo-Byzantine relations at the beginning of the tenth century may be connected with the treaty concluded after the invasion of 860–861.   In 910 the great naval expedition against the Eastern and Cretan Arabs was organized with Himerius at its head.[10] In the exact account of the composition of the troops of this expedition Constantine Porphyrogenitus speaks of the presence of 700 Russians.[11] It is known that in the treaty of 911 there is a special clause which allows the Russians 'desirous of honoring the Emperor' to come at any time and to remain in his service; 'they shall be permitted in this respect to act according to their desire' (transl. by Cross, p. 153).   In 1902 I tried to explain the presence of 700 Russians in the Byzantine troops in 910 by the fact that the clause just quoted, which was included in the final text of the treaty of 911, had already existed in the preliminary treaty, perhaps

[8] F. Dvorník, *Les Slaves, Byzance et Rome au IXe siècle* (Paris, 1926), p. 146, n. 3.

[9] The *Primary (Laurentian) Chronicle* under the year 6420 (912), and later versions.   Prof. S. H. Cross translates this passage into English as follows: 'for the maintenance and proclamation of the long-standing amity which joins Greeks and Russes' (p. 151).

[10] On the date of the expedition, A. Vasiliev, *Byzantium and the Arabs*, ii (St Petersburg, 1902), pp. 166–168 (in Russian).   The year 910 for the former 902 of the expedition has now been accepted. S. G. Ostrogorsky, 'L'expédition du prince Oleg contre Constantinople en 907,' *Annales de l'Institut Kondakov*, xi (1939), 53, no. 20.   *Idem, Geschichte des byzantinischen Staates* (Munich, 1940), pp. 181–182.

[11] Constantini Porphyrogeniti *De cerimoniis*, p. 651.

oral, which had been made immediately after the end of the war with Oleg.[12]   But we have no exact idea of the terms of the preliminary treaty, nor are we even sure that such a treaty was ever made.   In his account of the 700 Russians Constantine Porphyrogenitus mentions their presence in the army as a matter of course.   I am now inclined to believe that the right of the Russians to serve the Emperor as mercenaries goes back to a more distant past, namely to the first Russian attack on Constantinople and to the first amicable treaty or treaties which were concluded in 861 or soon after.   Bury was right in writing in 1912: 'The treaty which was concluded between A.D. 860 and 866 led probably to other consequences. We may surmise that it led to the admission of Norse mercenaries into the Imperial fleet — a notable event, because it was the beginning of the famous Varangian service at Constantinople, which was ultimately to include the Norsemen of Scandinavia as well as of Russia, and even Englishmen.'[13]

Here I wish to come back to Photius' encyclical letter to the Eastern Patriarchs, which has been quoted several times above.   In the letter Photius, among other things, says that the Russians have adopted Christianity and placed themselves in the ranks of ὑπηκόων and προξένων.[14]   If the first word ὑπήκοος refers to ecclesiastical dependence, the second word πρόξενος, in its original meaning *public guest* or *friend*, deals also with a *friendly relation between a State and an individual of another State*, in other words, this term refers to political friendship.[15]   And I am inclined to believe that this is the first indirect indication of new relations between Byzantium and Russians, which, among other things, resulted in the right of Russians if they wished to enter the Imperial army as mercenaries; so that the clause on this subject which we find in the treaty of 911 is merely the formal confirmation of the custom which had in practice already existed since the end of the first Russian invasion of 860–861.   Referring to some words of Photius Lamanski wrote, 'One may conclude that even before Oleg the Russians were seeking and asking for admission into the service of Byzantium.'[16]

The interpretation of our scanty evidence thus provides a direct link between the first Russian attack on the Empire in 860–861 and Oleg's campaign on Constantinople in 907 and his final treaty with Byzantium in 911.

---

[12] A. Vasiliev, *Byzantium and the Arabs*, II, pp. 166–167 (in Russian).

[13] Bury, *op. cit.*, p. 422.

[14] The exact reference has been given above.

[15] Here it is not amiss to remember the Russian envoys who were sent in 839 to the Emperor Theophilus *amicitiae causa*.

[16] Lamanski, *The Slavonic Life of St Cyril* (Petrograd, 1915), p. 153 (in Russian).

PEACE AND COMMERCE AFTER 860–861

RUSSIAN devastations were evidently soon forgotten, and economic life recovered, for instance on the southern shores of the Euxine. In this respect the *Eulogy on St Hyacinthus of Amastris*, compiled by Nicetas Paphlagon after 860–861 (he died in 880–890) and already twice noted above, is very interesting. From this *Eulogy* we learn that the Paphlagonian city of Amastris, 'which lacked little of being the eye of the Universe,' having powerful walls and a fine harbor which evidently had not been damaged by the Russians in 860–861, was a very brisk commercial center (ἐμπόριον), where the Scythians from the northern shores of the Euxine, i.e., the Russians, and the people from the south of the city assembled together to transact commercial business.[1]

The conditions of trade and commerce which were established between Byzantium and Oleg at the beginning of the tenth century do not impress us as new and unusual; the treaty merely regulated and gave definite form to the customs which had existed before, during the period of 'the long-standing amity which joined Greeks and Russians.' The same treaty says that the Russians who arrive in Constantinople 'shall dwell in the St. Mamas quarter.' It is almost certain that this suburb of St Mamas where the Russian traders and envoys were lodged, and which was located on the European shore of the Bosphorus, at the modern Beshik-tash,[2] had been designated for this particular purpose not in 907 or 911 but much earlier, according to the agreement made with the Russians after their campaign of 860–861, or even perhaps farther back in the year 838, when the Russian envoys had come to Constantinople 'for the purpose of friendship' (*amicitiae causa*).

The evidence of the *Eulogy on St Hyacinthus of Amastris* and the treaty between Byzantium and Oleg supply us, as has been noted above, with an indirect indication that the Russian expedition of 860–861 in the reign of Michael III, and probably negotiations with the Russians in the opening years of the reign of Basil I as well, resulted in the conclusion of an amicable agreement, one of the clauses of which, as we know, was that the Russians 'desirous of honoring the Emperor' were allowed 'to come at any time and to remain in his service.'

[1] Nicetae Paphlagonis *Oratio XIX*. In laudem S. Hyacinthi Amastreni, Migne, *P. G.*, cv, col. 421, § 4: Ἀμάστρα, ὁ τῆς Παφλαγονίας, μᾶλλον δὲ τῆς οἰκουμένης, ὀλίγου δεῖν, ὀφθαλμός, εἰς ἣν οἵ τε τὸ βόρειον τοῦ Εὐξείνου μέρος περιοικοῦντες Σκύθαι, καὶ οἱ πρὸς νότον δὲ κείμενοι, ὥσπερ εἴς τι κοινὸν συντρέχοντες ἐμπόριον, τὰ παρ' ἑαυτῶν τε συνεισφέρουσι, καὶ τῶν παρ'αὐτῆς ἀντιλαμβάνουσι.

[2] See F. Uspenski, *The Rule (Typikon) of the Monastery of St Mamas in Constantinople.* *Annals (Letopis)* of the Historico-Philological Society at the University of Novorossisk. ii. Byzantine Section (Odessa, 1892), pp. 83–84 (in Russian). J. Pargoire, 'Le Saint-Mamas de Constantinople,' *Transactions (Izvestiya)* of the Russian Archaeological Institute in Constantinople, ix, nos. 1–3 (1904), p. 302. *Idem*, 'St Mamas, le quartier russe de Constantinople,' *Echos d'Orient*, xi (1908), pp. 203–210.

RORIK OF JUTLAND AND RURIK OF THE RUSSIAN ANNALS

AS we know, in 860–861 the two Norman movements towards Constantinople, one from the south and one from the north, almost met each other under the walls of the capital of the Byzantine Empire. The question arises whether these almost simultaneous enterprises were a mere coincidence, or are to be explained by a general plan organized by one man who held in his hands the threads of all Viking expeditions both in Western Europe and in the Mediterranean, and in the Euxine as well. In 1906, in his accurate study on *The Normans and the Frankish State*, W. Vogel wrote: 'In 859 the Vikings began their great drive in the Mediterranean which brought them first to Spain, then after 844 through the Straits of Gibraltar, as far as Italy. At that time, then, the ring drawn by the expeditions of the Normans around Europe nearly closed fast: in 866 the Swedish Ros (Russians) beleaguered Constantinople.'[1] In connection with the Norman approach to Constantinople simultaneously from the south and north, the opinion has been brought forward that the leading spirit of all Norman expeditions at that time, both in the West and in the East, was the so-called founder of the Russian State in Novgorod, Rurik.

But before discussing this very debatable question, I wish to say a few words about the possible identity of the Russian prince Rurik with Rorik of Jutland, his very well known contemporary. Here are some episodes of the latter's long and disturbed life. The Jutish-Danish prince, Rorik of Friesland, who was born about 800, began his military activities relatively late, at the age of about forty (in 841). In the middle of the ninth century, he harassed the Frankish shores and took part in several raids both on the continent, for instance in maritime expeditions to South Friesland or to Northern France and even to England; he failed in 855 to seize the throne of Denmark, was for a while a vassal of Charles the Bald (843–877), but later took an oath of eternal fidelity to Louis the German (843–876) at Aachen in 873. This meeting with Louis the German is the last record of Rorik's life in Western annals. He died about 875–876, in any case before 882.[2]

---

[1] W. Vogel, *Die Normannen und das fränkische Reich bis zur Gründung der Normandie* (799–911), Heidelberg, 1906, pp. 171–172. (*Heidelberger Abhandlungen zur mittleren und neueren Geschichte*, no. 14.) Vogel erroneously ascribes the Russian attack to the year 866.

[2] In this summary of Rorik's life I have followed Vogel's study indicated in the previous note. On his death p. 246, 408; a genealogical table on p. 409. See also a brief sketch of Rorik's life in N. Beliaev, 'Rorik of Jutland and Rurik of Original (Russian) Annals,' *Seminarium Kondakovianum*, III (1929), pp. 238–239, 269–270, and *passim* (in Russian); and in G. Vernadsky, *Ancient Russia* (New Haven, 1943), pp. 337–339, 365–366.

For the opening pages of Russian history the years 867–870 in Rorik's life are very important and very intriguing.   We know that he was expelled from Friesland in 867; and then we see him back at his possessions in that country in 870.   These three years are the most obscure period of Rorik's life: our Western evidence fails to give any definite information on that time.   Rorik seems to have vanished from the West.[3]   But these years are extremely important for Russian history.   It was the time when, according to the Russian annals, Rurik was acting in Novgorod as the first ruler of the northern Russian principality.   Rurik's stay and work beyond the Baltic so far East, from the point of view of Western chroniclers, indeed in the Far East, may have easily escaped their attention and knowledge, and they may merely have failed to mention his Eastern experiences at all.

Over a hundred years ago, in 1836 to be exact, F. Kruse first suggested the identification of Rurik of Novgorod with Rorik of Jutland or Friesland.   Both bore the same name; the obscure years of Rorik's life in the Western evidence coincide with Rurik's activities in the East.   Finally, some Western chronicles state that Rorik did not remain all the time in Germany and Belgium, but also visited a great number of oversea regions ('transmarinas regiones plurimas').[4]

Kunik immediately opposed Kruse's opinion, and flatly denied the latter's identification of these two princes.[5]   Recently N. Beliaev has revived Kruse's theory and revealed himself a convinced supporter of the identity of Rurik of Russia with Rorik of Jutland.[6]   In his review of Beliaev's study, V. Mošin remarked that his hypothesis of the identity of Rurik of Russia with Rorik of Jutland does not seem to him sufficiently well-established, but is, however, in no way incredible.[7]   In 1938 an American historian, S. R. Tompkins, calling this theory a tempting hypothesis, ascribes it entirely to Beliaev without mentioning Kruse's study.[8]   More recently, G. Vernadsky, referring to Beliaev's study, says that the latter 'approached the problem once more, and with the use of

---

[3] On the years 867–870 see Vogel, *op. cit.*, pp. 225–226.

[4] F. Kruse, 'On the Origin of Rurik,' *Journal of the Ministry of Public Instruction*, January, 1836, p. 56, 72; the whole article, pp. 43–73.   F. Kruse, *Chronicon Nortmannorum, Wariago-Russorum nec non Danorum* . . . (Hamburg and Gotha, 1851), pp. 289–290.

[5] Kunik, 'Kritische Bemerkungen zu den Rafn'schen *Antiquités Russes* und zu dem Kruse'schen *Chronicon Nordmannorum.*' Erster Beitrag. *Bulletin* de la classe des sciences historiques, philologiques et politiques de l'Académie des Sciences de Saint-Pétersbourg, VII (1850), pp. 135–136; on p. 136 Kunik gives a full bibliography of Kruse's studies, which are very little known.   This study of Kunik is often referred to as *Remarques critiques*. . . .

[6] N. Beliaev, *op. cit.*, p. 270.

[7] V. Mošin, in *Seminarium Kondakovianum*, v (Prague, 1932), p. 338.

[8] Stuart R. Tompkins, 'The Varangians in Russian History,' *Medieval and Historiographical Essays in honor of James Westfall Thompson* (Chicago, 1938), p. 485.

some new materials and certain new arguments fully confirmed Kruse's theory. The identification is certainly valid.'[9]

Of course it is still possible to say that the identification of the two men has not been definitely determined. But considering the general trend of the well known life of Rorik of Jutland and the scanty evidence on Rurik of the Russian Annals, with especial emphasis on the obscure years 867–870 in Rorik's life, which may be those of his activities in the East, at Novgorod, I am inclined to accept the theory of Kruse and his followers, and I believe that the identification of Rurik of Novgorod with Rorik of Jutland or of Friesland may be fruitful for the opening pages of Russian history.

But it is a different proposition to assume that all Norman expeditions in the middle of the ninth century, both in the East and in the West, were carried out according to one general plan directed by Rorik-Rurik.

The most ardent supporter of this idea is N. Beliaev who, developing Vogel's opinion along the same lines, wrote that we may state almost with certainty that Rorik's hand was felt behind all Viking raids of that period, and that he himself organized and directed them from somewhere in his possessions.[10] 'It is hard to admit,' Beliaev says in another place, 'that this coincidence (of the two expeditions on Constantinople) was mere chance; all the data speak for the fact that either both attacks were planned by an experienced hand to coincide with each other, or that there was a simultaneous tendency towards the same goal by two rivals, one coming around Spain, the other from Novgorod by the rivers Volkhov and Dnieper. We have no evidence that any rivalry existed between Rurik and Rognar Lodbrok's sons. On the contrary, everything indicates that Rurik's directing hand had been felt in all great former raids and inroads. All necessary means and resources were also at Rurik's command, and all the threads of the Western and Eastern commerce of Friesland converged towards him alone. Only he could have had enough horizon and breadth of conception to devise and carry out such a plan as the discovery of the great trade route. In a word, all leads us to assume that . . . taking advantage of his relationship with Björn, he directed him to Constantinople by the better known southern route, and himself, after having organized a base in Novgorod, sent an expedition with Askold on Constantinople by the river route, down the Dnieper.'[11] Ravndal, as I have already noted above, very cautiously says that it would amost seem as if Vikings and Varings (Varangians) had planned to touch hands at Constantinople.[12]

[9] G. Vernadsky, *Ancient Russia*, p. 337.

[10] Beliaev, *op. cit.*, p. 231 (in Russian).   [11] Beliaev, *op. cit.*, p. 241.

[12] G. Bie Ravndal, *Stories of the East-Vikings* (Minneapolis, Minnesota, 1938), p. 191.

In his review of Beliaev's study V. Mošin writes that his statement that Hasting's expedition into the Mediterranean in 859 and the siege of Tsargrad by Russia in 860 were organized by Rorik is totally groundless.[13]

In this respect I believe Mošin is right. The directing hand of Rorik-Rurik in the south and in the north as well would of course have supplied the Norman expeditions around 860–861 with the idea of unity and premeditation. But our evidence fails to give us the slightest ground for this theory, and though we recognize that the almost simultaneous operations of the Normans from south and north are unexpected and even amazing, we have no solid evidence for considering this anything but an unusual coincidence.

[13] V. Mošin, in *Seminarium Kondakovianum*, v (Prague, 1932), p. 336.

APPENDICES

I

THE ICON OF THE MOTHER OF GOD FROM JERUSALEM

IN *The Complete Liturgical Calendar (Menologium) of the Orient* of the Archbishop Sergius I have come across a story of the transportation of an icon of the Mother of God from Constantinople to Russia, which has some connection with the Russian danger to that city.[1] The Archbishop Sergius reproduces the story from an anonymous pamphlet entitled *Glory of our Holy Lady*. The story runs as follows: 'In 453 this icon had been brought from Jerusalem to Tsargrad and stood in the Church of the Mother of God, which was called Piguii;[2] later, it was placed in the Church of Blachernae, and was very famous on account of many miracles. In 898 (*sic*), because of the invasion of the Russians on Constantinople, it was brought to Kherson (in the Crimea). Vladimir, after he had been baptized at Kherson, took this holy icon and sent it to Novgorod, where it stood in the Cathedral of St Sophia till the conquest of Novgorod by the Tsar Ivan Vasilyevich (Ivan III, 1462–1505). Then the icon was brought to the Uspenski Cathedral (the Cathedral of the Assumption) in Moscow. During the invasion of Napoleon this icon was stolen, and in its stead a very good, old copy of it was placed.'

According to some information, there was a Greek legend on the icon. In Tsargrad the icon had been considered the cause of the miraculous defeat of the Scythians.

Of course this story as it has been reproduced by the Archbishop Sergius is not a true historical document; and the year 898 is inaccurate. But I have recounted the story in this study, because it has never before been mentioned in this connection; and it may imply that under the pressure of imminent danger, some precious works were removed from Constantinople to safer places, as has been frequently done in modern times. The Mother of God on the Jerusalem icon under review has been commemorated by the Greek-Orthodox Church on October 12 (Archbp. Sergius, II, 1, sec. ed., p. 316).

---

[1] Arch. Sergius, *op. cit.*, II, 2, first ed. (Moscow, 1876), p. 328; sec. ed. (Vladimir, 1901), p. 424.

[2] This is the Greek name Πηγαί — the Springs, one of the suburbs of Constantinople; there was also the gate of the Pegé (Πηγή), i.e., that of the Spring, because it led to the celebrated Holy Springs (now Baloukli), about half a mile to the west. This place is still held in great repute among devotees.

II

THE PATRIARCH JOHN THE GRAMMARIAN

THE Russian danger which started in 860 has survived in curious legendary form in Byzantium. One such legend may be connected with the first Russian invasion. Under the Emperor Theophilus (829–842), Michael III's predecessor, the patriarchal throne of Constantinople was occupied by John the Grammarian, the iconoclast patriarch, who was deposed in 842 or 843 after Theophilus' death when, under his mother Theodora, icon veneration was restored. As one of the most learned men of his day, John the Grammarian, like many other learned men in the Middle Ages, among them the future Patriarch Photius, was accused of practicing the black art and was considered a messenger and coadjutor of the devil. An interesting legend concerning his black magic is related and may have some connection with the Russian invasion of 860. Here is the legend.[1]

A pagan and harsh people under three leaders were overrunning and harassing the Empire. Theophilus, unable to repel them, was in despair, when John came to the rescue by his magic art. A three-headed statue was made under his direction and placed among the statues of bronze which adorned the Hippodrome. Three men of immense physical strength, furnished with huge iron hammers, were stationed by the statue in the dark hours of the night, and instructed, at a given sign, simultaneously to raise their hammers and smite off the heads. John, concealing his identity under the disguise of a layman, recited a magical incantation which translated the vital strength of the three foemen into the statue, and then ordered the men to strike. They struck; two heads fell to the ground; but the third blow was less forceful, and bent the head without severing it. The event corresponded to the performance of the rite. The hostile leaders fell out among themselves; two were slain by the third, who was wounded, but survived; and the enemy left the Roman borders for their own country in flight and defeat.

Of course this is only a legend. John the Grammarian was Patriarch under Michael's predecessor; but he died during Michael's reign. It is

---

[1] *Theoph. Continuatus*, lib. IV, c. 7; ed. Bonn., pp. 155–156. F. Uspenski reproduced this legend in Russian in three places: 'Patriarch John VII the Grammarian and Rus-Dromitai with Symeon Magister,' *Journal of the Ministry of Public Instruction*, 1890, January, pp. 7 and 24–25; 'The First Pages of the Russian Annals and Byzantine Legends,' *Zapiski* of the Odessa Society of History and Antiquities, XXXII (Odessa, 1914), pp. 11–12 (pagination of an offprint); *History of the Byzantine Empire*, II, 1 (Leningrad, 1927), pp. 322–323. In English, J. Bury, *A History of the Eastern Roman Empire* (London, 1912), pp. 443–444. I am using here Bury's condensed version with a few changes at the beginning and the end.

impossible to determine positively the identity of this pagan and harsh people (ἔθνους . . . ἀπίστου τε καὶ σκληροῦ) who returned to their own country in flight and defeat (μετὰ φυγῆς ἀφώρμα καὶ συμφορᾶς). But proceeding from the assumption that most legends have some historical background, the description of 'a pagan and harsh people who returned to their own country in flight and defeat' suggests the Russian attack and rout of 860–861. By mere coincidence the end of the legend where one leader kills the two others and himself survives reminds me of the story of the Russian annals, in which Prince Oleg killed in Kiev two leaders, Askold and Dir.

It is not to be forgotten that the famous Madrid Scylitzes Manuscript contains a series of miniatures referring to Russian relations with Byzantium, beginning with the legend of the Gospel which, cast into the fire by a missionary-bishop in the presence of a Russian prince, failed to burn.[2] Among these miniatures there is one which represents the destruction of the three-headed statue through John the Grammarian's magic incantations.[3]

[2] *Theoph. Cont.*, v, c. 97, pp. 343–344 (under Basil ɪ).

[3] See this miniature in L. de Beylié, *L'habitation byzantine. Recherches sur l'architecture civile des Byzantins et son influence en Europe* (Paris, Grenoble, 1902), p. 106.

III

INSCRIPTION ON THE FORUM OF TAURUS

SINCE the attack of 860 was the starting point of the Russian danger
to Byzantium, it very deeply affected the imagination of the masses
of the Byzantine population.   In this connection a little book on the
origin of Constantinople, Πάτρια Κωσταντινουπόλεως, which was compiled
at the close of the tenth century, contains interesting material.   Its text
is full of descriptions of many Constantinopolitan monuments which, according to the interpretation of the superstitious masses of the capital,
referred to its future and unavoidable ruin.   Mysterious inscriptions and
obscure bas-reliefs on the monuments announced the last days of the city.
Among other monuments, on the forum of Taurus stood an equestrian
statue that had been brought from 'Great Antioch.'   In the rider some
identified Bellerophon, others Joshua the son of Nun; but everybody
agreed that the bas-reliefs sculptured on the pedestal of the statue fore-
told 'stories of the last days of the city when the Russians should destroy
Constantinople.'[1]   The prediction that the Russians would destroy Constantinople is very interesting.   It shows that at the close of the tenth
century, when the *Patria* was compiled, danger from Russia was stronger
in the popular imagination than danger from Bulgaria or the Arabs.   In
spite of the amicable visit of the Russian Grand Princess Olga to Constantinople in 957, in spite of the marriage of the Russian Prince Vladimir
to Anna, sister of the Emperors Basil II and Constantine VIII, and the
conversion of Russia to Orthodox Christianity, nevertheless the devastating though unsuccessful attack of 860–861, then the victorious campaign
upon Constantinople of the Russian Prince Oleg in 907, and Sviatoslav's
brilliant though temporary military successes in the seventies of the same
century were not yet effaced from the memory of the Empire.   The Russian attack of 860–861 laid the foundation for this mysterious belief that
the Russians finally would take and destroy Constantinople.

---

[1] *Scriptores originum Constantinopolitanarum*, recensuit Th. Preger, II (Leipzig, 1907), p. 176.
See Ch. Diehl, 'De quelques croyances byzantines sur la fin de Constantinople,' *Byzantinische Zeitschrift*, XXX (1929–1930), p. 195.   Also F. Uspenski, *Rus and Byzantium in the tenth century* (Odessa,
1888), p. 11 (in Russian).   A Vasiliev, 'Medieval Ideas of the End of the World: East and West,'
Byzantion, XVI, 2 (1942–1943), 493–494.

IV

TWO BYZANTINE RIDDLES

PAGAN Russia, i.e., Russia before its conversion to Christianity under Vladimir in 988 or 989,[1] may have made an impression upon the daily life of Byzantium. From Byzantine literature two riddles, probably connected, as some scholars think, with pagan Russia, have come down to us. In the first riddle 'a pagan people' or 'a people foreign in appearance' (ἐθνικὸν ὄψει γένος) are given, and in its solution we have 'the Russians with their whole army' (εὐθὺς πανστρατὶ τοὺς 'Ρῶς ἔχεις). In the second riddle 'a barbarian Scythian, a domestic slave or domestic servant or menial' (βάρβαρον ἐκφαίνουσιν οἰκέτην Σκύθην) is given, and in the solution of this riddle we have 'the Russian race' ('Ρωσικὸν βλέπω γένος).[2] In literary tradition these two riddles are ascribed to the writer Eustathius Macrembolites, whose dating has varied from the seventh to the twelfth century; ultimately it has been proved that he lived in the second half of the twelfth century, and Maximus Holobolus (his secular name was Manuel), whose name is connected with the solution of the riddles, lived in the thirteenth century.[3] Since these writers lived in so late a period, even if they are really the writers who compiled and solved the riddles, their significance for the ninth and tenth century cannot be very great, unless the riddles go back to old literary tradition, which is quite possible. In addition, the combination of the words ἐθνικὸν ὄψει γένος may signify not 'a pagan people,' but 'a people foreign in appear-

---

[1] I omit here the partial conversion of some Russians under the Patriarch Photius, an event which is still obscure.

[2] Eustathii Macrembolitae protonobilissimi de Hysmines et Hysminiae Amoribus libri XI. Rec. Isidorus Hilberg. Accedunt ejusdem auctoris aenigmata cum Maximi Holoboli protosyncelli solutionibus nunc primum edita (Vienna, 1876), pp. 203–206 (on the basis of twenty-two manuscripts). Eustathii Macrembolitae quae feruntur aenigmata, ed. M. Treu (Breslau, 1893), pp. 1–4 (Treu added four new manuscripts). These two riddles were discussed for the first time by F. Uspenski in his studies Rus and Byzantium in the tenth century (Odessa, 1888), p. 11. 'The First Pages of Russian History' (Odessa, 1914), pp. 15–16 (pagination of an offprint from Zapiski of the Odessa Society of History and Antiquities, vol. xxxii). Evidently Uspenski was not acquainted with Hilberg's and Treu's editions, because he used the text of the two riddles from the papers of the late distinguished French philologist Ch.-B. Hase (1780–1864), which are preserved in the Bibliothèque Nationale of Paris. The text which was employed by Uspenski apparently differs from that of Hilberg and Treu, because in the latter's texts I was unable to find the words given by Uspenski: 'a proud, arrogant, pagan race' in the first riddle, and 'a barbarian Scythian of arrogant pride' in the second. On Byzantine riddles see an interesting Russian article by G. Destunis, 'Sketches in Greek Riddles from Ancient Times to Modern,' Journal of the Ministry of Public Instruction, vol. cclxx (1890), pp. 262–263 (Destunis' statements on Byzantine riddles need to be revised). I myself mentioned the Byzantine riddles under review in my French article 'La Russie primitive et Byzance, L'art byzantin chez les Slaves,' Les Balkans. Premier recueil dedié à la mémoire de T. Uspenski (Paris, 1930), p. 14.

[3] Krumbacher, Geschichte der byzantinischen Literatur, pp. 764–766; 770–773.

ance.'   In any case, Destunis' phrase that two Byzantine high officials of the ninth–tenth century, Eustathius Macrembolites and Maximus Holobolus, half-jokingly half-seriously amused themselves by proposing and solving these riddles, cannot be maintained and is to be discarded.[4]   But I have taken the liberty of dwelling on these riddles because, even if they belong to a much later period, they show that 'Russian warriors' (πανστρατί) and 'Russian barbarians,' often known as Scythians, (βάρβαρος οἰκέτης Σκύθης) made a deep and lasting impression on the minds of Byzantine writers and the Byzantine people in general.   The attack of 860 was the starting point of this impression.

[4] G. Destunis, *op. cit.*, p. 263 (in Russian).

V

A. J. TOYNBEE'S SPECULATIONS ON THE VIKINGS

WITH vivid imagination the British writer A. J. Toynbee draws a picture of the possible general situation in the Mediaeval world had the Vikings, instead of failing, succeeded in their gigantic enterprises. 'Let us suppose,' Toynbee writes, 'that the Vikings captured Constantinople in 860, Paris in 885–886, and London in 895; let us suppose that Rollo had not been converted in 911 nor Svyatoslav defeated by John Tzimisces in 972; let us suppose that, at the turn of the tenth and eleventh centuries, the Scandinavian settlers in Greenland had just managed, instead of just failing, to gain a footing on the North American Continent; and let us suppose that the Scandinavian settlers in Russia, having actually made themselves masters of the Dnieper and the Volga waterways, had proceeded to make use of these key-positions, not merely for occasional raids upon the Caspian provinces of the Abbasid Caliphate, but for the exploration and mastery of the whole network of waterways that gives access to the Far East across the face of Eurasia.' And then Toynbee says: 'None of these seven suppositions are at all far-fetched or fantastic; and if we allow ourselves to postulate all of them, or even a majority of them, in imagination, we shall obtain a reconstruction of the course of history which will perhaps surprise us.' Toynbee then traces a picture of the Mediaeval world had the Vikings succeeded in their expeditions. 'We shall see the Vikings trampling the nascent civilizations of Roman and Orthodox Christendom out of existence as thoroughly as the Achaeans actually crushed the decadent Minoan and the rising Hittite society. . . . We shall then see this new Scandinavian Civilization reigning supreme in Europe in Christendom's stead, and marching with the Arabic Civilization across the Mediterranean, and with the Iranic Civilization across the Caspian. . . . '[1]

Of course Toynbee's suppositions, however ingenious, do not belong to history. But it is interesting for us to note that in this imaginary picture which tries to present what would have happened in the Mediaeval world had the Vikings succeeded in their stupendous enterprises, the starting point for Toynbee's picture in the East is the Russian attack of 860, when, as he says, the Vikings only just failed to take Constantinople.

---

[1] A. J. Toynbee, *A Study of History*, ii (London, 1934), pp. 438–439; also p. 443.